Frederic P. Miller, Agnes F. Vandome,
John McBrewster (Ed.)

Battle of Cable Street

Cable Street, East End of London,
Metropolitan Police Service, British Union
of Fascists, Oswald Mosley, Anti- fascist

Alphascript Publishing

Frederic P. Miller, Agnes F. Vandome,
John McBrewster (Ed.)

Contents

Articles

References

Article Licenses

Battle of Cable Street

The **Battle of Cable Street** took place on Sunday 4 October 1936 in Cable Street in the East End of London. It was a clash between the Metropolitan Police Service, overseeing a legal march by the British Union of Fascists, led by Oswald Mosley, and anti-fascists, including local Jewish, socialist, anarchist, Irish and communist groups. The majority of both marchers and counter-protesters travelled into the area for this purpose. Mosley planned to send thousands of marchers dressed in uniforms styled on those of Blackshirts through the East End of London, which had a large Jewish population.

Background

The Board of Deputies of British Jews denounced the march as anti-semitic baiting and urged Jewish people to stay well away. The Communist Party of Great Britain also tried to stop its members from taking part. Forbidden from confronting the blackshirts, party members had to operate under the cover of the ex-Serviceman's Association. On the day, the Communist Party produced a leaflet for an anti-fascist demonstration in Trafalgar Square, to draw people away from the East End. Stepney communist Joe Jacobs, who played a leading role, was expelled for 'street fighting'.[1]

Despite the strong likelihood of violence, the government refused to ban the march and a large escort of police was provided in an attempt to prevent anti-fascist protestors disrupting the march.

Leaflet directing supporters away from Cable Street - overprinted with an Aldgate meeting place by local members

Events

The anti-fascist groups erected roadblocks in an attempt to prevent the march from taking place. The barricades were erected near the junction with Christian Street, towards the west end of this long street. An estimated 300,000 anti-fascist demonstrators turned out.

Over 10,000 police, including 4,000 on horseback, attempted to clear the road to permit the march to proceed. The demonstrators fought back with sticks, rocks, chair legs and other improvised weapons. Rubbish, rotten vegetables and the contents of chamber pots were thrown at the police by women in houses along the street. After a series of running battles, Mosley agreed to abandon the march to prevent bloodshed. The BUF marchers were dispersed towards Hyde Park instead while the Anti-fascists rioted with Police. 150 demonstrators were arrested, although some escaped with the help of other demonstrators. Several members of the police were kidnapped by demonstrators. Around 100 people were injured including police, women and children.

Aftermath

Many of the arrested demonstrators reported harsh treatment at the hands of the police. Most were charged with the minor offence of obstructing police and fined £5, however several of the ringleaders were found guilty of affray and sentenced to 3 months' hard labour.

The Battle of Cable Street was a major factor leading to the passage of the Public Order Act 1936, which required police consent for political marches and forbade the wearing of political uniforms in public. This is widely considered to be a significant factor in the BUF's political decline prior to World War II.

In the 1980s, a large mural depicting the Battle was painted on the side of St. George's Town Hall. This building was originally the Vestry Hall for the area and later the Town Hall of Stepney Borough Council.It stands in Cable Street, about 150 yards west of Shadwell underground station. A red plaque in Dock Street commemorates the incident.

Red commemorative plaque in Dock Street

Steven Berkoff's *East* (1975) includes a depiction of the event; an eponymous play commemorating the events was written by Simon Blumenfeld and first performed in 1987; and in 2006 a short film was produced featuring a remembrance from a grandfather to his grandson.

See also

- National Socialist Party of America v. Village of Skokie

External links

- News footage from the day [2] News reel from youtube.com
- video for the Ghosts of Cable Street by TMTCH set to images of the battle [3]
- The Battle of Cable Street [4] as told by the Communist Party of Britain.
- "Fascists and Police Routed at Cable Street" [5] a personal account of the battle by a participant.
- Cable Street and the Battle of Cable Street [6].
- Does Cable Street still matter? [7]. BBC News Magazine, 4 October 2006
- *The Battle of Cable Street: Myths and Realities* [8] – by Richard Price and Martin Sullivan; a leftist but non-CPGB perspective. Originally published in Workers News, March-April 1994.
- Virtual reality panorama photograph and mural information [9] from the 70th anniversary celebrations, October 2006

From *eastendtalking.org.uk*

- Introduction to the Battle of Cable Street [10]
- More on the Battle of Cable Street [11]
- About the mural [12]
- Large photo of the mural [13]

From *The Guardian* newspaper

- The Guardian - Audrey Gillan - Day the East End said 'No pasaran' to Blackshirts, September 30th, 2006 [14]
- The Guardian - From The Archives - Fascist march stopped after disorderly scenes, October 5th, 1936 [15]
- Interview with witness William Fishman, aged 85. MP3 audio file [16]
- Interview with witness Max Levitas, aged 91. MP3 audio file [17]

From the BBC

- The Today Programme, BBC Radio 4, 4 October 2006. Interview with anti-fascist Aubrey Morris, who was present at the event and Nicholas Mosley, son of Oswald Mosley, leader of the British Union of Fascists. RealAudio stream [18]

Geographical coordinates: 51°30′39″N 0°03′08″W

References

[1] Joe Jacobs, *Out of the Ghetto*, Phoenix Press, 1991

[2] http://www.youtube.com/watch?v=-AQDOjQGZuA

[3] http://youtube.com/watch?v=GzKv5gjOzTA

[4] http://communist-party.org.uk/index.php?file=history&his=cs_intro.txt

[5] http://libcom.org/library/fascists-and-police-routed-battle-cable-street

[6] http://www.britannia.com/travel/london/cockney/cable.html

[7] http://news.bbc.co.uk/1/hi/magazine/5405598.stm

[8] http://www.whatnextjournal.co.uk/Pages/History/Cable.html

[9] http://www.battleofcablestreet.co.uk/

[10] http://www.eastendtalking.org.uk/OurHistory/legends/default.asp?ID=11

[11] http://www.eastendtalking.org.uk/OurHistory/CableStreet/battle.asp

[12] http://www.eastendtalking.org.uk/OurHistory/CableStreet/mural.asp

[13] http://www.eastendtalking.org.uk/OurHistory/CableStreet/images/mural/CableStreetMural.htm

[14] http://www.guardian.co.uk/farright/story/0,,1884440,00.html

[15] http://www.guardian.co.uk/fromthearchive/story/0,,1884280,00.html

[16] http://download.guardian.co.uk/sys-audio/Guardian/audio/2006/09/29/firstedit_1.mp3

[17] http://download.guardian.co.uk/sys-audio/Guardian/audio/2006/09/29/firstedit2.mp3

[18] http://www.bbc.co.uk/radio4/today/listenagain/ram/today5_cable_20061004.ram

Cable Street

Cable Street is a mile-long road in the East End of London, with several historic landmarks nearby, made famous by "the Battle of Cable Street" of 1936.

Location

Cable Street runs between the edge of The City and Limehouse: parallel to, and south of, the Docklands Light Railway and Commercial Road, and north of The Highway.

The area is close to Wapping and Shadwell Basin (to the south), Tower Hill (to the west), and Whitechapel and Stepney (to the north). Since many Londoners now define their locality by the nearest tube stations, this area is often referred to as Shadwell.

Cable Street is in the London Borough of Tower Hamlets, in postal district E1. It lies within the parliamentary constituencies of Bethnal Green and Bow and Poplar and Canning Town, currently represented by George Galloway and Jim Fitzpatrick.

History

Cable Street started as a straight path along which hemp ropes were twisted into ships cables (ie ropes). These supplied the many ships that would anchor in the nearby Pool of London, between London Bridge and Wapping & Rotherhithe. The length of rope needed for the sails on the ships was a mile in length and this is why Cable Street is exactly one mile long. Many other "rope walks" can be seen on later maps, showing how demand for ropes grew as shipping increased.

Until Victorian times, the current Cable Street had different names for each of its sections. From west to east these ran: "Cable Street", "Knock Fergus", "New Road", "Back Lane", "Blue Gate Fields", "Sun Tavern Fields", "Brook Street".

Knock Fergus is probably a reference to the large numbers of Irish residents there then. Also, in the 19th century, the area at the western end was identified as "near Wellclose Square", as this was a well-known landmark, where nautical items were sold. The whole of the central area of the current street was named after St George in the East church and its parish.

From Victorian times through to the 1950s, Cable Street had a reputation for cheap lodgings, brothels, drinking inns and opium dens.

The last occasion in England when a stake was hammered through a sinner's heart at an official burial, took place at the junction of Cable Street and Cannon Street Road. John Williams was found hanged in his cell, after being arrested as a suspect in the Ratcliff Highway murders. Local people went along with the claim that he had committed suicide, from guilt of the crimes. At the time, 1812, suicide was considered to be sinful, and justified him being buried upside down with a stake through his heart. His skull was found when new gas mains were being laid in the 1960s, and was on display for many years in The Crown and Dolphin pub opposite.

In 1936, a violent confrontation between the police and local communities, was later named the Battle of Cable Street. Communist, Anarchist, Labour and Jewish groups joined with locals to resist a planned march through the East End by the British Union of Fascists. A large mural on St George's Town Hall next to Library Place, depicts scenes from the day. A red plaque in Dock Street commemorates the incident.

Red plaque in Dock Street

Landmarks

(west to east)

- Wilton's Music Hall - the world's oldest surviving grand music hall
- Wellclose Square
- The Crown and Dolphin (ex-pub)
- Church of St George in the East
- terrace of Georgian Houses, nos. 192-232
- The Britannia (ex-pub)
- St George's Recreation Ground
- Mural of the Battle of Cable Street
- St George's Hall - the old town hall
- St Georges Swimming Pool
- Shadwell tube station
- Shadwell DLR station
- Watney Market

- Shadwell Fire Station
- Blue Gate fields primary school
- St Mary's church
- terrace of Georgian cottages
- Kings Arms - the only pub left in the street
- Cable Street Studios - artists workshops

Transport

Road

The whole street allows motor traffic to travel one-way: mostly west-bound, but east-bound east of Brodlove Lane. It lies outside of the London congestion charge zone.

A separate cycle path runs along the whole street, and is well used by cycling commuters.

Bus

Buses 100 and D3 both pass west-bound through the central part of Cable Street:

- **100** connects to Wapping, Liverpool Street, St Pauls and Elephant and Castle.
- **D3** connects to Isle of Dogs, Limehouse, Wapping and Bethnal Green.
- **339** connects to Mile End, Bow and Old Ford - from next to the DLR station.

Rail

The district falls within Transport for London's Travelcard Zone 2. The nearest London Underground station is Tower Hill. Opening in 2010, the nearest London Overground stations are Shadwell and Wapping on the East London line.

The nearest Docklands Light Railway stations are *Shadwell* and *Limehouse*

National Rail stations:

- **Limehouse** railway station

People

People associated with the area:

Politicians

Members of Parliament, for Bethnal Green and Bow :

- George Galloway, Respect (MP 2005-)
- Oona King, Labour (MP 1997-2005)

Members of Parliament, for Poplar and Canning Town :

- Jim Fitzpatrick, Labour (MP 1997-)

Science and Medicine

- **Dr Hannah Billig** (1901-1987) - a local doctor who became known as "**The Angel of Cable Street**". A blue plaque marks her home surgery at number 198, near Cannon Street Road.

- **Sir William Henry Perkin** (1838–1907) chemist who
  discovered aniline purple dye, mauveine, in a hut in the garden
  of his family's Cable Street home. A blue plaque marks the site,
  by the junction with King David Lane.

Sports

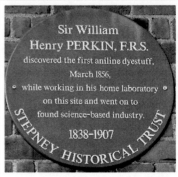

Blue plaque for William Perkin

- **Jack 'Kid' Berg** (1909–1991) - Lightweight Champion Boxer,
  born in Cable Street, by Noble Court

Literary figures

Victorian Era:

- **Oscar Wilde** visited the opium dens off Cable Street, near
  Dellow Street
- **Arthur Conan Doyle** visited the opium dens as research for his
  detective character Sherlock Holmes.

Edwardian Era:

- **Isaac Rosenburg** (1890-1918), poet & painter, lived at 47
  Cable Street from 1897 to 1900, when he attended St. Paul's
  School in Wellclose Square.

Blue plaque for Jack Kid Berg

People inspiring local street names

- Thomas **Barnardo** - Victorian philanthropist who established homes for destitute children
- Nicholas **Hawksmoor** - architect who designed the church of St George in the East
- Nathaniel **Heckford** - a young doctor who founded a local children's hospital
- Harriet **Martineau** - Victorian journalist and writer: populariser of political economy
- Daniel **Solander** - Swedish botanist who travelled with James Cook exploring the Pacific islands
- Emanuel **Swedenborg** - Swedish scientist, philosopher and mystic, in the Georgian era

Neighbouring Streets

west of Cable Street

- Royal Mint Street - formerly Rosemary Lane (in 1830)

north of Cable Street starting from the west:

- Leman Street - formerly White Lion Street, leading to Leman Street, (in 1830)
- Mill Yard
- Back Church Lane
- Pinchin Street - formerly Thomas Street (in 1862). *Historically noteworthy for its curve and arches, showing where the branch of the railway used to run, towards the goods yard to the north west.*
- Stute Street
- Christian Street - the barricade created during the Battle of Cable Street, was near this street's junction with Cable Street
- Golding Street - formerly Low Grove Street (in 1862)
- Cannon Street Road
- Watney Market - formerly Watney Street (in 1862)
- Watney Street - formerly Charles Street (in 1862)
- Cornwall Street - formerly Upper Cornwall Street (in 1862)
- Shadwell Gardens
- Shadwell Place - formerly Lower Cornwall Street and Sun Court (in 1862)
- Sutton Street - formerly Church Road (in 1862)
- Martineau Street
- Johnson Street
- Poonah Street
- Hardinge Street
- Hardinge Lane
- Devonport Street
- Barnado Street - formerly James Place (in 1862)
- Stepney Causeway
- Pitsea Street - formerly Dorset Street (in 1862)
- Caroline Street
- Ratcliffe Cross Street - formerly Ratcliffe Square and Periwinkle Street (in 1862)
- Boulcott Street - formerly George Street (in 1862)
- Commercial Road - major radial route into Aldgate - runs parallel to Cable Street

east of Cable Street

- Butcher Row - formerly Butcher Row and White Horse Street (in 1862)
- Narrow Street

south of Cable Street, starting from the west:

- Dock Street - already existed as Dock Street in 1830
- Ensign Street - formerly Well Street (in 1862)
- Graces Alley - between Ensign Street and Wellclose Square - home to Wilton's Music Hall
- Fletcher Street - formerly Shorter Street (in 1830 & 1862)
- Wellclose Square - already existed as Wellclose Square in 1830 & 1862
- Hindmarsh Close
- Swedenbourg Gardens
- Betts Street - formerly connected Cable Street to The Highway (in 1862)

- Crowder Street - formerly Denmark Street (in 1862)
- Cannon Street Road
- Hawksmoor Mews
- Bluegate Mews - formerly St George's Place (in 1830)
- Library Place - formerly Prospect Place (in 1862)
- Angel Court - in 1862, Angel Gardens was where Bewley Street is now.
- Dellow Street
- Bewley Street - formerly Albert Street (in 1862)
- Sage Street
- Lowood Street
- Solander Gardens
- Twine Court
- King David Lane
- Juniper Street - formerly Juniper Row (in 1862)
- Tarbert Walk
- Glamis Road
- Redcastle Close - formerly Carriage Way (in 1862)
- Glamis Place
- Brodlove Lane - formerly Love Lane (in 1862)
- Elf Row - formerly Elm Row (in 1862)
- Glasshouse Fields - formerly Glasshouse Street (in 1862)
- Schoolhouse Lane
- Heckford Street - formerly Burlington Place (in 1862). *No longer connected to Cable Street*
- Cranford Street - formerly Harris Court (in 1862)
- Bere Street - formerly connected through to Butcher Row (in 1862)
- Ratcliffe Orchard - formerly The Orchard (in 1862)
- The Highway - formerly Ratcliff Highway. Then St. George's Street, High Street (Shadwell), Cock Hill and Broad Street (in 1862).

See also

- Battle of Cable Street
- The Highway
- St George in the East

External links

- Wiltons Music Hall [1]
- Cable Street on Google Maps [2]

Geographical coordinates: 51°30′39″N 0°3′20″W

References

[1] http://www.wiltons.org.uk/

[2] http://maps.google.co.uk/maps?f=q&hl=en&geocode=&q=cable+street,+london&sll=54.162434,-3.647461&sspn=9.658919,29.
179688&ie=UTF8&z=16&iwloc=addr

East End of London

The **East End of London**, known vernacularly as the **East End**, is the area of London, England, east of the medieval walled City of London and north of the River Thames, although it is not defined by universally accepted formal boundaries. Use of the term in a pejorative sense began in the late 19th century,[1] as the expansion of the population of London led to extreme overcrowding throughout the area and a concentration of poor people and immigrants in the East End.[2] These problems were exacerbated with the construction of St Katharine Docks (1827)[3] and the central London railway termini (1840–1875) that caused the clearance of former slums and rookeries, with many of the displaced people moving into the East End. Over the course of a century, the East End became synonymous with poverty, overcrowding, disease and criminality.[4]

Christ Church, Spitalfields

The East End developed rapidly during the 19th century. Originally it was an area characterised by villages clustered around the City walls or along the main roads, surrounded by farmland, with marshes and small communities by the River, serving the needs of shipping and the Royal Navy. Until the arrival of formal docks, shipping was required to land its goods in the Pool of London, but industries related to construction, repair, and victualling of ships flourished in the area from Tudor times. The area attracted large numbers of rural people looking for employment. Successive waves of foreign immigration began with Huguenot refugees creating a new extramural suburb in Spitalfields in the 17th century.[5] They were followed by Irish weavers,[6] Ashkenazi Jews[7] and, in the 20th century, Bangladeshis.[8] Many of these immigrants worked in the clothing industry. The abundance of semi- and unskilled labour led to low wages and poor conditions throughout the East End. This brought the attentions of social reformers during the mid-18th century and led to the formation of unions and workers associations at the end of the century. The radicalism of the East End contributed to the formation of the Labour Party and demands for the enfranchisement of women.

Official attempts to address the overcrowded housing began at the beginning of the 20th century under the London County Council. World War II devastated much of the East End, with its docks, railways and industry forming a continual target, leading to dispersal of the population to new suburbs, and new housing being built in the 1950s.[4] The closure of the last of the East End docks in the Port of London in 1980 created further challenges and led to attempts at regeneration and the formation of the London Docklands Development Corporation. The Canary Wharf development, improved infrastructure, and the Olympic Park[9] mean that the East End is undergoing further change, but some of its parts continue to contain some of the worst poverty in Britain.[10]

Origin and scope

The term 'East End' was first applied to the districts immediately to the east of, and entirely outside, the medieval walled City of London and north of the River Thames; these included Whitechapel and Stepney. By the late 19th century, the East End roughly corresponded to the Tower division of Middlesex, which from 1900 formed the metropolitan boroughs of Stepney, Bethnal Green, Poplar and Shoreditch in the County of London. Today it corresponds to the London Borough of Tower Hamlets and the southern part of Hackney.[4]

> [The] invention about 1880 of the term 'East End' was rapidly taken up by the new halfpenny press, and in the pulpit and the music hall ... A shabby man from Paddington, St Marylebone or Battersea might pass muster as one of the respectable poor. But the same man coming from Bethnal Green, Shadwell or Wapping was an 'East Ender', the box of Keating's bug powder must be reached for, and the spoons locked up. In the long run this cruel stigma came to do good. It was a final incentive to the poorest to get out of the 'East End' at all costs, and it became a concentrated reminder to the public conscience that nothing to be found in the 'East End' should be tolerated in a Christian country.
>
> —The Nineteenth Century XXIV (1888)[11]

Parts of the London boroughs of Newham and Waltham Forest, formerly in an area of Essex known as 'London over the border', are sometimes considered to be in the East End.[12] However, the River Lee is usually considered to be the eastern boundary of the East End[13] and this definition would exclude the boroughs but place them in East London.[14] This extension of the term further east is due to the 'diaspora' of East Enders who moved to West Ham about 1886[15] and East Ham about 1894[16] to service the new docks and industries established there. In the inter-war period, migration occurred to new estates built to alleviate conditions in the East End, in particular at Becontree and Harold Hill, or out of London entirely.

The extent of the East End has always been difficult to define. When Jack London came to London in 1902 his Hackney carriage driver did not know the way and he observed, *Thomas Cook and Son, path-finders and trail-clearers, living sign-posts to all the World.... knew not the way to the East End.*[17]

Many East Enders are 'Cockneys', although this term has both a geographic and a linguistic connotation. A traditional definition is that to be a Cockney, one had to be born within the sound of Bow Bells, situated in Cheapside. In general, the sound pattern would cover most of the City, and parts of the near East End such as Aldgate and Whitechapel. In practice, with no maternity hospitals in the district, today few would be born in the area. The origin of the term is lost, but a plausible explanation is given by Websters.[18] London was referred to by the Normans as the "Land of Sugar Cake" (Old French: *pais de cocaigne*), an imaginary land of idleness and luxury. A humorous appellation, the word "Cocaigne" referred to all of London and its suburbs, and over time had a number of spellings: *Cocagne, Cockayne'*, and in Middle English, *Cocknay* and *Cockney*.

Its linguistic use is more identifiable, with lexical borrowings from Yiddish, Romani, and costermonger slang, and a distinctive accent that features T-glottalization, a loss of dental fricatives and diphthong alterations, amongst others. The accent is said to be a remnant of early English London speech, modified by the many immigrants to the area.[19] The Cockney accent has suffered a long decline, beginning with the introduction in the 20th century of received pronunciation, and the more recent adoption of Estuary English, which itself contains many features of Cockney English.[20]

History

The East End came into being as the separate villages east of London spread and the fields between them were built upon, a process that occurred in the late 18th and early 19th centuries. From the beginning, the East End has always contained some of the poorest areas of London. The main reasons for this include the following:

1745 Roque Map of the East End. London is expanding, but there are still large areas of fields to the East of the City.

- the medieval system of copyhold, which prevailed throughout the East End, into the 19th century. Essentially, there was little point in developing land that was held on short leases.[4]

- the siting of noxious industries, such as tanning and fulling outside the boundaries of the City, and therefore beyond complaints and official controls.

- the low paid employment in the docks and related industries, made worse by the trade practices of outwork, piecework and casual labour.
- and the concentration of the ruling court and national political epicentre in Westminster, on the opposite western side of the City of London.

Historically, the East End is conterminous with the Manor of Stepney. This manor was held by the Bishop of London, in compensation for his duties in maintaining and garrisoning the Tower of London. Further ecclesiastic holdings came about from the need to enclose the marshes and create flood defences along the Thames. Edward VI passed the land to the Wentworth family, and thence to their descendants, the Earls of Cleveland. The ecclesiastic system of copyhold, whereby land was leased to tenants for terms as short as seven years, prevailed throughout the manor. This severely limited scope for improvement of the land and new building until the estate was broken up in the 19th century.[21]

In medieval times, trades were carried out in workshops in and around the owners' premises, in the City. By the time of the Great Fire, these were becoming industries and some were particularly noisome for instance the processing of urine to perform tanning, or required large amounts of space, such as drying clothes after process and dying in fields known as tentergrounds and rope making. Some were dangerous, such as the manufacture of gun powder, or the proving of guns. These activities came to be performed outside the City walls in the near suburbs of the East End. Later, when lead making, bone processing for soap and china came to established, they too located in the East End, rather than the crowded streets of the City.[4]

The lands to the east of the City had always been used as hunting grounds for bishops and royalty, with King John establishing a palace at Bow. The Cistercian Stratford Langthorne Abbey became the court of Henry III in 1267, for the visitation of the Papal legates, and it was here that he made peace with the barons under the terms of the Dictum of Kenilworth. It became the fifth largest Abbey in the country, visited by monarchs and providing a popular retreat (and final resting place) for the nobility.[22] The Palace of Placentia at Greenwich, to the south of the river, was built by the Regent to Henry V, Humphrey, Duke of Gloucester and Henry VIII established a hunting lodge at Bromley Hall.[23] These Royal connections continued until after the Interregnum, when the Court established itself in the Palace of Whitehall, and the offices of politics congregated around them. The East End also lay on the main road to Barking Abbey, important as a religious centre since Norman times and where William the Conqueror had first established his English court.[24]

Politics and social reform

At the end of the 17th century, large numbers of Huguenot weavers arrived in the East End, settling to service an industry that grew up around the new estate at Spitalfields, where master weavers were based. They brought with them a tradition of 'reading clubs', where books were read, often in public houses. The authorities were suspicious of immigrants meeting, and in some ways they were right, as these grew into workers' associations and political organisations. When, towards the middle of the 18th century, the silk industry fell into a decline - partly due to the introduction of printed calico cloth - riots ensued. These 'Spitalfield Riots' of 1769 were actually centred to the east, and were put down with considerable force, culminating in

1882 Reynolds Map of the East End.
Development has now eliminated the open fields.

two men being hanged in front of the Salmon and Ball public house at Bethnal Green. One was John Doyle (an Irish weaver), the other John Valline (of Huguenot descent).[25]

In 1844, "An Association for promoting Cleanliness among the Poor" was established, and they built a bath-house and laundry in Glasshouse Yard, East Smithfield. This cost a single penny for bathing or washing, and by June 1847 was receiving 4,284 people a year. This led to an Act of Parliament to encourage other municipalities to build their own, and the model spread quickly throughout the East End. Timbs noted that "... so strong was the love of cleanliness thus encouraged that women often toiled to wash their own and their children's clothing, who had been compelled to *sell their hair* to purchase food to satisfy the cravings of hunger".[26]

William Booth founded the Salvation Army, in Whitechapel, in 1878

William Booth began his 'Christian Revival Society' in 1865, preaching the gospel in a tent erected in the 'Friends Burial Ground', Thomas Street, Whitechapel. Others joined his 'Christian Mission', and on 7 August 1878 the Salvation Army was formed at a meeting held at 272 Whitechapel Road.[27] A statue commemorates both his mission and his work in helping the poor. A Dubliner, Thomas John Barnardo came to the London Hospital, Whitechapel to train for medical missionary work in China. Soon after his arrival in 1866, a cholera epidemic swept the East End, killing 3,000 people. Many families were left destitute, with thousands of children orphaned and forced to beg or find work in the factories. In 1867, Barnardo set up a Ragged School to provide a basic education but was shown the many children sleeping rough. His first home for boys was established at 18 Stepney Causeway in 1870. When a boy died after being turned away (the home was full), the policy was instituted that 'No Destitute Child Ever Refused Admission'.[28]

In 1884, the Settlement movement was founded, with settlements such as Toynbee Hall[29] and Oxford House, to encourage university students to live and work in the slums, experience the conditions and try to alleviate some of the poverty and misery in the East End. Notable residents of Toynbee Hall included R. H. Tawney, Clement Attlee, Guglielmo Marconi, and William Beveridge. The Hall continues to exert considerable influence, with the Workers Educational Association (1903), Citizens Advice Bureau (1949) and Child Poverty Action Group (1965) all being founded or influenced by it.[30] In 1888, the matchgirls of Bryant and May in Bow went on strike for better working conditions. This, combined with the many dock strikes in the same era, made the East End a key element in the foundation of modern socialist and trade union organisations, as well as the Suffragette movement.[31]

Towards the end of the 19th century, a new wave of radicalism came to the East End, arriving both with Jewish émigrés fleeing from Eastern European persecution, and Russian and German radicals avoiding arrest. A German émigré, Rudolf Rocker, began writing in Yiddish for *Arbayter Fraynd* (Workers' Friend). By 1912 he had organised a London garment workers' strike for better conditions and an end to 'sweating'.[32] Amongst the Russians was Peter Kropotkin, the anarchist, who helped found the Freedom Press in Whitechapel. Afanasy Matushenko, one of the leaders of the Potemkin mutiny, fled the failure of the Russian Revolution of 1905 to seek sanctuary in Stepney Green.[33] Leon Trotsky and Vladimir Lenin attended meetings of the newspaper *Iskra* in 1903. in Whitechapel; and in 1907 Lenin and Joseph Stalin[34] [35] attended the Fifth Congress of the Russian Social Democratic Labour Party held in a Hoxton church. That congress consolidated the leadership of Lenin's Bolshevik faction and debated strategy for the communist revolution in Russia.[36] Trotsky noted, in his memoires, meeting Maxim Gorky and Rosa Luxembourg at the conference.[37]

By the 1880s, the casual system caused Dock workers to unionise under Ben Tillett and John Burns.[38] This led to a demand for '6d per hour' (*The Docker's Tanner*),[39] and an end to casual labour in the docks.[40] Colonel G. R. Birt, the general manager at Millwall Docks, gave evidence to a Parliamentary committee, on the physical condition of the workers:

> *The poor fellows are miserably clad, scarcely with a boot on their foot, in a most miserable state.... These are men who come to work in our docks who come on without having a bit of food in their stomachs, perhaps since the previous day; they have worked for an hour and have earned 5d. [2p]; their hunger will not allow them to continue: they take the 5d. in order that they may get food, perhaps the first food they have had for twenty-four hours.*

—Col. G. R. Birt, in evidence to the Parliamentary Committee (1889)[40]

These conditions earned dockers much public sympathy, and after a bitter struggle, the London Dock Strike of 1889 was settled with victory for the strikers, and established a national movement for the unionisation of casual workers, as opposed to the craft unions that already existed.

The philanthropist Angela Burdett-Coutts was active in the East End, alleviating poverty by founding a sewing school for ex-weavers in Spitalfields and building the ornate Columbia Market in Bethnal Green. She helped to inaugurate the London Society for the Prevention of Cruelty to Children, was a keen supporter of the 'Ragged School Union',[41] and founded institutions such as the East End Dwelling Company. This latter led to the foundation of organisations such as the '4% Dwelling Company', where investors received a financial return on their philanthropy.[42] Between the 1890s and 1903, when the work was published, the social campaigner Charles Booth instigated an investigation into the life of London poor (based at Toynbee Hall), much of which was centred on the poverty and conditions in the East End.[43] Further investigations were instigated by the 'Royal Commission on the Poor Laws and Relief of Distress 1905-09', the Commission found it difficult to agree, beyond that change was necessary and produced separate minority and majority reports. The minority report was the

Lady Angela Burdett-Coutts

work of Booth with the founders of the London School of Economics Sidney and Beatrice Webb. They advocated focusing on the causes of poverty and the radical notion of poverty being involuntary, rather than the result of innate indolence. At the time their work was rejected but was gradually adopted as policy by successive governments.[44]

Sylvia Pankhurst 1882–1960

Sylvia Pankhurst became increasingly disillusioned with the suffragette movement's inability to engage with the needs of working class women, so in 1912 she formed her own breakaway movement, the East London Federation of Suffragettes. She based it at a baker's shop at Bow emblazoned with the famous slogan, "Votes for Women," in large gold letters. The local Member of Parliament, George Lansbury, resigned his seat in the House of Commons to stand for election on a platform of women's enfranchisement. Pankhurst supported him in this, and Bow Road became the campaign office, culminating in a huge rally in nearby Victoria Park. Lansbury was narrowly defeated in the election, however, and support for the project in the East End was withdrawn. Pankhurst refocused her efforts, and with the outbreak of World War I, she began a nursery, clinic and cost price canteen for the poor at the bakery. A paper, the *Women's Dreadnought*, was published to bring her campaign to a wider audience. Pankhurst spent twelve years in Bow fighting for women's rights. During this time, she risked constant arrest and spent many months in Holloway Prison, often on hunger strike. She finally achieved her aim of full adult female suffrage in 1928, and along the way she alleviated some of the poverty and misery, and improved social conditions for all in the East End.[45]

The alleviation of widespread unemployment and hunger in Poplar had to be funded from money raised by the borough itself under the Poor Law. The poverty of the borough made this patently unfair and lead to the 1921 conflict between government and the local councillors known as the Poplar Rates Rebellion. Council meetings were for a time held in Brixton prison, and the councillors received wide support.[46] Ultimately, this led to the abolition of the Poor Laws through the Local Government Act 1929.

The General Strike had begun as a dispute between miners and their employers outside London in 1925. On 1 May 1926 the Trades Union Congress called out workers all over the country, including the London dockers. The government had had over a year to prepare and deployed troops to break the dockers' picket lines. Armed food convoys, accompanied by armoured cars drove down the East India Dock Road. By 10 May, a meeting was brokered at Toynbee Hall to end the strike. The TUC were forced into a humiliating climbdown and the general strike ended on 11 May, with the miners holding out until November.[47]

Industry and built environment

Industries associated with the sea developed throughout the East End, including rope making and shipbuilding. The former location of roperies can still be identified from their long straight, narrow profile in the modern streets, for instance Ropery Street near Mile End. Shipbuilding was important from the time when Henry VIII caused ships to be built at Rotherhithe as a part of his expansion of the Royal Navy. On 31 January 1858, the largest ship of that time, the SS Great Eastern, designed by Isambard Kingdom Brunel, was launched from the yard of Messrs Scott Russell & Co, of Millwall. The 692-foot (211 m) vessel was too long to fit across the river, and so the ship had to be launched sideways. Due to the technical difficulties of the launch, this was the last big ship to be built on the River, and the industry fell into a long decline.[48] Smaller ships, including battleships, continued to be built at the Thames Ironworks and Shipbuilding Company at Blackwall until the beginning of the 20th century.

The famous Howlett photo of Isambard Kingdom Brunel against the launching chains of the *Great Eastern* at Millwall in 1857

West India Docks by Pugin and Rowlandson from Ackermann's *Microcosm of London, or, London in Miniature* (1808-11)

The West India Docks were established in 1803, providing berths for larger ships and a model for future London dock building. Imported produce from the West Indies was unloaded directly into quayside warehouses. Ships were limited to 6000 tons.[49] The old Brunswick Dock, a shipyard at Blackwall became the basis for the East India Company's East India Docks established there in 1806.[50] The London Docks were built in 1805, and the waste soil and rubble from the construction was carried by barge to west London, to build up the marshy area of Pimlico. These docks imported tobacco, wine, wool and other goods into guarded warehouses within high walls (some of which still remain). They were able to berth over 300 sailing vessels simultaneously, but by 1971 they closed, no longer able to accommodate modern shipping.[51] The most central docks, St Katharine Docks, were built in 1828 to accommodate luxury goods, clearing the slums that lay in the area of the former Hospital of St Katharine. They were not successful commercially, as they were unable to accommodate the largest ships, and in 1864, management of the docks was amalgamated with that of the London Docks.[52] The Millwall Docks were created in 1868, predominantly for the import of grain and timber. These docks housed the first purpose built granary for the Baltic grain market, a local landmark that remained until it was demolished to improve access for the London City Airport.[53]

The first railway ('The Commercial Railway') to be built, in 1840, was a passenger service based on cable haulage by stationary steam engines that ran the 3.5 miles (5.6 km) from Minories to Blackwall on a pair of tracks. It required 14 miles (22.5 km) of hemp rope, and 'dropped' carriages as it arrived at stations, which were reattached to the cable for the return journey, and the train 'reassembling' itself at the terminus.[54] The line was converted to standard gauge in 1859, and steam locomotives adopted. The building of London termini at Fenchurch Street (1841),[55] and Bishopsgate (1840) provided access to new suburbs across the River Lee, again resulting in the destruction of housing and increased overcrowding in the slums. After the opening of

Minories station on the LBR, c. 1840. Winding drums and Cooke-Wheatstone "needle" telegraph shown in left foreground

Liverpool Street station (1874), Bishopsgate railway station became a goods yard, in 1881, to bring imports from Eastern ports. With the introduction of containerisation, the station declined, suffered a fire in 1964 that destroyed the station buildings, and it was finally demolished in 2004 for the extension of the East London Line. In the 19th century, the area north of Bow Road became a major railway centre for the North London Railway, with marshalling yards and a maintenance depot serving both the City and the West India docks. Nearby Bow railway station opened in 1850 and was rebuilt in 1870 in a grand style, featuring a concert hall. The line and yards closed in 1944, after severe bomb damage, and never reopened, as goods became less significant, and cheaper facilities were concentrated in Essex.[56]

The River Lee was a smaller boundary than the Thames, but it was a significant one. The building of the Royal Docks consisting of the Royal Victoria Dock (1855), able to berth vessels of up to 8000 tons;[57] Royal Albert Dock (1880), up to 12,000 tons;[58] and King George V Dock (1921), up to 30,000 tons,[59] on the estuary marshes, extended the continuous development of London across the Lee into Essex for the first time.[60] The railways gave access to a passenger terminal at Gallions Reach and new suburbs created in West Ham, which quickly became a major manufacturing town, with 30,000 houses built between 1871 and 1901.[15] Soon afterwards, East Ham was built up to serve the new Gas Light and Coke Company and Bazalgette's grand sewage works at Beckton.[16]

From the mid-20th century, the docks declined in use and were finally closed in 1980, leading to the setting up of the London Docklands Development Corporation in 1981.[61] London's main port is now at Tilbury, further down the Thames estuary, outside the boundary of Greater London. The dock had been established in 1886 to bring bulk goods by rail to London, but being nearer the sea and able to accommodate vessels of 50,000 tons, they were more easily converted to the needs of modern container ships in 1968, and so they survived the closure of the inner docks.[62] Various wharves along the river continue in use but on a much smaller scale.

Settlement

During the Middle Ages, settlements had been established predominantly along the lines of the existing roads, and the principal villages were Stepney, Whitechapel and Bow. Settlements along the river began at this time to service the needs of shipping on the Thames, but the City of London retained its right to actually land the goods. The riverside became more active in Tudor times, as the Royal Navy was expanded and international trading developed. Downstream, a major fishing port developed at Barking to provide fish to the City.

James Cook, portrait by Nathaniel
Dance, c. 1775, National Maritime
Museum, Greenwich

Whereas royalty such as King John had had a hunting lodge at Bromley-by-Bow, and the Bishop of London had a palace at Bethnal Green, later these estates began to be split up, and estates of fine houses for captains, merchants and owners of manufacturers began to be built. Samuel Pepys moved his family and goods to Bethnal Green during the Great Fire of London, and Captain Cook moved from Shadwell to Stepney Green, a place where a school and assembly rooms had been established (commemorated by *Assembly Passage*, and a plaque on the site of Cook's house on the Mile End Road). Mile End Old Town also acquired some fine buildings, and the New Town began to be built. As the area became built up and more crowded, the wealthy sold their plots for sub-division and moved further afield. Into the 18th and 19th centuries, there were still attempts to build fine houses, for example Tredegar Square (1830), and the open fields around Mile End New Town were used for the construction of estates of workers' cottages in 1820.[63]

Globe Town was established from 1800 to provide for the expanding population of weavers around Bethnal Green, attracted by improving prospects in silk weaving. The population of Bethnal Green trebled between 1801 and 1831, operating 20,000 looms in their own homes. By 1824, with restrictions on importation of French silks relaxed, up to half these looms became idle, and prices were driven down. With many importing warehouses already established in the district, the abundance of cheap labour was turned to boot, furniture and clothing manufacture.[2] Globe Town continued its expansion into the 1860s, long after the decline of the silk industry.

During the 19th century, building on an adhoc basis could never keep up with the needs of the expanding population. Henry Mayhew visited Bethnal Green in 1850 and wrote for the *Morning Chronicle*, as a part of a series forming the basis for *London Labour and the London Poor* (1851), that the trades in the area included tailors, costermongers, shoemakers, dustmen, sawyers, carpenters, cabinet makers and silkweavers. He noted that in the area:

Boundary Estate bandstand, built on
the rubble from the clearance of the
'Old Nichol' slum

  roads were unmade, often mere alleys, houses small and without foundations, subdivided and often around unpaved courts. An almost total lack of drainage and sewerage was made worse by the ponds formed by the excavation of brickearth. Pigs and cows in back yards, noxious trades like boiling tripe, melting tallow, or preparing cat's meat, and slaughter houses, dustheaps, and 'lakes of putrefying night soil' added to the filth

—Henry Mayhew London Labour and London Poor (1851)[64]

A movement began to clear the slums – with Burdett-Coutts building Columbia Market in 1869 and with the passing of the "Artisans' and Labourers' Dwelling Act" in 1876 to provide powers to seize slums from landlords and provide access to public funds to build new housing.[65] Housing associations such as the Peabody Trust were formed to provide philanthropic homes for the poor and clearing the slums generally. Expansion work by the railway companies, such as the London and Blackwall Railway and Great Eastern Railway caused large areas of slum housing to be demolished. The "Working Classes Dwellings Act" in 1890 placed a new responsibility to house the displaced residents and this led to the building of new "philanthropic housing" such as Blackwall Buildings and Great Eastern Buildings.[66]

By 1890 official slum clearance programmes had begun. One was the creation of the world's first council housing, the LCC Boundary Estate, which replaced the neglected and crowded streets of Friars Mount, better known as The Old Nichol Street Rookery.[67] Between 1918 and 1939 the LCC continued replacing East End housing with five or six storey flats, despite residents preferring houses with gardens and opposition from shopkeepers who were forced to relocate to new, more expensive premises. The Second World War brought an end to further slum clearance.[68]

Second World War

Dornier Do 17 bombers of the Luftwaffe over
West Ham on 7 September 1940. (Air Ministry
photograph)

❝ ❝Hardest of all, the Luftwaffe will smash Stepney. I know the East End! Those dirty Jews and Cockneys will run like rabbits into their ❞ ❞
holes.[69]

—Germany Calling - Lord Haw-Haw, collaborator and broadcaster

Initially, the German commanders were reluctant to bomb London, fearing retaliation against Berlin. On 24 August 1940, a single aircraft, tasked to bomb Tilbury, accidentally bombed Stepney, Bethnal Green and the City. The following night the RAF retaliated by mounting a forty aircraft raid on Berlin, with a second attack three days later. The Luftwaffe changed its strategy from attacking shipping and airfields to attacking cities. The City and West End were designated 'Target Area B'; the East End and docks were 'Target Area A'. The first raid occurred at 4:30 p.m. on 7 September and consisted of 150 Dornier and Heinkel bombers and large numbers of fighters. This was followed by a second wave of 170 bombers. Silvertown and Canning Town bore the brunt of this first attack.[4]

Between 7 September 1940 and 10 May 1941, a sustained bombing campaign was mounted. It began with the bombing of London for 57 successive nights[70], an era known as 'the Blitz'. East London was targeted because the area was a centre for imports and storage of raw materials for the war effort, and the German military command felt that support for the war could be damaged among the mainly working class inhabitants. On the first night of the blitz, 430 civilians were killed and 1600 seriously wounded.[70] The populace responded by evacuating children and the vulnerable to the country[71] and digging in, constructing Anderson shelters in their gardens and Morrison shelters in their houses, or going to communal shelters built in local public spaces.[72] On 10 September 1940, 400 civilians, including women and children preparing for evacuation, were killed when a bomb hit the South Hallsville School in Canning Town.[73]

The effect of the intensive bombing worried the authorities and 'Mass-Observation' was deployed to gauge attitudes and provide policy suggestions,[74] as before the war they had investigated local attitudes to anti-Semitism.[75] The organisation noted that close family and friendship links within the East End were providing the population with a surprising resilience under fire. Propaganda was issued, reinforcing the image of the 'brave chirpy Cockney'. On the Sunday after the Blitz began, Winston Churchill himself toured the bombed areas of Stepney and Poplar. Anti-aircraft installations were built in public parks, such as Victoria Park and the Mudchute on the Isle of Dogs, and along the line of the Thames, as this was used by the aircraft to guide them to their target.

Children of an eastern suburb of London, made homeless by the Blitz

The authorities were initially wary of opening the London Underground for shelter, fearing the effect on morale elsewhere in London and hampering normal operations. On 12 September, having suffered five days of heavy bombing, the people of the East End took the matter into their own hands and invaded tube stations with pillows and blankets. The government relented and opened the partially completed Central line as a shelter. Many deep tube stations remained in use as shelters until the end of the war.[4] Aerial mines were deployed on 19 September 1940. These exploded at roof top height, causing severe damage to buildings over a wider radius than the impact bombs. By now, the Port of London had sustained heavy damage with a third of its warehouses destroyed, and the West India and St Katherine Docks had been badly hit and put out of action. Bizarre events occurred when the River Lee burned with an eerie blue flame, caused by a hit on a gin factory at Three Mills, and the Thames itself burnt fiercely when Tate & Lyle's Silvertown sugar refinery was hit.[4]

On 3 March 1943 at 8:27 p.m., the unopened Bethnal Green tube station was the site of a wartime disaster. Families had crowded into the underground station due to an air raid siren at 8:17, one of 10 that day. There was a panic at 8:27 coinciding with the sound of an anti-aircraft battery (possibly the recently installed Z battery) being fired at nearby Victoria Park. In the wet, dark conditions, a woman slipped on the entrance stairs and 173 people died in the resulting crush. The truth was suppressed, and a report appeared that there had been a direct hit by a German bomb. The results of the official investigation were not released until 1946.[76] There is now a plaque at the entrance to the tube station, which commemorates the event as the "worst civilian disaster of World War II". The first V-1 flying bomb struck in Grove Road, Mile End, on 13 June 1944, killing six, injuring 30, and making 200 people homeless.[63] The area remained derelict for many years until it was cleared to extend Mile End Park. Before demolition, local artist Rachel Whiteread made a cast of the inside of 193 Grove Road. Despite attracting controversy, the exhibit won her the Turner Prize for 1993.[77]

Prefabricated post-war home at Chiltern Open Air Museum: Universal House, steel frame clad with corrugated asbestos cement

By the end of the war, it is estimated that 80 tons of bombs fell on the Metropolitan Borough of Bethnal Green alone, affecting 21,700 houses, destroying 2,233 and making a further 893 uninhabitable. In Bethnal Green, 555 people were killed, and 400 were seriously injured.[68] For the whole of Tower Hamlets, a total of 2,221 civilians were killed, and 7,472 were injured, with 46,482 houses destroyed and 47,574 damaged.[78] So badly battered was the East End that when Buckingham Palace was hit during the height of the bombing, Queen Elizabeth observed that "It makes me feel I can look the East End in the face."[79] [80] By the end of the war, the East End was a scene of devastation, with large areas derelict and depopulated. War production was changed quickly to making prefabricated housing,[81] and many were installed in the bombed areas and remained common into the 1970s. Today, 1950s and 1960s architecture dominates the housing estates of the area such as the Lansbury Estate in Poplar, much of which was built as a show-piece of the 1951 Festival of Britain.[82]

Population

Throughout history, the area has absorbed waves of immigrants who have each added a new dimension to the culture and history of the area, most notably the French Protestant Huguenots in the 17th century,[5] the Irish in the 18th century,[6] Ashkenazi Jews fleeing pogroms in Eastern Europe towards the end of the 19th century,[7] and the Bangladeshi[8] community settling in the East End from the 1960s.

Brick Lane has been a centre for new immigration through the centuries (Sep 2005)

Immigration

Immigrant communities first developed in the riverside settlements. From the Tudor era until the 20th century, ships crew were employed on a casual basis. New and replacement crew would be found wherever they were available, local sailors being particularly prized for their knowledge of currents and hazards in foreign ports. Crews would be paid off at the end of their voyage. Inevitably, permanent communities became established, including colonies of Lascars and Africans from the Guinea Coast. Large Chinatowns at both Shadwell and Limehouse developed, associated with the crews of merchantmen in the opium and tea trades. It was only after the devastation of World War II that this predominantly Han Chinese community relocated to Soho.[83]

In 1786, the Committee for the Relief of the Black Poor was formed, by citizens concerned at the size of London's indigent Black population, many of whom had been expelled from North America as Black Loyalists — former slaves who had fought on the side of the British, in the War of Independence. Others were discharged sailors, and some a legacy of British involvement in the slave trade, The committee distributed food, clothing, medical aid and found work for the (predominantly) men from the White Raven tavern in Mile End.[84] They also helped the men to go abroad, some to Canada. In October 1786, the Committee funded an ill-fated expedition of 280 Black men, 40 Black women and 70 White women (mainly wives and girlfriends) to settle in Sierra Leone.[85] From the late 19th century, a large African mariner community was established in Canning Town as a result of new shipping links to the Caribbean and West Africa.[86]

Immigrants have not always been readily accepted and, in 1517, the Evil May Day riots, where foreign owned property was attacked, resulted in the deaths of 135 Flemings in Stepney. The Gordon Riots of 1780 began with burnings of the houses of Catholics and their chapels in Poplar and Spitalfields.[87]

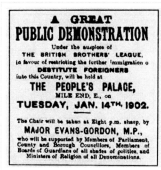

A GREAT
PUBLIC DEMONSTRATION
Under the auspices of
THE BRITISH BROTHERS' LEAGUE,
in favour of restricting the further immigration o
DESTITUTE FOREIGNERS
into this Country, will be held at
THE PEOPLE'S PALACE,
MILE END, E., on
TUESDAY, JAN. 14TH, 1902.

The Chair will be taken at Eight p.m. sharp, by
MAJOR EVANS-GORDON, M.P.,
who will be supported by Members of Parliament,
County and Borough Councillors, Members of
Boards of Guardians of all shades of politics, and
Ministers of Religion of all Denominations.

Anti-immigration poster, from 1902

In the 1870 and 80s, so many Jewish émigrés were arriving that over 150 synagogues were built. Today, there are only four active synagogues remaining in Tower Hamlets, the Congregation of Jacob Synagogue (1903 – Kehillas Ya'akov), the East London Central Synagogue (1922), the Fieldgate Street Great Synagogue (1899) and Sandys Row Synagogue (1766).[88] Jewish immigration to the East End peaked in the 1890s, leading to anti-foreigner agitation by the British Brothers League, formed in 1902 by Captain William Stanley Shaw and the Conservative MP for Stepney, Major Evans-Gordon, who had overturned a Liberal majority in the 1900 General Election on a platform of limiting immigration. In Parliament, in 1902, Evans-Gordon claimed that *"not a day passes but English families are ruthlessly turned out to make room for foreign invaders. The rates are burdened with the education of thousands of foreign children".*[89] Jewish immigration only slowed with the passing of the Aliens Act 1905, that gave the Home Secretary powers to regulate and control immigration.[90]

Community tensions were again raised by an anti-semitic Fascist march that took place in 1936 and was blocked by residents and activists at the Battle of Cable Street.[91] From the mid-1970s, anti-Asian violence occurred,[92] culminating in the murder on 4 May 1978, of a 25–year old clothing worker named Altab Ali, by three white teenagers, in a racially motivated attack. Bangladeshi groups mobilised for self-defence, 7,000 people marched to Hyde Park in protest, and the community became more politically involved.[93] The former churchyard of St Mary's Whitechapel, near where the attack occurred, was renamed "Altab Ali Park", in 1998 as a commemoration of his death. Inter-racial tension has continued with occasional outbreaks of violence; and in 1993 there was a council seat win for the British National Party (since lost).[94] A 1999 bombing in Brick Lane was part of a series that targeted ethnic minorities, gays and "multiculturalists".[95]

Demographics

The population of the East End increased inexorably throughout the 19th century. House building could not keep pace, and overcrowding was rife. It was not until the interwar period that there was a decline caused by migration to new Essex suburbs, like the Becontree estate, built by the London County Council between 1921 and 1932, and to areas outside London.[96] This depopulation accelerated after World War II and has only recently begun to reverse.

These population figures reflect the area that now forms the London Borough of Tower Hamlets only:

Borough	1811[97]	1841[97]	1871[97]	1901[98]	1931[98]	1961[98]	1971[99]	1991	2001[100]
Bethnal Green	33,619	74,088	120,104	129,680	108,194	47,078	n/a	n/a	n/a
Poplar	13,548	31,122	116,376	168,882	155,089	66,604			
Stepney	131,606	203,802	275,467	298,600	225,238	92,000			
Total	**178,773**	**309,012**	**511,947**	**597,102**	**488,611**	**205,682**	165,791	161,064	196,106

By comparison, in 1801 the population of England and Wales was 9 million; by 1851 it had more than doubled to 18 million, and by the end of the century had reached 40 million.[63] Today, Bangladeshis form the largest minority population in Tower Hamlets; constituting 33.5% of the borough population at the 2001 census; and is the largest Bangladeshi community in Britain.[101] The 2006 estimates, show a decline in this group to 29.8% of the population; reflecting a movement to better economic circumstances and the larger houses available in the eastern suburbs.[102] In this, the latest group of migrants are following a pattern established for over three centuries.

Crime

The high levels of poverty in the East End have, throughout history, corresponded with a high incidence of crime. From earliest times, crime depended, as did labour, on the importing of goods to London, and their interception in transit. Theft occurred in the river, on the quayside and in transit to the City warehouses. This was why, in the 17th century, the East India Company built high-walled, guarded docks at Blackwall to minimise the vulnerability of their cargoes. Armed convoys would then take the goods to the company's secure compound in the City. The practice led to the creation of ever larger docks throughout the area, and for large roads to be driven through the crowded 19th century slums to carry goods from the docks.[4]

No police force operated in London before the 1750s. Crime and disorder were dealt with by a system of magistrates and volunteer parish constables, with strictly limited jurisdiction. Salaried constables were introduced by 1792, although they were few in number and their power and jurisdiction continued to derive from local magistrates, who *in extremis* could be backed by militias. In 1798, England's first Marine Police Force was formed by magistrate Patrick Colquhoun and a Master Mariner, John Harriott to tackle theft and looting from ships anchored in the Pool of London and the lower reaches of the river. Its base was (and remains) in Wapping High Street. It is now known as the Marine Support Unit.[103] In 1829, the Metropolitan Police Force were formed, with a remit to patrol within 7 miles (11 km) of Charing

The 'Gabriel Franks', of the Marine Support Unit of the Metropolitan Police, named after the first marine police officer killed in the line of duty

Cross, with a force of 1,000 men in 17 divisions, including 'H' division, based in Stepney. Each division was controlled by a superintendent, under whom were four inspectors and sixteen sergeants. The regulations demanded that recruits should be under thirty-five years of age, well built, at least 5-foot-7-inch (1.70 m) in height, literate and of good character.[104] Unlike the former constables, the police were recruited widely and so were initially disliked. The force took until the mid-19th century to be established in the East End. Unusually, Joseph Sadler Thomas, a Metropolitan Police superintendent of 'F' (Covent Garden) Division appears to have mounted the first local investigation (in Bethnal Green), in November 1830 of the London Burkers.[105] In 1841, a specific Dockyard division of the Metropolitan force was formed to assume responsibility for shore patrols within the docks,[106] a detective department was formed in 1842, and in 1865, 'J' division was established in Bethnal Green.[104]

William Hogarth's depiction of London vice, Gin Lane (1751)

One of the East End industries that serviced ships moored off the Pool of London was prostitution, and in the 17th century, this was centred on the Ratcliffe Highway, a long street lying on the high ground above the riverside settlements. In 1600, it was described by the antiquarian John Stow as 'a continual street, or filthy straight passage, with alleys of small tenements or cottages builded, inhabited by sailors and victuallers.' Crews were 'paid off' at the end of a long voyage, and would spend their earnings on drink in the local taverns. One madame described as 'the great bawd of the seamen' by Samuel Pepys was Damaris Page. Born in Stepney in 1620, she had moved from prostitution to running brothels, including one on the Highway that catered for ordinary seaman and a further establishment nearby that catered for the more expensive tastes amongst the officers and gentry. She died wealthy, in 1669, in a house on the Highway, despite charges being brought against her and time spent in Newgate prison.[107]

By the 19th century, an attitude of toleration had changed, and the social reformer William Acton described the riverside prostitutes as a 'horde of human tigresses who swarm the pestilent dens by the riverside at Ratcliffe and Shadwell'. The 'Society for the Suppression of Vice' estimated that between the Houndsditch, Whitechapel and Ratcliffe area there were 1803 prostitutes; and between Mile End, Shadwell and Blackwall 963 women in the trade. They were often victims of circumstance, there being no welfare state and a high mortality rate amongst the inhabitants that left wives and daughters destitute, with no other means of income.[108] At the same time, religious reformers began to introduce 'Seamans' Missions' throughout the dock areas that both sought to provide for seafarer's physical needs and to keep them away from the temptations of drink and women. Eventually, the passage of the 'Contagious Diseases Act' in 1864 allowed policemen to arrest prostitutes and detain them in hospital. The act was repealed in 1886, after agitation by early feminists, such as Josephine Butler and Elizabeth Wolstenholme led to the formation of the Ladies National Association for the Repeal of the Contagious Diseases Acts.[109]

Notable crimes in the area include the Ratcliff Highway murders (1813);[110] the killings committed by the London Burkers (apparently inspired by Burke and Hare) in Bethnal Green (1831);[111] the notorious serial killings of prostitutes by Jack the Ripper[31] (1888); and the Sidney Street Siege (1911) (in which anarchists, inspired by the legendary Peter the Painter, took on Home Secretary Winston Churchill, and the army).[112] In the 1960s the East End was the area most associated with gangster activity, most notably that of the Kray twins.[113] The 1996 Docklands bombing caused significant damage around South Quay Station, to the south of the main Canary Wharf development. Two people were killed and thirty-nine injured in one of Mainland Britain's biggest bomb attacks by the Provisional Irish Republican Army.[114] This led to the introduction of Police checkpoints controlling access to the Isle of Dogs, reminiscent of the City's 'Ring of steel'.

Disasters

Many disasters have befallen the residents of the East End, both in war and in peace. In particular, as a maritime port, plague and pestilence have disproportionately fallen on the residents of the East End. The area most afflicted by the Great Plague (1665) was in Spitalfields,[115] and cholera epidemics broke out in Limehouse in 1832 and struck again in 1848 and 1854.[87] Typhus and tuberculosis were also common in the crowded 19th century tenements. The *Princess Alice* was a passenger steamer crowded with day trippers returning from Gravesend to Woolwich and London Bridge. On the evening of 3 September 1878, she collided with the steam collier *Bywell Castle* (named for Bywell Castle) and sank into the Thames in under four minutes. Of the approximately 700 passengers, over 600 were lost.[116]

1878 drawing. The *Bywell Castle* bears down upon the *Princess Alice*.

During World War I, on 19 January 1917 73 people died, including 14 workers, and more than 400 were injured, in a TNT explosion in the Brunner-Mond munitions factory in Silvertown. Much of the area was flattened, and the shock wave was felt throughout the city and much of Essex. This was the largest explosion in London history, and was heard in Southampton and Norwich. Andreas Angel, chief chemist at the plant, was posthumously awarded the Edward Medal for trying to extinguish the fire that caused the blast.[117] The same year, on 13 June, a bomb from a German Gotha bomber killed 18 children in their primary school in Upper North Street, Poplar. This event is commemorated by the local war memorial erected in Poplar Recreation Ground,[118] [119] but during the war a total of 120 children and 104 adults were killed in the East End by aerial bombing, with many more injured.[120]

Another tragedy occurred on the morning of 16 May 1968 when Ronan Point, a 23-storey tower block in Newham, suffered a structural collapse due to a natural gas explosion. Four people were killed in the disaster and seventeen were injured, as an entire corner of the building slid away. The collapse caused major changes in UK building regulations and led to the decline of further building of high rise council flats that had characterised 1960s public architecture.[121]

Entertainment

Inn-yard theatres were first established in the Tudor period, with the Boar's Head Inn (1557) in Whitechapel, the George in Stepney and a purpose built, but short lived, John Brayne's Red Lion Theatre (1567), nearby.[122] The first permanent theatres with resident companies were constructed in Shoreditch, with James Burbage's The Theatre (1576) and Henry Lanman's Curtain Theatre (1577) standing close together. On the night of 28 December 1598 Burbage's sons dismantled The Theatre, and moved it piece by piece across the Thames to construct the Globe Theatre.[123]

Curtain Theatre, c. 1600 (some sources identify this as a depiction of The Theatre, the other Elizabethan theatre in Shoreditch)

The Goodman's Fields Theatre was established in 1727, and it was here that David Garrick made his successful début as *Richard III*, in 1741. In the 19th century the theatres of the East End rivalled in their grandiosity and seating capacity those of the West End. The first of this era was the ill-fated Brunswick Theatre (1828), which collapsed three days after opening, killing 15 people. This was followed by the opening of the Pavilion (1828) in Whitechapel, the Garrick (1831) in Leman Street, the Effingham (1834) in Whitechapel, the Standard (1835) in Shoreditch, the City of London (1837) in Norton Folgate, then the Grecian and the Britannia Theatre in Hoxton (1840).[124] Though very popular for a time, from the 1860s onwards these theatres, one by one, began to close, the buildings were demolished and their very memory began to fade.[125]

1867 Poster from the National Standard Theatre, Shoreditch

There were also many Yiddish theatres, particularly around Whitechapel. These developed into professional companies, after the arrival of Jacob Adler in 1884 and the formation of his 'Russian Jewish Operatic Company' that first performed in Beaumont Hall,[126] Stepney, and then found homes both in the Prescott Street Club, Stepney, and in Princelet Street in Spitalfields.[127] The Pavilion became an exclusively Yiddish theatre in 1906, finally closing in 1936 and being demolished in 1960. Other important Jewish theatres were Feinmans, The Jewish National Theatre and the Grand Palais. Performances were in Yiddish, and predominantly melodrama.[88] These declined, as audience and actors left for New York and the more prosperous parts of London.[128]

The once popular music halls of the East End have mostly met the same fate as the theatres. Prominent examples included the London Music Hall (1856–1935), 95-99 Shoreditch High Street, and the Royal Cambridge Music Hall (1864–1936), 136 Commercial Street. An example of a 'giant pub hall', Wilton's Music Hall (1858), remains in Grace's Alley, off Cable Street and the early 'saloon style' Hoxton Hall (1863) survives in Hoxton Street, Hoxton.[129] Many popular music hall stars came from the East End, including Marie Lloyd.

The music hall tradition of live entertainment lingers on in East End public houses, with music and singing. This is complemented by less respectable amusements such as striptease, which, since the 1950s has become a fixture of certain East End pubs, particularly in the area of Shoreditch, despite being a target of local authority restraints.[130]

Novelist and social commentator Walter Besant proposed a 'Palace of Delight'[131] with concert halls, reading rooms, picture galleries, an art school and various classes, social rooms and frequent fêtes and dances. This coincided with a project by the philanthropist businessman, Edmund Hay Currie to use the money from the winding up of the 'Beaumont Trust',[132] together with subscriptions to build a 'People's Palace' in the East End. Five acres of land were secured on the Mile End Road, and the *Queen's Hall* was opened by Queen Victoria on 14 May 1887. The complex was completed with a library, swimming pool, gymnasium and winter garden, by 1892, providing an eclectic mix of populist entertainment and education. A peak of 8000 'tickets' were sold for classes in 1892, and by 1900, a Bachelor of Science degree awarded by the University of London was introduced.[133] In 1931, the building was destroyed by fire, but the Draper's Company, major donors to the original scheme, invested more to rebuild the technical college and create Queen Mary's College in December 1934.[134] A new 'People's Palace' was constructed, in 1937, by the Metropolitan Borough of Stepney, in St Helen's Terrace. This finally closed in 1954.[135]

Hoxton Hall, still an active community resource and performance space

Professional theatre returned briefly to the East End in 1972, with the formation of the Half Moon Theatre in a rented former synagogue in Aldgate. In 1979, they moved to a former Methodist chapel, near Stepney Green and built a new theatre on the site, opening in May 1985, with a production of *Sweeney Todd*. The theatre enjoyed success, with premières by Dario Fo, Edward Bond and Steven Berkoff, but by the mid-1980s, the theatre suffered a financial crisis and closed. After years of disuse, it has been converted to a public house.[136] The theatre spawned two further arts projects: the *Half Moon Photography Workshop*, exhibiting in the theatre and locally, and from 1976 publishing *Camerwork*,[137] and the 'Half Moon Young People's Theatre', which remains active in Tower Hamlets.[138]

Today

Historically, the East End has suffered from under-investment in both housing stock and infrastructure. From the 1950s, the East End represented the structural and social changes affecting the UK economy in a microcosm. The area had one of the highest concentrations of council housing, the legacy both of slum clearance and war time destruction.[139] The progressive closure of docks, cutbacks in railways and the closure and relocation of industry contributed to a long term decline, removing many of the traditional sources of low- and semi-skilled jobs. However, beginning with the LDDC, in the 1980s, there have been a number of urban regeneration

Redevelopment of Isle of Dogs

projects, most notably Canary Wharf, a huge commercial and housing development on the Isle of Dogs. Many of the 1960s tower blocks have been demolished or renovated, replaced by low rise housing, often in private ownership, or owned by housing associations.[140]

The area around Old Spitalfields market and Brick Lane has been extensively regenerated and is famous, amongst other things, as "London's curry capital", and has been dubbed as *Bangla Town*.[141] The contribution of Bangladeshi people to British life was recognised in 1998, when Pola Uddin, Baroness Uddin of Bethnal Green became the first Bangladeshi-born Briton to enter the House of Lords; and the first Muslim peer to swear her oath of allegiance in the name of her own faith.[142]

The area is also home to a number of commercial and public art galleries; including the newly expanded Whitechapel Gallery. The artists Gilbert and George have long made their home and workshop in Spitalfields,[143] and the neighbourhood around Hoxton Square has become a centre for modern British art, including the White Cube gallery, with many artists from the Young British Artists movement living and working in the area. This has made the area around Hoxton and Shoreditch fashionable, with many former residents and artists now driven out by higher property prices, and a busy nightlife has developed, with over 80 licensed premises around Shoreditch.[144]

By the mid-1980s, both the District Line (extended to the East End in 1884 and 1902)[145] and Central Line (1946)[146] were running beyond their capacity, and the Docklands Light Railway (1987) and Jubilee Line (1999) were constructed to improve rail communications through the riverside district. There was a long standing plan to provide London with an inner motorway box, the East Cross Route. Apart from a short section, this was never built,[147] but road communications were improved by the completion of the Limehouse Link tunnel under Limehouse Basin in 1993 and the extension of the A12 connecting to the Blackwall tunnel with an upgraded carriageway in the 1990s. The extension of the East London line to the north, on the border between Islington and Hackney, is scheduled to provide further travel links in 2010. From 2017, Crossrail line 1 is expected to create a fast railway service across London, from east to west, with a major interchange at Whitechapel. New river crossings are planned at Beckton, (the Thames Gateway Bridge)[148] and the proposed Silvertown Link road tunnel, to supplement the existing Blackwall Tunnel.[149]

Graphic of the proposed 2012 Summer Olympics stadium

The 2012 Summer Olympics will be held in an Olympic Park created on former industrial land around the River Lee. It is intended that this should leave a legacy of new sports facilities, housing, and industrial and technical infrastructure that will further help regenerate the area.[9] This is linked to a new Stratford International station in the Newham, and the future Stratford City development.[150] Also in Newham is London City Airport, built in 1986 in the former King George V Dock, a small airport serving short-haul domestic and European destinations. In the same area, the University of East London has developed a new campus, and the Queen Mary campus has expanded into new accommodation both adjacent to its existing site at Mile End, and with specialist medical campuses at the Royal London Hospital, Whitechapel and at Charterhouse Square in the City. Whitechapel is the base for the London Air Ambulance, and the hospital's clinical facilities are undergoing a £1 billion refurbishment and expansion.[151]

Much of the area remains, however, one of the poorest in Britain and contains some of the capital's worst deprivation. This is in spite of rising property prices and the extensive building of luxury apartments centred largely around the former dock areas and alongside the Thames. With rising costs elsewhere in the capital and the availability of brownfield land, the East End has become a desirable place for business.[10]

In popular culture

The East End has been the subject of parliamentary commissions and other examinations of social conditions since the 19th century, as seen in Henry Mayhew's *London Labour and the London Poor* (1851)[152] and Charles Booth's *Life and Labour of the People in London* (third, expanded edition 1902-3, in 17 volumes).[43] Narrative accounts of experiences amongst the East End poor were also written by Jack London in *The People of the Abyss* (1903), by George Orwell in parts of his novel *Down and Out in Paris and London*, recounting his own experiences in the 1930s, as well as the Jewish writer Emanuel Litvinoff in his autobiographical novel Journey Through A Small Planet set in the 1930s. A further detailed study of Bethnal Green was carried out in the 1950s by sociologists Michael Young and Peter Willmott, in *Family and Kinship in East London*.[153]

Gus Elen, *The Coster's Mansion*,
1899 sheet music

Themes from these social investigations have been drawn out in fiction. Crime, poverty, vice, sexual transgression, drugs, class-conflict and multi-cultural encounters and fantasies involving Jewish, Chinese and Indian immigrants are major themes. Though the area has been productive of local writing talent, from the time of Oscar Wilde's *The Picture of Dorian Gray* (1891) the idea of 'slumming it' in the 'forbidden' East End has held a fascination for a coterie of the literati.[154]

The image of the East Ender changed dramatically between the 19th century and the 20th. From the 1870s they were characterised in culture as often shiftless, untrustworthy and responsible for their own poverty.[153] However, many East Enders worked in lowly but respectable occupations such as carters, porters and costermongers. This later group particularly became the subject of music hall songs at the turn of the century, with performers such as Marie Lloyd, Gus Elen and Albert Chevalier establishing the image of the humorous East End Cockney and highlighting the conditions of ordinary workers.[155] This image, buoyed by close family and social links, and the community's fortitude in the war, came to be represented in literature and film. However, with the rise of the Kray twins, in the 1960s, the dark side of East End character returned, with a new emphasis on criminality and gangsterism.

See also

- Compare to West End of London
- Historical immigration to Great Britain
- Arrival of black immigrants in London
- History of Bangladeshi immigrants in London
- History of Bangladeshis in the United Kingdom

Museums of local history

- Island History Trust
- Museum in Docklands
- Ragged School Museum
- V&A Museum of Childhood

References

[1] *Oxford Dictionary of London Place Names* A Mills (2000)

[2] From 1801 to 1821, the population of Bethnal Green more than doubled, and by 1831, it had trebled (see table in population section). These incomers were principally weavers. For further details, see Andrew August *Poor Women's Lives: Gender, Work, and Poverty in Late-Victorian London* pp 35-6 (Fairleigh Dickinson University Press, 1999) ISBN 0838638074

[3] By the early 19th century, over 11,000 people were crammed into insanitary slums in an area, which took its name from the former Hospital of St Catherine that had stood on the site since the 12th century.

[4] *The East End* Alan Palmer, (John Murray, London 1989) ISBN 071955666X

[5] *Bethnal Green: Settlement and Building to 1836*, A History of the County of Middlesex: Volume 11: Stepney, Bethnal Green (1998), pp. 91–5 (http://www.british-history.ac.uk/report.asp?compid=22743) Date accessed: 17 April 2007

[6] *Irish in Britain* John A. Jackson, p. 137–9, 150 (Routledge & Kegan Paul, 1964)

[7] *The Jews*, A History of the County of Middlesex: Volume 1: Physique, Archaeology, Domesday, Ecclesiastical Organization, The Jews, Religious Houses, Education of Working Classes to 1870, Private Education from Sixteenth Century (1969), pp. 149–51 (http://www.british-history.ac.uk/report.asp?compid=22113) Date accessed: 17 April 2007

[8] *The Spatial Form of Bangladeshi Community in London's East End* Iza Aftab (http://www.spacesyntax.tudelft.nl/media/prcdngsabstracts/izaaftab.pdf) (UCL) (particularly background of Bangladeshi immigration to the East End). Date accessed: 17 April 2007

[9] *Olympic Park: Legacy* (http://www.london2012.com/plans/olympic-park/legacy/index.php) (London 2012) accessed 20 September 2007

[10] Chris Hammett *Unequal City: London in the Global Arena* (2003) Routledge ISBN 0-415-31730-4

[11] The Nineteenth Century XXIV (1888) p.292; in *East End 1888* William Fishman (1998) p.1

[12] 'Londoners Over the Border', in *Household Words* Charles Dickens 390 (http://apps.newham.gov.uk/history_canningtown/cdickens.htm) 12 September 1857 (Newham archives) accessed 18 September 2007

[13] The New Oxford Dictionary of English (1998) ISBN 0-19-861-263-x - p.582 "**East End** the part of London east of the City as far as the River Lea, including the Docklands"

[14] Fishman (1998) defines the boundaries as being Tower Hamlets and the southern part of Hackney. By contrast, Palmer (2000) writing about a later period includes the dock areas of Newham.

[15] *West Ham: Introduction*, A History of the County of Essex: Volume 6 (1973), pp. 43-50 (http://www.british-history.ac.uk/report.aspx?compid=42748) accessed: 23 February 2008

[16] *Becontree hundred: East Ham*, A History of the County of Essex: Volume 6 (1973), pp. 1-8 (http://www.british-history.ac.uk/report.asp?compid=42740) 18 September 2007

[17] Jack London, *The People of the Abyss* (1903). *The People of the Abyss* (http://www.gutenberg.org/etext/1688) at Project Gutenberg

[18] *New Universal Unabridged Dictionary*

[19] *Concise Oxford Companion to the English Language* Ed. Tom McArthur (Oxford University Press, 2005)

[20] *Estuary English* David Rosewarne (http://www.phon.ucl.ac.uk/home/estuary/rosew.htm) *Times Educational Supplement*, (19 October 1984) accessed 20 November 2007

[21] *Stepney, Old and New London: Volume 2* (1878), pp. 137-142 (http://www.british-history.ac.uk/report.aspx?compid=45083) accessed: 17 November 2007

[22] *Houses of Cistercian monks: Abbey of Stratford Langthorne*, A History of the County of Essex: Volume 2 (1907), pp. 129-133 (http://www.british-history.ac.uk/report.aspx?compid=39836) accessed: 30 April 2008.

[23] *Stepney: Manors and Estates*, A History of the County of Middlesex: Volume 11: Stepney, Bethnal Green (1998), pp. 19-52 (http://www.british-history.ac.uk/report.aspx?compid=22734) accessed: 20 November 2007

[24] *The ancient parish of Barking: Introduction*, A History of the County of Essex: Volume 5 (1966), pp. 184-190 (http://www.british-history.ac.uk/report.aspx?compid=42722) accessed: 20 November 2007

[25] *The Spitalfields Riots 1769* (http://www.cityoflondon.gov.uk/corporation/lma_learning/schoolmate/Irish/sm_irish_stories_detail.asp?ID=246) London Metropolitan Archives accessed on 10 November 2006

[26] *Curiosities of London: Exhibiting the Most Rare and Remarkable* John Timbs, pp. 33 (London, 1855)

[27] *1878 Foundation Deed Of The Salvation Army* (http://www1.salvationarmy.org/heritage.nsf/titles/1878_Foundation_Deed_Of_The_Salvation_Army) (Salvation Army history) accessed 15 February 2007

[28] *History of Barnardo's Homes* (http://www.barnardos.org.uk/who_we_are/history.htm) (Barnardo's 2007) accessed 29 May 2007

[29] Toynbee Hall, named for Arnold Toynbee was founded in 1884 in Commercial Street as a centre for social reform by Samuel and Henrietta Barnett with support from Balliol and Wadham College, Oxford; its work continues today.

[30] *Toynbee Hall* (http://www.spartacus.schoolnet.co.uk/EDtoynbeeH.htm) (Sparticus Educational) accessed 26 September 2007

[31] *East End 1888* William Fishman (Duckworth 1998) ISBN 0-7156-2174-2

[32] *East End Jewish Radicals 1875-1914* William J Fishman (Five Leaves Publications, 2004) ISBN 0 9071234 57

[33] *The Battleship Potemkin and Stepney Green* (http://www.eastlondonhistory.com/battleship potemkin.htm) (East London History Society) accessed on 10 November 2006

[34] *Stalin, Man of the Borderlands* Alfred J. Rieber (http://www.historycooperative.org/journals/ahr/106.5/ah0501001651.html) *The American Historical Review*, **106.5** December 2001 (The History Cooperative)

[35] Lenin stayed in Bloomsbury. Stalin, then known as Joseph Djugashvili, was the delegate from Tbilisi. He did not speak at the conference,
      and did not refer to it in his own memoires. An account of the conference under his name appeared in the Bolshevik newspaper *Bakinskii
      proletarii* (but was excised from the second edition of his collected works). He stayed in Tower House, a hostel for itinerant workers near the
      London Hospital, for two weeks, paying sixpence a night for a cubicle. Jack London and George Orwell, in their respective periods, also
      stayed at the hostel writing on the poor conditions. Today, the hostel provides luxury housing for City workers. *(see Guardian, below)*
[36] *Luxury beckons for East End's house of history* Mark Gould and Jo Revill (http://www.guardian.co.uk/society/2004/oct/24/
      housingpolicy.books) 24 October 2004 *The Guardian* accessed 25 February 2007
[37] *Chapter 16: My Second Foreign Exile: German Socialism* (http://www.marxists.org/archive/trotsky/1930/mylife/ch16.htm) Trotsky,
      Leon *My Life* (Charles Schribner's Sons, NY, 1930) Marxist Internet Archive, accessed 27 February 2008
[38] John Burns is commemorated in the name given to a current Woolwich Ferry)
[39] 2.5p in modern coinage
[40] *The Great Dock Strike of 1889* (http://www.bardaglea.org.uk/docklands/8-strikes-the.html) Smith and Nash, *The Story of the Dockers'
      Strike* (1889) in London Docklands History for GCSE, accessed 18 September 2007
[41] *Angela Georgina Burdett-Coutts* (http://www.nndb.com/people/257/000102948/) in *National Dictionary of Biography* accessed 3
      February 2007
[42] *Social Policy: From the Victorians to the Present Day* Susan Morris (http://fathom.lse.ac.uk/Seminars/21701744/index.html) (LSE
      seminars) accessed 10 November 2006
[43] *Life and Labour of the People in London* (London: Macmillan, 1902-1903) at (http://booth.lse.ac.uk/) The Charles Booth on-line archive
      accessed 10 November 2006
[44] *The Webbs: Beatrice (1858-1943) and Sidney (1859-1947)* (http://www.lse.ac.uk/resources/LSEHistory/webbs.htm) (The history of
      the LSE) accessed 15 November 2007
[45] Barbara Castle, *Sylvia and Christabel Pankhurst* (Penguin Books, 1987) ISBN 0-14-008761-3
[46] *Poplarism, 1919-25: George Lansbury and the Councillors' Revolt* Noreen Branson (Lawrence & Wishart, 1980) ISBN 0-85-315434-1
[47] *Breaking the General Strike* (http://www.eastlondonhistory.com/breaking the general strike.htm) (East London History Society)
      accessed 15 November 2007
[48] *Building the Great Eastern* (http://www.portcities.org.uk/london/server/show/ConNarrative.61/chapterId/1225/
      The-Great-Eastern-as-a-passenger-liner.html) Port Cities: London, accessed 17 April 2007
[49] *West India Docks (1803-1980)* (http://www.portcities.org.uk/london/server/show/ConFactFile.83/West-India-Docks.html) Port
      Cities: London, accessed 29 September 2007
[50] *East India Docks (1806-1967)* (http://www.portcities.org.uk/london/server/show/ConFactFile.69/East-India-Docks.html) Port Cities:
      London, accessed 29 September 2007
[51] *London Docks (1805-1971)* (http://www.portcities.org.uk/london/server/show/ConFactFile.78/London-Docks.html) Port Cities:
      London, accessed 29 September 2007
[52] *St Katharine Docks (1828-1969)* (http://www.portcities.org.uk/london/server/show/ConFactFile.77/St-Katharine-Docks.html) Port
      Cities: London, accessed 29 September 2007
[53] *Millwall Docks (1868-1980)* (http://www.portcities.org.uk/london/server/show/ConFactFile.79/Millwall-Docks.html) Port Cities:
      London, accessed 29 September 2007
[54] *Our Home Railways* (Volume 2) W.J. Gordon (1910, Frederick Warne & Co, London)
[55] *Basildon's Railway Stations* (http://www.basildon.com/history/railway/railway.html) Basildon History On-line, accessed 23 October
      2007
[56] *Bow* (http://www.subbrit.org.uk/sb-sites/stations/b/bow/index.shtml) Disused stations, site record, Subterranea Britannica, accessed
      23 October 2007
[57] *Royal Victoria Dock (1855-1981)* (http://www.portcities.org.uk/london/server/show/ConFactFile.73/Royal-Victoria-Dock.html) Port
      Cities: London, accessed 29 September 2007
[58] *Royal Albert Dock (1880-1980)* (http://www.portcities.org.uk/london/server/show/ConFactFile.72/Royal-Albert-Dock.html) Port
      Cities: London, accessed 29 September 2007
[59] *King George V Dock (1921-1981)* (http://www.portcities.org.uk/london/server/show/ConFactFile.71/King-George-V-Dock.html)
      Port Cities: London, accessed 29 September 2007
[60] *Royal Docks - a short History* (http://www.royaldockstrust.org.uk/rdhist.htm) Royal Docks Trust (2006) accessed 18 September 2007
[61] *The London Docklands Development Corporation 1981–1998* (2007) (http://www.lddc-history.org.uk/index.html) LDDC accessed 18
      September 2007
[62] *Tilbury Dock (1886-1981)* (http://www.portcities.org.uk/london/server/show/ConFactFile.82/Tilbury-Dock.html) Port
      Cities:London, accessed 29 September 2007
[63] *What lies beneath ... East End of London* (http://www.eastlondonhistory.com/meotra.htm) East London History Society accessed 5 Oct
      2007
[64] 'Bethnal Green: Building and Social Conditions from 1837 to 1875', A History of the County of Middlesex: Volume 11: Stepney, Bethnal
      Green (1998), pp. 120-26 (http://www.british-history.ac.uk/report.asp?compid=22751) accessed: 14 November 2006.
[65] *Hovels to High Rise: State Housing in Europe Since 1850* Anne Power (Routeledge, 1993) ISBN 0415089352

[66] *The estate of Sir Charles Wheler and the Wilkes family* (http://www.british-history.ac.uk/report.aspx?compid=50161), Survey of London: volume 27: Spitalfields and Mile End New Town Great Eastern Buildings (1957), pp. 108-115. accessed 17 May 2008

[67] *Walks Through History: Exploring the East End*, Taylor, Rosemary (Breedon Books 2001) ISBN 1 8598327 09

[68] *Bethnal Green: Building and Social Conditions from 1915 to 1945*, A History of the County of Middlesex: Volume 11: Stepney, Bethnal Green (1998), pp. 132-135 (http://www.british-history.ac.uk/report.aspx?compid=22753) accessed: 10 October 2007

[69] *From Here to Obscurity* Yoel Sheridan (Tenterbooks, 2001) ISBN 0954081102

[70] The weather closed in on the night of 2 November 1940, otherwise London would have been bombed for 76 successive nights. *Docklands at War - The Blitz* (http://www.museumindocklands.org.uk/English/EventsExhibitions/Themes/DocklandsWar/Docklandsatwar1.htm) The Museum in Docklands accessed 27 February 2008

[71] An earlier planned evacuation had been met with intense distrust in the East End, families preferring to remain united and in their own homes (see Palmer, 1989).

[72] The man responsible for the shelter programme was Charles Kay MP, London's Joint Regional Commissioner, and a former councillor and Mayor of Poplar. Elected on a pro-war ticket within the first 30 weeks of war (see Palmer, 1989, p. 139)

[73] *Remembering the East End:The Second World War* (http://www.age-exchange.org.uk/eastend/secondworldwar/index.html) Age-exchange accessed 14 November 2007

[74] *Mass-Observation Archive: Topic Collections:Air Raids 1938-45* (Box TC23/9/T) (http://www.sussex.ac.uk/library/speccoll/collection_catalogues/tclists/tc23.html) University of Sussex, special collections accessed 15 November 2007

[75] *Mass-Observation Archive: Topic Collections:Anti-Semitism survey 1939-51* (http://www.sussex.ac.uk/library/speccoll/collection_catalogues/tclists/tc62.html) University of Sussex, special collections accessed 15 November 2007

[76] *Bethnal Green tube disaster* (http://www.bbc.co.uk/homeground/archive/2003/bethnal-green-tube-disaster.shtml) (BBC Homeground) accessed 15 February 2007

[77] *Best and worst of art bites the dust* (http://www.libraryofmu.org/display-resource.php?id=375) Roberts, Alison *The Times*, London, 12 January 1994 accessed 5 October 2007

[78] *The East End at War* Rosemary Taylor and Christopher Lloyd (Sutton Publishing, 2007) ISBN 0750949139

[79] "Biography of Queen Elizabeth, the Queen Mother" (http://www.britainexpress.com/royals/queen-mother.htm). BritainExpress. . Retrieved 2007-02-13.

[80] Jennifer Wilding. "The Will to Fight" (http://www.onwar.com/articles/0205.htm). On War. . Retrieved 2007-02-13.

[81] Pre-fabricated housing was constructed under the auspices of the Burt Committee and the Housing (Temporary Accommodation) Act 1944.

[82] *The Lansbury Estate: Introduction and the Festival of Britain exhibition*, Survey of London: volumes 43 and 44: Poplar, Blackwall and Isle of Dogs (1994), pp. 212-23 (http://www.british-history.ac.uk/report.asp?compid=46490) accessed: 18 September 2007

[83] *London's First Chinatown* (http://www.portcities.org.uk/london/server/show/ConNarrative.127/chapterId/2614/Chinese-in-the-Port-of-London.html) Port Cities: London, accessed 29 May 2007

[84] Further relief was distributed at the Yorkshire Stingo, on the south side of Marylebone Road, with other centres of Black poor being the rookery of Seven Dials and Marylebone.

[85] Braidwood, Stephen *Black Poor and White Philanthropists: London's Blacks and the Foundation of the Sierra Leone Settlement 1786 - 1791* (Liverpool University Press, 1994)

[86] Geoffrey Bell, *The other Eastenders : Kamal Chunchie and West Ham's early black community* (Stratford: Eastside Community Heritage, 2002)

[87] *London from the Air* (http://www.eastlondonhistory.com/london from the air.htm) East London History Society accessed 5 July 2007

[88] *Exploring the vanishing Jewish East End* (http://www.visiteastlondon.co.uk/downloads/Leaflets/Jewish History walk pdf.pdf) London Borough of Tower Hamlets accessed 26 Sep 2007

[89] *Dispersing the Myths about Asylum* Helen Shooter, March 2003 (http://www.socialistreview.org.uk/article.php?articlenumber=8365) (Socialist Review) accessed 1 October 2007

[90] *Aliens Act 1905 (5 Edward VII c.13)* (UK Government Acts) available online at Moving Here (http://www.movinghere.org.uk/search/catalogue.asp?RecordID=77093&ResourceTypeID=2&sequence=6)

[91] *Day the East End said 'No pasaran' to Blackshirts* (http://www.guardian.co.uk/farright/story/0,,1884440,00.html) by Audrey Gillan, *The Guardian*, 30 September 2006. Retrieved 17 April 2007

[92] Bethnal Green and Stepney Trades Council *Blood on the Streets* (report published 1978)

[93] Troyna, Barry and Carrington, Bruce *Education, Racism and Reform* pp. 30–31 (Taylor & Francis, 1990) ISBN 041503826X

[94] *On this day* report (http://news.bbc.co.uk/onthisday/hi/dates/stories/september/17/newsid_2520000/2520085.stm) BBC accessed: 17 April 2007

[95] *Life sentence for London nailbomber* (http://www.met.police.uk/news/stories/copeland/job/1.htm), *The Job*, published by the London Metropolitan Police, 30 June 2000; accessed: 17 April 2007

[96] *Metropolitan Essex since 1919: Suburban growth*, A History of the County of Essex: Volume 5 (1966), pp. 63-74 (http://www.british-history.ac.uk/report.aspx?compid=42708) accessed: 18 October 2007

[97] *Population data for Civil Parishes* Statistical Abstract for London Vol IV (London County Council 1901)

[98] *A vision of Britain between 1801 and 2001. Including maps, statistical trends and historical descriptions* Vision of Britain - Population data: *Metropolitan Borough of Bethnal Green* (http://vision.edina.ac.uk/data_cube_table_page.jsp?data_theme=T_POP&data_cube=N_TPop&u_id=10186353&c_id=10001043&add=N), *Metropolitan Borough of Poplar* (http://vision.edina.ac.uk/data_cube_table_page.

jsp?data_theme=T_POP&data_cube=N_TPop&u_id=10088628&c_id=10001043&add=N), *Metropolitan Borough of Stepney* (http://
vision.edina.ac.uk/data_cube_table_page.jsp?data_theme=T_POP&data_cube=N_TPop&u_id=10207101&c_id=10001043&add=N)

[99] Vision of Britain (http://vision.edina.ac.uk/data_cube_table_page.jsp?data_theme=T_POP&data_cube=N_TPop&u_id=10108275&
c_id=10001043&add=N) (LB Tower Hamlets Population) accessed 22 February 2008

[100] *Neighbourhood Statistics* (http://www.neighbourhood.statistics.gov.uk/dissemination/LeadDatasetList.do?a=3&b=276772&c=E1+
4LP&d=13&g=346818&i=1001x1003&m=0&enc=1&domainId=46) - LB Tower Hamlets statistics (National Statistics) accessed 22
February 2008

[101] 2001 Census (29 April 2001). "Census 2001 Profiles — Tower Hamlets" (http://www.statistics.gov.uk/census2001/profiles/00bg.
asp). National Statistics Online. . Retrieved 200-03-26.

[102] *Bangladeshi population estimates* (http://www.neighbourhood.statistics.gov.uk/dissemination/LeadTrendView.do?a=7&b=276772&
c=tower+hamlets&d=13&e=13&f=24451&g=346968&i=1001x1003x1004x1005&l=1812&o=254&m=0&r=1&s=1237123476500&
enc=1&adminCompId=24451&variableFamilyIds=6374&xW=1010) - Tower Hamlets Neighbourhood Statistics (Office for National
Statistics). (13 July 2006). Retrieved on 2009-03-27.

[103] *History of the Marine Support Unit* (http://www.met.police.uk/msu/history.htm) (Metropolitan Police) accessed 24 January 2007

[104] *Records of Service* (http://www.met.police.uk/history/records.htm) (Metropolitan Police) accessed 23 Oct 2007

[105] *Early Murder Investigations* (http://www.historybytheyard.co.uk/early_murder_investigations.htm) The Official Encyclopaedia of
Scotland Yard, accessed 23 October 2007

[106] *History of the Metropolitan Police: Time Line 1829 - 1849* (http://www.met.police.uk/history/timeline1829-1849.htm) (Metropolitan
Police) accessed 23 October 2007

[107] *Prostitution in maritime London* (http://www.portcities.org.uk/london/server/show/ConNarrative.111/chapterId/2339/
Prostitution-in-maritime-London.html) Port Cities: London, accessed 29 September 2007

[108] *19th century responses to prostitution* (http://www.portcities.org.uk/london/server/show/ConNarrative.111/chapterId/2347/
Prostitution-in-maritime-London.html) Port Cities: London, accessed 29 September 2007

[109] *Prostitution in maritime London* (http://www.portcities.org.uk/london/server/show/ConNarrative.111/chapterId/2349/
Prostitution-in-maritime-London.html) Port Cities: London, accessed 29 September 2007

[110] *Ratcliffe Highway Murders* (http://www.thamespolicemuseum.org.uk/h_ratcliffehighwaymurders_1.html) (Thames Police Museum)
accessed 15 Feb 2007

[111] *Sarah Wise - The Italian Boy: A Tale of Murder and Body Snatching in 1830s London* (Metropolitan Books, 2004) ISBN 0805075372

[112] *The Houndsditch Murders and the Siege of Sidney Street*, Donald Rumbelow, ISBN 0-491-03178-5

[113] *Inside the Firm: The Untold Story of the Krays' Reign of Terror* Tony Lambrianou (Pan Books 2002) ISBN 0-330-49014-1

[114] *Statement in Lord's Northern Ireland debate* The Lord Privy Seal (Viscount Cranborne) (http://www.publications.parliament.uk/pa/
ld199596/ldhansrd/vo960212/text/60212-07.htm) 12 February 1996 (*Lord's Hansard*, UK Parliament) accessed 26 September 2007

[115] Plague deaths measured at more than 3000 deaths per 478 sq yards in Spitalfields in 1665 (source: *London from the Air*)

[116] *Princess Alice Disaster* (http://www.thamespolicemuseum.org.uk/h_alice_1.html) Thames Police Museum accessed 19 September
2007

[117] *The Silvertown Explosion: London 1917* Graham Hill and Howard Bloch (Stroud: Tempus Publishing 2003). ISBN 0-7524-3053-X.

[118] The *Poplar War Memorial* is an exclusively civilian memorial, reflecting the pacifism of the Mayor Will Crooks and local MP George
Lansbury.

[119] *East London in Mourning* (http://www.ppu.org.uk/memorial/children/index.html) (Peace Pledge Union) accessed 2 April 2007

[120] *The East End at War* (http://www.eastlondonhistory.com/east end at war.htm) East London History Society accessed 14 November
2007

[121] *Collapse: Why Buildings Fall Down* Phil Wearne (Channel 4 books) ISBN 0-7522-1817-4

[122] *Red Lion Theatre, Whitechapel* Christopher Phillpotts (CrossRail Documentary Report, prepare by MoLAS (http://billdocuments.
crossrail.co.uk/files/Home/Home3/04.STRs/STR02_Archaeology/Part 2 Central Route Section/03_Appendix 3 Red Lion Theatre,
Whitechapel, Documentary Researc/0004_R_ RedLionTheatre.pdf) accessed 17 Nov 2007

[123] *William Shakespeare: A Compact Documentary Life* Samuel Schoenbaum (Oxford University Press, 1987) ISBN 0195051610

[124] Haycroft, Jack Adams and the troupe moved to Hoxton from premises in Shoreditch, that had operated from the early 1830s, *The Making
of the Britannia Theatre* Alan D. Craxford and Reg Moore, from *Sam and Sallie: A novel of the theatre* Alfred L. Crauford, (London: Cranley
and Day 1933) (http://www.craxford-family.co.uk/crauart1.php) accessed 22 September 2007

[125] *Theatre in the Victorian Age* Michael Booth (CUP 1991) pp. 4-6

[126] *Yiddish Theatre and music hall in London: 1880 - 1905* (http://www.jewishmuseum.org.uk/whatson/exhibitions/y3.asp) The Jewish
Museum (2004) accessed on 31 March 2007

[127] *A Life on the Stage: A Memoir* Jacob Adler translated and with commentary by Lulla Rosenfeld, (Knopf NY 1999) ISBN 0-679-41351-0

[128] *The end of Yiddish theatre* (http://www.eastlondonhistory.com/yiddish theatre.htm) East London History Society accessed on 29 April
2007

[129] *The Last Empires: A Music Hall Companion* ed. Benny Green (London, Pavilion Books Ltd. in association with Michael Joseph Ltd.,
1986)

[130] Lara Clifton *Baby Oil and Ice: Striptease in East London* (DoNotPress, 2002) ISBN 1 899 344 85 3

[131] In Walter Besant *All Sorts and Conditions of Men* (1882)

[132] In 1841, John Barber Beaumont died and left property in Beaumont Square, Stepney to provide for the 'education and entertainment' of people from the neighbourhood. The charity - and its property - was becoming moribund by the 1870s, and in 1878 it was wound up by the Charity Commissioners, providing its new chair, Sir Edmund Hay Currie, with £120,000 to invest in a similar project. He raised a further £50,000 and secured continued funding from the Draper's Company for ten years (The Whitechapel Society, below)

[133] *From Palace to College - An illustrated account of Queen Mary College* G. P. Moss and M. V. Saville pp. 39-48 (University of London 1985) ISBN 0-902238-06-X

[134] *The People's Palace* (http://www.whitechapelsociety.com/London/life_leisure/peoples_palace.htm) The Whitechapel Society (2006), accessed 5 July 2007

[135] *Origins and History* (http://www.qmul.ac.uk/alumni/alumninetwork/qmandw/qm_origins_history.pdf) Queen Mary, University of London Alumni Booklet (2005) accessed 5 July 2007

[136] Royal Holloway *Half Moon Theatre archive* (http://www.aim25.ac.uk/cgi-bin/search2?coll_id=7092&inst_id=11) Archives in M25, accessed 23 October 2007

[137] British Photography 1945-80: Part 4: Britain in the 70s (http://photography.about.com/library/weekly/aa112000d.htm) *The New York Times* online, accessed 23 May 2007

[138] *About Us* (http://www.halfmoon.org.uk/aboutus.html) Half Moon Young People's Theatre accessed 23 October 2007

[139] *Poverty, Housing Tenure and Social Exclusion* Peter Lee and Alan Murie, (The Policy Press in association with the Joseph Rowntree Foundation, 1997) ISBN 1 86134 063 X

[140] Housing associations, also known as *registered social landlords*, active in the East End, include: BGVPHA (Bethnal Green and Victoria Park Housing Association, Tower Hamlets Community Housing, Poplar HARCA and EastendHomes.

[141] *The taste of Banglatown* Paul Barker 13 April 2004 (http://www.guardian.co.uk/comment/story/0,,1190643,00.html) *The Guardian* accessed 18 September 2007

[142] *Bangladeshi London* (http://www.20thcenturylondon.org.uk/server.php?show=conInformationRecord.294) (Exploring 20th century London) accessed 26 March 2009

[143] *Gilbert & George: The Complete Pictures*, Rudi Fuchs (Tate Publishing, 2007) ISBN 9781854376817

[144] *Draft Statement of Licensing Policy* (s5.2) - London Borough of Hackney (2007)

[145] *District line facts* (http://www.tfl.gov.uk/tfl/corporate/modesoftransport/tube/linefacts/?line=district) TfL accessed 23 October 2007

[146] *An extended history of the Central line* (http://www.tfl.gov.uk/tfl/corporate/modesoftransport/tube/linefacts/?line=central#history) TfL accessed 23 October 2007

[147] *East Cross Route* (http://www.cbrd.co.uk/histories/ringways/ringway1.shtml#ecr) (Chris's British Road Directory) accessed 23 Oct 2007

[148] *Thames Gateway Bridge* Transport Projects in London (http://www.alwaystouchout.com/project/41) (alwaystouchout) accessed 20 July 2007

[149] *Silvertown Link* Transport Projects in London (http://www.alwaystouchout.com/project/41) (alwaystouchout) accessed 20 July 2007

[150] Webster, Ben (2006-04-21). "Ghost train station that cost £210 m" (http://www.timesonline.co.uk/article/0,,2-2144275,00.html) (in en-GB). *The Times* (London). . Retrieved 2007-07-24.

[151] Ben Bradshaw, written Parliamentary answer (http://www.publications.parliament.uk/pa/cm200607/cmhansrd/cm070903/text/70903w0070.htm#0709051009754), *Hansard* 3 September 2007 accessed 18 September 2007

[152] Henry Mayhew, *London Labour and the London Poor* (London: Griffin, Bohn, and Company, Stationers' Hall Court) in Volume 1 (1861) (http://nils.lib.tufts.edu/cgi-bin/ptext?doc=Perseus:text:4000.01.0140), Volume 2 (http://nils.lib.tufts.edu/cgi-bin/ptext?doc=Perseus:text:4000.01.0141), Volume 3 (http://nils.lib.tufts.edu/cgi-bin/ptext?doc=Perseus:text:4000.01.0142), and an additional Volume (1862) (http://nils.lib.tufts.edu/cgi-bin/ptext?doc=Perseus:text:4000.01.0143) all accessed 14 November 2007

[153] *Family and Kinship in East London* Michael Young and Peter Willmott (1957) ISBN 978-0140205954

[154] William Taylor (2001) *This Bright Field: A Travel Book in One Place*

[155] *Vaudeville, Old and New: An Encyclopedia of Variety Performers in America* pp 351-2, Frank Cullen, Florence Hackman, Donald P. McNeilly (Routledge 2006) (http://books.google.com/books?id=XFnfnKg6BcAC&pg=PA351&lpg=PA351&dq="gus+elen"&source=web&ots=5svEnNz8A-&sig=N1coxv6YYj5jafbpSFvtDhbaFLQ#PPA352,M1) ISBN 0415938538 accessed 22 October 2007

- *This article incorporates text from the 1901–1906 Jewish Encyclopedia, a publication now in the public domain.*

Further reading

- Geoffrey Bell, *The other Eastenders : Kamal Chunchie and West Ham's early black community* (Stratford: Eastside Community Heritage, 2002)
- Walter Besant. *All Sorts and Conditions of Men* (1882)
- Gerry Black *Jewish London: An Illustrated History* (Breedon) ISBN 1-85983-363-2
- William J. Fishman, *East End 1888: Life in a London Borough Among the Laboring Poor* (1989)
- William J. Fishman, *Streets of East London* (1992) (with photographs by Nicholas Breach)
- William J. Fishman, *East End Jewish Radicals 1875-1914* (2004)
- Gretchen Gerzina, *Black London: Life Before Emancipation* (New Jersey, 1995)
- Tony Lambrianou, *Inside the Firm: The Untold Story of the Krays' Reign of Terror* - (2002)
- Nigel Glendinning, Joan Griffiths, Jim Hardiman, Christopher Lloyd and Victoria Poland, *Changing Places: a short history of the Mile End Old Town RA area (Mile End Old Town Residents' Association, 2001)*
- Derek Morris, *Mile End Old Town 1740-1780: A social history of an early modern London Suburb* (East London History Society, 2007) ISBN 978-0-9506258-6-7
- Alan Palmer, *The East End* (John Murray, London 1989)

External links

London/East End travel guide from Wikitravel

- East End Film Society (http://www.eastendfilmsociety.co.uk/)
- The East End of London (http://www.bbc.co.uk/h2g2/guide/A513596) on h2g2
- East London History Society (http://www.eastlondonhistory.com/)
- Jewish East End of London (http://www.jewisheastend.com/london.html)
- *Stepney and Bethnal Green* Victoria County History of Middlesex Vol 11 (http://www.british-history.ac.uk/source.asp?pubid=92)

Geographical coordinates: 51°31′N 0°03′W

Metropolitan Police Service

Metropolitan Police Service	
Metropolitan Police Force	
Common name	The Met[1]
Abbreviation	MPS[2]
Working together for a safer London	
Logo of the Metropolitan Police Service.	
Flag of the Metropolitan Police Service.	
Motto	Working together for a safer London[1]
Agency overview	
Formed	29 September, 1829[3]
Preceding agencies	• Bow Street Runners[4] • Marine Police Force[5]
Employees	50,000
Volunteers	797[6]
Annual budget	£3.5bn[7]
Legal personality	Governmental: Government agency
Jurisdictional structure	
Operations jurisdiction*	Police area of Metropolitan Police District in the country of England, UK

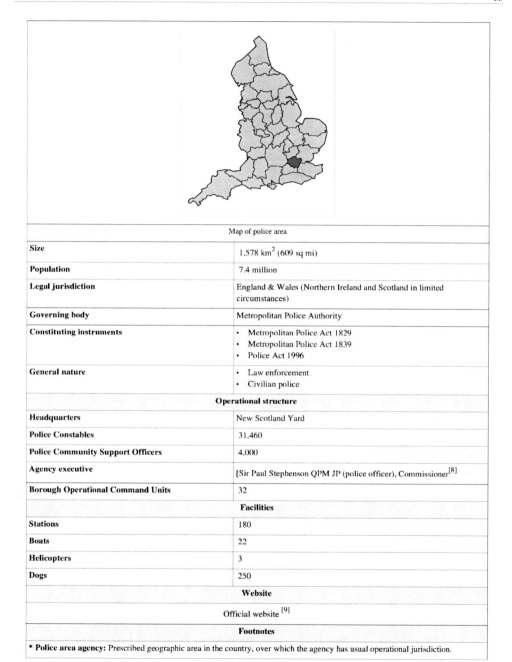

Map of police area	
Size	1,578 km^2 (609 sq mi)
Population	7.4 million
Legal jurisdiction	England & Wales (Northern Ireland and Scotland in limited circumstances)
Governing body	Metropolitan Police Authority
Constituting instruments	• Metropolitan Police Act 1829 • Metropolitan Police Act 1839 • Police Act 1996
General nature	• Law enforcement • Civilian police
Operational structure	
Headquarters	New Scotland Yard
Police Constables	31,460
Police Community Support Officers	4,000
Agency executive	[Sir Paul Stephenson QPM JP (police officer), Commissioner[8]
Borough Operational Command Units	32
Facilities	
Stations	180
Boats	22
Helicopters	3
Dogs	250
Website	
Official website [9]	
Footnotes	
* **Police area agency:** Prescribed geographic area in the country, over which the agency has usual operational jurisdiction.	

The **Metropolitan Police Service** (**MPS**) is the territorial police force responsible for policing within Greater London, excluding the 'square mile' of the City of London which is the responsibility of the City of London

Police.[10]

A number of informal names and abbreviations exist for the Metropolitan Police, such as "the Met" and "MPS". In statutes it is referred to in the lower case as the "metropolitan police force" or the "metropolitan police", without the appendage "service". The MPS is also referred to as **Scotland Yard** after the location of its original headquarters buildings in and around Great Scotland Yard, Whitehall.[10] [11] [12] [13] In 1890, the purpose-built Norman Shaw Building overlooking the River Thames on the Victoria Embankment became the new headquarters and was known as New Scotland Yard.[14] However, the building was cramped so a large twin-towered office block on the corner of Victoria Street and Broadway was leased and the title, New Scotland Yard, transferred there; it remains the official headquarters to this day.[15] Administrative functions are increasingly based at the Empress State Building (ESB), and since late 2007 all command and control functions have been transferred to the three Metcall complexes, rather than New Scotland Yard.

In the period 2007/08, the MPS employed 31,460 police officers, 2,510 Special Constables, 14,085 police staff, and 4,247 Police Community Support Officers.[16] This makes it the largest police force within the United Kingdom, and the second largest in the world after the NYPD.[17] The Commissioner of Police of the Metropolis, known commonly as Commissioner, is the overall head of the force, responsible to the Metropolitan Police Authority. The post of Commissioner was first held jointly by Sir Charles Rowan and Sir Richard Mayne. The Commissioner since 27 January 2009 is Sir Paul Stephenson, QPM who had previously been the Acting Commissioner since 1 December 2008.[18]

Area covered and other forces

The geographical area policed by the MPS, is known as the Metropolitan Police District. In terms of geographic policing the MPS is divided into 32 Borough Operational Command Units which directly align with the London Boroughs, excluding the City of London which is a separate police area and the responsibility of the City of London Police.

The Ministry of Defence Police are responsible for policing of Ministry of Defence property throughout the United Kingdom, including the MoD headquarters in Whitehall and other MoD establishments across the MPS district.[19]

The British Transport Police is responsible for policing of the rail network in the United Kingdom, including London. Within London, they are also responsible for policing of the London Underground, Tramlink and the Docklands Light Railway.[20]

The English part of the Royal Parks Constabulary, which patrolled a number of Greater London's major parks, was merged with the Metropolitan Police in 2004 and is now policed by the Royal Parks Operational Command Unit.[21] There is also a small park police forces, the Kew Constabulary, responsible for the Botanic Gardens) whose officers have full police powers within the park. Some London borough councils maintain their own borough park constabularies, such as the Newham Parks Constabulary in East London; their remit only extends to park by-laws, and although they are sworn as constables under laws applicable to parks, their powers are not equal to those of constables appointed under the Police Acts, meaning that they are not police officers.[22]

It should be noted that despite these specialist police forces the Metropolitan Police is statutorily responsible for law and order throughout the Metropolitan Police District and can take on primacy of any incident or investigation within the MPD.

Metropolitan Police Officers have legal jurisdiction throughout all of England and Wales, including areas which have their own special police forces, such as the Ministry of Defence, as do all police officers of territorial police forces. Officers also have limited powers in Scotland and Northern Ireland. Within the Metropolitan Police District, the Metropolitan Police will take over the investigation of any serious crime from the British Transport Police and Ministry of Defence Police if it is deemed appropriate. Terrorist incidents and complex murder enquiries will always be investigated by the Metropolitan Police, with the assistance of the relevant specialist force, even if they are committed on railway or Ministry of Defence property. (A minor oddity to the normal jurisdiction of territorial police officers in England & Wales is that Metropolitan Police Officers involved in protection duties of Royal family and other VIPs have full police powers in Scotland and Northern Ireland in connection with those duties.)

Police ranks

The Metropolitan Police uses the standard UK police ranks, indicated by shoulder boards, up to Chief Superintendent, but it has five ranks above that level instead of the standard three.[23]

The Metropolian Police approved the use of name badges in October 2003, with new recruits wearing the Velcro badges from September 2004. The badge consists of the wearer's rank, followed by their surname.[24]

Following controversy over alleged assaults by uniformed officers with concealed shoulder identification numbers[25] during the G20 summit, Metropolitan Police Commissioner Sir Paul Stephenson stated that "The public has a right to be able to identify any uniformed officer whilst performing their duty" by their shoulder identification numbers.[26]

- Police Constable (PC) (Divisional call sign and shoulder number)
- Sergeant (Sgt or PS) (three point down chevrons above divisional call sign and Shoulder Number) - an "acting" Sergeant, i.e. a substantive constable being paid an allowance to undertake the duties of a sergeant for a short period of time, displays two point down chevrons above divisional call sign, and Shoulder Number. *The use of the three chevrons of a substantive Sergeant is incorrect, and should only be used during a period of temporary promotion.*
- Inspector (Insp) (two Order of the Bath stars, informally known as "pips")
- Chief Inspector (Ch Insp) (three pips in a line)
- Superintendent (Supt) (single crown)
- Chief Superintendent (Ch Supt) (crown over one pip)
- Commander (Cmdr) (crossed tipstaves in a bayleaf wreath); the first ACPO rank.
- Deputy Assistant Commissioner (DAC) (one pip over Commander's badge)
- Assistant Commissioner (AC) (crown over Commander's badge);
- Deputy Commissioner (crown above two side-by-side small pips, above Commander's badge)
- Commissioner (crown above one pip above Commander's badge)

London Metropolitan Police ranks

Police Constable	Sergeant	Inspector	Chief Inspector	Super-intendent	Chief Super-intendent	Commander	Deputy Assistant Commissioner	Assistant Commissioner	Deputy Commissioner	Commissioner
DF 638	RW 79									

For a comparison of these ranks with other British police forces (in and out of London) see Police ranks of the United Kingdom.

The Metropolitan Police also has several active Volunteer Police Cadet units, which maintain their own internal rank structure.[27] The Metropolitan Special Constabulary is a contingent of part-time volunteer police officers and is attached to most Borough Operational Command Units. The MSC has its own internal rank structure.

Newly employed PCs in the MPS are paid a starting salary of £28,605 (including London weighting), rising to £31,176 after the initial training and probationary period as of 1 September 2008. This continues to rise, with the amount of time the officer has served, rising to a ceiling level of £39,373 after ten years.[28]

The prefix 'Woman' in front of female officers' ranks has been obsolete since 1999. Members of the Criminal Investigation Department (CID) up to and including the rank of Chief Superintendent prefix their ranks with 'Detective'. Other departments, such as Special Branch and Child Protection, award non-detectives 'Branch Detective' status, allowing them to use the 'Detective' prefix. Detective ranks are abbreviated as DC, DS, DI, etc, and are equivalent in rank to their uniform counterparts.

Police numbers

MPS employees consist of uniformed police officers, Special Constables, civilian staff, and Police Community Support Officers[29]. The MPS was the first force to introduce these.

Uniformed traffic wardens, who wear a uniform with yellow and black markings, are a distinct body from local authority civil enforcement officers. The former have greater powers that include being able to stop vehicles and redirect traffic at an incident.[30]

MPS constables policing an event at Trafalgar Square

Total numbers 2009

- Regular Police Officers: 33,000[31]
- Police Community Support Officers: 4,700[31]
- Special Constables: 2,500[31]
- Traffic wardens: 470[31]
- Other police staff: 14,200[31]

Historic numbers

- 2009 – 35,804 (June 9: full time equiv. strength including Special Constables)[32]
- 2004 – 31,000 (approx)[33]
- 2003 – 28,000 (approx)[33]
- 2001 – 25,000 (approx)[34]
- 1984 – 27,000 (approx)[35]
- 1965 – 18,016[36]
- 1952 – 16,400[37]
- 1912 – 20,529[38]

MPS officers protecting World Cup revellers in London, 2006

Cost of the service

Annual expenditure for single years, selected by quarter centuries.[39]

- 1829/30 – £194,126
- 1848 – £437,441
- 1873 – £1,118,785

- 1898 – £1,812,735
- 1923 – £7,838,251
- 1948 – £12,601,263
- 1973 – £95,000,000
- 1998/9 – £2,033,000,000

Crime figures

Crimes reported within the Metropolitan Police District, selected by quarter centuries.[40]

- 1829/30 – 20,000
- 1848 – 15,000
- 1873 – 20,000
- 1898 – 18,838
- 1923 – 15,383
- 1948 – 126,597
- 1973 – 355,258
- 1998/9 – 934,254

Past Commissioners

See Commissioners of Police of the Metropolis, from the MPS's inception in 1829, to 2009.[10]

Police stations

In addition to the Headquarters at New Scotland Yard, there are 140 police stations in London.[41] These range from large borough headquarters staffed around the clock every day to smaller stations which may be open to the public only during normal business hours, or on certain days of the week.

The oldest police station, which opened in Bow Street in 1881, closed in 1992 and the adjoining Bow Street Magistrates Court heard its last case on 14 July 2006.[42] The oldest operational police station is in Wapping, and opened in 1908. It is the headquarters of the Marine Support Unit (formerly known as Thames Division), which is responsible for policing the River Thames. It also houses a mortuary and the River Police Museum.

The Metropolitan Police station in Paddington Green has received much publicity for its housing of terrorism suspects in an underground complex.

Most police stations can easily be identified from one or more blue lamps located outside the entrance, which were introduced in 1861.

Metropolitan police stations may have:

A traditional blue lamp as seen outside most police stations. This one is outside Bow Street Police Station

- Uniformed police officers who are responsible for attending emergency calls.
- Uniformed police officers who make up safer neighbourhood team policing a specific area.
- Police Community Support Officers responsible for a general presence in the community, assisting in policing duties.
- Metropolitan Police employed Traffic wardens who enforce parking regulations.
- Non-police Crime Reduction Officer who are responsible for attending public functions with advice, visiting households, and handing out items such as personal alarms.

- Non-police Firearms Enquiries Officer responsible for issuing firearms certificates and related duties.
- Non-police Station Reception Officer or Station PCSO who are responsible for interaction with members of the public who enter the front office of a police station, along with general administration.
- Non-police Fingerprinting and identification staff who are responsible for maintaining criminal identities, and archives.
- Police cadets assisting police officers, PCSOs or other police staff in non-confrontational duties
- Metropolitan Police Specials may also be present.
- CID detectives concerned with criminal investigations. Detective Constables, Detective Sergeants and Detective Inspectors may be present, headed by a Detective Chief Inspector.
- Most stations have temporary holding cells where an arrested person can be held until either released without charge, bailed to appear at court on a later date, or remanded until escort to a Court of Law.

In 2004 there was a call from the Institute for Public Policy Research for more imaginative planning of police stations to aid in improving relations between police forces and the wider community.[43]

Notable incidents and investigations

Notable major incidents and investigations in which the Metropolitan Police Service has been involved:

- 1888-91 - Whitechapel Murders - Suspected to have been carried out by Jack the Ripper who killed 5 prostitutes, with another 6 being suspected but unconfirmed. In the same period a dismembered corpse was found in the construction site of Scotland Yard which was believed to have been perpetrated by Jack the Ripper, known as The Whitehall Mystery. No suspect was ever charged with the murders, and to this day the exact identity of the killer remains unknown, with the crime unsolved.
- 2 January 1911 - Siege of Sidney Street - Involved members of a Latvian gang taking a couple hostage after an unsuccessful attempt to rob a jeweller's, Home Secretary Winston Churchill later arrived to take charge of the siege, and authorised a detachment of Scots Guards to assist police from the Tower of London.[44]
- 1970-1990s - IRA bombing campaign - Throughout the last quarter of the 20th century, several bombings were carried out by the Provisional Irish Republican Army. The bombings which the PIRA carried out within the Metropolitan Police District, and those planted in central London can be found here.[45]
- 28 February 1975 - Moorgate Tube Train Crash - A London Underground train failed to stop and crashed into the buffers at the end of a tunnel, recorded as the largest loss of life in peacetime on the Tube, over 42 people killed.[46]
- 30 August 1976 - Notting Hill Carnival Riot - After MPS officers attempted to arrest a "pickpocket", a riot ensued leading to over 100 officers being admitted to hospital.[47]
- 6–12 December 1975 - Balcombe Street Siege - Occurred when PIRA members took a couple hostage in their home, while on the run from police.[48]
- 18 September 1975 - Spaghetti House Siege - The Spaghetti House Siege occurred when members of the "Black Liberation Front" attempted to commit an armed robbery at Spaghetti House Restaurant to gain publicity for their cause. However, the robbery was discovered by police, and the would-be robbers initiated a siege by taking hostages.[49]
- 1978-1983 - Muswell Hill Murders - Mass murderer Dennis Nilsen murdered at least 15 men over a period of five years, disposing of the body parts by burning or in drains, he was also found to have many remains in his home at Muswell Hill when police apprehended him.[50]
- Blair Peach April 1979 - Peach was fatally injured in April 1979 during a demonstration in Southall by the Anti-Nazi League against a National Front election meeting taking place in the town hall. He was knocked unconscious and died the next day in hospital. Police brutality was never proven to be a contributory factor in his death, but it was claimed that he had fallen to a blow from a rubberised police radio belonging to the Metropolitan Police's Special Patrol Group.[51]

- 1980 Iranian Embassy Siege - The Iranian Embassy Siege involved members of a terrorist group calling themselves the "Democratic Revolutionary Movement for the Liberation of Arabistan (DRMLA)" took the embassy staff hostage, the Metropolitan Police were heavily involved in the hostage negotiation, but after six days, negotiations were terminated, preceded by an assault by the British Army's Special Air Service.[52]
- April 11, 1981 - Brixton Riot - During the early 1980s the Metropolitan Police began "Operation Swamp" which was implemented to cut street crime by the use of the Stop Under Suspicion which legally allowed officers to stop people on the suspicion of wrong doing. Tensions rose within the black community after a black youth was stabbed, leading to severe rioting.[53]
- 1982-86 Railway Rapists - John Duffy and David Mulcahy committed 18 rapes of women and young girls near railway stations in London and the South East, murdering three of their victims. Metropolitan Police officers worked with neighbouring forces to solve the crimes. Duffy was convicted in 1988, but Mulcahy was not brought to justice until almost 10 years later.[54]
- 28 September 1985 - Brixton Riot - Rioting erupted in Brixton, sparked by the shooting of Dorothy 'Cherry' Groce by police seeking her son Michael Groce in relation to a suspected firearms offence believed to be hiding in his mother's home. He was not there at the time, and Groce was part-paralysed by the bullet.[55]
- 6 October 1985 - Broadwater Farm Riot - A week after the Brixton riot of 28 September 1985, while tensions among the black community were still high, riots broke out in Tottenham after the mother of a black man whose house was being searched died of a heart attack during the operation. In the course of the riot, PC Keith Blakelock was murdered.[56]
- 1986 - Stockwell Strangler - Kenneth Erskine carried out a series of attacks in Stockwell on elderly men and women, breaking into their homes and strangling them to death. Most were sexually assaulted.[57]
- 18 November 1987 - King's Cross Fire - Fire broke out under a wooden escalator leading from one of the underground station platforms to the surface. The blaze and resulting smoke claimed 31 lives, including that of a senior firefighter.[58]
- 12 December 1988 - Clapham Train Crash - A packed commuter train passed a defective signal and ran into the back of a second train, derailing it into the path of a third coming the other way. The crash killed 35 people and seriously injured 69 others.[59]
- 20 August 1989 - Sinking of the Marchioness - Pleasure boat the Marchioness was struck by the dredger *Bowbelle*, killing 30 people.[60]
- 31 March 1990 - Trafalgar Square Riot - Also known as the Poll Tax Riot, this was triggered by growing unrest against the Community Charge, and grew from a legitimate demonstration which had taken place that morning. An estimated £400,000-worth of damage was caused.[61]
- 8 January 1991 - Cannon Street Train Crash - Two people were killed and over 500 injured.[62]
- 1993 - "Gay Slayer" - Former soldier Colin Ireland murdered five homosexual men in a deliberate bid to get notoriety - he had read an article that said to be a serial killer you must have killed five times or more.[63]
- 1993 - Stephen Lawrence and the MacPherson Inquiry - A series of operations failed to convict the killers of schoolboy Stephen Lawrence, despite substantial evidence. The resulting MacPherson inquiry found that the Metropolitan Police was 'institutionally racist'.[64]
- December 1995 - Brixton Riot - A large gathering protested outside Brixton Police Station over the death of a local man in police custody, leading to a riot. Three police officers were injured with a two mile exclusion zone set-up around Brixton, later reports showed that the male in custody died of heart failure, said to be brought on because of difficulties restraining him.[65]
- April 1999 - London Nailbomber - Lone bomber David Copeland carried out a series of hate attacks on ethnic minority areas and on a pub frequented by the homosexual community.[66]
- 18 June 1999 - Anti-capitalist Riot - Previously peaceful anti-capitalist demonstrations ended with disorder in The City, which caused widespread damage, particularly to businesses in the financial district identified with global capitalism.[67]

- 1 May 2001 - May Day protest - In an attempt to control crowds, the police employed the tactic of "kettling", and were criticised for detaining innocent bystanders for long periods of time.[68]
- 21 September 2001 - Thames murder case - A dismembered body of a young boy believed to have been between the ages of four and seven was spotted floating in the River Thames, named by police as *Adam* in the absence of a confirmed name. During the investigation a Commander and a Detective Chief Inspector met with Nelson Mandela.[69] The case was never solved.[70]
- 2004 Pro-hunting protests - demonstrators protesting against the Hunting Act 2004 outside the UK Parliament were involved in violent confrontations with the Metropolitan Police.[71]
- 7 July 2005 - London Bombings - Multiple bombings across London, in which MPS worked to a Major Incident Plan to provide coordination, control and forensic and investigative resources.[72]
- 21 July 2005 - Attempted London Bombings - Multiple attempted bombings across London, in which MPS officers worked to a similar plan to that used two weeks previously. In the aftermath of these events, Jean Charles de Menezes was mistakenly targeted as a potential terrorist and shot dead in a deployment of Operation Kratos.[73]
- 2006 - TransAtlantic Aircraft Bomb Plots - The Metropolitan Police continue to investigate alleged aircraft bombing plots and other related terrorist activities by militant Islamists.[74] [75]
- 13 September 2006 - Operation Mokpo - Officers from Operation Trident make the MPS's largest seizure of firearms after a series of raids in Dartford, Kent. A senior officer was quoted as saying: *"This operation has resulted in hundreds of guns being taken out of circulation."*[76]
- 10 October 2006 - Operation Minstead - Detectives from the Specialist Crime Directorate issued an appeal for the subject of the UK's most extensive rape investigation to surrender himself to police.[77]

A Fast Response Targa 31 boat of the Marine Support Unit of the MPS, on the River Thames in London

Following continuing investigation a man was arrested in November 2009 in relation to Operation Minstead, charged with several offences and currently is on remand for trial in 2010.

- 29 June 2007 - London car bombs - Attempted car bombings in Central London. One of the devices, in a car outside a nightclub, was initially reported by an LAS paramedic dealing with an unrelated incident nearby. MPS bomb disposal officers diffused this device and another device located in an underground car park. Subsequent investigation led to convictions of those involved.
- Autumn 2008 - National Black Police Association Boycott - declared against the police force on the grounds of racial discrimination within the police. This followed high profile controversies involving high ranking black officers, including allegations of racism made by Tarique Ghaffur - the highest ranking Asian officer - against Commissioner Ian Blair.
- 2009 G-20 London summit protests - the police once more used the "kettling" technique to contain large numbers of demonstrators during the G-20 protests. The tactic was criticised for its indiscriminate detention of demonstrators. Ian Tomlinson, a bystander to the protests, died after being pushed to the ground by a police officer.[78] A sergeant in the Territorial Support Group has been suspended after being filmed striking a woman across the face.[79] The tactics used in the policing of mass protests are now under review following these incidents.[80]

Notable convictions

Notable major trials in which the Metropolitan Police Service has been convicted:

Jean Charles de Menezes death

Jean Charles de Menezes (7 January 1978 – 22 July 2005) was a Brazilian national shot dead by police at Stockwell tube station in London, England. He was shot in the head at close range by Metropolitan Police. The Met faced criminal charges under sections 3 (1) and 33 (1)(a) of the Health and Safety at Work etc. Act 1974 for "failing to provide for the health, safety and welfare of Jean Charles de Menezes". It entered a not guilty plea to the charges, "after the most careful consideration".[81] The trial started on 1 October 2007.[82]

On 1 November 2007 The Metropolitan Police were found guilty of the above offences, and were fined £175,000, with £385,000 legal costs.[83] The Met published a terse release about this decision,[84] and Len Duvall, Chair of the Metropolitan Police Authority, asked that the full report on the investigation be published.[85]

See also

* Crimint - The Metropolitan Police Service's Intelligence Database
* London Ambulance Service
* London Air Ambulance (HEMS)
* London Emergency Services Liaison Panel
* London Fire Brigade
* Police National E-Crime Unit
* Hendon Police College
* Project Griffin
* Shoulder Number
* Royal National Lifeboat Institution (RNLI)

External links

* **Metropolitan Police website** [9]
* **Metropolitan Police Crime Academy** [86]
* **Metropolitan Police Leadership Academy** [87]
* **Metropolitan Police Specialist Training Centre - Gravesend** [88]
* **Metropolitan Police Federation** [89]
* **Metropolitan Police Youtube site** [90]

References

[1] "Metropolitan Police Service - Homepage" (http://www.met.police.uk/). Met.police.uk. 2009-04-02. . Retrieved 2009-05-06.

[2] (http://www.mpa.gov.uk/contact/policecontacts/)

[3] "Metropolitan Police Service - History of the Metropolitan Police Service" (http://www.met.police.uk/history/timeline1829-1849.htm). Met.police.uk. . Retrieved 2009-05-06.

[4] "The Bow street runners - Victorian Policeman by Simon Dell OBE QCB - Devon & Cornwall Constabulary" (http://www.devon-cornwall. police.uk/v3/about/history/vicpolice/bow.htm). Devon-cornwall.police.uk. . Retrieved 2009-05-06.

[5] "Policing the Port of London - Crime and punishment" (http://www.portcities.org.uk/london/server/show/ConNarrative.125/chapterId/ 2588/Policing-the-Port-of-London.html). Port Cities. . Retrieved 2009-05-06.

[6] "Working as a Volunteer - Metropolitan Police Service" (http://cms.met.police.uk/met/boroughs/kingston_upon_thames/ 03working_with_the_community/kingston_police_volunteers). Cms.met.police.uk. 1970-01-01. . Retrieved 2009-05-06.

[7] "Met Police budget settlement to put more police on beat in London" (http://www.personneltoday.com/articles/2008/02/14/44429/ met-police-budget-settlement-to-put-more-police-on-beat-in-london.html). Personneltoday.com. 2008-02-14. . Retrieved 2009-05-06.

[8] Last Updated: 7:47AM GMT 1 Dec 2008 (2008-12-01). "Sir Paul Stephenson profile" (http://www.telegraph.co.uk/news/uknews/ 3537956/Sir-Paul-Stephenson-profile.html). Telegraph. . Retrieved 2009-05-06.

[9] http://www.met.police.uk/

[10] (http://www.robinsonlibrary.com/social/pathology/criminal/police/scotyard.htm)

[11] Sir Ronald Howe (1965) *The Rise of Scotland Yard*

[12] Douglas Browne (1956) *The Rise of Scotland Yard: A History of the Metropolitan Police*

[13] Martin Fido and Keith Skinner (1999) *The Official Encyclopedia of Scotland Yard*

[14] "MPS - Brief history and definition of policing" (http://www.met.police.uk/history/definition.htm). met.police.uk. . Retrieved 2009-09-29.

[15] "MPS - New Scotland Yard" (http://www.met.police.uk/history/New_Scotland_Yard.htm). met.police.uk. . Retrieved 2009-09-29.

[16] "Metropolitan Police | Home Office" (http://police.homeoffice.gov.uk/performance-and-measurement/performance-assessment/assessments-2007-2008/metropolitan-police). Police.homeoffice.gov.uk. 2008-11-28. . Retrieved 2009-05-06.

[17] "Metropolitan Police Authority" (http://www.mpa.gov.uk/default.htm). *MPA*. . Retrieved 2006-07-20.

[18] "Metropolitan Police Service - Deputy Commissioner Paul Stephenson" (http://www.met.police.uk/about/stephenson.htm). Met.police.uk. . Retrieved 2009-05-06.

[19] "Ministry of Defence Police" (http://www.modpoliceofficers.co.uk). MOD. . Retrieved 2008-12-28.

[20] "British Transport Police" (http://www.btp.police.uk/). *BTP*. 2006-07-19. . Retrieved 2006-07-19.

[21] "Policing the Royal Parks - keeping you safe in the Royal Parks" (http://www.royalparks.org.uk/about/police.cfm). Royalparks.org.uk. 2004-04-01. . Retrieved 2009-05-06.

[22] The Committee Office, House of Lords. "House of Lords - Unopposed Bill Committee - Minutes of Evidence" (http://www.publications.parliament.uk/pa/ld200203/ldselect/ldllauno/30219/3021909.htm). Publications.parliament.uk. . Retrieved 2009-05-06.

[23] "Metropolitan Police: Ranks" (http://www.met.police.uk/about/ranks.htm). *Met Police*. . Retrieved 2006-07-19.

[24] http://www.mpa.gov.uk/committees/x-cop/2003/031020/04/

[25] "England | London | Met suspends G20 footage officer" (http://news.bbc.co.uk/1/hi/england/london/7999277.stm). BBC News. 2009-04-15. . Retrieved 2009-05-06.

[26] "England | London | Police begin G20 tactics review" (http://news.bbc.co.uk/1/hi/in_depth/8000246.stm). BBC News. 2009-04-16. . Retrieved 2009-05-06.

[27] "Metropolitan Police: Cadets" (http://www.met.police.uk/cadets/). *Met Police*. . Retrieved 2006-07-19.

[28] "Police Pay" (http://www.police-information.co.uk/policepay.htm). Police-information.co.uk. . Retrieved 2009-05-06.

[29] Metropolitan Police PCSO (http://www.met.police.uk/careers/pcso/)

[30] "Metropolitan Police Authority website, home-page" (http://www.mpa.gov.uk/default.htm). Mpa.gov.uk. 2005-07-22. . Retrieved 2009-06-08.

[31] "Metropolitan Police Service - About the Met" (http://www.met.police.uk/about/). Met.police.uk. . Retrieved 2009-05-06.

[32] "Police officer, staff and PCSO numbers: June 2009" (http://www.mpa.gov.uk/statistics/police-numbers/). . Retrieved 2009-10-04.

[33] GLA press release (http://www.london.gov.uk/view_press_release.jsp?releaseid=1657), 11 March 2003

[34] Hansard (http://www.publications.parliament.uk/pa/cm200001/cmhansrd/vo010423/text/10423w32.htm), 23 April 2001. London population at the time was 7,172,000.

[35] Hansard (http://www.publications.parliament.uk/pa/cm199596/cmhansrd/vo960226/text/60226w27.htm), 26 February 1996

[36] *The Thin Blue Line*, Police Council for Great Britain Staff Side Claim for Undermanning Supplements, 1965

[37] Report of the Commissioner of Police of the Metropolis for the Year 1952. Included 35 Chief Superintendents (including one woman), 12 Detective Chief Superintendents, 62 Superintendents (including one woman), 16 Detective Superintendents, 128 Chief Inspectors (including five women), 64 Detective Chief Inspectors (including one woman), 20 Station Inspectors, 465 Inspectors (including four women), 140 Detective Inspectors (including one woman), 441 Station Sergeants, 202 1st Class Detective Sergeants, 1,834 Sergeants (including 32 women), 414 2nd Class Detective Sergeants (including six women), 11,951 Constables (including 310 women), and 615 Detective Constables (including 27 women). The official establishment was 20,045.

[38] Raymond B. Fosdick, *European Police Systems*, 1915. Figures at 31 December 1912, including 33 Superintendents, 607 Chief Inspectors and Inspectors, 2,747 Sergeants and 17,142 Constables.

[39] Fido, Martin; Keith Skinner (2000). *Official Encyclopedia of Scotland Yard*. Virgin. p. 56. ISBN 1852277122.

[40] Fido, Martin; Keith Skinner (2000). *Official Encyclopedia of Scotland Yard*. Virgin. p. 57. ISBN 1852277122.

[41] "Met Police stations: A-Z Directory" (http://www.met.police.uk/contacts/AZPhonenumbers.htm). Met.police.uk. . Retrieved 2009-06-08.

[42] "BBC: Bow Street court closes its doors" (http://news.bbc.co.uk/1/hi/england/london/5179270.stm). BBC News. 2006-07-14. . Retrieved 2009-06-08.

[43] Institute for Public Policy Research: Re-inventing the police station (http://www.ippr.org.uk/ecomm/files/reinventing_police_station.pdf) (PDF)

[44] "Metropolitan Police Service - History of the Metropolitan Police Service" (http://www.met.police.uk/history/sidney_street.htm). Met.police.uk. . Retrieved 2009-05-06.

[45] "TERROR IN LONDON: LONDON UNDER ATTACK: THE IRA CAMPAIGN | Independent, The (London) | Find Articles at BNET" (http://findarticles.com/p/articles/mi_qn4158/is_/ai_n14726815). Findarticles.com. . Retrieved 2009-05-06.

[46] "website: on this day 28 February 1975" (http://news.bbc.co.uk/onthisday/hi/witness/february/28/newsid_4298000/4298307.stm). BBC News. 1975-02-28. . Retrieved 2009-06-08.

[47] "website: on this day 30 August 1975" (http://news.bbc.co.uk/onthisday/hi/dates/stories/august/30/newsid_2511000/2511059.stm).
      BBC News. 1976-08-30. . Retrieved 2009-06-08.
[48] "BBC ON THIS DAY | 6 | 1975: Couple under siege in Balcombe Street" (http://news.bbc.co.uk/onthisday/hi/dates/stories/december/
      6/newsid_4261000/4261478.stm). BBC News. 1975-12-06. . Retrieved 2009-05-06.
[49] "BBC ON THIS DAY | 3 | 1975: London's Spaghetti House siege ends" (http://news.bbc.co.uk/onthisday/hi/dates/stories/october/3/
      newsid_4286000/4286414.stm). BBC News. 1995-10-03. . Retrieved 2009-05-06.
[50] "Famous Criminals: Dennis Nilsen" (http://www.crimeandinvestigation.co.uk/famous_criminal/14/biography/1/Dennis_Nilsen.htm).
      Crimeandinvestigation.co.uk. . Retrieved 2009-06-08.
[51] 4:00AM Monday Mar 9, 2009 (2009-03-09). "Activists to mark death of teacher - World - NZ Herald News" (http://www.nzherald.co.nz/
      world/news/article.cfm?c_id=2&objectid=10560632). Nzherald.co.nz. . Retrieved 2009-05-06.
[52] Peter Taylor (2002-07-24). "Six days that shook Britain" (http://www.guardian.co.uk/Archive/Article/0,4273,4467433,00.html). The
      Guardian. . Retrieved 2009-06-11.
[53] "website: on this day 25 November 1981" (http://news.bbc.co.uk/onthisday/hi/dates/stories/november/25/newsid_2546000/2546233.
      stm). BBC News. 1963-11-25. . Retrieved 2009-06-08.
[54] "website: Life for depraved killer" (http://news.bbc.co.uk/1/hi/uk/1146657.stm). BBC News. 2001-02-02. . Retrieved 2009-06-08.
[55] "On this day 28 September 1985" (http://news.bbc.co.uk/onthisday/hi/dates/stories/september/28/newsid_2540000/2540397.stm).
      BBC News. 1995-09-28. . Retrieved 2009-06-08.
[56] "On this day 6 October 1985" (http://news.bbc.co.uk/onthisday/hi/dates/stories/october/6/newsid_4094000/4094928.stm). BBC
      News. . Retrieved 2009-06-08.
[57] Serial Killers: Kenneth Erskine (http://www.serialkillers.nl/kenneth-erskine/kenneth-erskine.htm)
[58] "On this day 18 November 1987" (http://news.bbc.co.uk/onthisday/hi/dates/stories/november/18/newsid_2519000/2519675.stm).
      BBC News. . Retrieved 2009-06-08.
[59] "On this day 12 December 1988" (http://news.bbc.co.uk/onthisday/hi/dates/stories/december/12/newsid_2547000/2547561.stm).
      BBC News. . Retrieved 2009-06-08.
[60] "On this day 20 August 1989" (http://news.bbc.co.uk/onthisday/hi/dates/stories/august/20/newsid_2500000/2500211.stm). BBC
      News. . Retrieved 2009-06-08.
[61] "BBC ON THIS DAY | 31 | 1990: Violence flares in poll tax demonstration" (http://news.bbc.co.uk/onthisday/hi/dates/stories/march/
      31/newsid_2530000/2530763.stm). BBC News. 1966-03-31. . Retrieved 2009-05-06.
[62] "On this day 8 January 1991" (http://news.bbc.co.uk/onthisday/hi/dates/stories/january/8/newsid_4091000/4091741.stm). BBC
      News. . Retrieved 2009-06-08.
[63] "Colin Ireland" (http://www.crimelibrary.com/serial_killers/predators/ireland/story_1.html). Crime Library. . Retrieved 2009-06-08.
[64] "The Stephen Lawrence Inquiry" (http://www.archive.official-documents.co.uk/document/cm42/4262/sli-01.htm).
      Archive.official-documents.co.uk. . Retrieved 2009-05-06.
[65] "On this day 13 December 1995" (http://news.bbc.co.uk/onthisday/hi/dates/stories/december/13/newsid_2559000/2559341.stm).
      BBC News. . Retrieved 2009-06-08.
[66] The Job: Life sentence for London nailbomber (http://www.met.police.uk/news/stories/copeland/job/1.htm)
[67] "On this day 18 June 1999" (http://news.bbc.co.uk/onthisday/hi/dates/stories/june/18/newsid_2515000/2515679.stm). BBC News. .
      Retrieved 2009-06-08.
[68] "Met pressured for May Day 'apology'" (http://news.bbc.co.uk/1/hi/uk/1383846.stm). BBC News. 2001-06-11. . Retrieved
      2009-04-16.
[69] "ENGLAND | Thames torso police meet occult experts" (http://news.bbc.co.uk/1/hi/england/1930359.stm). BBC News. 2002-04-15. .
      Retrieved 2009-05-06.
[70] "Focus: Torso in the Thames - MUTI: THE STORY OF ADAM | Independent on Sunday, The | Find Articles at BNET" (http://findarticles.
      com/p/articles/mi_qn4159/is_20030803/ai_n12743122). Findarticles.com. . Retrieved 2009-05-06.
[71] Griffiths, Emma (2004-09-15). "Anger and defiance at hunt rally" (http://news.bbc.co.uk/1/hi/uk/3659030.stm). BBC News. .
      Retrieved 2009-04-16.
[72] "On this day 7 July 2005" (http://news.bbc.co.uk/onthisday/hi/dates/stories/july/7/newsid_4942000/4942238.stm). BBC News. .
      Retrieved 2009-06-08.
[73] "Indepth | London Attacks" (http://news.bbc.co.uk/1/shared/spl/hi/uk/05/london_blasts/tube_shooting/html/default.stm). BBC
      News. 2005-07-22. . Retrieved 2009-05-06.
[74] "UK | 'Airlines terror plot' disrupted" (http://news.bbc.co.uk/1/hi/uk/4778575.stm). BBC News. 2006-08-10. . Retrieved 2009-05-06.
[75] "PM pays tribute to police and security services" (http://www.number10.gov.uk/Page9970). Number10.gov.uk. 2006-08-10. . Retrieved
      2009-05-06.
[76] "'Biggest ever' gun haul" (http://www.thisislocallondon.co.uk/display.var.918059.0.biggest_ever_gun_haul_found_opposite_school.
      php). This is Local London. 2006-09-13. . Retrieved 2009-06-08.
[77] "Surrender plea to serial rapist" (http://news.bbc.co.uk/1/hi/england/london/6036013.stm). BBC News. 2006-10-10. . Retrieved
      2009-06-08.
[78] Lewis, Paul (2009-04-07). "Video reveals G20 police assault on man who died" (http://www.guardian.co.uk/uk/2009/apr/07/
      video-g20-police-assault). The Guardian. . Retrieved 7 April 2009.

[79] "Met suspends G20 footage officer" (http://news.bbc.co.uk/1/hi/england/london/7999277.stm). BBC News. 2009-04-15. . Retrieved 2009-04-16.

[80] "Police 'kettle' tactic feels the heat" (http://news.bbc.co.uk/1/hi/uk/8000641.stm). BBC News. 2009-04-16. . Retrieved 2009-04-16.

[81] "Met not guilty plea over Menezes" (http://news.bbc.co.uk/1/hi/uk/5359500.stm). BBC News. 19 September 2006. .

[82] "Timeline: the Stockwell shooting" (http://www.guardian.co.uk/menezes/story/0,,2181230,00.html). Guardian. 1 October 2007. .

[83] BBC News. Police guilty over Menezes case (http://news.bbc.co.uk/1/hi/uk/7069796.stm). Last updated 1 November 2007. Retrieved 22 January 2008.

[84] Metropolitan Police. Health and Safety trial result (http://cms.met.police.uk/news/met_comment/health_and_safety_trial_result) 1 November 2007. Retrieved 22 January 2008.

[85] Metropolitan Police. MPA and ACPO on Health and Safety verdict (http://cms.met.police.uk/news/met_comment/mpa_and_acpo_on_health_and_safety_verdict). 1 November 2007. Retrieved 22 January 2008.

[86] http://www.teammet.com/crime_academy/index.html

[87] http://www.teammet.com/leadership/index.php

[88] http://www.laing.com/documents_new/Met_Firearms__sustainability_.pdf

[89] http://www.metfed.org/

[90] http://www.youtube.com/user/metpoliceservice

British Union of Fascists

British Union of Fascists	
Founded	1932
Dissolved	1940
Preceded by	New Party British Fascisti
Succeeded by	Union Movement
Ideology	Fascism, British Nationalism, British Imperialism, National Corporatism
Political position	Far right
International affiliation	N/A
Official colours	Flash and Circle

The **British Union of Fascists** (BUF) was a political party in the United Kingdom formed in 1932 by Sir Oswald Mosley, who had previously sat as an MP for both the Labour and Conservative parties.

Background

Oswald Mosley had been a minister in Ramsay MacDonald's Labour government advising on rising unemployment. In 1930 he issued his 'Mosley Memorandum': a proto-Keynesian programme of policies designed to tackle the unemployment problem. He resigned in early 1931 when his plans were rejected, and immediately formed the New Party, with policies based on his memorandum. Despite winning 16% of the vote at a by-election in Ashton-under-Lyne in early 1931, the party failed to achieve electoral success.

During 1931 New Party policies became increasingly influenced by Fascism.[1] In January 1932, Mosley's conversion to Fascism was confirmed when he visited Benito Mussolini in Italy. He wound up the New Party in April 1932 but kept its youth movement going. He spent summer that year writing a Fascist programme, *The Greater Britain*. The BUF was launched in October 1932.[1]

Character

Imagery

Mosley modelled himself on Benito Mussolini and the BUF on Mussolini's National Fascist Party in Italy. Mussolini and, later, Mosley instituted black uniforms for members, earning them the nickname "Blackshirts." The BUF was anti-communist and protectionist, and proposed replacing parliamentary democracy with elected executives having jurisdiction over specific industries – a system similar to the corporatism of the Italian fascists. Unlike the Italian system, British fascist corporatism planned a democracy that would replace the House of Lords with elected executives drawn from major industries, the clergy, and colonies. The House of Commons was to be reduced to allow for a faster, "less factionist" democracy.[2]

The BUF's programme and ideology were outlined in Mosley's *Great Britain* (1932), and A. Raven Thompson's *The Coming Corporate State* (1938).

Many BUF policies were built on isolationism, prohibiting trade by British nationals outside the British Empire. Mosley proposed this would protect the British economy from the flux of the world market, especially during the Great Depression, and prevent "cheap slave competition from abroad." [3]

The BUF and Suffragettes

In a January 2010 documentary, "Mother Was A Blackshirt," on the BBC, James Maw reported on how in 1914 Norah Elam was placed in a Holloway prison cell with Emmeline Pankhurst for her involvement with the Suffragette movement, yet in 1940 she returned to the same prison with Diana Mosley, but this time for her involvement with the fascist movement. Another leading suffragette, Mary Raleigh Richardson, became head of the Women's section of the BUF.

The report described how Elam's fascist philosophy grew from her suffragette experiences, how the British fascist movement became largely driven by women, how they targeted young women from an early age, how the first British fascist movement was founded by a woman, and how the leading lights of the Suffragettes who, with Oswald Mosley, founded the BUF.[4]

The BUF never won any Parliamentary seats during its existence, but although not putting up any candidates for the 1935 election did campaign under the slogan 'Fascism Next Time'. Elam being a good loyal fascist hung a huge banner across the entire frontage of her home with the slogan Fascism Next Time in huge letters. Mosley's electoral strategy was to prepare for the election after 1935 and in 1936 announced a list of BUF candidates for that election, with Elam nominated to stand for Northampton. Mosley accompanied Elam to Northampton to introduce her to her electorate at a meeting in the Town Hall. At that meeting Mosley announced that 'He was glad indeed to have the opportunity of introducing the first candidate, and it killed for all time the suggestion that National Socialism proposed putting British women back into the home. Mrs Elam, he went on, had fought in the past for women's suffrage ... and was a great example of the emancipation of women in Britain'.[5]

Prominence

The BUF claimed 50,000 members at one point[6] and the *Daily Mail* was an early supporter, running the headline *"Hurrah for the Blackshirts!"*[7] .

Despite considerable and sometimes violent resistance from Jewish people, the Labour Party, Liberals, democrats and the Communist Party of Great Britain, the BUF found a following in the East End of London, where in the London County Council elections of 1937 it obtained reasonably good results in Bethnal Green, Shoreditch and Limehouse, although none of its candidates was actually elected.[8] However, the BUF never faced a General Election. Having lost the funding of newspaper magnate, Lord Rothermere, that it previously enjoyed, at the 1935 General Election the party urged voters to abstain, offering *"Fascism Next Time"*.[9] There never was a "next time", as the next General Election was not held until July 1945, by which time World War II in Europe had ended and fascism had been discredited.

Towards the middle of the 1930s, the BUF's violent activities and its perceived alignment with the German Nazi Party began to alienate some middle-class supporters and membership decreased. At the Olympia rally in London, in 1934, BUF stewards were in a violent confrontation with anti-fascist activists, in which one of the Anti-fascist protesters lost an eye, and this caused the *Daily Mail* to withdraw support. The level of violence shown at the rally shocked many with the effect of turning even neutral parties against the BUF and contributing to Anti-fascist support. As one observer remarked *I came to the conclusion that Mosley was a political maniac, and that all decent*

English people must combine to kill his movement[10] . The reaction to the Olympia rally can be illustrated in the growth in British Communist parties from 1935 onwards.[11]

Final years and legacy

With lack of electoral success, the party drew away from mainstream politics and towards extreme antisemitism over 1934-1935, which saw the resignation of members such as Dr. Robert Forgan. It organised anti-immigration marches and protests in London, recalling tactics of predecessors such as the British Brothers League, like the one which resulted in the Battle of Cable Street in October 1936.

Membership fell to below 8,000 by the end of 1935. The government was sufficiently concerned, however, to pass the Public Order Act 1936, which banned political uniforms and required police consent for political marches. This act hindered BUF activity, although in the years building up to the war they enjoyed brief success on the back of their 'Peace Campaign' to prevent conflict with Germany. In May 1940, the BUF was banned outright by the government, and Mosley, along with 740 other fascists, was interned for much of World War II. After the war, Mosley made several unsuccessful attempts of reviving his brand of fascism, notably in the Union Movement.

The BUF in popular culture

The television serial *Mosley* featured the BUF and Oswald Mosley, through his political career to the internment of the BUF.

In the film *It Happened Here*, the BUF appears to be the ruling party of German-occupied Britain. A Mosley speech is heard on the radio in the scene before everyone goes to the movies.

Harry Turtledove's alternate history novel, *In the Presence of Mine Enemies*, is set in 2010 in a world where the Nazis were triumphant, the BUF governs Britain — and the first stirrings of the reform movement come from there. The BUF and Mosley also appear as background influences in Turtledove's Colonization trilogy which follows the Worldwar tetralogy and is set in the 1960s.

In Ken Follett's novel *Night Over Water*, several of the main characters are BUF members.

The BUF is also in Guy Walters book *The Leader* (2003), where Mosely is the dictator of Britain leading up to World War II.

Emblem of P.G. Wodehouse's fictional *Black Shorts* movement, featured in the television series *Jeeves and Wooster*.

British humorous writer P.G. Wodehouse satirized the BUF in books and short stories. The BUF was satirized as "The Black Shorts" (shorts being worn as all the best shirt colours were already taken) and their leader was Roderick Spode, owner of a ladies' underwear shop.

In the 1992 Acorn Media production of Agatha Christie's *One, Two, Buckle My Shoe* with David Suchet and Philip Jackson, one of the supporting characters (Played by actor Christopher Eccleston) secures a paid position as a rank-and-file member of the BUF.

The BUF and Oswald Mosley are also alluded to in Kazuo Ishiguro's novel *The Remains of the Day*.

Mark Gatiss's second Lucifer Box novel *The Devil In Amber*'s main villain is a thinly-veiled version of Mosley named Olympus Mons.

BUF Anthem

The BUF Anthem resembles the German *Horst-Wessel-Lied*, the anthem of the NSDAP or Nazi Party, which is now banned in Germany, and was set to the same tune.

The lyrics are as follows:

> *Comrades, the voices of the dead battalions,*
>
> *Of those who fell that Britain might be great,*
>
> *Join in our song, for they still march in spirit with us,*
>
> *And urge us on to gain the fascist state!*
>
> (Repeat Last Two Lines)
>
> *We're of their blood, and spirit of their spirit,*
>
> *Sprung from that soil for whose dear sake they bled,*
>
> *Against vested powers, Red Front, and massed ranks of reaction,*
>
> *We lead the fight for freedom and for bread!*
>
> (Repeat Last Two Lines)
>
> *The streets are still, the final struggle's ended;*
>
> *Flushed with the fight we proudly hail the dawn!*
>
> *See, over all the streets the fascist banners waving,*
>
> *Triumphant standards of our race reborn!*
>
> (Repeat Last Two Lines)

Prominent members

Despite the short period of operation the BUF attracted prominent members and supporters. These included:

- Hastings Russell, 12th Duke of Bedford
- Josslyn Hay, 22nd Earl of Erroll
- Harold Sidney Harmsworth, 1st Viscount Rothermere
- David Freeman-Mitford, 2nd Baron Redesdale
- Admiral Sir Barry Edward Domvile KBE CB CMG
- Group Captain Sir Louis Leisler Greig, KBE, CVO was a British naval surgeon, courtier and intimate of King George VI.
- Brigadier-General Sir Ormonde de l'Épée Winter KBE CB CMG DSO
- Sir Alliott Verdon Roe
- Sir Reginald Goodall
- Major General John Frederick Charles Fuller CB, CBE, DSO
- John Francis Ashley Erskine, Lord Erskine, GCSI, GCIE, was the Conservative and Unionist MP for Weston-super-Mare and Brighton and assistant Government whip.
- Lieutenant-Colonel Lord William Walter Montagu Douglas Scott, MC, was the Conservative and Unionist MP for Roxburgh and Selkirk
- Major Sir William Eden Evans-Gordon, was the Conservative and Unionist MP for Stepney
- John Beckett MP, was the Labour MP for Member of Parliament for Peckham
- Robert Forgan MP, was the Labour MP for West Renfrewshire
- William Edward David Allen, was the Unionist Member of Parliament (MP) for Belfast West.
- A. K. Chesterton MC
- Neil Francis Hawkins

- Arthur Gilligan
- Jeffrey Hamm
- William Joyce
- Tommy Moran
- Alexander Raven Thomson
- Henry Williamson
- William Ford

See also

- Battle of Cable Street
- List of British fascist parties
- Blueshirts
- Mosley (1997)
- Diana Mosley - Wife of BUF leader Oswald Mosley
- People's Action Party - The ruling party of Singapore, whose ideology and logo are modeled on the BUF

Further reading

- *Blackshirt: Sir Oswald Mosley and British Fascism* by Stephen Dorril
- *'Hurrah for the Blackshirts!': Fascists and Fascism in Britain between the Wars*, Martin Pugh (Random House, 2005)

External links

- OswaldMosley.com The Friends of Oswald Mosley [12]

References

[1] Thorpe, Andrew. (1995) *Britain In The 1930s*, Blackwell Publishers, ISBN 0-613-17411-7

[2] Tomorrow We Live (1938)

[3] Tomorrow We Live (1938), by Sir Oswald Mosley and http://www.oswaldmosley.com/audio/speeches.html entitled http://www.oswaldmosley.com/audio/speeches.html'

[4] http://www.bbc.co.uk/iplayer/episode/b00pk7zp/Mother_Was_A_Blackshirt/?from=r&id=35227e69-fcbf-45d7-8295-2c78e9703b74.0

[5] McPherson, Angela; McPherson, Susan (2010). *Mosley's Old Suffragette - A Biography of Norah Elam* (http://www.oldsuffragette.mcpherson.org.uk). ISBN 978-1-4452-7308-2. .

[6] Andrzej Olechnowicz, 'Liberal Anti-Fascism in the 1930s: The Case of Sir Ernest Barker' in Albion: A Quarterly Journal Concerned with British Studies, (Vol. 36, No. 4, Winter, 2004), p. 643.

[7] [http://www.voiceoftheturtle.org/dictionary/dict_h1.php#hurrah Hurrah for the Blackshirts

[8] R. Benewick, *Political Violence and Public Order*, London: Allan Lane, 1969, pp. 279-282

[9] 1932-1938 Fascism rises - March of the Blackshirts (http://www.searchlightmagazine.com/features/century/cbf.php?include=page3)

[10] LLOYD. G, Yorkshire Post 9 June 1934

[11] STEVENSON. J, Britain in the Depression (Longman Group UK LTD: 1994) p155

[12] http://www.oswaldmosley.com

Oswald Mosley

Sir Oswald Mosley, Bt.	
Sir Oswald Mosley, Bt.	
Member of Parliament for Harrow	
In office 1918 – 1924	
Preceded by	Harry Mallaby-Deeley
Succeeded by	Sir Isidore Salmon
Member of Parliament for Smethwick	
In office 1926 – 1931	
Preceded by	John Davison
Succeeded by	Roy Wise
Born	16 November 1896 London, England
Died	3 December 1980 (aged 84) Orsay, France
Nationality	British
Political party	Conservative (until 1924) Labour / Independent Labour Party (1924-1931) New Party (1931-1932) British Union of Fascists (1932-1940?) Union Movement (1948?-1962) National Party of Europe (1962-1980)
Spouse(s)	Lady Cynthia Mosley (1920-1933) Diana Mitford (1936-1980)
Children	Vivien Mosley Nicholas Mosley Michael Mosley (Oswald) Alexander Mosley Max Mosley

Sir Oswald Ernald Mosley, 6th Baronet (16 November 1896 – 3 December 1980) was a British politician, known principally as the founder of the British Union of Fascists. He was a member of Parliament for Harrow from 1918 to 1923 and for Smethwick from 1926 to 1931.

Biography

Family and early life

Mosley was the eldest of three sons of Sir Oswald Mosley, 5th Baronet of Ancoats (1874–1928), and his wife Katharine Maud Edwards-Heathcote (1874–1950), the second child of Captain Justinian Edwards-Heathcote, of Market Drayton, Shropshire. Mosley's family were Anglo-Irish but his branch were prosperous landowners in Staffordshire.

Mosley was born at Rolleston Hall, near Burton-on-Trent. When his parents separated he was brought up by his mother, who initially went to live at Betton Hall near Market Drayton, and his paternal grandfather, Sir Oswald Mosley, 4th Baronet of Ancoats. Within the family and among intimate friends, he was always called 'Tom'. He lived for many years at Apedale Hall near Newcastle-under-Lyme.

He was educated at West Downs in Winchester, and Winchester College. In January 1914 he entered the Royal Military Academy Sandhurst but was expelled in June for a 'riotous act of retaliation' against a fellow student.[1] During World War I he was commissioned in the 16th The Queen's Lancers and fought on the Western Front. He transferred to the Royal Flying Corps as an observer but while showing off in front of his mother and sister he crashed, which left him with a permanent limp. He returned to the trenches before the injury was fully healed and, at the Battle of Loos, he passed out at his post from the pain. He spent the remainder of the war at desk jobs in the Ministry of Munitions and in the Foreign Office.[1]

Personal life

Mosley was a noted philanderer and had numerous affairs, including, before his first marriage, a short romance with his first wife's elder sister Mary Irene Curzon.

In May 1920 he married Lady Cynthia Curzon (known as 'Cimmie'), second daughter of George Curzon, Lord Curzon of Kedleston and Lord Curzon's first wife, the American mercantile heiress, the former Mary Victoria Leiter. Lord Curzon had to be persuaded that Mosley was a suitable husband, as he suspected Mosley was largely motivated by social advancement and her inheritance. The wedding was the social event of the year, attended by many branches of European royalty, including King George V and Queen Mary.

He had three children by Cynthia: Vivien (b. 1921), Nicholas Mosley (b. 1923), a successful novelist who wrote a biography of his father and edited his memoirs for publication, and Michael (b. 1932).

During this marriage he had an extended affair with his wife's younger sister Lady Alexandra Metcalfe, and with their stepmother, Grace Curzon, Marchioness Curzon of Kedleston, the American-born second wife and widow of Lord Curzon of Kedleston.

Cynthia died of peritonitis in 1933, after which Mosley married his mistress Diana Guinness, née Mitford, (one of the celebrated Mitford sisters). They married in secret in 1936, in the Berlin home of Nazi propaganda chief Joseph Goebbels. Adolf Hitler was one of the guests. By Diana Mitford, he had two sons: Alexander (b. 1938) and Max Mosley (b. 1940), who was president of the Fédération Internationale de l'Automobile (FIA) for 16 years.

Mosley spent large amounts of his private fortune on the British Union of Fascists (BUF) and tried to establish it on a firm financial footing by negotiating, through Diana, with Adolf Hitler for permission to broadcast commercial radio to Britain from Germany. Mosley also reportedly in 1937 struck a deal with Francis William Lionel Collings Beaumont, the heir to the Seigneur of Sark, to set up a privately owned radio station on Sark.[2] [3]

Elected Member of Parliament

At the end of World War I Mosley decided to go into politics as a Conservative Member of Parliament (MP), although he was only 21 years old and had not fully developed his politics. He was driven by a passionate conviction to avoid any future war and this motivated his career. Largely because of his family background, he was considered by several constituencies; a vacancy near the family estates seemed to be the best prospect. Unexpectedly, he was selected for Harrow first. In the general election of 1918 he faced no serious opposition and was elected easily. He was the youngest member of the House of Commons to take his seat (there was an abstentionist Sinn Féin MP who was younger). He soon distinguished himself as an orator and political player, one marked by extreme self-confidence. He made a point of speaking in the House of Commons without notes.

Crossing the floor

Mosley was at this time falling out with the Conservatives over the issue of Irish policy, and the use of the Black and Tans to suppress the Irish population. Eventually he 'crossed the floor' and sat as an Independent MP on the opposition side of the House of Commons. Having built up a following in his constituency, he retained it against a Conservative challenge in the 1922 and 1923 general elections. The liberal *Westminster Gazette* wrote that he was "the most polished literary speaker in the Commons, words flow from him in graceful epigrammatic phrases that have a sting in them for the government and the conservatives. To listen to him is an education in the English language, also in the art of delicate but deadly repartee. He has human sympathies, courage and brains."[4] By 1924 he was growing increasingly attracted to the Labour Party, which had just formed a government, and in March he joined. He immediately joined the Independent Labour Party (ILP) as well and allied himself with the left.

When the government fell in October, Mosley had to choose a new seat as he believed that Harrow would not re-elect him as a Labour candidate. He therefore decided to oppose Neville Chamberlain in Birmingham Ladywood. An energetic campaign led to a knife-edge result but Mosley was defeated by 77 votes. His period outside Parliament was used to develop a new economic policy for the ILP, which eventually became known as the Birmingham Proposals; they continued to form the basis of Mosley's economics until the end of his political career. In 1926, the Labour-held seat of Smethwick fell vacant and Mosley returned to Parliament after winning the resulting by-election on 21 December.

Mosley and his wife Cynthia were ardent Fabian Socialists in the 1920s and 1930s. Mosley appears in a list of names of Fabians from Fabian News and Fabian Society Annual Report 1929–31. He was Kingsway Hall lecturer in 1924 and Livingstone Hall lecturer in 1931.

Office

Mosley then made a bold bid for political advancement within the Labour Party. He was close to Ramsay MacDonald and hoped for one of the great offices of state, but when Labour won the 1929 general election he was appointed only to the post of Chancellor of the Duchy of Lancaster, de facto Minister without Portfolio, outside the Cabinet. He was given responsibility for solving the unemployment problem, but found that his radical proposals were blocked either by his superior James Henry Thomas or by the Cabinet. Mosley was always impatient and eventually put forward a whole scheme in the 'Mosley Memorandum' to find it rejected by the Cabinet; he then resigned in May 1930. At the time, the weekly liberal paper *The Nation* described his move: "The resignation of Sir Oswald Mosley is an event of capital importance in domestic politics...We feel that Sir Oswald has acted rightly-as he has certainly acted courageously-in declining to share any longer in the responsibility for inertia."[4] He attempted to persuade the Labour Party Conference in October, but was defeated again. The memorandum called for high tariffs to protect British industries from international finance, for state nationalisation of industry and a programme of public works to solve unemployment. Thirty years later, in 1961, R. H. S. Crossman described the memorandum: "... this brilliant memorandum was a whole generation ahead of Labour thinking".[4]

New Party

Determined that the Labour Party was no longer suitable, Mosley quickly founded the New Party. Its early parliamentary contests, in the Ashton-under-Lyne by-election, 1931 and subsequent by-elections, were successful only in splitting the vote and allowing the Conservative candidate to win. Despite this, the organisation gained support among many Labour and Conservative MPs, who agreed with his corporatist economic policy - among those who agreed were Aneurin Bevan and Harold Macmillan. It also gained the endorsement of the *Daily Mail* newspaper. The New Party increasingly inclined to fascist policies, but Mosley was denied the opportunity to get his party established when the 1931 election was suddenly called. All its candidates, including Mosley, lost their seats. As the New Party gradually became more radical and authoritarian, many previous supporters defected from it. Shortly after the election, he was described by the Manchester Guardian:

> "When Sir Oswald Mosley sat down after his Free Trade Hall speech in Manchester and the audience, stirred as an audience rarely is, rose and swept a storm of applause towards the platform-who could doubt that here was one of those root-and-branch men who have been thrown up from time to time in the religious, political and business story of England. First that gripping audience is arrested, then stirred and finally, as we have said, swept off its feet by a tornado of peroration yelled at the defiant high pitch of a tremendous voice."
> —*Manchester Guardian*[4]

Fascism

After his failure in 1931 Mosley went on a study tour of the 'new movements' of Italy's Benito Mussolini and other fascists, and returned convinced that it was the way forward for him and for Britain. He determined to unite the existing fascist movements and created the British Union of Fascists (BUF) in 1932. The BUF was anti-communist and protectionist. It claimed membership as high as 50,000, and had the *Daily Mail*[5] and *Daily Mirror*[6] among its earliest supporters. Among his followers were the novelist Henry Williamson, military theorist J.F.C. Fuller and the future "Lord Haw Haw", William Joyce.

Flag of the British Union of Fascists.

Mosley had found problems with disruption of New Party meetings, and instituted a corps of black-uniformed paramilitary stewards, nicknamed *blackshirts*. The party was frequently involved in violent confrontations, particularly with Communist and Jewish groups and especially in London. At a large Mosley rally at Olympia on 7 June 1934 mass brawling broke out when hecklers were removed by blackshirts, resulting in bad publicity. This and the Night of the Long Knives in Germany led to the loss of most of the BUF's mass support. The party was unable to fight the 1935 general election.

Plaque commemorating the Battle of Cable Street.

In October 1936 Mosley and the BUF attempted to march through an area with a high proportion of Jewish residents, and violence resulted between local and nationally organised protesters trying to block the march and police trying to force it through, since called the Battle of Cable Street. An eyewitness, Bill Fishman, 15 at the time of the battle, recalled: "I was moved to tears to see bearded Jews and Irish Catholic dockers standing up to stop Mosley. I shall never forget that as long as I live, how working-class people could get together to oppose the evil of racism."[7] At length Sir Philip Game the Police Commissioner disallowed the march from going ahead and the BUF abandoned it. Mosley continued to organise marches policed by the blackshirts, and the government was sufficiently concerned to pass the Public Order Act 1936, which, amongst other things, banned political uniforms and quasi-military style organisations and came into effect on 1 January 1937.

In the London County Council elections in 1937 the BUF stood in three of its East London strongholds, polling up to a quarter of the vote. Mosley then made most of the employees redundant, some of whom then defected from the party with William Joyce. As the European situation moved towards war, the BUF began nominating Parliamentary candidates and launched campaigns on the theme of 'Mind Britain's Business'. After the outbreak of war he led the campaign for a negotiated peace. He was at first received well but, after the invasion of Norway, public opinion of him gave way to hostility and Mosley was nearly assaulted.

He was a friend of Edward VIII, who approved of the BUF campaign for Edward to keep his throne.

Internment

On 23 May 1940 Mosley, who had continued his peace campaign, was interned under Defence Regulation 18B, along with most active fascists in Britain, and the BUF was later proscribed. His wife Diana Mitford was also interned, shortly after the birth of their son Max; they lived together for most of the war in a house in the grounds of Holloway prison. Mosley used the time to read extensively on classical civilisations. Mosley refused visits from most BUF members, but on 18th March 1943 Dudley and Norah Elam (who had been released by then) accompanied Unity Mitford to see her sister Diana. Mosley agreed to be present because he mistakenly believed Diana and Unity's mother Lady Redesdale was accompanying Unity[8] . The Mosleys were released in November 1943, when Mosley was suffering with phlebitis, and spent the rest of the war under house arrest. On his release from prison he stayed with his sister-in-law Pamela Mitford, followed shortly by a stay at the Shaven Crown Hotel in Shipton-under-Wychwood. He then purchased Crux Easton, near Newbury, with Diana. He and his wife were the subject of much media attention.[9] The war ended what remained of his political reputation.

Post-war politics

After the war Mosley was contacted by his former supporters and persuaded to rejoin active politics. He formed the Union Movement, calling for a single nation-state covering the continent of Europe (known as Europe a Nation), and later attempted to launch a National Party of Europe to this end. The Union Movement's meetings were often physically disrupted, as Mosley's meetings had been before the war, and largely by the same opponents. This led to Mosley's decision, in 1951, to leave Britain and live in Ireland. He later moved to Paris. Of his decision to leave, he said, "You don't clear up a dungheap from underneath it."

Mosley briefly returned to Britain in order to fight the 1959 general election at Kensington North, shortly after the 1958 Notting Hill race riots. Concerns over immigration were beginning to come into the spotlight for the first time and Mosley led his campaign on this issue. When Mosley's final share of the vote was less than he expected, he launched a legal challenge to the election on the basis that the result had been rigged. The result was upheld. In 1961 he took part in a debate at University College London about Commonwealth immigration, seconded by a young David Irving.[10] He contested the 1966 general election at Shoreditch and Finsbury, where he fared even worse than he had in 1959. He wrote his autobiography, *My Life* (1968), and made a number of television appearances before retiring. In 1977, by which time he was suffering from Parkinson's disease, he was nominated for the post of Rector of the University of Glasgow. In the subsequent election he polled over 100 votes but finished bottom of the poll.

Death

Mosley died of natural causes on 3 December 1980 in his Orsay home, aged 84. He was cremated in Paris and his ashes were scattered on the pond at Orsay. His papers are housed at the University of Birmingham Special Collections.

Cultural impact

Mosley's rising influence before the Second World War provoked alarm and reaction against would-be populist dictators by major cultural figures of the time:

- Aldous Huxley's *Point Counter Point* features Everard Webley, a character modelled on Mosley.
- A character in the novel *The Holy Terror* (1939) by H. G. Wells is a bombastic British fascist with an aristocratic background, strikingly similar to Mosley.
- "Sir Roderick Spode" in P.G. Wodehouse's novels parodies Mosley. Spode, a blustering bully who is described as an "amateur dictator", heads a British fascist "Black Shorts" organization.

Mosley's attempts to promote his views after the war resulted in continued critical reaction:

- In 2006 he was selected by the *BBC History Magazine* as the 20th century's worst Briton.[11]
- In 1997 Channel Four Television produced a mini-series about him called *Mosley*, starring Jonathan Cake.
- In the 1986 film version of Colin MacInnes's book *Absolute Beginners*, Steven Berkoff appears as a Mosley-esque character billed as "The Fanatic", who delivers a (rhyming) hate speech at a fascist election rally; it is generally assumed this is meant to be Mosley during his brief resurgence in 1958.
- In the film *It Happened Here*, Mosley and the BUF are implied to be the rulers of German-occupied Britain in 1944.
- In Harry Turtledove's Southern Victory Series of alternate history novels, Mosley and Winston Churchill lead a fascist Britain after the Allies lose the First World War. Mosley is also referenced in Turtledove's Colonization trilogy, where MP Mosley introduces legislation to revoke the citizenship of the country's Jews. Mosley is also referenced in Turtledove's novel, *In the Presence of Mine Enemies*, where he was given control of Britain after the Nazis won World War II.
- In Philip Roth's alternate history novel *The Plot Against America*, a secret pact between President Charles Lindbergh and Hitler is said to include an agreement to impose Mosley as the ruler of a German-occupied Britain with America's blessing after a sham attempt by Lindbergh to convince Churchill to negotiate peace with Hitler would fail.
- In Guy Walters's alternate history novel *The Leader*, Mosley has taken power as "The Leader" of Great Britain in 1937. King Edward VIII is still on the throne, Winston Churchill is a prisoner on the Isle of Man, and Prime Minister Mosley is conspiring with Adolf Hitler about the fate of Britain's Jewish population.
- In Kim Newman's alternate history novel *The Bloody Red Baron*, Mosley is shot down in 1918 by Erich von Stalhein (from the *Biggles* series by W. E. Johns), with a character later commenting that "a career has been ended before it was begun."

- The indulgent tone of Mosley's newspaper obituaries was lampooned by the satirical television programme *Not The Nine O'Clock News* in the song "Baronet Oswald Ernald Mosley" by Peter Brewis, which featured Mel Smith, Pamela Stephenson and Griff Rhys Jones all dressed as Nazi Skinheads, singing his eulogy and reading some of the more positive remarks of newspapers from all sides of the political spectrum, including *The Times* and *The Guardian*.[12]
- The original version of the Elvis Costello song "Less Than Zero" is an attack on Mosley and his politics, but US listeners assumed that the "Mr Oswald" referred to was Lee Harvey Oswald and Costello obligingly wrote an alternative lyric in which it was.[13] :74,84
- In Kazuo Ishiguro's *The Remains of the Day* and James Ivory's film adaptation Mosley is portrayed as Sir Geoffrey Wren.
- In the popular BBC science fiction sitcom *Goodnight Sweetheart*, 1990s time traveller Gary Sparrow attempts to educate 1940s East End barmaid Phoebe Bamford on the subject of racism, only to have Phoebe rebut him by saying: "You can be a right twit sometimes Gary. Me and dad were down Cable Street in '36 standing up to Mosley and his Blackshirts. I know all about Fascists, thank you very much!" (Series 3, Episode 25, "The Yanks are Coming"). Gary recognises his blunder and humbly apologises to her.

Bibliography

- *My Life*, Mosley's autobiography.
- *Oswald Mosley*, Robert Skidelsky
- *Fascism in Britain*, Richard Thurlow
- *Blackshirt*, Stephen Dorril, Viking Publishing, ISBN 0-670-86999-6
- *Rules of the Game, Beyond the Pale*, Nicholas Mosley, ISBN 0-7126-6536-6
- *Haw-Haw: the tragedy of William and Margaret Joyce*, Nigel Farndale, Macmillan, London, 2005
- *'Hurrah for the Blackshirts!': Fascists and Fascism in Britain between the Wars*, Martin Pugh, Random House, 2005

ISBN 0-224-06439-8

See also

- *The European*

External links

- Hansard 1803–2005: contributions in Parliament by Oswald Mosley [14]
- Friends of Oswald Mosley [15], containing archives of his speeches and books
- Portraits at the National Portrait Gallery [16]
- BBC report on MI5 surveillance of Mosley [17]
- Metropolitan Police records of the incident at the British Union of Fascists Meeting at Olympia on 7 June 1934 including eyewitness accounts [18]
- GeoCache near Cable Street [19]
- Oswald Mosley [20] at the Notable Names Database
- Oswald Mosley [21] at the Internet Movie Database

Parliament of the United Kingdom		
Preceded by **Harry Mallaby-Deeley**	**Member of Parliament for Harrow** 1918–1924	Succeeded by **Sir Isidore Salmon**
Preceded by **John Davison**	**Member of Parliament for Smethwick** 1926–1931	Succeeded by **Roy Wise**
Political offices		
Preceded by **The Lord Cushendun**	**Chancellor of the Duchy of Lancaster** 1929–1930	Succeeded by **Clement Attlee**
Baronetage of Great Britain		
Preceded by **Oswald Mosley**	**Baronet** (of Ancoats) 1928–1980	Succeeded by **Nicholas Mosley**

References

[1] Philip Rees. Biographical Dictionary of the Extreme Right Since 1890. University Press. Cambridge.

[2] Amato quotes national archive document HO 283/11, which states that among the property seized following Mosley's arrest by the British government in 1940 was correspondence between Mosely and Beaumont dating from 1937. Amato, Joseph Anthony (2002). *Rethinking home: a case for writing local history* (http://books.google.com/books?id=3b2g1RD5fUAC&pg=PA278&lpg=PA278&dq=buster+beaumont& source=bl&ots=aPWKwoQf1R&sig=0OeG8fWMUMCJVNC1_vs73-huxpY&hl=en&ei=TRcoSrnNIIzm6gOaqlipAQ&sa=X& oi=book_result&ct=result&resnum=5#PPA278,M1). Berkeley: University of California Press. pp. 278–79. 9780520232938. .

[3] Barnes, James J.; Patience P. Barnes (2005). *Nazis in pre-war London, 1930-1939: the fate and role of German party members and British sympathizers* (http://books.google.com/books?id=RvzUAubHJ9IC&pg=PA139&dq=beaumont+station+sark#PPA139,M1). Brighton: Sussex Academic Press. 9781845190538. .

[4] Mosley, Diana (1977). *A Life of Contrasts*. Hamish Hamilton.

[5] "Daily Mail" (http://www.britishpapers.co.uk/midmarket/daily-mail/). British Newspapers Online. .

[6] Chris Horrie, Revealed: the fascist past of the Daily Mirror (http://www.independent.co.uk/news/media/ revealed-the-fascist-past-of-the-daily-mirror-735366.html), *The Independent*, 11 November 2003

[7] Day the East End said 'No pasaran' to Blackshirts (http://www.guardian.co.uk/farright/story/0,,1884440,00.html) by Audrey Gillan, *The Guardian*, 30 September 2006. Retrieved 23 October 2006.

[8] McPherson & McPherson 2010, Mosley's Old Suffragette: A Biography of Norah Elam (http://www.oldsuffragette.mcpherson.org.uk)

[9] *Rules of the Game, Beyond the Pale* by Nicholas Mosley p503

[10] http://www.fpp.co.uk/online/08/03/images/Mosley_at_UCL.gif

[11] 'Worst' historical Britons list (http://news.bbc.co.uk/1/low/uk/4561624.stm)

[12] Not The Nine O'Clock News: "Baronet Oswald Ernald Mosley" (http://web.ukonline.co.uk/sotcaa/sotcaa.html?/sotcaa/archive/ greatmoments01.html), *Some of the Corpses are Amusing*

[13] Thomson, Graeme (2004). *Complicated Shadows: The Life and Music of Elvis Costello*. New York: Canongate. ISBN 9781841957968.

[14] http://hansard.millbanksystems.com/people/mr-oswald-mosley

[15] http://www.oswaldmosley.com/

[16] http://www.npg.org.uk/live/search/person.asp?search=ss&sText=mosley&LinkID=mp05636

[17] http://news.bbc.co.uk/1/hi/uk/2518271.stm

[18] http://www.nationalarchives.gov.uk/catalogue/displaycataloguedetails.asp?CATLN=6&CATID=7988806&SearchInit=4& CATREF=MEPO+2%2F10978

[19] http://www.geocaching.com/seek/cache_details.aspx?guid=4a1749d0-c8c3-4e02-9d83-e2f5b5b14ae6

[20] http://www.nndb.com/people/533/000114191

[21] http://www.imdb.com/name/nm0608846/

Anti-fascist

Anti-fascism is the opposition to fascist ideologies, governments, groups and individuals. The related term **antifa** derives from *Antifaschismus*, which is German for anti-fascism. It refers to individuals and groups that are dedicated to fighting fascism. Most major resistance movements during World War II were anti-fascist.

According to an article published by the Anarchist Federation, militant anti-fascists advocate the use of violence against fascists.[1] Writer Dave Renton argues, however, that "for anti-fascists, violence is not part of their world view", and calls militants "professional anti-fascists."[2]

Dutch Resistance members with American 101st Airborne troops in Eindhoven in September 1944.

Anti-fascist demonstration in Switzerland in 2006.

France

In the 1920s and 1930s in France, anti-fascists confronted aggressive far right groups such as the Action Française movement in France, which dominated the Latin Quarter students' neighborhood.[3] In France, quite a few people who joined the Resistance against the pro-Nazi Vichy regime came from far right nationalist and royalist backgrounds. They abandoned the Vichy regime and started fighting against the German occupiers when they saw that Vichy leader Philippe Pétain was subservient to Nazi Germany, and had no intent to stop collaboration.[4]

Maquis members in 1944.

Germany

Symbol of the Iron Front

In the 1920s and 1930s in Germany, Communist Party and Social Democratic Party members advocated violence and mass agitation amongst the working class to stop Adolf Hitler's Nazi Party and the *Freikorps*. Leon Trotsky wrote:

"fighting squads must be created ... nothing increases the insolence of the fascists so much as 'flabby pacifism' on the part of the workers' organisations ... [It is] political cowardice [to deny that] without organised combat detachments, the most heroic masses will be smashed bit by bit by fascist gangs."[5]

Logo of Antifaschistische Aktion.

After German reunification in 1990, many anti-fascist groups formed in reaction to a rise in far right extremism and violence, such as the Solingen arson attack of 1993.[6] According to the German intelligence agency Bundesamt für Verfassungsschutz, the contemporary anti-fascist movement in Germany includes extremists who are willing to use violence.[7]

Italy

In Italy in the 1920s, anti-fascists — many from the workers' movement — fought against the violent Blackshirts, and against the rise of fascist leader Benito Mussolini. After the Italian Socialist Party (PSI) signed a pacification pact with the National Fascist Party on August 3, 1921, and trade unions adopted a legalist and pacified strategy, members of the workers' movement who disagreed with this strategy formed the *Arditi del popolo*. The General Confederation of Labour (CGT) and the PSI refused to officially recognize the anti-fascist militia, while the Italian Communist Party (PCI) ordered its members to quit the organization. The PCI organized some militant groups, but their actions were relatively minor, and the party maintained a non-violent, legalist strategy. The Italian anarchist Severino Di Giovanni, who exiled himself to Argentina following the 1922 March on Rome, organized several bombings against the Italian fascist community.[8]

Italian liberal anti-fascist Benedetto Croce wrote *Manifesto of the Anti-Fascist Intellectuals*, which was published in 1925.[9] Another notable Italian liberal anti-fascist around that time was Piero Gobetti.[10]

Between 1920 and 1943, several anti-fascist movements were active among the Slovenes and Croats in the territories annexed to Italy after World War I.[11] [12] The most influential was the militant insurgent organization TIGR, which carried out numerous sabotages, as well as attacks on representatives of the Fascist Party and the military.[13] [14] Most of the underground structure of the organization was discovered and dismantled by the Organization for Vigilance and Repression of Anti-Fascism (OVRA) in 1940 and 1941,[15] and after June 1941, most of its former activists joined the Liberation Front of the Slovenian People.

During World War II, many members of the Italian resistance left their houses and went to live in the mountainside, fighting against both Italian fascists and German Nazi soldiers. Many cities in northern Italy, including Turin and Milan, were freed by anti-fascist uprisings.[16]

Spain

Large-scale anti-fascist movements were first seen in the 1930s, during the Spanish Civil War. The Republican army, the International Brigades, the Workers' Party of Marxist Unification (POUM) and Spanish anarchist militias such as the Iron Column fought the rise of Francisco Franco with military force. The Friends of Durruti were a particularly militant group, associated with the Federación Anarquista Ibérica (FAI). Thousands of people from many countries went to Spain in support of the anti-fascist cause, joining units such as the Abraham Lincoln Brigade, the British Battalion, the Dabrowski Battalion, the Mackenzie-Papineau Battalion and the Naftali Botwin Company. Notable anti-fascists who worked internationally against Franco included: George Orwell (who fought in the POUM militia and wrote *Homage to Catalonia* about this experience), Ernest Hemingway (a supporter of the International Brigades who wrote *For Whom the Bell Tolls* about this experience), and radical journalist Martha Gellhorn.

Spanish anarchist guerrilla Francesc Sabaté Llopart fought against Franco's regime until the 1960s, from a base in France. The Spanish Maquis also fought the Franco regime from a base in France, long after the Spanish Civil war had ended.

Sweden

Antifasistiskt Aktion (AFA) is an anti-fascist group founded in Sweden in 1993. AFA's *Activity Guide* advocates violence against neo-Nazis.[17] Some in the mainstream media have called them "left extremists".[18] [19] [20] An editorial in the tabloid newspaper *Expressen* argued that the label *anti-fascist* was misleading, because of the organization's methods,[21] such as stealing the subscriber list of the National Democrats newspaper, and threatening the subscribers.[21] . Other critics say the group does not respect freedom of speech, because some members have attacked fascists and other nationalists.[22] [23]

United Kingdom

The rise of Oswald Mosley's British Union of Fascists (BUF) was challenged by the Communist Party of Great Britain, socialists in the Labour Party and Independent Labour Party, anarchists, Irish Catholic dockmen and working class Jews in London's east end. A high point in the struggle was the Battle of Cable Street, when thousands of eastenders and others turned out to stop the BUF from marching. Initially, the national Communist Party leadership wanted a mass demonstration at Hyde Park in solidarity with Republican Spain, instead of a mobilisation against the BUF, but local party activists argued against this. Activists rallied support with the slogan *They shall not pass,* adopted from Republican Spain.

There were debates within the anti-fascist movement over tactics. While many east end ex-servicemen participated in violence against fascists,[24] Communist Party leader Phil Piratin denounced these tactics and instead called for large demonstrations.[25] In addition to the militant anti-fascist movement, there was a smaller current of liberal anti-fascism in Britain; Sir Ernest Barker, for example, was a notable English liberal anti-fascist in the 1930s.[26]

After World War II, Jewish war veterans in the 43 Group continued the tradition of militant confrontations with the BUF. In the 1960s, the 62 Group continued the struggle against neo-Nazis.[27]

1970s and later

In the 1970s, fascist and far right parties such as the National Front (NF) and British Movement were making significant gains electorally, and were increasingly bold in their public appearances. This was challenged in 1977 with the Battle of Lewisham, when thousands of black and white people physically stopped an NF march in South London.[28] Soon after this, the Anti-Nazi League (ANL) was launched by the Socialist Workers Party (SWP). The ANL had a large-scale propaganda campaign and squads that attacked NF meetings and paper sales. The success of the ANL's campaigns contributed to the end of the NF's period of growth.

Tony Cliff of the SWP disbanded the ANL, but many squad members refused to stop their activities. They were expelled from the SWP in 1981, many going on to found Red Action. The SWP used the term squadism to dismiss these militant anti-fascists as thugs. In 1985, some members of Red Action and the anarcho-syndicalist Direct Action Movement launched Anti-Fascist Action (AFA). Their founding document said "we are not fighting Fascism to maintain the status quo but to defend the interests of the working class".[29] [30] Thousands of people took part in militant AFA mobilisations, such as Remembrance Day demonstrations in 1986 and 1987, the Unity Carnival, the Battle of Cable Street's 55th anniversary march in 1991, and the *Battle of Waterloo* against Blood and Honour in 1992.[31] [32]

After 1995, some anti-fascist mobilisations still occurred, such as against the NF in Dover in 1997 and 1998. In 1997, an AFA statement officially banned members from associating with *Searchlight* magazine, and in 1998, Leeds and Huddersfield AFA chapters were expelled by AFA officials for ignoring this policy. By 2001, AFA barely existed as a national organisation.

In 2001, some former AFA members founded the militant anti-fascist group No Platform, but this group soon disbanded. In 2004, members of the Anarchist Federation, Class War, and No Platform founded the organisation Antifa. This predominantly anarchist group has imitated AFA's stance of physical and ideological confrontation with fascists. In 2003, Unite Against Fascism (UAF) formed in response to electoral successes of the British National Party (BNP). Antifa and UAF have held many demonstrations against far right groups such as the BNP and the English Defence League, some of which resulted in violent confrontations and arrests.

United States

Premature anti-fascism is a term that was used in the United States to describe the views of those who opposed fascism at a time when the US government was on relatively friendly terms with fascist Italy and (to a lesser extent) Nazi Germany.[33] The term was applied especially to supporters of the Second Spanish Republic in the Spanish Civil War, including members of the Abraham Lincoln Brigade.

See also

- Antifascist Circle
- Anti-racism
- List of anti-fascists
- Resistance during World War II
- Resistance movement
- Redskin (subculture)
- Slovak National Uprising
- Squadism

Antifa graffiti in Trnava, Slovakia.

Further reading

- Key, Anna (ed.), ed. *Beating Fascism: Anarchist Anti-Fascism in Theory and Practice*. ISBN 1-873605-88-9.

External links

- Against unveiling monument to Nazi troops [34]
- 'Fascism or Revolution !' Anarchism and Antifascism in France, 1933-39 [35]
- Anti-fascism from Avtonom [36]
- "Anti-Fascist Action 1985-2001" [37]
- Gilles Dauve/Jean Barrot on liberal anti-fascism [38]
- "Bash the Fash: Anti-Fascist Recollections 1984-1993" [39]
- Interview from *Beating Fascism: Anarchist Anti-Fascism in Theory and Practice* [40]
- "Intellectuals and Anti-Fascism: For a Critical Historization" [41] *New Politics*, vol. 9, no. 4 (new series), whole no. 36, Winter 2004
- Liberal anti-fascism page at Red Action [42]
- Remembering the Anarchist Resistance to fascism [43]

References

[1] *ORGANISE! for revolutionary anarchism* (http://www.afed.org.uk/org/issue70/antifa_bash_the_fash.html), Magazine of the Anarchist Federation, Summer 2008, Issue 70

[2] Fascism: Theory and Practice. Pluto Press, ISBN 0-7453-1470-8 (http://www.dkrenton.co.uk/books/theory.html)

[3] Worker Insurgency and Statist Containment in Portugal and Spain, 1974-1977 - Loren Goldner (http://libcom.org/library/worker-insurgency-portugal-spain)

[4] Chicago Journals - The Journal of Modern History (http://www.journals.uchicago.edu/doi/abs/10.1086/422933?journalCode=jmh)

[5] quoted *Fighting Talk* no.22 October 1999, p.11

[6] (German) Opfer-Rechter-Gewalt (http://www.opfer-rechter-gewalt.de/)

[7] (German) Verfassungsschutz-bericht 2004 (http://www.verfassungsschutz.de/download/SHOW/vsbericht_2004.pdf), p. 168-172

[8] Anarchist Century (http://anarchist_century.tripod.com/timeline.html)

[9] David Ward *Antifascisms: Cultural Politics in Italy, 1943-1946*

[10] James Martin, 'Piero Gobetti's Agonistic Liberalism', *History of European Ideas*, vol. 32, (2006), 205-222.

[11] Milica Kacin Wohinz, Jože Pirjevec, *Storia degli sloveni in Italia : 1866-1998* (Venice: Marsilio, 1998)

[12] Milica Kacin Wohinz, *Narodnoobrambno gibanje primorskih Slovencev : 1921-1928* (Trieste: Založništvo tržaškega tiska, 1977)

[13] Milica Kacin Wohinz, *Prvi antifašizem v Evropi* (Koper: Lipa, 1990)

[14] Mira Cenčič, *TIGR : Slovenci pod Italijo in TIGR na okopih v boju za narodni obstoj* (Ljubljana: Mladinska knjiga, 1997)

[15] Vid Vremec, Pinko Tomažič in drugi tržaški proces 1941 (Trieste: Založništvo tržaškega tiska, 1989)

[16] Intelligence and Operational Support for the Anti-Nazi Resistance (http://darbysrangers.tripod.com/id102.htm)

[17] (Swedish) AFA - Aktivitetsguide för antifascister (http://www.antifa.se/files/aktivitetsguide.pdf), Antifa.se, 2004, pp. 9-11

[18] (Swedish) http://svt.se/2.33538/1.1750213/polisen_afa_bakom_upplopp_i_fittja&from=rss?utm_source=feedburner&utm_medium=feed&utm_campaign=Feed%3A+Svtse-NyheterABC+%28svt.se+-+Nyheter+ABC%29

[19] http://mobil.svt.se/2.33538/1.1752021/10_afa-anhangare_begardes_haktade

[20] (Swedish) http://www.aftonbladet.se/nyheter/article5784027.ab

[21] (Swedish) http://www.expressen.se/ledare/1.1466908/090215-stoppa-afa

[22] (Swedish) Poohl, Daniel (2006-10-18). "Ta avstånd från våldet mot SD" (http://www.expo.se/index_1.php?pg=http://www.expo.se/www/1_1735.html). EXPO. . Retrieved 2006-12-08.

[23] (Swedish) "Vänsterextrema infiltrerade IOGT-NTO" (http://www.svd.se/dynamiskt/inrikes/did_10487676.asp). Svenska Dagbladet. 2006-09-07. . Retrieved 2006-12-08.

[24] Jacobs, Joe *Out of the Ghetto*. London: Phoenix Press, 1991 (originally published in 1977). http://libcom.org/tags/joe-jacobs

[25] Phil Piratin *Our Flag Stays Red*. London: Lawrence & Wishart, 2006.

[26] Andrzej Olechnowicz, 'Liberal anti-fascism in the 1930s the case of Sir Ernest Barker', *Albion* 36, 2005, pp. 636-660

[27] Diethelm Prowe, 'Classic' Fascism... (http://www.jstor.org/pss/20081528)

[28] Lewisham '77 history site (http://lewisham77.blogspot.com/)

[29] Anti-Fascist Action: Radical resistance or rent-a-mob? (http://www.amielandmelburn.org.uk/collections/soundings/14_53.pdf)" *Soundings* issue 14 Spring 2000

[30] AFA (London) Constitution Part 1.4

[31] It Woz AFA Wot Done It! (http://www.redaction.org/anti-fascism/it_woz_afa.html)

[32] Diamond in the Dust - The Ian Stuart Biography (http://www.skrewdriver.net/diamond.html)

[33] *Politics and politicians in American film* by Phillip L. Gianos p.62.

[34] http://www.dcestonian.com/estonews/articles/05/mon042705.htm

[35] http://raforum.info/article.php3?id_article=238

[36] http://www.ainfos.ca/05/jul/ainfos00075.html

[37] http://www.libcom.org/history/1985-2001-anti-fascist-action-afa

[38] http://libcom.org/dst

[39] http://www.libcom.org/library/bash-the-fash-anti-fascist-recollections-1984-1993

[40] http://www.anarkismo.net/newswire.php?story_id=1583

[41] http://www.wpunj.edu/newpol/issue36/Traverso36.htm

[42] http://www.redaction.org/anti-fascism/liberal.html

[43] http://www.anarkismo.net/newswire.php?story_id=87

Jew

For the Jewish way of life, including religion, law, culture, and philosophy, see Judaism. "Jew" redirects here;
for other uses, see Jew (disambiguation).

Jews

יהודים (*Yehudim*)

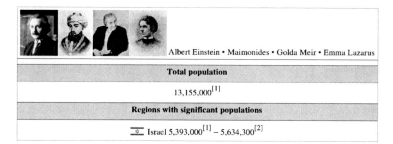

Albert Einstein • Maimonides • Golda Meir • Emma Lazarus

Total population
13,155,000[1]
Regions with significant populations
Israel 5,393,000[1] – 5,634,300[2]

United States	5,275,000[1] – 6,444,000	[3]
France	490,000	[1]
Canada	374,000	[1]
United Kingdom	295,000	[1]
Russia	225,000	[1]
Argentina	184,000	[1]
Germany	120,000	[1]
Australia	104,000	[1]
Brazil	96,000	[1]
Ukraine	77,000	[1]
South Africa	72,000	[1]
Hungary	49,000	[1]
Mexico	40,000	[1]
Belgium	31,200	[4]
Netherlands	30,000	[4]
Italy	28,600	[4]
Chile	20,700	[4]
Belarus	18,200	[4]
Uruguay	18,000	[4]
Switzerland	17,900	[4]
Turkey	17,800	[4]
Venezuela	15,400	[4]
Sweden	15,000	[4]
Spain	12,000	[4]
Iran	10,800	[4]
Romania	10,100	[4]
Latvia	9,800	[4]
Austria	9,000	[4]
Azerbaijan	6,800	[4]
Denmark	6,400	[4]
Panama	5,000	[4]

Languages
Historical Jewish languages Hebrew · Yiddish · Ladino · others
Liturgical languages Hebrew · Aramaic
Predominant spoken languages Hebrew, English, Russian, the vernacular languages of other countries in the Jewish diaspora.

Religion
Judaism

Part of a series of articles on

Jews and Judaism

Who is a Jew? · Etymology · Culture

The **Jews** (Hebrew: יְהוּדִים, *Yehudim*), also known as the **Jewish people**, are an ethnoreligious group originating in the Israelites or Hebrews of the Ancient Near East. The Jewish ethnicity, nationality, and religion are strongly interrelated, as Judaism is the traditional faith of the Jewish nation.[5] [6] [7] Converts to Judaism, whose status as Jews within the Jewish ethnos is equal to those born into it, have been absorbed into the Jewish people throughout the millennia.

In Jewish tradition, Jewish ancestry is traced to the Biblical patriarchs Abraham, Isaac and Jacob in the second millennium BCE. The Jews have experienced three periods of political autonomy in their national homeland, the Land of Israel, twice during ancient history, and currently once again, since 1948, with the establishment of the modern State of Israel. The first of the two ancient eras spanned from 1350 to 586 BCE, and encompassed the periods of the Judges, the United Monarchy, and the Divided Monarchy of the Kingdoms of Israel and Judah, ending with the destruction of the First Temple. The second era was the period of the Hasmonean Kingdom spanning from 140 to 37 BCE. Since the destruction of the First Temple, the diaspora has been the home of most of the world's Jews.[8] Except in the modern State of Israel, Jews are a minority in every country in which they live, and they have frequently experienced persecution throughout history, resulting in a population that fluctuated both in numbers and distribution over the centuries.

According to the Jewish Agency for Israel, as of 2007 there were 13.2 million Jews worldwide, 5.4 million of whom lived in Israel, 5.3 million in the United States, and the remainder distributed in communities of varying sizes around the world; this represents 0.2% of the current estimated world population.[1] (Other sources cite higher estimates. For example, the Israel Central Bureau of Statistics estimates the number of Israeli Jews to be 5.6 million and the U.S. Census Bureau estimates the American Jewish population to be as many as 6.4 million.[2] [3]) These numbers include all those who consider themselves Jews whether or not affiliated with a Jewish organization.[9] The total world Jewish population, however, is difficult to measure. In addition to *halakhic* considerations, there are secular, political, and ancestral identification factors in defining who is a Jew that increase the figure considerably.[9]

Name and etymology

The English word *Jew* continues Middle English *Gyw, Iewe*, a loan from Old French *giu*, earlier *juieu*, ultimately from Latin *Iudaeum*. The Latin *Iudaeus* simply means *Judaean*, "from the land of *Judaea*". The Latin term itself, like the corresponding Greek Ἰουδαῖος, is a loan from Aramaic *Y'hūdāi*, corresponding to Hebrew: יְהוּדִי, *Yehudi* (sg.); יְהוּדִים, *Yehudim* (pl.), in origin the term for a member of the tribe of Judah or the people of the kingdom of Judah. The Hebrew word for Jew, יְהוּדִי, is pronounced Hebrew pronunciation: [jəhuˈdiː], with the stress on the final syllable.[10]

The Ladino name is גֿיודיו, *Djudio* (sg.); סׄוׄיׄדׄיׄוׄס, *Djudios* (pl.); Yiddish: ייִד: *Yid* (sg.); ייִדן, *Yidn* (pl.).
The etymological equivalent is in use in other languages, e.g., "Jude" in German, "juif" in French, "jøde" in Danish, "judío" in Spanish, etc., but derivations of the word "Hebrew" are also in use to describe a Jewish person, e.g., in Italian (Ebreo), and Russian: Еврей, (*Yevrey*).[11] The German word "Jude" is pronounced German pronunciation: [ˈjuːdə], and is the origin of the word Yiddish.[12] (See Jewish ethnonyms for a full overview.)

According to the The American Heritage Dictionary of the English Language, Fourth Edition (2000):

> It is widely recognized that the attributive use of the noun *Jew*, in phrases such as *Jew lawyer* or *Jew ethics*, is both vulgar and highly offensive. In such contexts *Jewish* is the only acceptable possibility. Some people, however, have become so wary of this construction that they have extended the stigma to any use of *Jew* as a noun, a practice that carries risks of its own. In a sentence such as *There are now several Jews on the council*, which is unobjectionable, the substitution of a circumlocution like *Jewish people* or *persons of Jewish background* may in itself cause offense for seeming to imply that Jew has a negative connotation when used as a noun.[13]

Judaism

Judaism guides its adherents in both practice and belief, and has been called not only a religion, but also a "way of life,"[14] which has made drawing a clear distinction between Judaism, Jewish culture, and Jewish identity rather difficult. Throughout history, in eras and places as diverse as the ancient Hellenic world,[15] in Europe before and after The Age of Enlightenment (see Haskalah),[16] in Islamic Spain and Portugal,[17] in North Africa and the Middle East,[17] India,[18] and China,[19] or the contemporary United States[20] and Israel,[21] cultural phenomena have developed that are in some sense characteristically Jewish without being at all specifically religious. Some factors in this come from within Judaism, others from the interaction of Jews or specific communities of Jews with their surroundings, others from the inner social and cultural dynamics of the community, as opposed to from the religion itself. This phenomenon has led to considerably different Jewish cultures unique to their own communities, each as authentically Jewish as the next.[22]

Who is a Jew?

Judaism shares some of the characteristics of a nation, an ethnicity, a religion, and a culture, making the definition of who is a Jew vary slightly depending on whether a religious or national approach to identity is used.[23] Generally, in modern secular usage, Jews include three groups: people who were born to a Jewish family regardless of whether or not they follow the religion, those who have some Jewish ancestral background or lineage (sometimes including those who do not have strictly matrilineal descent), and people without any Jewish ancestral background or lineage who have formally converted to Judaism and therefore are followers of the religion.[24] At times conversion has accounted for a substantial part of Jewish population growth. In the first century of the Christian era, for example, the population more than doubled, from 4 to 8–10 million within the confines of the Roman Empire, in good part as a result of a wave of conversion.[25]

Historical definitions of Jewish identity have traditionally been based on *halakhic* definitions of matrilineal descent, and halakhic conversions. Historical definitions of who is a Jew date back to the codification of the oral tradition into the Babylonian Talmud. Interpretations of sections of the Tanakh, such as Deuteronomy 7:1–5, by learned Jewish sages, are used as a warning against intermarriage between Jews and non-Jews because "[the non-Jewish male spouse] will cause your child to turn away from Me and they will worship the gods of others." Leviticus 24:10 says that the son in a marriage between a Hebrew woman and an Egyptian man is "of the community of Israel." This contrasts with Ezra 10:2–3, where Israelites returning from Babylon vow to put aside their gentile wives and their children.[26] [27] Since the *Haskalah*, these *halakhic* interpretations of Jewish identity have been challenged.[28]

Ethnic divisions

Within the world's Jewish population there are distinct ethnic divisions, most of which are primarily the result of geographic branching from an originating Israelite population, and subsequent independent evolutions. An array of Jewish communities were established by Jewish settlers in various places around the Old World, often at great distances from one another resulting in effective and often long-term isolation from each other. During the millennia of the Jewish diaspora the communities would develop under the influence of their local environments; political, cultural, natural, and populational. Today, manifestation of these differences among the Jews can be observed in Jewish cultural expressions of each community, including Jewish linguistic diversity, culinary preferences, liturgical practices, religious interpretations, as well as degrees and sources of genetic admixture.[29]

Ashkenazi Jews of late 19th century Eastern Europe portrayed in *Jews Praying in the Synagogue on Yom Kippur* (1878), by Maurycy Gottlieb.

Jews are often identified as belonging to one of two major groups: the *Ashkenazim*, or "Germanics" (Ashkenaz meaning "Germany" in Medieval Hebrew, denoting their Central European base), and the *Sephardim*, or "Hispanics" (Sefarad meaning "Spain/Hispania" or "Iberia" in Hebrew, denoting their Spanish, and Portuguese, base). The *Mizrahim*, or "Easterners" (Mizrach being "East" in Hebrew), that is, the diverse collection of Middle Eastern and North African Jews, constitute a third major group, although they are sometimes termed *Sephardi* for liturgical reasons.[30]

Smaller groups include, but are not restricted to, Indian Jews such as the Bene Israel, Bnei Menashe, Cochin Jews, and Bene Ephraim; the Romaniotes of Greece; the Italian Jews ("Italkim" or "Bené Roma"); the Teimanim from Yemen and Oman; various African Jews, including most numerously the Beta Israel of Ethiopia; and Chinese Jews, most notably the Kaifeng Jews, as well as various other distinct but now almost extinct communities.[31]

The divisions between all these groups are approximate and their boundaries are not always clear. The Mizrahim for example, are a heterogeneous collection of North African, Central Asian, Caucasian, and Middle Eastern Jewish communities that are often as unrelated to each other as they are to any of the earlier mentioned Jewish groups. In modern usage, however, the Mizrahim are sometimes termed *Sephardi* due to similar styles of liturgy, despite independent development from Sephardim proper. Thus, among Mizrahim there are Iraqi Jews, Egyptian Jews, Berber Jews, Lebanese Jews, Kurdish Jews, Libyan Jews, Syrian Jews, Bukharian Jews, Mountain Jews, Georgian Jews, and various others. The Teimanim from Yemen and Oman are sometimes included, although their style of liturgy is unique and they differ in respect to the admixture found among them to that found in Mizrahim. In addition, there is a differentiation made between Sephardi migrants who established themselves in the Middle East and North Africa after the expulsion of the Jews from Spain and Portugal in the 1490s and the pre-existing Jewish communities in those regions.[31]

Despite this diversity, Ashkenazi Jews represent the bulk of modern Jewry, with at least 70% of Jews worldwide (and up to 90% prior to World War II and the Holocaust). As a result of their emigration from Europe, Ashkenazim also represent the overwhelming majority of Jews in the New World continents, in countries such as the United States, Canada, Argentina, Australia, and Brazil. In France, emigration of Mizrahim from North Africa has led them to outnumber the Ashkenazim and Sephardim.[32] Only in Israel is the Jewish population representative of all groups, a melting pot independent of each group's proportion within the overall world Jewish population.[33]

Jewish languages

Hebrew is the liturgical language of Judaism (termed *lashon ha-kodesh*, "the holy tongue"), the language in which the Hebrew scriptures (Tanakh) were composed, and the daily speech of the Jewish people for centuries. By the fifth century BCE, Aramaic, a closely related tongue, joined Hebrew as the spoken language in Judea.[34] By the third century BCE, Jews of the diaspora were speaking Greek.[35] Modern Hebrew is now one of the two official languages of the State of Israel along with Arabic.[36]

Hebrew was revived as a spoken language by Eliezer ben Yehuda, who arrived in Palestine in 1881. It hadn't been used as a mother tongue since Tannaic times.[34] For over sixteen centuries Hebrew was used almost exclusively as a liturgical language, and as the language in which most books had been written on Judaism, with a few speaking only Hebrew on the Sabbath.[37] For centuries, Jews worldwide have spoken the local or dominant languages of the regions they migrated to, often developing distinctive dialectal forms or branching off as independent languages. Yiddish is the Judæo-German language developed by Ashkenazi Jews who migrated to Central Europe, and Ladino is the Judæo-Spanish language developed by Sephardic Jews who migrated to the Iberian peninsula. Due to many factors, including the impact of the Holocaust on European Jewry, the Jewish exodus from Arab lands, and widespread emigration from other Jewish communities around the world, ancient and distinct Jewish languages of several communities, including Gruzinic, Judæo-Arabic, Judæo-Berber, Krymchak, Judæo-Malayalam and many others, have largely fallen out of use.[38]

The three most commonly spoken languages among Jews today are Hebrew, English and Russian. Some Romance languages, such as French, and Spanish are also widely used.[38]

Yiddish has been spoken by more Jews in history than any other language, closely followed by English and Hebrew (if modern and biblical are counted as one variety).

Genetic studies

Genetic studies indicate various lineages found in modern Jewish populations, however, most of these populations share a lineage in common, traceable to an ancient population that underwent geographic branching and subsequent independent evolutions.[39] While DNA tests have demonstrated inter-marriage in all of the various Jewish ethnic divisions over the last 3,000 years, it was substantially less than in other populations.[40] The findings lend support to traditional Jewish accounts accrediting their founding to exiled Israelite populations, and counters theories that many or most of the world's Jewish populations were founded entirely by local populations that adopted the Jewish faith, devoid of any actual Israelite genetic input.[40] [41]

DNA analysis further determined that modern Jews of the priesthood tribe—"Kohanim"—share an ancestor dating back about 3,000 years.[42] This result is consistent for all Jewish populations around the world.[42] The researchers estimated that the most recent common ancestor of modern Kohanim lived between 1000 BCE (roughly the time of the Biblical Exodus) and 586 BCE, when the Babylonians destroyed the First Temple.[43] They found similar results analyzing DNA from Ashkenazi and Sephardi Jews.[43] The scientists estimated the date of the original priest based on genetic mutations, which indicated that the priest lived roughly 106 generations ago, between 2,650 and 3,180 years ago depending whether one counts a generation as 25 or 30 years.[43]

Although individual and groups of converts to Judaism have historically been absorbed into contemporary Jewish populations — in the Khazars' case, absorbed into the Ashkenazim — it is unlikely that they formed a large percentage of the ancestors of modern Jewish groups, and much less that they represented their genesis as Jewish communities.[44]

Male lineages: Y chromosomal DNA

A study published by the National Academy of Sciences found that "the paternal gene pools of Jewish communities from Europe, North Africa, and the Middle East descended from a common Middle Eastern ancestral population", and suggested that "most Jewish communities have remained relatively isolated from neighboring non-Jewish communities during and after the Diaspora".[39] Researchers expressed surprise at the remarkable genetic uniformity they found among modern Jews, no matter where the diaspora has become dispersed around the world.[39]

Other Y-chromosome findings show that the world's Jewish communities are closely related to Kurds, Syrians and Palestinians.[42] [45] Skorecki and colleague wrote that "the extremely close affinity of Jewish and non-Jewish Middle Eastern populations observed ... supports the hypothesis of a common Middle Eastern origin".[42] According to another study of the same year, more than 70% of Jewish men and half of the Arab men (inhabitants of Israel and the territories only) whose DNA was studied inherited their Y-chromosomes from the same paternal ancestors who lived in the region within the last few thousand years. The results are consistent with the Biblical account of Jews and Arabs having a common ancestor. About two-thirds of Israeli Arabs and Arabs in the territories and a similar proportion of Israeli Jews are the descendants of at least three common ancestors who lived in the Middle East in the Neolithic period. However, the Palestinian Arab clade includes two Arab modal haplotypes which are found at only very low frequency among Jews, reflecting divergence and/or large scale admixture from non-local populations to the Palestinians.[46]

Points in which Jewish groups differ is largely in the source and proportion of genetic contribution from host populations.[47] [48] The proportion of male indigenous European genetic admixture in Ashkenazi Jews amounts to around 0.5% per generation over an estimated 80 generations, and a total admixture estimate "very similar to Motulsky's average estimate of 12.5%."[39] More recent study estimates an even lower European male contribution, and that only 5%–8% of the Ashkenazi gene pool is of European origin.[39]

Female lineages: Mitochondrial DNA

Before 2006, geneticists largely attributed the genesis of most of the world's Jewish populations to founding acts by males who migrated from the Middle East and "by the women from each local population whom they took as wives and converted to Judaism." However, more recent findings of studies of maternally inherited mitochondrial DNA, at least in Ashkenazi Jews, has led to a review of this archetype.[49] This research has suggested that, in addition to Israelite male, significant female founder ancestry might also derive from the Middle East.[49] In addition, Behar (2006) suggested that the rest of Ashkenazi mtDNA is originated from about 150 women, most of those were probably of Middle Eastern origin.[50]

Research in 2008 found significant founder effects in many non-Asheknazi Jewish populations. In Belmonte, Azerbaijani, Georgian, Bene Israel and Libyan Jewish communities "a single mother was sufficient to explain at least 40% of their present-day mtDNA variation". In addition, "the Cochin and Tunisian Jewish communities show an attenuated pattern with two founding mothers explaining >30% of the variation." In contrast, Bulgarian, Turkish, Moroccan and Ethiopian Jews were heterogeneous with no evidence "for a narrow founder effect or depletion of mtDNA variation attributable to drift". The authors noted that "the first three of these communities were established following the Spanish expulsion and/or received large influxes of individuals from the Iberian Peninsula and high variation presently observed, probably reflects high overall mtDNA diversity among Jews of Spanish descent. Likewise, the mtDNA pool of Ethiopian Jews reflects the rich maternal lineage variety of East Africa." Jewish communities from Iraq, Iran, and Yemen showed a "third and intermediate pattern... consistent with a founding event, but not a narrow one".[51]

In this and other studies Yemenite Jews differ from other Mizrahim, as well as from Ashkenazim, in the proportion of sub-Saharan African gene types which have entered their gene pools.[47] African-specific Hg L(xM,N) lineages were found only in Yemenite and Ethiopian Jewish populations.[51] Among Yemenites, the average stands at 35% lineages within the past 3,000 years.[47]

Demographics

Population centres

There are an estimated 13.2 million Jews worldwide.[1] The table below lists countries with significant populations. Please note that these populations represent low-end estimates of the worldwide Jewish population, accounting for around 0.2% of the world's population.

Country or Region	Jewish population	Total Population	% Jewish	Notes
Israel	5,393,000	7,117,000	75.8%	[1]
United States	5,275,000	301,469,000	1.7%	[1]
Europe	1,506,000	710,000,000	0.2%	[4]
France	490,000	64,102,000	0.8%	[1]
Canada	374,000	32,874,000	1.1%	[1]
United Kingdom	295,000	60,609,000	0.5%	[1]
Russia	225,000	142,400,000	0.2%	[1]
Argentina	184,000	39,922,000	0.5%	[1]
Germany	120,000	82,310,000	0.1%	[1]
Australia	104,000	20,788,000	0.5%	[1]
Brazil	96,000	188,078,000	0.05%	[1]
Ukraine	77,000	46,481,000	0.2%	[1]
South Africa	72,000	47,432,000	0.2%	[1]
Hungary	49,000	10,053,000	0.5%	[1]
Mexico	40,000	108,700,000	0.04%	[1]
Asia (excl. Israel)	39,500	3,900,000,000	0.001%	[4]
Belgium	31,200	10,419,000	0.3%	[4]
Italy	28,600	58,884,000	0.05%	[4]
Turkey	17,800	72,600,000	0.02%	[4]
Iran	10,800	68,467,000	0.02%	[4]
Romania	10,100	21,500,000	0.05%	[4]
New Zealand	7,000	4,306,400	0.2%	[4]
Greece	5,500	11,100,000	0.05%	[4]

Cuba	1,500	11,450,000	0.013%	[52]
Total	**13,156,500**	**6,455,078,000**	**0.2%**	[1]

State of Israel

Israel, the Jewish nation-state, is the only country in which Jews make up a majority of the citizens.[53] [54] Israel was established as an independent democratic state on May 14, 1948.[55] Of the 120 members in its parliament, the Knesset,[56] currently, 12 members of the Knesset are Arab citizens of Israel, most representing Arab political parties and one of Israel's Supreme Court judges is a Palestinian Arab.[57] Between 1948 and 1958, the Jewish population rose from 800,000 to two million.[58] Currently, Jews account for 75.8% of the Israeli population, or 5.4 million people.[1] The early years of the state of Israel were marked by the mass immigration of Holocaust survivors and Jews fleeing Arab lands.[59] Israel also has a large population of Ethiopian Jews, many of whom were airlifted to Israel in the late 1980s

David Ben Gurion (First Prime Minister of Israel) publicly pronouncing the Declaration of the Establishment of the State of Israel, May 14, 1948

and early 1990s.[60] Between 1974 and 1979 nearly 227,258 immigrants arrived in Israel, about half being from the Soviet Union.[61] This period also saw an increase in immigration to Israel from Western Europe, Latin America, and the United States[62] A trickle of immigrants from other communities has also arrived, including Indian Jews and others, as well as some descendants of Ashkenazi Holocaust survivors who had settled in countries such as the United States, Argentina, Australia and South Africa. Some Jews have emigrated from Israel elsewhere, due to economic problems or disillusionment with political conditions and the continuing Arab-Israeli conflict. Jewish Israeli emigrants are known as yordim.[63]

Diaspora (outside Israel)

The waves of immigration to the United States and elsewhere at the turn of the nineteenth century, the founding of Zionism and later events, including pogroms in Russia, the massacre of European Jewry during the Holocaust, and the founding of the state of Israel, with the subsequent Jewish exodus from Arab lands, all resulted in substantial shifts in the population centers of world Jewry by the end of the twentieth century.[64]

Currently, the largest Jewish community in the world is located in the United States, with 5.3 million or 6.4 million Jews by various estimates. Elsewhere in the Americas, there are also large Jewish populations in Canada, Argentina, and Brazil, and smaller populations in Mexico, Uruguay, Venezuela, Chile, and several other countries (see History of the Jews in Latin America).[1] [3]

Western Europe's largest Jewish community can be found in France, home to 490,000 Jews, the majority of whom are immigrants or refugees from North African Arab countries such as Algeria, Morocco, and Tunisia (or their descendants).[66] There are 295,000 Jews in the United Kingdom. In Eastern Europe, there are anywhere from 350,000 to one million Jews living in the former Soviet Union, but exact figures are difficult to establish. The fastest-growing Jewish community in the world, outside Israel, is the one in Germany, especially in Berlin, its capital. Tens of thousands of Jews from the former Eastern Bloc have settled in Germany since the fall of the Berlin Wall.[67]

The Arab countries of North Africa and the Middle East were home to around 900,000 Jews in 1945. Fueled by anti-Zionism[68] after the founding of Israel, systematic persecution caused almost all of these Jews to flee to Israel, North America, and Europe in the 1950s (see Jewish exodus from Arab lands). Today, around 8,000 Jews remain in all Arab nations combined.[4]

In this Rosh Hashana greeting card from the early 1900s, Russian Jews, packs in hand, gaze at the American relatives beckoning them to the United States. Over two million Jews would flee the pogroms of the Russian Empire to the safety of the US from 1881–1924.[65]

Iran is home to around 10,800 Jews, down from a population of 100,000 Jews before the 1979 revolution. After the revolution some of the Iranian Jews emigrated to Israel or Europe but most of them emigrated (with their non-Jewish Iranian compatriots) to the United States (especially Los Angeles, where the principal community is called "Tehrangeles").[4] [69]

Outside Europe, the Americas, the Middle East, and the rest of Asia, there are significant Jewish populations in Australia and South Africa.[4]

Demographic changes

Assimilation

Since at least the time of the Ancient Greeks, a proportion of Jews have assimilated into the wider non-Jewish society around them, by either choice or force, ceasing to practice Judaism and losing their Jewish identity.[70] Assimilation took place in all areas, and during all time periods,[70] with some Jewish communities, for example the Kaifeng Jews of China, disappearing entirely.[71] The advent of the Jewish Enlightenment of the 1700s (see

Haskalah) and the subsequent emancipation of the Jewish populations of Europe and America in the 1800s, accelerated the situation, encouraging Jews to increasingly participate in, and become part of, secular society. The result has been a growing trend of assimilation, as Jews marry non-Jewish spouses and stop participating in the Jewish community.[72] Rates of interreligious marriage vary widely: In the United States, they are just under 50%,[73] in the United Kingdom, around 53%, in France, around 30%,[74] and in Australia and Mexico, as low as 10%.[75] [76] In the United States, only about a third of children from intermarriages affiliate themselves with Jewish religious practice.[77] The result is that most countries in the Diaspora have steady or slightly declining religiously Jewish populations as Jews continue to assimilate into the countries in which they live.

War and persecution

Related articles: Antisemitism, History of antisemitism, New antisemitism

The Jewish people and Judaism have experienced various persecutions throughout Jewish history. During late Antiquity and the early Middle Ages the Roman Empire (in its later phases known as the Byzantine Empire) repeatedly repressed the Jewish population, first by ejecting them from their homelands during the pagan Roman era and later by officially establishing them as second-class citizens during the Christian Roman era.[78] [79] According to James Carroll, "Jews accounted for 10% of the total population of the Roman Empire. By that ratio, if other factors had not intervened, there would be 200 million Jews in the world today, instead of something like 13 million."[80] Of course, there are many other complex demographic factors involved; the rate of population growth, epidemics, migration, assimilation, and conversion could all have played major roles in the current size of the global Jewish population.

Jews (identifiable by the distinctive hats that they were required to wear) being killed by Christian knights. French Bible illustration from 1255.

Later in medieval Western Europe, further persecutions of Jews in the name of Christianity occurred, notably during the Crusades—when Jews all over Germany were massacred—and a series of expulsions from England, Germany, France, and, in the largest expulsion of all, Spain and Portugal after the Reconquista (the Catholic Reconquest of the Iberian Peninsula), where both unbaptized Sephardic Jews and the ruling Muslim Moors were expelled.[81] [82] In the Papal States, which existed until 1870, Jews were required to live only in specified neighborhoods called ghettos.[83] In the 19th and (before the end of World War II) 20th centuries, the Roman Catholic Church adhered to a distinction between "good antisemitism" and "bad antisemitism". The "bad" kind promoted hatred of Jews because of their descent. This was considered un-Christian because the Christian

THE JEWS THE WORLD OVER LOVE LIBERTY HAVE FOUGHT FOR IT & WILL FIGHT FOR IT.

BRITAIN EXPECTS EVERY SON OF ISRAEL TO DO HIS DUTY

ENLIST WITH THE INFANTRY REINFORCEMENTS FOR OVERSEAS

Under the Command of

Capt. FREEDMAN

Headquarters-

786 ST. LAWRENCE BOULEVARD. MONTREAL.

WW I poster shows a soldier cutting the bonds from a Jewish man, who says, "...now let me help you set others free!"

message was intended for all of humanity regardless of ethnicity; anyone could become a Christian. The "good" kind criticized alleged Jewish conspiracies to control newspapers, banks, and other institutions, to care only about accumulation of wealth, etc.[84]

Islam and Judaism have a complex relationship. Traditionally Jews and Christians living in Muslim lands, known as dhimmis, were allowed to practice their religions and to administer their internal affairs, but subject to certain conditions.[85] They had to pay the jizya (a per capita tax imposed on free adult non-Muslim males) to the Islamic state.[85] Dhimmis had an inferior status under Islamic rule. They had several social and legal disabilities such as prohibitions against bearing arms or giving testimony in courts in cases involving Muslims.[86] Many of the disabilities were highly symbolic. The one described by Bernard Lewis as "most degrading"[87] was the requirement of distinctive clothing, not found in the Qur'an or hadith but invented in early medieval Baghdad; its enforcement was highly erratic.[87] On the other hand, Jews rarely faced martyrdom or exile, or forced compulsion to change their religion, and they were mostly free in their choice of residence and profession.[88] Notable exceptions include the massacre of Jews and/or forcible conversion of some Jews by the rulers of the Almohad dynasty in Al-Andalus in the 12th century,[89] as well as in Islamic Persia,[90] and the forced confinement of Morrocan Jews to walled quarters known as mellahs beginning from the 15th century and especially in the early 19th century.[91] In modern times, it has become commonplace for standard antisemitic themes to be conflated with anti-Zionist publications and pronouncements of Islamic movements such as Hezbollah and Hamas, in the pronouncements of various agencies of the Islamic Republic of Iran, and even in the newspapers and other publications of Turkish Refah Partisi."[92]

Throughout history, many rulers, empires and nations have oppressed their Jewish populations or sought to eliminate them entirely. Methods employed ranged from expulsion to outright genocide; within nations, often the threat of these extreme methods was sufficient to silence dissent. The history of antisemitism includes the First Crusade which resulted in the massacre of Jews;[81] the Spanish Inquisition (led by Torquemada) and the Portuguese Inquisition, with their persecution and *Auto de fé* against the New Christians and Marrano Jews;[93] the Bohdan Chmielnicki Cossack massacres in Ukraine;[94] the Pogroms backed by the Russian Tsars;[95] as well as expulsions from Spain, Portugal, England, France, Germany, and other countries in which the Jews had settled.[82] The persecution reached a peak in Adolf Hitler's Final Solution, which led to the Holocaust and the slaughter of approximately 6 million Jews from 1939 to 1945.[96] According to a recent study published in the American Journal of Human Genetics 19.8% of the modern Iberian population has Sephardic Jewish ancestry,[97] indicating that the number of conversos may have been much higher than originally thought.[98]

The most notable modern day persecution of Jews remains the Holocaust — the state-led systematic persecution and genocide of European Jews (and certain communities of North African Jews in European controlled North Africa) and other minority groups of Europe during World War II by Nazi Germany and its collaborators.[99] The persecution and genocide were accomplished in stages. Legislation to remove the Jews from civil society was enacted years before the outbreak of World War II.[100] Concentration camps were established in which inmates were used as slave labour until they died of exhaustion or disease.[101] Where the Third Reich conquered new territory in eastern Europe, specialized units called Einsatzgruppen murdered Jews and political opponents in mass shootings.[102] Jews and Roma were crammed into ghettos before being transported hundreds of miles by freight train to extermination camps where, if they survived the journey, the majority of them were killed in gas chambers.[103] Virtually every arm of Germany's bureaucracy was involved in the logistics of the mass murder, turning the country into what one Holocaust scholar has called "a genocidal nation."[104]

Migrations

Throughout Jewish history, Jews have repeatedly been directly or indirectly expelled from both their original homeland, and the areas in which they have resided. This experience as both immigrants and emigrants (see: Jewish refugees) have shaped Jewish identity and religious practice in many ways, and are thus a major element of Jewish history.[106] An incomplete list of such migrations includes:

Etching of the expulsion of the Jews from Frankfurt on August 23, 1614. The text says: "1380 persons old and young were counted at the exit of the gate"

- The patriarch Abraham was a migrant to the land of Canaan from Ur of the Chaldees.[107]
- The Children of Israel experienced the Exodus (meaning "departure" or "exit" in Greek) from ancient Egypt, as recorded in the Book of Exodus.[108]
- The Kingdom of Israel was sent into permanent exile and scattered all over the world (or at least to unknown locations) by Assyria.[109]
- The Kingdom of Judah was exiled by Babylonia,[110] then returned to Judea by Cyrus the Great of the Persian Achaemenid Empire,[111] and then many were exiled again by the Roman Empire.[112]
- The 2,000 year dispersion of the Jewish diaspora beginning under the Roman Empire, as Jews were spread throughout the Roman world and, driven from land to land, and settled wherever they could live freely enough to practice their religion. Over the course of the diaspora the center of Jewish life moved from Babylonia[113] to the Iberian Peninsula[114] to Poland[115] to the United States[116] and, as a result of Zionism, to Israel.[117]

Jewish refugees in Shanghai, China during World War II. Shanghai offered unconditional asylum for tens of thousands of Jewish refugees from Europe escaping the Holocaust.[105]

- Many expulsions during the Middle Ages and Enlightenment in Europe, including: 1290, 16,000 Jews were expelled from England, see the *(Statute of Jewry)*; in 1396, 100,000 from France; in 1421 thousands were expelled from Austria. Many of these Jews settled in Eastern Europe, especially Poland.[118]
- Following the Spanish Inquisition in 1492, the Spanish population of around 200,000 Sephardic Jews were expelled by the Spanish crown and Catholic church, followed by expulsions in 1493 in Sicily (37,000 Jews) and Portugal in 1496. The expelled Jews fled mainly to the Ottoman Empire, the Netherlands, and North Africa, others migrating to Southern Europe and the Middle East.[119]

- During the 19th century, France's policies of equal citizenship regardless of religion led to the immigration of Jews (especially from Eastern and Central Europe).[120]
- The arrival of millions of Jews in the New World, including immigration of over two million Eastern European Jews to the United States from 1880–1925, see History of the Jews in the United States and History of the Jews in Russia and the Soviet Union.[121]
- The Pogroms in Eastern Europe,[95] the rise of modern antisemitism,[122] the Holocaust,[123] and the rise of Arab nationalism[124] all served to fuel the movements and migrations of huge segments of Jewry from land to land and continent to continent, until they arrived back in large numbers at their original historical homeland in Israel.[117]
- The Islamic Revolution of Iran forced many Iranian Jews to flee Iran. Most found refuge in the US (particularly Los Angeles, CA) and Israel. Smaller communities of Persian Jews exist in Canada and Western Europe.[125]
- When the Soviet Union collapsed, many of the Jews in the affected territory (who had been refuseniks) were suddenly allowed to leave. This produced a wave of migration to Israel in the early 1990s.[63]

Growth

Israel is the only country with a consistently growing Jewish population due to natural population increase, though the Jewish populations of other countries in Europe and North America have recently increased due to immigration. In the Diaspora, in almost every country the Jewish population in general is either declining or steady, but Orthodox and Haredi Jewish communities, whose members often shun birth control for religious reasons, have experienced rapid population growth.[126]

Orthodox and Conservative Judaism discourage proselytization to non-Jews, but many Jewish groups have tried to reach out to the assimilated Jewish communities of the Diaspora in order for them to reconnect to their Jewish roots. Additionally, while in principle Reform Judaism favors seeking new members for the faith, this position has not translated into active proselytism, instead taking the form of an effort to reach out to non-Jewish spouses of intermarried couples.[127] There is also a trend of Orthodox movements pursuing secular Jews in order to give them a stronger Jewish identity so there is less chance of intermarriage. As a result of the efforts by these and other Jewish groups over the past twenty-five years, there has been a trend of secular Jews becoming more religiously observant, known as the *Baal Teshuva* movement, though the demographic implications of the trend are unknown.[128] Additionally, there is also a growing movement of Jews by Choice by gentiles who make the decision to head in the direction of becoming Jews.[129]

Jewish leadership

There is no single governing body for the Jewish community, nor a single authority with responsibility for religious doctrine.[130] Instead, a variety of secular and religious institutions at the local, national, and international levels lead various parts of the Jewish community on a variety of issues.[131]

Notable Jews

Jews have made contributions in a broad range of human endeavors, including the sciences, arts, politics, and business.[132] [133] The number of Jewish Nobel prize winners is far out of proportion to the percentage of Jews in the world's population.[134] [133]

See also

More complete guides to topics related to the Jews is available from the guide at the top or bottom of this page. Some topics of interest include:

References

- Baron, Salo Wittmayer (1952). *A Social and Religious History of the Jews,* Volume II, *Ancient Times,* Part II. Philadelphia: Jewish Publication Society of America.
- Carr, David R. (2003) [2000]. "Judaism in Christendom". in Neusner, Jacob; Avery-Peck, Alan J.. *The Blackwell Companion to Judaism*. Malden, Mass.: Blackwell Publishing. ISBN 1-57718-058-5.
- Cowling, Geoffrey (2005). *Introduction to World Religions*. Singapore: First Fortress Press. ISBN 0-8006-3714-3.
- Danzger, M. Herbert (2003) [2000]. "The "Return" to Traditional Judaism at the End of the Twentieth Century: Cross-Cultural Comparisons". in Neusner, Jacob; Avery-Peck, Alan J.. *The Blackwell Companion to Judaism*. Malden, Mass.: Blackwell Publishing. ISBN 1-57718-058-5.
- Dekmejian, R. Hrair (1975). *Patterns of Political Leadership: Egypt, Israel, Lebanon*. State University of New York Press. ISBN 087395291X.
- de Lange, Nicholas (2002) [2000]. *An Introduction to Judaism*. Cambridge: Cambridge University Press. ISBN 0-521-46073-5.
- Dosick, Wayne (2007). *Living Judaism*. New York: HarperCollins. ISBN 0-06-062179-6.
- Elazar, Daniel J. (2003) [2000]. "Judaism as a Theopolitical Phenomenon". in Neusner, Jacob; Avery-Peck, Alan J.. *The Blackwell Companion to Judaism*. Malden, Mass.: Blackwell Publishing. ISBN 1-57718-058-5.
- Feldman, Louis H. (2006). *Judaism and Hellenism Reconsidered*. Leiden, The Netherlands: Brill. ISBN 90-04-14906-6.
- Gartner, Lloyd P. (2001). *History of the Jews in Modern Times*. Oxford: Oxford University Press. ISBN 0-19-289259-2.
- Goldenberg, Robert (2007). *The Origins of Judaism: From Canaan to the Rise of Islam*. Cambridge: Cambridge University Press. ISBN 0-521-84453-3.
- Goldstein, Joseph (1995). *Jewish History in Modern Times*. Sussex Academic Press. ISBN 1898723060.
- Johnson, Paul (1987). *A History of the Jews*. New York: HarperCollins. ISBN 0-06-091533-1.
- Kaplan, Dana Evan (2003) [2000]. "Reform Judaism". in Neusner, Jacob; Avery-Peck, Alan J.. *The Blackwell Companion to Judaism*. Malden, Mass.: Blackwell Publishing. ISBN 1-57718-058-5.
- Katz, Shmuel (1974). *Battleground: Fact and Fantasy in Palestine*. Taylor Productions. ISBN 0-929093-13-5.
- Lewis, Bernard (1984). *The Jews of Islam*. Princeton: Princeton University Press. ISBN 0-691-00807-8

- Lewis, Bernard (1999). *Semites and Anti-Semites: An Inquiry into Conflict and Prejudice*. W. W. Norton & Co. ISBN 0-393-31839-7
- Littman, David (1979). "Jews Under Muslim Rule: The Case Of Persia". *The Wiener Library Bulletin* **XXXII** (New series 49/50).
- Neusner, Jacob (1991). *Studying Classical Judaism: A Primer*. Westminster John Knox Press. ISBN 0664251366.
- Poliakov, Leon (1974). *The History of Anti-semitism*. New York: The Vanguard Press.
- Sharot, Stephen (1997). "Religious Syncretism and Religious Distinctiveness: A Comparative Analysis of Pre-Modern Jewish Communities". in Endelman, Todd M.. *Comparing Jewish Societies*. Ann Arbor, Mich.: University of Michigan Press. ISBN 0-472-06592-0.
- Stillman, Norman (1979). *The Jews of Arab Lands: A History and Source Book*. Philadelphia: Jewish Publication Society of America. ISBN 0-8276-0198-0
- Sweeney, Marvin A. (2003) [2000]. "The Religious World of Ancient Israel to 586 BCE". in Neusner, Jacob; Avery-Peck, Alan J.. *The Blackwell Companion to Judaism*. Malden, Mass.: Blackwell Publishing. ISBN 1-57718-058-5.

External links

General

- Jewish Virtual Library [135]
- Judaism 101 [136]
- Maps related to Jewish history [137]

Secular organizations

- American Jewish Committee [138]
- American Jewish Congress [139]
- Anti-Defamation League [140]
- B'nai B'rith International [141]
- Hillel: The Foundation for Jewish Campus Life [142]
- United Jewish Communities: The Federations of North America [143]

Religious organizations

- Aish HaTorah [144] (Orthodox)
- ALEPH: Alliance for Jewish Renewal [145] (Renewal)
- American Sephardi Federation [146] (Sephardic)
- Chabad Lubavitch [147] (Chabad)
- Jewish Reconstructionist Federation [148] (Reconstructionist)

- The Karaite Korner [149] (Karaite)
- The Orthodox Union [150] (Orthodox)
- Society for Humanistic Judaism [151] (Humanistic)
- Union for Reform Judaism [152] (Reform)
- The United Synagogue of Conservative Judaism [153] (Conservative)

Zionist organizations

- Ameinu [154]
- Hadassah: the Women's Zionist Organization of America [155]
- The Jewish Agency for Israel [156]
- Religious Zionists of America [157]

- World Mizrachi Movement [158]
- World Zionist Organization [159]
- Zionist Organization of America [160]

References

[1] (PDF) *Annual Assessment* (http://www.jpppi.org.il/JPPPI/SendFile.asp?DBID=1&LNGID=1&GID=489), Jewish People Policy Planning Institute (Jewish Agency for Israel), 2007, p. 15, , based on *American Jewish Year Book* (http://www.ajcarchives.org/main. php?GroupingId=10142). **106**. American Jewish Committee. 2006. .

[2] (DOC) *Statistical Abstract of Israel* (http://www1.cbs.gov.il/www/hodaot2009n/11_09_208b.doc), Central Bureau of Statistics, 2009,

[3] (PDF) *Statistical Abstract* (http://www.census.gov/compendia/statab/tables/09s0076.pdf), U.S. Census Bureau, 2007,

[4] "The Jewish Population of the World (2006)" (http://www.jewishvirtuallibrary.org/jsource/Judaism/jewpop.html). *Jewish Virtual Library*. ., based on *American Jewish Year Book* (http://www.ajcarchives.org/main.php?GroupingId=10142). **106**. American Jewish Committee. 2006. .

[5] (http://www.law.louisville.edu/library/collections/brandeis/node/234) "The Jewish Problem: How To Solve It," U.S. Supreme Court Justice Louis D. Brandeis, "Jews are a distinctive nationality of which every Jew, whatever his country, his station or shade of belief, is necessarily a member" (April 25, 1915), University of Louisville Louis D. Brandeis School of Law, Retrieved on June 15, 2009

[6] (http://books.google.com/books?id=pPcOAAAAYAAJ&pg=PA3&lpg=PA3&dq="jewish+nation"+people&source=bl& ots=mwcd98d6Hx&sig=snSbv5ryENiSr-a9Kkfc4Ycs7h4&hl=en&ei=A0o2SvmeI-PBtwed0qj5Dg&sa=X&oi=book_result&ct=result& resnum=33) Palmer, Henry, *A History of the Jewish Nation* (1875), D. Lothrop & Co., Retrieved on June 15, 2009

[7] (http://press.princeton.edu/einstein/materials/jewish_nationality.pdf) "The Collected Papers of Albert Einstein, Vol. 7: Berlin Years," U.S. Supreme Court Justice Louis D. Brandeis, "The Jewish Nation is a living fact" (June 21, 1921), Princeton University Press, Retrieved on June 15, 2009

[8] Johnson (1987), p. 82.

[9] Pfeffer, Anshel (September 12, 2007). "Jewish Agency: 13.2 million Jews worldwide on eve of Rosh Hashanah, 5768" (http://www.haaretz. com/hasen/spages/903585.html). *Haaretz*. . Retrieved January 24, 2009.

[10] Grintz, Yehoshua M. (2007). "Jew". in Fred Skolnik. *Encyclopaedia Judaica*. **11** (2d ed.). Farmington Hills, Mich.: Thomson Gale. p. 253. ISBN 0-02-865928-2.

[11] Falk, Avner (1996). *A Psychoanalytic History of the Jews*. Madison, N.J.: Fairleigh Dickinson University Press. p. 131. ISBN 0-8386-3660-8.

[12] "Yiddish". *Merriam-Webster's Collegiate Dictionary* (11th ed.). Springfield, Mass.: Merriam-Webster. 2004. p. 1453. ISBN 0-87779-809-5.

[13] "Jew" (http://web.archive.org/web/20080621020359/http://www.bartleby.com/61/75/J0037500.html), The American Heritage Dictionary of the English Language, Fourth Edition (2000). Archived from the original (http://www.bartleby.com/61/75/J0037500.html) on June 21, 2008. Retrieved on October 26, 2009.

[14] Neusner (1991) p. 64

[15] Patai, Raphael (1996) [1977]. *The Jewish Mind*. Detroit: Wayne State University Press. p. 7. ISBN 0-8143-2651-X.

[16] Johnson, Lonnie R. (1996). *Central Europe: Enemies, Neighbors, Friends*. Oxford: Oxford University Press. p. 145. ISBN 0-19-510071-9.

[17] Sharot (1997), pp. 29–30.

[18] Sharot (1997), pp. 42–43.

[19] Sharot (1997), p. 42.

[20] Fishman, Sylvia Barack (2000). *Jewish Life and American Culture*. Albany, N.Y.: State University of New York Press. p. 38. ISBN 0-7914-4546-1.

[21] Kimmerling, Baruch (1996). *The Israeli State and Society: Boundaries and Frontiers*. Albany, N.Y.: State University of New York Press. p. 169. ISBN 0-88706-849-9.

[22] Lowenstein, Steven M. (2000). *The Jewish Cultural Tapestry: International Jewish Folk Traditions*. Oxford: Oxford University Press. p. 228. ISBN 0-19-513425-7.

[23] Weiner, Rebecca (2007). "Who is a Jew?" (http://www.jewishvirtuallibrary.org/jsource/Judaism/whojew1.html). Jewish Virtual Library. . Retrieved 2007-10-06.

[24] Fowler, Jeaneane D. (1997). *World Religions: An Introduction for Students*. Sussex Academic Press. pp. 7. ISBN 1898723486.

[25] Bauer, Yehuda. "Problems of Contemporary Anti-Semitism" (http://web.archive.org/web/20030705131522/http://humanities.ucsc. edu/JewishStudies/docs/YBauerLecture.pdf), 2003, p. 2. Retrieved February 24, 2008.

[26] "What is the origin of Matrilineal Descent?" (http://www.shamash.org/lists/scj-faq/HTML/faq/10-11.html). Shamash.org. September 4, 2003. . Retrieved January 9, 2009.

[27] "What is the source of the law that a child is Jewish only if its mother is Jewish?" (http://www.torah.org/qanda/seequanda.php?id=318). Torah.org. . Retrieved January 9, 2009.

[28] Dosick (2007), pp. 56–57.

[29] Dosick (2007), p. 60.

[30] Dosick (2007), p. 59.

[31] Schmelz, Usiel Oscar; Sergio DellaPergola (2007). "Demography". in Fred Skolnik. *Encyclopaedia Judaica*. **5** (2d ed. ed.). Farmington Hills, Mich.: Thomson Gale. p. 571. ISBN 0-02-865928-2.

[32] Schmelz, Usiel Oscar; Sergio DellaPergola (2007). "Demography". in Fred Skolnik. *Encyclopaedia Judaica*. **5** (2d ed. ed.). Farmington Hills, Mich.: Thomson Gale. pp. 571–572. ISBN 0-02-865928-2.

[33] Dosick (2007), p. 61.

[34] Grintz, Jehoshua M. "Hebrew as the Spoken and Written Language in the Last Days of the Second Temple." (http://links.jstor.org/ sici?sici=0021-9231(196003)79:1<32:HATSAW>2.0.CO;2-M) *Journal of Biblical Literature*. March, 1960.

[35] Feldman (2006), p. 54.

[36] "Language and Literature" (http://www.israelemb.org/US-Israel-Relations/landl.html). Embassy of Israel. . Retrieved January 10, 2009.

[37] Parfitt, T. V. "The Use of Hebrew in Palestine 1800–1822." *Journal of Semitic Studies* , 1972.

[38] "Jewish Languages" (http://www.bh.org.il/links/jewishlangs.asp). Beth Hatefutsoth, The Nahum Goldmann Museum of the Jewish Diaspora. . Retrieved 2008-07-03.

[39] Hammer, Mf; Redd, Aj; Wood, Et; Bonner, Mr; Jarjanazi, H; Karafet, T; Santachiara-Benerecetti, S; Oppenheim, A; Jobling, Ma; Jenkins, T; Ostrer, H; Bonne-Tamir, B (Jun 2000). "Jewish and Middle Eastern non-Jewish populations share a common pool of Y-chromosome biallelic haplotypes." (http://www.pnas.org/cgi/pmidlookup?view=long&pmid=10801975) (Free full text). *Proceedings of the National Academy of Sciences of the United States of America* **97** (12): 6769–74. doi: 10.1073/pnas.100115997 (http://dx.doi.org/10.1073/pnas. 100115997). ISSN 0027-8424 (http://worldcat.org/issn/0027-8424). PMID 10801975 (http://www.ncbi.nlm.nih.gov/pubmed/ 10801975). PMC 18733 (http://www.pubmedcentral.nih.gov/articlerender.fcgi?tool=pmcentrez&artid=18733). .

[40] "Y Chromosome Bears Witness to Story of the Jewish Diaspora" (http://query.nytimes.com/gst/fullpage. html?res=9D02E0D71338F93AA35756C0A9669C8B63). *New York Times*. May 9 2000. .

[41] Diana Muir Appelbaum and Paul S. Appelbaum (February 11, 2008). "Genetics and the Jewish identity" (http://www.jpost.com/servlet/ Satellite?apage=1&cid=1202742130771&pagename=JPost/JPArticle/ShowFull). *The Jerusalem Post*. .

[42] Skorecki, K; Selig, S; Blazer, S; Bradman, R; Bradman, N; Waburton, Pj; Ismajlowicz, M; Hammer, Mf (Jan 1997). "Y chromosomes of Jewish priests.". *Nature* **385** (6611): 32. doi: 10.1038/385032a0 (http://dx.doi.org/10.1038/385032a0). ISSN 0028-0836 (http://worldcat. org/issn/0028-0836). PMID 8985243 (http://www.ncbi.nlm.nih.gov/pubmed/8985243).

[43] "Priestly Gene Shared By Widely Dispersed Jews" (http://www.sciencedaily.com/releases/1998/07/980714071409.htm). *American Society for Technion, Israel Institute of Technology*. July 14 1998. .

[44] Nebel, A; Filon, D; Brinkmann, B; Majumder, Pp; Faerman, M; Oppenheim, A (Nov 2001). "The Y chromosome pool of Jews as part of the genetic landscape of the Middle East." (http://www.pubmedcentral.nih.gov/articlerender.fcgi?tool=pmcentrez&artid=1274378). *American journal of human genetics* **69** (5): 1095–112. doi: 10.1086/324070 (http://dx.doi.org/10.1086/324070). ISSN 0002-9297 (http:// worldcat.org/issn/0002-9297). PMID 11573163 (http://www.ncbi.nlm.nih.gov/pubmed/11573163).

[45] Appelbaum, Diana Muir; Paul S. Appelbaum (12 February 2008). "Genetics and the Jewish identity" (http://pqasb.pqarchiver.com/jpost/ access/1428186701.html?dids=1428186701:1428186701&FMT=ABS&FMTS=ABS:FT). *Jerusalem Post*. . Retrieved 25 September 2009.

[46] Nebel, Almut; Filon, Dvora; Weiss, Deborah A.; Weale, Michael; Faerman, Marina; Oppenheim, Ariella; Thomas, Mark G. (2000). "High-resolution Y chromosome haplotypes of Israeli and Palestinian Arabs reveal geographic substructure and substantial overlap with haplotypes of Jews". *Human Genetics* **107**: 630. doi: 10.1007/s004390000426 (http://dx.doi.org/10.1007/s004390000426).

[47] Richards, M; Rengo, C; Cruciani, F; Gratrix, F; Wilson, Jf; Scozzari, R; Macaulay, V; Torroni, A (Apr 2003). "Extensive female-mediated gene flow from sub-Saharan Africa into near eastern Arab populations." (http://www.pubmedcentral.nih.gov/articlerender. fcgi?tool=pmcentrez&artid=1180338). *American journal of human genetics* **72** (4): 1058–64. doi: 10.1086/374384 (http://dx.doi.org/10. 1086/374384). ISSN 0002-9297 (http://worldcat.org/issn/0002-9297). PMID 12629598 (http://www.ncbi.nlm.nih.gov/pubmed/ 12629598).

[48] Ariella Oppenheim and Michael Hammer. *Jewish Genetics: Abstracts and Summaries* (http://www.khazaria.com/genetics/abstracts. html). Khazaria InfoCenter. .

[49] Wade, Nicholas (January 14 2006). "New Light on Origins of Ashkenazi in Europe" (http://www.nytimes.com/2006/01/14/science/ 14gene.html?_r=1&oref=slogin). *The New York Times*. . Retrieved 2006-05-24.

[50] Behar, Dm; Metspalu, E; Kivisild, T; Achilli, A; Hadid, Y; Tzur, S; Pereira, L; Amorim, A; Quintana-Murci, L; Majamaa, K; Herrnstadt, C; Howell, N; Balanovsky, O; Kutuev, I; Pshenichnov, A; Gurwitz, D; Bonne-Tamir, B; Torroni, A; Villems, R; Skorecki, K (Mar 2006). "The matrilineal ancestry of Ashkenazi Jewry: portrait of a recent founder event." (http://www.pubmedcentral.nih.gov/articlerender. fcgi?tool=pmcentrez&artid=1380291). *American journal of human genetics* **78** (3): 487–97. doi: 10.1086/500307 (http://dx.doi.org/10. 1086/500307). ISSN 0002-9297 (http://worldcat.org/issn/0002-9297). PMID 16404693 (http://www.ncbi.nlm.nih.gov/pubmed/ 16404693).

[51] Behar, Dm; Metspalu, E; Kivisild, T; Rosset, S; Tzur, S; Hadid, Y; Yudkovsky, G; Rosengarten, D; Pereira, L; Amorim, A; Kutuev, I; Gurwitz, D; Bonne-Tamir, B; Villems, R; Skorecki, K (Apr 2008). "Counting the founders: the matrilineal genetic ancestry of the Jewish Diaspora" (http://dx.plos.org/10.1371/journal.pone.0002062) (Free full text). *PloS one* **3** (4): e2062. doi: 10.1371/journal.pone.0002062

(http://dx.doi.org/10.1371/journal.pone.0002062). PMID 18446216 (http://www.ncbi.nlm.nih.gov/pubmed/18446216). PMC 2323359 (http://www.pubmedcentral.nih.gov/articlerender.fcgi?tool=pmcentrez&artid=2323359). .

[52] on October 28, 2009 (http://noti.hebreos.net/enlinea/2008/03/16/2562/Retrieved)

[53] Telahoun, Tesfu (2008-03-11). "Israel at 60" (http://www.capitalethiopia.com/archive/2008/march/week2/feature.htm). *Capital Ethiopia*. . Retrieved 2008-07-03.

[54] Naggar, David (2006-11-07). "The Case for a Larger Israel" (http://web.israelinsider.com/Views/9811.htm). israelinsider.com. . Retrieved 2008-07-03.

[55] "Israel" (https://www.cia.gov/library/publications/the-world-factbook/geos/is.html). *The World Factbook*. Central Intelligence Agency. 2007-06-19. . Retrieved 2007-07-20.

[56] "The Electoral System in Israel" (http://www.knesset.gov.il/description/eng/eng_mimshal_beh.htm). The Knesset. . Retrieved 2007-08-08.

[57] "Country's Report Israel" (http://www.freedomhouse.org/template.cfm?page=22&year=2006&country=6985). Freedom House. .

[58] "Population, by Religion and Population Group" (http://www1.cbs.gov.il/reader/shnaton/templ_shnaton_e.html?num_tab=st02_01& CYear=2006). Israel Central Bureau of Statistics. 2006. . Retrieved 2007-08-07.

[59] Dekmejian 1975, p. 247. "And most [Oriental-Sephardic Jews] came... because of Arab persecution resulting from the very attempt to establish a Jewish state in Palestine."

[60] "airlifted tens of thousands of Ethiopian Jews" (http://www.jewishvirtuallibrary.org/jsource/Judaism/ejhist.html#operation1/). . Retrieved July 7, 2005.

[61] *History of Dissident Movement in the USSR* (http://www.memo.ru/history/diss/books/ALEXEEWA/alexeeva_toc.htm) by Ludmila Alekseyeva. Vilnius, 1992 **(Russian)**

[62] Goldstein (1995) p. 24

[63] Dosick (2007), p. 340.

[64] Gartner (2001), p. 213.

[65] Gurock, Jeffrey S. (1998). *East European Jews in America, 1880-1920: Immigration and Adaptation*. New York: Routledge. p. 54. ISBN 0-415-91924-X.

[66] Gartner (2001), pp. 410–410.

[67] Waxman, Chaim I. (2007). "Annual Assessment 2007" (http://www.jpppi.org.il/JPPPI/SendFile.asp?DBID=1&LNGID=1&GID=489) (PDF). Jewish People Policy Planning Institute (Jewish Agency for Israel). pp. 40–42. . Retrieved 2008-07-03.

[68] "The Ingathering of the Exiles" (http://www.mfa.gov.il/MFA/History/Modern History/Israel at 50/The Ingathering of the Exiles). Israel Ministry of Foreign Affairs. .

[69] Littman (1979), p. 5.

[70] Johnson (1987), p. 171.

[71] Edinger, Bernard (December 2005). "Chinese Jews: Reverence for Ancestors" (http://www.hadassah.org/news/content/per_hadassah/archive/2005/05_DEC/feature_kaifeng.asp). *Hadassah Magazine*. Hadassah. . Retrieved January 9, 2009.

[72] Elazar (2003), p. 434.

[73] "NJPS: Intermarriage: Defining and Calculating Intermarriage" (http://www.ujc.org/content_display.html?ArticleID=83910). . Retrieved July 7, 2005.

[74] Cohen, Erik H.. "Les Juifs de France: La Lente Progression des Mariages Mixtes" (http://www.akadem.org/photos/contextuels/1027_357_Rapport_Erik_Cohen.pdf) (in French). . Retrieved March 25, 2009.

[75] "World Jewish Congress Online" (http://www.worldjewishcongress.org/communities/world/asia-oceania/australia.cfm). . Retrieved July 7, 2005.

[76] "The Virtual Jewish History Tour - Mexico" (http://www.jewishvirtuallibrary.org/jsource/vjw/Mexico.html). . Retrieved July 7, 2005.

[77] Waxman, Chaim I. (2007). "Annual Assessment 2007" (http://www.jpppi.org.il/JPPPI/SendFile.asp?DBID=1&LNGID=1&GID=489) (PDF). Jewish People Policy Planning Institute (Jewish Agency for Israel). p. 61. . Retrieved 2008-07-03.

[78] Goldenberg (2007), pp. 131, 135–136.

[79] Johnson (1987), pp. 164–165.

[80] Carroll, James. *Constantine's Sword* (Houghton Mifflin, 2001) ISBN 0-395-77927-8 p.26

[81] Johnson (1987), pp. 207–208.

[82] Johnson (1987), pp. 213, 229–231.

[83] Johnson (1987), pp. 243–244.

[84] "A Catholic Timeline of Events Relating to Jews, Anti-Judaism, Antisemitism, and the Holocaust, From the 3rd century to the Beginning of the Third Millennium" (http://www.sullivan-county.com/news/mine/timeline.htm)

[85] Lewis (1984), pp. 10, 20

[86] Lewis (1987), p. 9, 27

[87] Lewis (1999), p.131

[88] Lewis (1999), p.131; (1984), pp.8,62

[89] Lewis (1984), p. 52; Stillman (1979), p.77

[90] Lewis (1984), pp. 17–18, 94–95; Stillman (1979), p. 27

[91] Lewis (1984), p. 28.

[92] Muslim Anti-Semitism (http://www.meforum.org/article/396) by Bernard Lewis (Middle East Quarterly) June 1998

[93] Johnson (1987), pp. 226–229.

[94] Johnson (1987), pp. 259–260.

[95] Johnson (1987), pp. 364–365.

[96] Johnson (1987), p. 512.

[97] Study: 20 Percent of Spanish, Portuguese Have Jewish Ancestry (http://www.foxnews.com/story/0,2933,463564,00.html). FoxNews.com. December 8, 2008.

[98] DNA study shows 20 percent of Iberian population has Jewish ancestry (http://www.iht.com/articles/2008/12/04/europe/gene.php). The New York Times. December 4, 2008.

[99] Donald L Niewyk, *The Columbia Guide to the Holocaust,* Columbia University Press, 2000, p.45: "The Holocaust is commonly defined as the murder of more than 5,000,000 Jews by the Germans in World War II." However, the Holocaust usually includes all of the different victims who were systematically murdered.

[100] Johnson (1987), pp. 484–488.

[101] Johnson (1987), pp. 490–492.

[102] Ukrainian mass Jewish grave found (http://news.bbc.co.uk/2/hi/europe/6724481.stm)

[103] Johnson (1987), pp. 493–498.

[104] Berenbaum, Michael. *The World Must Know,"* United States Holocaust Museum, 2006, p. 103.

[105] Melvin, Sheila; Jindong Cai (2004). *Rhapsody in Red.* New York: Algora Publishing. pp. 103–104. ISBN 0-87586-179-2.

[106] de Lange (2002), pp. 41–43.

[107] Johnson (1987), p. 10.

[108] Johnson (1987), p. 30.

[109] Johnson (1987), pp. 70–71.

[110] Johnson (1987), pp. 78–79.

[111] Johnson (1987), pp. 85–86.

[112] Johnson (1987), p. 147.

[113] Johnson (1987), p. 163.

[114] Johnson (1987), p. 177.

[115] Johnson (1987), p. 231.

[116] Johnson (1987), p. 460.

[117] Gartner (2001), p. 431.

[118] Gartner (2001), pp. 11–12.

[119] Johnson (1987), pp. 229–231.

[120] Johnson (1987), p. 306.

[121] Johnson (1987), p. 370.

[122] Gartner (2001), pp. 213–215.

[123] Gartner (2001), pp. 357–370.

[124] Johnson (1987), pp. 529–530.

[125] Netzer, Amnon (2007). "Iran". in Fred Skolnik. *Encyclopaedia Judaica.* **10** (2d ed. ed.). Farmington Hills, Mich.: Thomson Gale. pp. 13. ISBN 0-02-865928-2.

[126] Gartner (2001), pp. 400–401.

[127] Kaplan (2003), p. 301.

[128] Danzger (2003), pp. 495–496.

[129] de Lange (2002), p. 220.

[130] Eisenstadt, S.N. (2004). *Explorations in Jewish Historical Experience: The Civilizational Dimension.* Leiden, The Netherlands: Brill. p. 75. ISBN 90-04-13693-2.

[131] Lewis, Hal M. (2006). *From Sanctuary to Boardroom: A Jewish Approach to Leadership.* Lanham, Md.: Rowman & Littlefield. p. 1. ISBN 0-7425-5229-2.

[132] Schwartz, Richard H. (2001). *Judaism and Global Survival.* New York: Lantern Books. p. 153. ISBN 1-930051-87-5.

[133] Brooks, David (January 12, 2010). "The Tel Aviv Cluster" (http://www.nytimes.com/2010/01/12/opinion/12brooks.html). *The New York Times.* p. A23. . Retrieved January 13, 2010. " Jews are a famously accomplished group. They make up 0.2 percent of the world population, but 54 percent of the world chess champions, 27 percent of the Nobel physics laureates and 31 percent of the medicine laureates. Jews make up 2 percent of the U.S. population, but 21 percent of the Ivy League student bodies, 26 percent of the Kennedy Center honorees, 37 percent of the Academy Award-winning directors, 38 percent of those on a recent Business Week list of leading philanthropists, 51 percent of the Pulitzer Prize winners for nonfiction."

[134] Dobbs, Stephen Mark (October 12, 2001). "As the Nobel Prize marks centennial, Jews constitute 1/5 of laureates" (http://www.jewishsf.com/content/2-0-/module/displaystory/story_id/17015/edition_id/335/format/html/displaystory.html). *j..* . Retrieved January 23, 2009. "Throughout the 20th century, Jews, more so than any other minority, ethnic or cultural group, have been recipients of the Nobel Prize -- perhaps the most distinguished award for human endeavor in the six fields for which it is given. Remarkably, Jews constitute almost one-fifth of all Nobel laureates. This, in a world in which Jews number just a fraction of 1 percent of the population."

[135] http://www.jewishvirtuallibrary.org
[136] http://www.jewfaq.org
[137] http://www.routledge.com/textbooks/0415236614/resources/indi.asp
[138] http://www.ajc.org
[139] http://www.ajcongress.org
[140] http://www.adl.org
[141] http://www.bnaibrith.org
[142] http://www.hillel.org
[143] http://www.ujc.org
[144] http://www.aish.com
[145] http://www.aleph.org
[146] http://www.americansephardifederation.org
[147] http://www.chabad.org
[148] http://www.jrf.org
[149] http://www.karaite-korner.org
[150] http://ou.org
[151] http://www.shj.org
[152] http://urj.org
[153] http://www.uscj.org
[154] http://www.ameinu.net
[155] http://www.hadassah.org
[156] http://www.jafi.org.il
[157] http://www.rza.org/
[158] http://www.mizrachi.org
[159] http://www.wzo.org.il/en/default.asp
[160] http://www.zoa.org

Socialist

Socialism refers to the various theories of economic organization advocating either public or direct worker ownership and administration of the means of production and allocation of resources.[1] [2] [3] A more comprehensive definition of socialism is an economic system that has transcended commodity production and wage labor, where economic activity is carried out to maximize use-value as opposed to exchange-value and thus a corresponding change in social and economic relations, including the organization of economic institutions and resource allocation;[4] often implying advocacy for a method of compensation based on the amount of labor expended.[5]

Most socialists share the view that capitalism unfairly concentrates power and wealth among a small segment of society that controls capital and derives its wealth through exploitation, creates an unequal society, does not provide equal opportunities for everyone to maximise their potential,[6] and does not utilise technology and resources to their maximum potential nor in the interests of the public.[7]

Many socialists, from Henri de Saint-Simon, one of the founders of early socialism (Utopian Socialism), to Friedrich Engels and Karl Marx, advocated for the creation of a society that allows for the widespread application of modern technology to rationalise economic activity by eliminating the anarchy of capitalist production.[8] [9] They reasoned that this would allow for wealth and power to be distributed based on the amount of work expended in production, although there is disagreement among socialists over how and to what extent this can be achieved.

Socialism is not a concrete philosophy of fixed doctrine and programme; its branches advocate a degree of social interventionism and economic rationalisation (usually in the form of economic planning), but sometimes oppose each other. A dividing feature of the socialist movement is the split between reformists and revolutionaries on how a socialist economy should be established. Some socialists advocate complete nationalisation of the means of production, distribution, and exchange; others advocate state control of capital within the framework of a market economy.

Socialists inspired by the Soviet model of economic development have advocated the creation of centrally planned economies directed by a state that owns all the means of production. Others, including Yugoslavian, Hungarian, German and Chinese communist governments in the 1970s and 1980s, have instituted various forms of market socialism, combining co-operative and state ownership models with the free market exchange and free price system (but not free prices for the means of production).[10] Modern social democrats propose selective nationalisation of key national industries in mixed economies, while maintaining private ownership of capital and private business enterprise. (In the 19th and early 20th century the term was used to refer to those who wanted to completely replace capitalism with socialism through reform.) Modern social democrats also promote tax-funded welfare programs and regulation of markets; many, particularly in European welfare states, refer to themselves as socialists, despite holding pro-capitalist viewpoints, thus adding ambiguity to the meaning of the term "socialist". Libertarian socialism (including social anarchism and libertarian Marxism) rejects state control and ownership of the economy altogether and advocates direct collective ownership of the means of production via co-operative workers' councils and workplace democracy.

Modern socialism originated in the late 18th-century intellectual and working class political movement that criticised the effects of industrialisation and private ownership on society. The utopian socialists, including Robert Owen (1771–1858), tried to found self-sustaining communes by secession from a capitalist society. Henri de Saint Simon (1760–1825), the first individual to coin the term *socialisme*, was the original thinker who advocated technocracy and industrial planning.[11] The first socialists predicted a world improved by harnessing technology and combining it with better social organisation, and many contemporary socialists share this same belief. Early socialist thinkers tended to favour an authentic meritocracy combined with rational social planning, while many modern socialists have a more egalitarian approach.

Vladimir Lenin, drawing on Karl Marx's ideas of "lower" and "upper" stages of socialism[12] defined socialism as a transitional stage between capitalism and communism.[13]

Origins

The English word *socialism* (1839) derives from the French *socialisme* (1832), the mainstream introduction of which usage is attributed, in France, to Pierre Leroux,[14] and to Marie Roch Louis Reybaud; and in Britain to Robert Owen in 1827, father of the cooperative movement.[15] [16] Although socialist models and ideas espousing common ownership have existed since antiquity with the classical Greek philosophers Plato and Aristotle[17] , the modern concept of socialism evolved in response to the development of industrial capitalism. Early socialism was seen as an extension of classical liberalism by extending liberty and rights to the industrial economic aspect of life, so that these values were compatible with the then-emerging industrial society.

The first advocates of socialism favoured social levelling in order to create a meritocratic or technocratic society based upon individual talent. Count Henri de Saint-Simon is regarded as the first individual to coin the term *socialism*.[11] Simon was fascinated by the enormous potential of science and technology and advocated a socialist society that would eliminate the disorderly aspects of capitalism and would be based upon equal opportunities.[18] He advocated the creation of a society in which each person was ranked according to his or her capacities and rewarded according to his or her work.[11] The key focus of Simon's socialism was on administrative efficiency and industrialism, and a belief that science was the key to progress.[1]

This was accompanied by a desire to implement a rationally-organised economy based on planning and geared towards large-scale scientific and material progress,[11] and thus embodied a desire for a more directed or planned economy. Other early socialist thinkers, such as Thomas Hodgkin and Charles Hall, based their ideas on David Ricardo's economic theories. They reasoned that the equilibrium value of commodities approximated to prices charged by the producer when those commodities were in elastic supply, and that these producer prices corresponded to the embodied labor — the cost of the labor (essentially the wages paid) that was required to produce the commodities. The Ricardian socialists viewed profit, interest and rent as deductions from this exchange-value.[19]

West European social critics, including Robert Owen, Charles Fourier, Pierre-Joseph Proudhon, Louis Blanc, Charles Hall and Saint-Simon, were the first modern socialists who criticised the excessive poverty and inequality of the Industrial Revolution. They advocated reform, with some such as Robert Owen advocating the transformation of society to small communities without private property. Robert Owen's contribution to modern socialism was his understanding that actions and characteristics of individuals were largely determined by the social environment they were raised in and exposed to.[1]

Linguistically, the contemporary connotation of the words *socialism* and *communism* accorded with the adherents' and opponents' cultural attitude towards religion. In Christian Europe, of the two, communism was believed the atheist way of life. In Protestant England, the word *communism* was too culturally and aurally close to the Roman Catholic *communion rite*, hence English atheists denoted themselves socialists.[20]

Friedrich Engels argued that in 1848, at the time when the Communist Manifesto was published, "socialism was respectable on the continent, while communism was not." The Owenites in England and the Fourierists in France were considered "respectable" socialists, while working-class movements that "proclaimed the necessity of total social change" denoted themselves communists. This latter branch of socialism produced the communist work of Étienne Cabet in France and Wilhelm Weitling in Germany.[21]

The Marxist conception of socialism is that of a specific historical phase that will displace capitalism and be a precursor to communism. The major characteristics of socialism (particularly as conceived by Marx and Engels after the Paris Commune of 1871), are that the proletariat will control the means of production through a workers' state erected by the workers in their interests. Economic activity is still organised through the use of incentive systems and social classes would still exist but to a lesser and diminishing extent than under capitalism.[22]

Karl Marx

For orthodox Marxists, socialism is the lower stage of communism based on the principle of "from each according to his ability, to each according to his contribution" while upper stage communism is based on the principle of "from each according to his ability, to each according to his need"; the upper stage becoming possible only after the socialist stage further develops economic efficiency and the automation of production has led to a superabundance of goods and services.[23] [24]

First International

Socialists made varying interpretations of The Communist Manifesto.

In 1864, the International Workingmen's Association (IWA) – the First International – was founded in London. Londoner Victor le Lubez, a French radical republican, invited Karl Marx to participate as a representative of German workers.[25] In 1865, the IWA had its preliminary conference, and its first congress, at Geneva, in 1866. Karl Marx was a member of the committee; he and Johann Georg Eccarius, a London tailor, were the two mainstays of the International, from its inception to its end; the First International was the premiere international forum promulgating socialism.

In 1869, under the influence of Marx and Engels, the Social Democratic Workers' Party of Germany was founded. In 1875, the SDW Party merged with the General German Workers' Association, of Ferdinand Lassalle, metamorphosing to the contemporary German Social Democratic Party (SPD). The SPD founded and constituted trade unions in Germany in the 1870s and in Austria, France, and other countries, socialist parties and anarchists did like-wise.

Socialists supported and advocated many branches of Socialism – the gradualism of trade unions, the radical revolution of Marx and Engels who emphasised a worker's state and central democratic planning of production, and the anarchists/libertarian socialists who emphasised direct worker control and local power – all co-existing, with Marxism becoming the most influential ideology in the form of Social Democracy on the continent of Europe. The anarchists, led by the Mikhail Bakunin, believed that capitalism and the state are inseparable and neither can be abolished without abolishing the other.

In 1871, in the wake of the Franco-Prussian War, an uprising in Paris established the Paris Commune. According to Marx and Engels, for a few weeks the Paris Commune provided a glimpse of a socialist society, before it was brutally suppressed by the French government. Large-scale industry was to be "based on the association of the workers" joined into "one great union", all posts in government were elected by universal franchise, elected officials took only the average worker's wage and were subject to recall. For Engels, this was what the Dictatorship of the proletariat – the political, democratic control or governance of the working class – looked like. Marx and Engels argued that the state is "nothing but a machine for the oppression of one class by another" and a new generation of socialists, "reared in new and free social conditions, will be able to throw the entire lumber of the state on the scrap-heap".[26]

After the Paris Commune, the differences between supporters of Marx and Engels and those of Bakunin were too great to bridge. The anarchist section of the First International was expelled from the International at the 1872 Hague Congress and they went on to form the Jura federation. The First International was disbanded in 1876.

Second International

As the ideas of Marx and Engels gained popularity, especially in central Europe, socialists founded the Second International in 1889, the centennial of the French Revolution. Three hundred socialist and labor union organisations from 20 countries sent 384 delegates.[27] The Second International expelled individuals and member organisations that it considered to have an anarchist outlook, most notably Swiss, Italian, and French anarcho-syndicalists such as Errico Malatesta and Mikhail Bakunin. This created a rift, lasting to this day in many parts of the world, between what anarchists describe as libertarian socialism and authoritarian socialism.

In 1890, The Social Democratic Party of Germany used the limited, universal, male suffrage to exercise the electoral strength necessary to compel rescission of Germany's Anti-Socialist Laws.[28] In 1893, the SPD received 1,787,000 votes, a quarter of the votes cast. Before the SPD published Engels's 1895 introduction to Karl Marx's *Class Struggles in France 1848–1850*, they deleted phrases that they felt were too revolutionary for mainstream readers.[29]

The Swedish Social Democratic Party, (Swedish: *Sveriges socialdemokratiska arbetareparti*, SAP, 'Social Democratic Labour Party of Sweden'), which today contests elections as 'Labour Party – Social Democrats' (Arbetarepartiet-Socialdemokraterna), is the oldest and largest political party in Sweden, founded in 1889. Commonly referred to as 'the Social Democrats' (Socialdemokraterna) or colloquially 'the Socials' (Sossarna), this party suffered a schism in 1917, when the communists and other Revolutionary Left factions split from the Social Democrats to form what is now the Left Party.

In the UK, politically moderate New Model Unions dominated unionised labor from the mid–nineteenth century until the founding of New Unionism, which arose after the successful London matchgirls' strike in 1888. Unskilled workers such as the Dockers and the Gas Workers were unionised through the activities of socialists such as Ben Tillett, a founder of the Independent Labour Party, Tom Mann (who together with Tillett founded the dockers union) and Will Thorne, who founded the Gas Workers union. Also under pressure from socialists such as Keir Hardie, the UK trade union movement broke from the Liberal Party and founded the Labour Party in the early twentieth century.

The first U.S. socialist party was founded in 1876, then metamorphosed to a Marxist party in 1890; the Socialist Labor Party exists today. An early leader of the Socialist Labor Party was Daniel De Leon. De Leon helped found the Industrial Workers of the World (IWW) which influenced the formation IWW unions beyond the United States.

When World War I began in 1914, the leaders of the most prominent European Socialist Parties organised under the banner of the Second International, at first vocal opponents, supported the belligerent aims of their national governments: the British, French, Belgian, and German social democratic parties discarded their political commitments to proletarian internationalism and worker solidarity to co-operate with their imperial governments.[30] [31] In Russia, by contrast, Vladimir Lenin denounced the Europeans' Great War as an imperialist conflict[32] and urged workers worldwide to use the war as an occasion for proletarian revolution.[33] The Second International dissolved during the war.[34] Lenin, Leon Trotsky, Karl Liebknecht, Rosa Luxemburg and other anti-war Marxists conferred in the Zimmerwald Conference in September 1915.[35] [36]

Revolutions of 1917–1923

Trotsky, Lenin, and Kamenev at the Second Communist Party Congress, 1919

By the year 1917, the patriotism of the First World War changed into political radicalism in most of Europe, the United States (cf. Socialism in the United States), and Australia. In February, popular revolution exploded in Russia when workers, soldiers, and peasants established soviets (councils), the monarchy fell and a Provisional Government convoked pending the election of a Constituent Assembly. In April, Lenin arrived in Russia from Switzerland, calling for "All power to the soviets." In October, his party (the Bolsheviks) won support of most soviets at the second All-Russian congress of Soviets of Workers' and Soldiers' Deputies, while he and Trotsky simultaneously led the October Revolution. On 25 January 1918, at the Petrograd Soviet, Lenin declared "Long live the world socialist revolution!"[37] , proposed an immediate armistice on all fronts, and transferred the land of the landed proprietors, the crown and the monasteries to the peasant committees without compensation.[38]

On 26 January, the day after assuming executive power, Lenin wrote *Draft Regulations on Workers' Control*, which granted workers control of businesses with more than five workers and office employees, and access to all books, documents, and stocks, and whose decisions were to be "binding upon the owners of the enterprises".[39] Governing through the elected soviets, and in alliance with the peasant-based Left Socialist-Revolutionaries, the Bolshevik government began nationalising banks, industry, and disavowed the national debts of the deposed Romanov royal régime. It sued for peace, withdrawing from the First World War, and convoked a Constituent Assembly in which the peasant Socialist-Revolutionary (SR) Party won a majority.[40] The Constituent Assembly elected Socialist-Revolutionary leader Victor Chernov President of a Russian republic, but rejected the Bolshevik proposal that it endorse the Soviet decrees on land, peace and workers' control, and acknowledge the power of the Soviets of Workers', Soldiers' and Peasants' Deputies. The next day, the Bolsheviks declared that the assembly was elected on outdated party lists[41] and the All-Russian Central Executive Committee of the Soviets dissolved it.[42] [43]

The Bolshevik Russian Revolution of January 1918 engendered Communist parties worldwide, and their concomitant revolutions of 1917-23. Few Communists doubted that the Russian success of socialism depended upon successful, working-class socialist revolutions in developed capitalist countries.[44] [45] In 1919, Lenin and Trotsky organised the world's Communist parties into a new international association of workers – the Communist International, (Comintern), also called the Third International.

In November 1918, the German Revolution deposed the monarchy; as in Russia, the councils of workers and soldiers were comprised mostly of SPD and USPD (Independent Social Democrats) revolutionaries installed to office as the Weimar republic; the SPD were in power, led by Friedrich Ebert. In January 1919 the left-wing Spartacist uprising challenged the SPD government, and President Ebert ordered the army and Freikorps mercenaries to violently suppress the workers' and soldiers' councils. Communist leaders Karl Liebknecht and Rosa Luxemburg were captured and summarily executed. Also that year, in Bavaria, the Communist régime of Kurt Eisner was suppressed. In Hungary, Béla Kun briefly headed a Hungarian Communist government. Throughout, popular socialist revolutions in Vienna, Italy's northern industrial cities, the German Ruhr (1920) and Saxony (1923) all failed in spreading revolutionary socialism to Europe's advanced, capitalist countries.

Rosa Luxemburg, prominent communist and leader of the German Spartacist uprising, 1919

In Russia in August 1918, assassin Fanya Kaplan shot Lenin in the neck, leaving him with wounds from which he never fully recovered. Earlier, in June, the Soviet government had implemented War Communism to repel the invasions by Germany, Britain, the United States and France, who were interfering in the Russian Civil War beside royalist White Russians. The great powers organised a crippling economic boycott of Russia. Under War Communism, private business was outlawed, strikers could be shot, the white collar classes were forced to work manually and peasants could be forced to provide to workers in cities.

By 1920, the Red Army, under its commander Trotsky, had largely defeated the royalist White Armies. In 1921, War Communism was ended and, under the New Economic Policy (NEP), private ownership was allowed for small and medium peasant enterprises. While industry remained largely state-controlled, Lenin acknowledged that the NEP was a necessary capitalist measure for a country unripe for socialism. Profiteering returned in the form of "NEP men" and rich peasants (Kulaks) gained power in the countryside.[46]

In 1922, the fourth congress of the Communist International took up the policy of the United Front, urging Communists to work with rank and file Social Democrats while remaining critical of their leaders, who they criticised for "betraying" the working class by supporting the war efforts of their respective capitalist classes. For their part, the social democrats pointed to the dislocation caused by revolution, and later, the growing authoritarianism of the Communist Parties. When the Communist Party of Great Britain applied to affiliate to the Labour Party in 1920 it was turned down.

In 1923, on seeing the Soviet State's growing coercive power, the dying Lenin said Russia had reverted to "a bourgeois tsarist machine... barely varnished with socialism."[47] After Lenin's death (January 1924), the Communist Party of the Soviet Union − then increasingly under the control of Joseph Stalin − rejected the theory that socialism could not be built solely in the Soviet Union with the Socialism in One Country slogan. Despite the marginalised Left Opposition's demand for the restoration of Soviet democracy, Stalin developed a bureaucratic, authoritarian government, that was condemned by democratic socialists, anarchists and Trotskyists for undermining the initial socialist ideals of the Bolshevik Russian Revolution.[48] [49]

The Russian Revolution of October 1917 brought about the definitive ideological division between Communists as denoted with a capital "C" on the one hand and other communist and socialist trends such as anarcho-communists and social democrats, on the other. The Left Opposition in the Soviet Union gave rise to Trotskyism which was to remain isolated and insignificant for another fifty years, except in Sri Lanka where Trotskyism gained the majority and the pro-Moscow wing was expelled from the Communist Party.

After World War II

In 1945, the world's three great powers met at the Yalta Conference to negotiate an amicable and stable peace. UK Prime Minister Winston Churchill joined USA President Franklin D. Roosevelt and Joseph Stalin, General Secretary of the Communist Party of the Soviet Union's Central Committee. With the relative decline of Britain compared to the two superpowers, the USA and the Soviet Union, however, many viewed the world as "bi-polar" − a world with two irreconcilable and antagonistic political and economic systems.

Joseph Stalin

Many termed the Soviet Union "socialist", not least the Soviet Union itself, but also commonly in the USA, China, Eastern Europe, and many parts of the world where Communist Parties had gained a mass base. In addition, scholarly critics of the Soviet Union, such as economist Friedrich Hayek were commonly cited as critics of socialism. This view was not universally shared, particularly in Europe, and especially in Britain, where the Communist Party was very weak.

In 1951, British Health Minister Aneurin Bevan expressed the view that, "It is probably true that Western Europe would have gone socialist after the war if Soviet behaviour had not given it too grim a visage. Soviet Communism and Socialism are not yet sufficiently distinguished in many minds."[50]

In 1951, the Socialist International was re-founded by the European social democratic parties. It declared: "Communism has split the International Labour Movement and has set back the realisation of Socialism in many countries for decades... Communism falsely claims a share in the Socialist tradition. In fact it has distorted that tradition beyond recognition. It has built up a rigid theology which is incompatible with the critical spirit of Marxism."[51]

The last quarter of the twentieth century marked a period of major crisis for Communists in the Soviet Union and the Eastern bloc, where the growing shortages of housing and consumer goods, combined with the lack of individual rights to assembly and speech, began to disillusion more and more Communist party members. With the rapid collapse of Communist party rule in the Soviet Union and Eastern Europe between 1989 and 1991, the Soviet version of socialism has effectively disappeared as a worldwide political force.

In the postwar years, socialism became increasingly influential throughout the so-called Third World. Countries in Africa, Asia, and Latin America frequently adopted socialist economic programmes. In many instances, these nations nationalised industries held by foreign owners. The Soviet Union had become a superpower through its adoption of a planned economy, albeit at enormous human cost. This achievement seemed hugely impressive from the outside, and convinced many nationalists in the former colonies, not necessarily communists or even socialists, of the virtues of state planning and state-guided models of social development. This was later to have important consequences in countries like China, India and Egypt, which tried to import some aspects of the Soviet model.

Social Democracy in power

In 1945, the British Labour Party, led by Clement Attlee, was elected to office based upon a radical, socialist programme. Social Democratic parties dominated the post-war French, Italian, Czechoslovakian, Belgian, Norwegian, and other, governments. In Sweden, the Social Democratic Party held power from 1936 to 1976 and then again from 1982 to 1991 and from 1994 to 2006. Labour parties governed Australia and New Zealand. In Germany, the Social Democrats lost in 1949. In Eastern Europe, the war-resistance unity, between 'Social Democrats and Communists, continued in the immediate postwar years, until Stalin imposed Communist régimes.

Clement Attlee, U.K. Prime Minister,
Labour Party government, 1945–51

In the UK, the Labour Party was influenced by the British social reformer William Beveridge, who had identified five "Giant Evils" afflicting the working class of the pre-war period: "want" (poverty), disease, "ignorance" (lack of access to education), "squalor" (poor housing), and "idleness" (unemployment).[52] Unemployment benefit, as well as national insurance and hence state pensions, were introduced by the 1945 Labour government. However Aneurin Bevan, who had introduced the Labour Party's National Health Service in 1948, criticised the Attlee Government for not progressing further, demanding that the "main streams of economic activity are brought under public direction" with economic planning, and criticising the implementation of nationalisation for not empowering the workers with democratic control of operations.

Bevan's *In Place of Fear* became the most widely read socialist book of the post-war period. It states: "A young miner in a South Wales colliery, my concern was with one practical question: Where does the power lie in this particular state of Great Britain, and how can it be attained by the workers?" [53] [54]

Socialists in Europe widely believed that fascism arose from capitalism. The *Frankfurt Declaration* of the re-founded Socialist International stated:

> 1. From the nineteenth century onwards, Capitalism has developed immense productive forces. It has done so at the cost of excluding the great majority of citizens from influence over production. It put the rights of ownership before the rights of Man. It created a new class of wage-earners without property or social rights. It sharpened the struggle between the classes.
>
> Although the world contains resources, which could be made to provide a decent life for everyone, Capitalism has been incapable of satisfying the elementary needs of the world's population. It proved unable to function without devastating crises and mass unemployment. It produced social insecurity and glaring contrasts between rich and poor. It resorted to imperialist expansion and colonial exploitation, thus making conflicts, between nations and races, more bitter. In some countries, powerful capitalist groups helped the barbarism of the past to raise its head again in the form of Fascism and Nazism.| The Frankfurt Declaration 1951[51]

The post-war social democratic governments introduced social reform and wealth redistribution via state welfare and taxation. The UK Labour Government nationalised major public utilities such as mines, gas, coal, electricity, rail, iron, steel, and the Bank of England.[55] France claimed to be the world's most State-controlled, capitalist country.[56] In the UK, the National Health Service provided free health care to all.[57] Working-class housing was provided in council housing estates, and university education available via a school grant system. Ellen Wilkinson, Minister for Education, introduced free milk in schools, saying, in a 1946 Labor Party conference: "Free milk will be provided in Hoxton and Shoreditch, in Eton and Harrow. What more social equality can you have than that?" Clement Attlee's biographer argued that this policy "contributed enormously to the defeat of childhood illnesses resulting from bad diet. Generations of poor children grew up stronger and healthier, because of this one, small, and inexpensive act of generosity, by the Attlee government".[58]

In 1956, Anthony Crosland said that 25 per cent of British industry was nationalised, and that public employees, including those in nationalised industries, constituted a similar percentage of the country's total employed population.[59] However, the Labour government did not seek to end capitalism, in terms of nationalising of the commanding heights of the economy, as Lenin had put it. In fact, the "government had not the smallest intention of bringing in the 'common ownership of the means of production, distribution, and exchange'",[60] yet this was the declared aim of the Labour Party, stated in its 'socialist clause', Clause 4 of the Labour Party Constitution. Cabinet minister Herbert Morrison argued that, "Socialism is what the Labour Government does."[60] Crosland claimed capitalism had ended: "To the question, 'Is this still capitalism?', I would answer 'No'."[61]

Social Democracy adopts free market policies

Many social democratic parties, particularly after the Cold war, adopted neoliberal-based market policies that include privatization, liberalization, deregulation and financialization; resulting in the abandonment of pursuing the development of moderate socialism in favor of market liberalism. Despite the name, these pro-capitalist policies are radically different from the many non-capitalist free-market socialist theories that have existed throughout history.

In 1959, the German Social Democratic Party adopted the Godesberg Program, rejecting class struggle and Marxism. In 1980, with the rise of conservative neoliberal politicians such as Ronald Reagan in the U.S., Margaret Thatcher in Britain and Brian Mulroney, in Canada, the Western, welfare state was attacked from within. Monetarists and neoliberalism attacked social welfare systems as impediments to private entrepreneurship at public expense.

In the 1980s and 1990s, western European socialists were pressured to reconcile their socialist economic programmes with a free-market-based communal European economy. In the UK, the Labour Party leader Neil Kinnock made a passionate and public attack against the Party's Militant Tendency at a Labour Party conference and repudiated the demands of the defeated striking miners after a year-long strike against pit closures. In the 1990s, released from the Left's pressure, the Labour Party, under Tony Blair, posited policies based upon the free market economy to deliver public services via private contractors.

In 1989, at Stockholm, the 18th Congress of the Socialist International adopted a new *Declaration of Principles*, saying that

> Democratic socialism is an international movement for freedom, social justice, and solidarity. Its goal is to achieve a peaceful world where these basic values can be enhanced and where each individual can live a meaningful life with the full development of his or her personality and talents, and with the guarantee of human and civil rights in a democratic framework of society.[62]

In 1995, the Labour Party re-defined its stance on socialism by re-wording clause IV of its constitution, effectively rejecting socialism by removing any and all references to public, direct worker or municipal ownership of the means of production.

The objectives of the Party of European Socialists, the European Parliament's socialist bloc, are now "to pursue international aims in respect of the principles on which the European Union is based, namely principles of freedom, equality, solidarity, democracy, respect of Human Rights and Fundamental Freedoms, and respect for the Rule of Law." As a result, today, the rallying cry of the French Revolution – "Egalité, Liberté, Fraternité" – which overthrew absolutism and ushered capitalism into French society, are promoted as essential socialist values.[63]

In 1995, the British Labour Party revised its political aims: "The Labour Party is a democratic socialist party. It believes that, by the strength of our common endeavour we achieve more than we achieve alone, so as to create, for each of us, the means to realise our true potential, and, for all of us, a community in which power, wealth, and opportunity are in the hands of the many, not the few."[64]

Socialism in the 21st century

Those who championed socialism in its various Marxist and class struggle forms sought out other arenas than the parties of social democracy at the turn of the 21st century. Anti-capitalism and anti-globalisation movements rose to prominence particularly through events such as the opposition to the WTO meeting of 1999 in Seattle. Socialist-inspired groups played an important role in these new movements, which nevertheless embraced much broader layers of the population, and were championed by figures such as Noam Chomsky. The 2003 invasion of Iraq led to a significant anti-war movement in which socialists argued their case.

The Financial crisis of 2007–2010 led to mainstream discussions as to whether "Marx was right".[65] [66] Time magazine ran an article 'Rethinking Marx' and put Karl Marx on the cover of its European edition in a special for the 28 January 2009 Davos meeting.[67] [68] While the mainstream media tended to conclude that Marx was wrong, this was not the view of socialists and left-leaning commentators.[69] [70]

A Globescan BBC poll on the twentieth anniversary of the fall of the Berlin Wall found that 23% of respondents believe capitalism is "fatally flawed and a different economic system is needed", with that figure rising to 40% of the population in some developed countries such as France; while a majority of respondents including over 50% of Americans believe capitalism "has problems that can be addressed through regulation and reform".[71] Opinions regarding the demise of the Soviet Union are also heavily divided between the developed and developing world, with the latter believing the disintegration of the Soviet Union was a bad thing.

Africa

African socialism continues to be a major ideology around the continent. In South Africa the African National Congress (ANC) abandoned its partial socialist allegiances after taking power, and followed a standard neoliberal route. From 2005 through to 2007, the country was wracked by many thousands of protests from poor communities. One of these gave rise to a mass movement of shack dwellers, Abahlali baseMjondolo that, despite major police suppression, continues to advocate for popular people's planning and against the creation of a market economy in land and housing.

Asia

The People's Republic of China, North Korea, Laos and Vietnam are Asian states remaining from the first wave of socialism in the 20th century. States with socialist economies have largely moved away from centralised economic planning in the 21st century, placing a greater emphasis on markets, in the case of the Chinese Socialist market economy and Vietnamese Socialist-oriented market economy, worker cooperatives as in Venezuela, and utilising state-owned corporate management models as opposed to modeling socialist enterprise off traditional management styles employed by government agencies.

In New China, the Chinese Communist Party has led a transition from the command economy of the Mao period to an economic program they term the socialist market economy or "socialism with Chinese characteristics." Under Deng Xiaoping, the leadership of China embarked upon a programme of market-based reform that was more sweeping than had been Soviet leader Mikhail Gorbachev's perestroika program of the late 1980s. Deng's programme, however, maintained state ownership rights over land, state or cooperative ownership of much of the heavy industrial and manufacturing sectors and state influence in the banking and financial sectors.

Elsewhere in Asia, some elected socialist parties and communist parties remain prominent, particularly in India and Nepal. The Communist Party of Nepal in particular calls for multi-party democracy, social equality, and economic prosperity.[72] In Singapore, a majority of the GDP is still generated from the state sector comprising government-linked companies.[73] In Japan, there has been a resurgent interest in the Japanese Communist Party among workers and youth.[74] [75] In Malaysia, the Socialist Party of Malaysia got its first Member of Parliament, Dr. Jeyakumar Devaraj, after the 2008 general election.

Europe

In Europe, the socialist Left Party in Germany grew in popularity[76] due to dissatisfaction with the increasingly neoliberal policies of the SPD, becoming the fourth biggest party in parliament in the general election on 27 September 2009.[77] Communist candidate Dimitris Christofias won a crucial presidential runoff in Cyprus, defeating his conservative rival with a majority of 53%.[78] In Greece, in the general election on 4 October 2009, the Panhellenic Socialist Movement (PASOK) won the elections with 43.92% of the votes, the Communist KKE got 7.5% and the new Socialist grouping, (Syriza or "Coalition of the Radical Left"), won 4.6% or 361,000 votes.[79]

In Ireland, in the 2009 European election, Joe Higgins of the Socialist Party took one of three seats in the capital Dublin European constituency. In Denmark, the Socialist People's Party (SF or Socialist Party for short) more than doubled its parliamentary representation to 23 seats from 11, making it the fourth largest party.[80]

In the UK, the National Union of Rail, Maritime and Transport Workers put forward a slate of candidates in the 2009 European Parliament elections under the banner of No to the EU – Yes to Democracy, a broad left-wing alter-globalisation coalition involving socialist groups such as the Socialist Party, aiming to offer an alternative to the "anti-foreigner" and pro-business policies of the UK Independence Party.[81] [82] [83]

In France, the Revolutionary Communist League (LCR) candidate in the 2007 presidential election, Olivier Besancenot, received 1,498,581 votes, 4.08%, double that of the Communist candidate.[84] The LCR abolished itself in 2009 to initiate a broad anti-capitalist party, the New Anticapitalist Party, whose stated aim is to "build a new socialist, democratic perspective for the twenty-first century".[85]

Latin America

In some Latin American countries, Third-world socialism has re-emerged in recent years, with a populist, anti-imperialist stance, the rejection of the policies of neoliberalism, and the nationalisation or partial nationalisation of oil production, land and other assets. Venezuelan President Hugo Chávez, Bolivian President Evo Morales, and Ecuadorian president Rafael Correa for instance, refer to their political programmes as socialist, combining it with populism.

Hugo Chávez

Chávez adopted the term Socialism of the 21st century. After winning re-election in December 2006, President Chávez said, "Now more than ever, I am obliged to move Venezuela's path towards socialism."[86]

United States

Socialist parties in the United States reached their zenith in the early twentieth century, but currently active parties and organizations include the Socialist Party USA, the Socialist Workers Party and the Democratic Socialists of America, which has approximately 10,000 members.[87]

A December 2008 Rasmussen poll found that when asked whether Americans supported a state-managed economy or a free-market economy, 70% preferred free-market capitalism, with only 15% preferring a state-managed economy.[88] An April 2009 Rasmussen Reports poll, conducted during the Financial crisis of 2007–2010, suggested that there had been a growth of support for socialism in the United States. The poll results stated that 53% of American adults thought capitalism was better than socialism, and that "Adults under 30 are essentially evenly divided: 37% prefer capitalism, 33% socialism, and 30% are undecided". The question posed by Rasmussen Reports did not define either capitalism or socialism, allowing for the possibility of confusing socialism with regulated capitalism, or socialism with authoritarian communism.[89]

Economics

"I am convinced there is only one way to eliminate (the) grave evils (of capitalism), namely through the establishment of a socialist economy, accompanied by an educational system which would be oriented toward social goals. In such an economy, the means of production are owned by society itself and are utilized in a planned fashion. A planned economy, which adjusts production to the needs of the community, would distribute the work to be done among all those able to work and would guarantee a livelihood to every man, woman, and child. The education of the individual, in addition to promoting his own innate abilities, would attempt to develop in him a sense of responsibility for his fellow-men in place of the glorification of power and success in our present society."

— Albert Einstein, *Why Socialism?*, 1949 [90]

Economically, socialism denotes an economic system of state ownership and/or worker ownership of the means of production and distribution. In the economy of the Soviet Union, state ownership of the means of production was combined with central planning, in relation to which goods and services to make and provide, how they were to be produced, the quantities, and the sale prices.

Soviet economic planning was an alternative to allowing the market (supply and demand) to determine prices and production. During the Great Depression, many socialists considered Soviet-style planned economies the remedy to capitalism's inherent flaws – monopoly, business cycles, unemployment, unequally distributed wealth, and the economic exploitation of workers.

In the West, neoclassical liberal economists such as Friedrich Hayek and Milton Friedman said that socialist planned economies would fail, because planners could not have the business information inherent to a market economy (cf. economic calculation problem), nor would managers in Soviet-style socialist economies match the motivation of profit. Consequent to Soviet economic stagnation in the 1970s and 1980s, socialists began to accept parts of their critique. Polish economist Oskar Lange, an early proponent of market socialism, proposed a central planning board establishing prices and controls of investment. The prices of producer goods would be determined through trial and error. The prices of consumer goods would be determined by supply and demand, with the supply coming from state-owned firms that would set their prices equal to the marginal cost, as in perfectly competitive markets. The central planning board would distribute a "social dividend" to ensure reasonable income equality.[91]

In western Europe, particularly in the period after World War II, many socialist and social democratic parties in government implemented what became known as mixed economies. In the biography of the 1945 UK Labour Party Prime Minister Clement Attlee, Francis Beckett states: "the government... wanted what would become known as a mixed economy".[92] Beckett also states that "Everyone called the 1945 government 'socialist'." These governments nationalised major and economically vital industries while permitting a free market to continue in the rest. These were most often monopolistic or infrastructural industries like mail, railways, power and other utilities. In some instances a number of small, competing and often relatively poorly financed companies in the same sector were nationalised to form one government monopoly for the purpose of competent management, of economic rescue (in the UK, British Leyland, Rolls Royce), or of competing on the world market.

Also in the UK, British Aerospace was a combination of major aircraft companies British Aircraft Corporation, Hawker Siddeley and others. British Shipbuilders was a combination of the major shipbuilding companies including Cammell Laird, Govan Shipbuilders, Swan Hunter, and Yarrow Shipbuilders Typically, this was achieved through compulsory purchase of the industry (i.e. with compensation). In the UK, the nationalisation of the coal mines in 1947 created a coal board charged with running the coal industry commercially so as to be able to meet the interest payable on the bonds which the former mine owners' shares had been converted into.[93] [94]

The modern socialist system in the People's Republic in China, formally titled the socialist market economy, combines a large state sector that comprises the 'commanding heights' of the economy with a growing private sector mainly engaged in commodity production and light industry, and is responsible from anywhere between 33%[95] (People's Daily Online 2005) to over 50% of GDP generated in 2005[96] . Directive centralized planning based on mandatory output requirements and production quotas have been displaced by the free-market mechanism for most of the economy and directive planning in some larger state industries.[97] Many political scientists liken this to Russia's policy of perestroika. One of the major changes between the old planned economy and the socialist market model is the corporatization of state institutions, with 150 of them reporting directly to the central government.[98] By 2008, these state-owned corporations have became increasingly dynamic and generated a large increase in revenue for the state[99] [100] , with the state-sector leading the recovery of economic growth in 2009 during the wake of the financial crises.[101] The Socialist Republic of Vietnam has adopted a similar model after the Doi Moi economic renovation, officially called the socialist-oriented market economy. This differs from the Chinese model in that the Vietnamese government retains firm control over the state sector and strategic industries, but allows for a considerable increase in private-sector activity for firms engaged in commodity production.[102]

Proponents of the socialist market economic system defend their it from a Marxist perspective, stating that a planned socialist economy can only become possible after first establishing the necessary comprehensive commodity market economy and letting it fully develop until it exhausts its historical stage and gradually transforms itself into a planned economy.[103] They distinguish themselves from market socialists who believe that economic planning is unattainable, undesirable or ineffective at distributing goods, viewing the market as the solution rather than a temporary phase in development of a socialist planned economy.

Some socialists propose various decentralised, worker-managed economic systems. One such system is the cooperative economy, a largely free market economy in which workers manage the firms and democratically determine remuneration levels and labour divisions. Productive resources would be legally owned by the cooperative and rented to the workers, who would enjoy usufruct rights.[104]

Another, more recent, variant is participatory economics, wherein the economy is planned by decentralised councils of workers and consumers. Workers would be remunerated solely according to effort and sacrifice, so that those engaged in dangerous, uncomfortable, and strenuous work would receive the highest incomes and could thereby work less.[105]

Some Marxists and anarcho-communists also propose a worker-managed economy based on workers councils, however in anarcho-communism, workers are remunerated according to their needs (which are largely self-determined in an anarcho-communist system). Recently socialists have also been working with the technocracy movement to promote such concepts as energy accounting.

Social and political theory

Marxist and non-Marxist social theorists agree that socialism developed in reaction to modern industrial capitalism, but disagree on the nature of their relationship.

Marxism

In the most influential of all socialist theories, Marx and Engels believed the consciousness of those who earn a wage or salary (the "working class" in the broadest Marxist sense) would be molded by their "conditions" of "wage-slavery", leading to a tendency to seek their freedom or "emancipation" by throwing off the capitalist ownership of society. For Marx and Engels, conditions determine consciousness and ending the role of the capitalist class leads eventually to a classless society in which the state would wither away.

> It is not the consciousness of [people] that determines their existence, but their social existence that determines their consciousness. - *Preface to A Contribution to the Critique of Political Economy, Karl Marx 1859*

Émile Durkheim, by contrast, posits that socialism is rooted in the desire to bring the state closer to the realm of individual activity, in countering the anomie of a capitalist society.

Marx argued that the material productive forces (in industry and commerce) brought into existence by capitalism predicated a cooperative society since production had become a mass social, collective activity of the working class to create commodities but with private ownership (the relations of production or property relations). This conflict between collective effort in large factories and private ownership would bring about a conscious desire in the working class to establish collective ownership commensurate with the collective efforts their daily experience. "At a certain stage of development, the material productive forces of society come into conflict with the existing relations of production or — this merely expresses the same thing in legal terms — with the property relations within the framework of which they have operated hitherto. Then begins an era of social revolution. The changes in the economic foundation lead sooner or later to the transformation of the whole immense superstructure." [106] A socialist society based on democratric cooperation thus arises.

By contrast, Che Guevara attempted to inspire the peasants of Bolivia by his own example into a change of consciousness. Guevara said in 1965,

> Socialism cannot exist without a change in consciousness resulting in a new fraternal attitude toward humanity, both at an individual level, within the societies where socialism is being built or has been built, and on a world scale, with regard to all peoples suffering from imperialist oppression.[107]

In the middle of the twentieth century, socialist intellectuals retained considerable influence in European philosophy. *Eros and Civilisation* (1955), by Herbert Marcuse, explicitly attempts to merge Marxism with Freudianism. The social science of structuralism had a significant influence on the socialist New Left in the 1960s and the 1970s.

Utopian versus scientific

The distinction between "utopian" and "scientific socialism" was first explicitly made by Friedrich Engels in *Socialism: Utopian and Scientific*, which contrasted the "utopian pictures of ideal social conditions" of social reformers with the Marxian concept of scientific socialism. Scientific socialism begins with the examination of social and economic phenomena—the empirical study of real processes in society and history.

For Marxists, the development of capitalism in western Europe provided a material basis for the possibility of bringing about socialism because, according to the *Communist Manifesto*, "What the bourgeoisie produces above all is its own grave diggers",[108] namely the working class, which must become conscious of the historical objectives set it by society. In *Capitalism, Socialism and Democracy*, Joseph Schumpeter, an Austrian economist, presents an alternative mechanism of how socialism will come about from a Weberian perspective: the increasing bureaucratization of society that occurs under capitalism will eventually necessitate state-control in order to better coordinate economic activity. Eduard Bernstein revised this theory to suggest that society is inevitably moving toward socialism, bringing in a mechanical and teleological element to Marxism and initiating the concept of evolutionary socialism.

Utopian socialists establish a set of ideals or goals and present socialism as an alternative to capitalism, with subjectively better attributes. Examples of this form of socialism include Robert Owen's New Harmony community.

Reform versus revolution

Reformists, such as classical social democrats, believe that a socialist system can be achieved by reforming capitalism. Socialism, in their view, can be reached through the existing political system by reforming private enterprise. Revolutionaries, such as Marxists, Leninists and Trotskyist, believe such methods will fail because the state ultimately acts in the interests of capitalist business interests. They believe that revolution is the only means to establish a new socio-economic system. Marxists do not necessarily define revolution as a violent insurrection, but instead as a thorough and rapid change.[109]

Socialism from above or below

Socialism from above refers to the viewpoint that reforms or revolutions for socialism will come from, or be led by, higher status members of society who desire a more rational, efficient economic system. Claude Henri de Saint-Simon believed that socialism would come from engineers, scientists and technicians who want to organize society and the economy in a rational, logical fashion. Social democracy is often advocated by intellectuals and the middle-class, as well as the working class segments of the population. *Socialism from below* refers to the position that socialism can only come from, and be led by, popular solidarity and political action from the lower classes, such as the working class and lower-middle class. Proponents of socialism from below — such as syndicalists, orthodox Marxists and Leninists — often liken socialism from above to elitism.

Technocratic management versus democratic management

The distinction between technocratic/scientific management and democratic management refers to positions on how state institutions and the economy are to be managed. Technocratic organizational management is distinct from bureaucratic and democratic techniques, with the state apparatus being transformed as an administration of economic affairs through technical management as opposed to the administration of people through the creation and enforcement of laws. Some proponents of technocratic socialism include Claude Henri de Saint-Simon, Alexander Bogdanov, Howard Scott and H. G. Wells. They include proponents of economic planning (except those, like the Trotskyists, who tend to emphasize the need for democratic workers control), and socialists inspired by Taylorism. They show a tendency to promote scientific management, whereby technical experts manage institutions and receive their position in society based on a demonstration of their technical expertise or merit, with the aim of creating a rational, effective and stable organization. Although scientific management is based on technocratic organization, elements of democracy can be present in the system, such as having democratically decided social goals that are executed by a technocratic state.

Proponents of democratic management propose workers' self-management: a system whereby management decisions are made democratically, or a manager is elected by all the members of the institution. Groups that promote democratic management include libertarian socialists, social anarchists and syndicalists. Many Trotskyists argue that the destruction of democratic workers' control of the economy through the workers' councils in Russia by Joseph Stalin was a critical juncture in the growth of the bureaucracy, and led to the poor performance of the planned economy in Russia. They demand a democratic plan of production developed through workers' committees.

Allocation of Resources

Resource allocation is the subject of intense debate between market socialists and proponents of planned economies.

Market socialists believe that the market mechanism is either the most efficient or the only viable means of allocating resources and determining what is to be produced. Examples of market socialism include Ricardian socialism, the New Economic Policy and the socialist market economy. Socialist theories that involve the market as the main arbitrator of economic decision-making are sometimes viewed as a temporary, transitional phase between capitalism and a fully planned economy.

Proponents of economic planning argue that the market is inherently irrational and prone to unstable cyclical fluctuations, fails to prioritize production according to a rational plan that conforms to macro-social goals and promotes short-term investment and uncoordinated economic activity. They argue that through either state directed administration or economic planning, the state can allocate resources more effectively than the market.

Proponents of democratic planning reject both state-led planning and the market, instead arguing for inclusive decision-making on what should be produced, with the distribution of the output being based on direct democracy or council democracy. Leon Trotsky held the view that central planners, regardless of their intellectual capacity, operated without the input and participation of the millions of people who participate in the economy and understand/respond to local conditions and changes in the economy would be unable to effectively coordinate all economic activity.[110]

Equality of opportunity versus equality of outcome

Proponents of equality of opportunity advocate a society in which there are equal opportunities and life chances for all individuals to maximize their potentials and attain positions in society. This would be made possible by equal access to the necessities of life. This position is held by technocratic socialists, Marxists and social democrats. *Equality of outcome* refers to a state where everyone receives equal amounts of rewards and an equal level of power in decision-making, with the belief that all roles in society are necessary and therefore none should be rewarded more than others. This view is shared by some communal utopian socialists and anarcho-communists.

Criticism

Criticisms of socialism range from claims that socialist economic and political models are inefficient or incompatible with civil liberties to condemnation of specific socialist states. In the economic calculation debate, classical liberal Friedrich Hayek argued that a socialist command economy could not adequately transmit information about prices and productive quotas due to the lack of a price mechanism, and as a result it could not make rational economic decisions. Ludwig von Mises argued that a socialist economy was not possible at all, because of the impossibility of rational pricing of capital goods in a socialist economy since the state is the only owner of the capital goods. Hayek further argued that the social control over distribution of wealth and private property advocated by socialists cannot be achieved without reduced prosperity for the general populace, and a loss of political and economic freedoms.

See also

- Anti-Globalisation
- Anti-capitalism
- Class struggle
- Commonwealth
- Communism
- Dictatorship of the proletariat
- Fabian Society
- Heaven on Earth: The Rise and Fall of Socialism
- History of socialism
- History of socialism in Great Britain
- Industrial revolution
- Labour movement
- List of communist ideologies
- List of socialist songs

- Market Socialism
- Marxism
- Nationalisation
- Nano socialism
- Proletariat
- Proletarian revolution
- Social democracy
- Socialist state
- Socialism in the United States
- State ownership or Public ownership
- Syndicalism
- To each according to his contribution
- Worker cooperative
- Workers' self-management

References and further reading

- Guy Ankerl, *Beyond Monopoly Capitalism and Monopoly Socialism*, Cambridge MA: Schenkman, 1978.
- Beckett, Francis, *Clem Attlee*, Politico's (2007) 978-1842751923
- G.D.H. Cole, *History of Socialist Thought, in 7 volumes*, Macmillan and St. Martin's Press, 1965; Palgrave Macmillan, 2003 reprint; 7 volumes, hardcover, 3160 pages, ISBN 1-4039-0264-X.
- Friedrich Engels, *Socialism: Utopian and Scientific*, Pathfinder; 2r.e. edition (December 1989) 978-0873485791
- Friedrich Engels, *The Origin of the Family, Private Property and the State*, Zurich, 1884. LCC HQ504 .E6 [111]
- Albert Fried and Ronald Sanders, eds., *Socialist Thought: A Documentary History*, Garden City, NY: Doubleday Anchor, 1964. LCCN 64-11312 [112].
- Phil Gasper [113], *The Communist Manifesto: A Road Map to History's Most Important Political Document*, Haymarket Books [114], paperback, 224 pages, 2005. ISBN 1-931859-25-6.
- Élie Halévy, *Histoire du Socialisme Européen*. Paris, Gallimard, 1948.
- Michael Harrington, *Socialism*, New York: Bantam, 1972. LCCN 76-154260 [115].
- Jesús Huerta de Soto, *Socialismo, cálculo económico y función empresarial* [116] (*Socialism, Economic Calculation, and Entrepreneurship*), Unión Editorial, 1992. ISBN 8472094200.
- Makoto Itoh, *Political Economy of Socialism*. London: Macmillan, 1995. ISBN 0333553373.
- Kitching, Gavin (1983). *Rethinking Socialism* [117]. Meuthen. ISBN 0416358403.
- Oskar Lange, *On the Economic Theory of Socialism*, Minneapolis, MN: University of Minnesota Press, 1938. LCCN 38-12882 [118].
- Michael Lebowitz, *Build It Now: Socialism for the 21st Century* [119], Monthly Review Press [120], 2006. ISBN 1-58367-145-5.
- Marx, Engels, *The Communist Manifesto*, Penguin Classics (2002) 978-0140447576
- Marx, Engels, *Selected works in one volume*, Lawrence and Wishart (1968) 978-0853151814
- Ludwig von Mises, *Socialism: An Economic and Sociological Analysis* [121], Liberty Fund, 1922. ISBN 0-913966-63-0.
- Joshua Muravchik, *Heaven on Earth: The Rise and Fall of Socialism* [122], San Francisco: Encounter Books, 2002. ISBN 1-893554-45-7.
- Michael Newman, *Socialism: A Very Short Introduction*, Oxford University Press, 2005. ISBN 0-19-280431-6.
- Bertell Ollman, ed., *Market Socialism: The Debate among Socialists*, Routledge, 1998. ISBN 0415919673
- Leo Panitch, *Renewing Socialism: Democracy, Strategy, and Imagination*. ISBN 0-8133-9821-5.
- Emile Perreau-Saussine, *What remains of socialism ?* [123], in Patrick Riordan (dir.), Values in Public life: aspects of common goods (Berlin, LIT Verlag, 2007), pp. 11–34

- Richard Pipes, *Property and Freedom*, Vintage, 2000. ISBN 0-375-70447-7.
- John Barkley Rosser and Marina V. Rosser, *Comparative Economics in a Transforming World Economy*. Cambridge, MA: MIT Press, 2004. ISBN 9780262182348.
- Maximilien Rubel and John Crump, *Non-Market Socialism in the Nineteenth and Twentieth Centuries*. ISBN 0-312-00524-5.
- David Selbourne, *Against Socialist Illusion*, London, 1985. ISBN 0-333-37095-3.
- Katherine Verdery, *What Was Socialism, What Comes Next*, Princeton. 1996. ISBN 0-691-01132-X
- James Weinstein, *Long Detour: The History and Future of the American Left*, Westview Press [124], 2003, hardcover, 272 pages. ISBN 0-8133-4104-3.
- Peter Wilberg, *Deep Socialism: A New Manifesto of Marxist Ethics and Economics* [125], 2003. ISBN 1-904519-02-4.
- Edmund Wilson, *To the Finland Station: A Study in the Writing and Acting of History*, Garden City, NY: Doubleday, 1940. LCCN 4-34338 [126].

External links

- "Socialism: Utopian and Scientific" [127] by Friedrich Engels
- "Why Socialism?" [128] by Albert Einstein
- "The Soul of Man under Socialism" [129] by Oscar Wilde
- "Socialism and Liberty" [130] by George Bernard Shaw
- Freedom Socialist Party website [131]
- What is Socialism? [132]
- History of socialism at Spartacus Educational [133]
- Modern History Sourcebook on socialism [134]
- Socialist history at *What Next?* [135]
- "The Two Souls of Socialism" [136] by Hal Draper
- "Approaching Socialism" [137] by Harry Magdoff and Fred Magdoff
- PBS television documentary: "Heaven on Earth: the Rise and Fall of Socialism" [138]
- *Towards a New Socialism* [139] by W. Paul Cockshott and Allin Cottrell
- 21st Century Socialism [140] web magazine
- New Ideas of Socialism [141]
- World Socialist Web Site [142]
- The Marxists Internet Archive [143] (online library of Marxist writers)
- Marxist.net [144] - a resource on socialist writers
- In Defense of Marxism [145]
- Reason in Revolt: Marxism and Modern Science By Alan Woods and Ted Grant [146]
- Science, Marxism & the Big Bang: A Critical Review of Reason in Revolt by Peter Mason [147]
- What Needs to be Done: A Socialist View [148] by Fred Magdoff and Michael D. Yates, *Monthly Review*, November 2009

References

[1] *Newman, Michael*. (2005) *Socialism: A Very Short Introduction*, Oxford University Press, ISBN 0-19-280431-6

[2] "1. A theory or policy of social organisation which aims at or advocates the ownership and control of the means of production, capital, land, property, etc., by the community as a whole, and their administration or distribution in the interests of all people

2. A state of society in which things are held or used in common."

[3] "Socialism".Merriam-Webster Unabridged Dictionary

[4] *Socialism and Calculation*, on worldsocialism.org. Retrieved February 15, 2010, from worldsocialism.org: http://www.worldsocialism.org/spgb/overview/calculation.pdf: "Although money, and so monetary calculation, will disappear in socialism this does not mean that there will no longer be any need to make choices, evaluations and calculations...Wealth will be produced and distributed in its natural form of useful things, of objects that can serve to satisfy some human need or other. Not being produced for sale on a market, items of wealth will not acquire an exchange-value in addition to their use-value. In socialism their value, in the normal non-economic sense of the word, will not be their selling price nor the time needed to produce them but their usefulness. It is for this that they will be appreciated, evaluated, wanted. . . and produced."

[5] *Critique of the Gotha Programme*, Karl Marx.

[6] Socialism, (2009), in Encyclopædia Britannica. Retrieved October 14, 2009, from Encyclopædia Britannica Online: http://www.britannica.com/EBchecked/topic/551569/socialism, "Main" summary: "Socialists complain that capitalism necessarily leads to unfair and exploitative concentrations of wealth and power in the hands of the relative few who emerge victorious from free-market competition—people who then use their wealth and power to reinforce their dominance in society."

[7] Marx and Engels Selected Works, Lawrence and Wishart, 1968, p. 40. Capitalist property relations put a "fetter" on the productive forces.

[8] Socialism: Utopian and Scientific (http://www.marxists.org/archive/marx/works/1880/soc-utop/ch03.htm) at Marxists.org

[9] Frederick Engels. *Socialism: Utopian and Scientific* (http://books.google.com/books?id=6avaAAAAMAAJ&pg=PA47&dq=Socialism:+Utopian+and+Scientific#v=onepage&q=anarchy&f=false). pp. 92–11. .Chapter III: Historical Materialism

[10] "Market socialism," *Dictionary of the Social Sciences*. Craig Calhoun, ed. Oxford University Press 2002; and "Market socialism" *The Concise Oxford Dictionary of Politics*. Ed. Iain McLean and Alistair McMillan. Oxford University Press, 2003. See also Joseph Stiglitz, "Whither Socialism?" Cambridge, MA: MIT Press, 1995 for a recent analysis of the market socialism model of mid–20th century economists Oskar R. Lange, Abba P. Lerner, and Fred M. Taylor.

[11] http://www.fsmitha.com/h3/h44-ph.html

[12] Lenin refers specifically to Marx's *Critique of the Gotha Program* in his 1917 book *State and Revolution*.

[13] "In striving for socialism, however, we are convinced that it will develop into communism", Lenin, *State and Revolution*, Selected Works, Progress publishers, Moscow, 1968, p. 320. (End of chapter four)

[14] Leroux: socialism is "the doctrine which would not give up any of the principles of Liberty, Equality, Fraternity" of the French Revolution of 1789. "Individualism and socialism" (1834)

[15] Oxford English Dictionary, etymology of socialism

[16] Russell, Bertrand (1972). A History of Western Philosophy. Touchstone. p. 781

[17] http://www.economictheories.org/2008/10/aristotle-and-plato-communism.html

[18] http://www.anu.edu.au/polsci/marx/contemp/pamsetc/socfrombel/sfb_2.htm

[19] http://cepa.newschool.edu/het/schools/utopia.htm

[20] Williams, Raymond (1976). *Keywords: a vocabulary of culture and society*. Fontana. ISBN 0006334792.

[21] Engels, Frederick, *Preface to the 1888 English Edition of the Communist Manifesto*, p202. Penguin (2002)

[22] http://www.economictheories.org/2008/07/karl-marx-socialism-and-scientific.html

[23] Schaff, Kory (2001). *Philosophy and the problems of work: a reader*. Lanham, Md: Rowman & Littlefield. pp. 224 (http://books.google.com/books?id=mdLh5EMehwgC&pg=PA224&dq=isbn=0742507955&source=gbs_search_r&cad=0_1&sig=ACfU3U2S6uiRNCig9mq_bY4yKB7877tY4A). ISBN 0-7425-0795-5.

[24] Walicki, Andrzej (1995). *Marxism and the leap to the kingdom of freedom: the rise and fall of the Communist utopia*. Stanford, Calif: Stanford University Press. p. 95. ISBN 0-8047-2384-2.

[25] MIA: Encyclopaedia of Marxism: Glossary of Organisations, *First International (International Workingmen's Association)*, accessed 5 July 2007 (http://www.marxists.org/glossary/orgs/f/i.htm#iwma)

[26] Engels' 1891 Preface to Marx, Civil War in France, Selected Works, Lawrence and Wishart, (1968), p256, p259

[27] *The Second (Socialist) International 1889–1923* (http://www.marxisthistory.org/subject/usa/eam/secondinternational.html) accessed 12 July 2007

[28] Engels, 1895 Introduction to Marx's *Class Struggles in France 1848–1850*

[29] cf Footnote 449 in *Marx Engels Collected Works* on Engels' 1895 Introduction to Marx's *Class Struggles in France 1848–1850*

[30] The Common People 1746-1946, Cole and Postgate, Menthuen 1987, p. 506.

[31] The Second International, 1889-1914, James Joll, p. 184

[32] "the war of 1914-18 was imperialist (that is, an annexationist, predatory, war of plunder) on the part of both sides; it was a war for the division of the world, for the partition and repartition of colonies and spheres of influence of finance capital, etc.", Vladimir Ilyich Lenin, Imperialism, the Highest Stage of Capitalism, Preface to the French and German editions.

[33] Dead Chauvinism and Living Socialism, How the International can be restored, V I Lenin, Lenin Collected Works, Progress Publishers, [197[4]], Moscow, Volume 21, pages 94-101, http://www.marxists.org/archive/lenin/works/1914/dec/12.htm

[34] The Second International, 1889-1914, James Joll, p. 184

[35] International Socialist Conference at Zimmerwald, September/October 1915, MIA History, http://www.marxists.org/history/international/social-democracy/zimmerwald/index.htm

[36] Manifesto of the International Socialist Conference at Zimmerwald, The Bolsheviks and War, by Sam Marcy, online at http://www.marxists.org/history/international/social-democracy/zimmerwald/manifesto-1915.htm.The Nashe Slovo representative, namely Trotsky, was commissioned to draft the Manifesto with the German delegation, and Lenin signed it (with reservations)

[37] Lenin, *Meeting of the Petrograd Soviet of workers and soldiers' deputies 25 January 1918*, Collected works, Vol 26, p239. Lawrence and Wishart, (1964)

[38] Lenin, *To workers Soldiers and Peasants*, Collected works, Vol 26, p247. Lawrence and Wishart, (1964)

[39] Lenin, *Collected Works*, Vol 26, pp. 264–5. Lawrence and Wishart (1964)

[40] Caplan, Brian. "Lenin and the First Communist Revolutions, IV" (http://www.gmu.edu/departments/economics/bcaplan/museum/his1d.htm). George Mason University. . Retrieved 2008-02-14. Strictly, the Right Socialist Revolutionaries won - the Left SR's were in alliance with the Bolsheviks.

[41] *Declaration of the RSDLP (Bolsheviks) group at the Constituent Assembly meeting January 5, 1918* Lenin, *Collected Works*, Vol 26, p. 429. Lawrence and Wishart (1964)

[42] *Draft Decree on the Dissolution of the Constituent Assembly* Lenin, *Collected Works*, Vol 26, p. 434. Lawrence and Wishart (1964)

[43] Payne, Robert; "The Life and Death of Lenin", Grafton: paperback pp. 425–440

[44] Bertil, Hessel, Introduction, *Theses, Resolutions and Manifestos of the first four congresses of the Third International*, pxiii, Ink Links (1980)

[45] "We have always proclaimed, and repeated, this elementary truth of Marxism, that the victory of socialism requires the joint efforts of workers in a number of advanced countries." Lenin, *Sochineniya* (Works), 5th ed. Vol. XLIV p. 418, Feb 1922. (Quoted by Mosche Lewin in *Lenin's Last Struggle*, p. 4. Pluto (1975))

[46] *Soviet history: NEPmen* (http://www.soviethistory.org/index.php?action=L2&SubjectID=1924nepmen&Year=1924)

[47] Serge, Victor, *From Lenin to Stalin*, p. 55.

[48] Serge, Victor, *From Lenin to Stalin*, p. 52.

[49] Brinton, Maurice (1975). "The Bolsheviks and Workers' Control 1917–1921 : The State and Counter-revolution" (http://www.spunk.org/texts/places/russia/sp001861/bolintro.html). Solidarity. . Retrieved 2007-01-22.

[50] Bevan, Aneurin, *In Place of Fear*, p 63, p91

[51] The Frankfurt Declaration (http://www.socialistinternational.org/5Congress/1-FRANKFURT/Frankfurtdecl-e.html)

[52] cf Beckett, Francis, *Clem Attlee*, Politico, 2007, p243. "Idleness" meant unemployment and hence the starvation of the worker and his/her family. It was not then a pejorative term.

[53] Crosland, Anthony, *The Future of Socialism*, p52

[54] Bevan, Aneurin, *In Place of Fear* p.50, pp.126–128, p.21 MacGibbon and Kee, second edition (1961)

[55] British Petroleum, privatised in 1987, was officially nationalised in 1951 per government archives (http://yourarchives.nationalarchives.gov.uk/index.php?title=Nationalisation_of_Anglo-Iranian_Oil_Company,_1951) with further government intervention during the 1974–79 Labour Government, cf 'The New Commanding Height: Labor Party Policy on North Sea Oil and Gas, 1964–74' in *Contemporary British History*, Volume 16, Issue 1 Spring 2002 , pages 89–118. Elements of these entities already were in public hands. Later Labour re-nationalised steel (1967, British Steel) after Conservatives denationalised it, and nationalised car production (1976, British Leyland), (http://www.uksteel.org.uk/history.htm). In 1977, major aircraft companies and shipbuilding were nationalised

[56] The nationalised public utilities include CDF (Charbonnages de France), EDF (Électricité de France), GDF (Gaz de France), airlines (Air France), banks (Banque de France), and Renault (Régie Nationale des Usines Renault) (http://www.sund.ac.uk/~os0tmc/contem/trente1.htm).

[57] "One of the consequences of the universality of the British Health Service is the free treatment of foreign visitors." Bevan, Aneurin, *In Place of Fear* p.104, MacGibbon and Kee, second edition (1961)

[58] Beckett, Francis, *Clem Attlee*, p247. Politico's (2007)

[59] Crosland, Anthony, *The Future of Socialism*, pp.9, 89. Constable (2006)

[60] Beckett, Francis, *Clem Attlee*, Politico, 2007, p243

[61] Crosland, Anthony, *The Future of Socialism* p46. Constable (2006)

[62] Socialist International - Progressive Politics For A Fairer World (http://www.socialistinternational.org/4Principles/dofpeng2.html)

[63] R Goodin and P Pettit (eds), *A Companion to Contemporary political philosophy*

[64] Labour Party Clause Four (http://www.labour.org.uk/labour_policies)

[65] *Karl Marx: did he get it all right?*, The Times (UK), October 21, 2008, http://www.timesonline.co.uk/tol/news/politics/article4981065.ece

[66] *Capitalism has proven Karl Marx right again*, The Herald (Scotland), 17 Sep 2008, http://www.heraldscotland.com/capitalism-has-proven-karl-marx-right-again-1.889708

[67] *Rethinking Marx*, Peter Gumbell, Time magazine, 28 January 2009, http://www.time.com/time/specials/packages/article/0,28804,1873191_1873190_1873188,00.html

[68] *Karl Marx makes cover of TIME magazine*, January 28, 2009, http://cogsciandtheworld.blogspot.com/2009/01/karl-marx-makes-cover-of-time-magazine.html

[69] *Capitalist crisis - Karl Marx was right* Editorial, The Socialist, 17 Sep 2008, www.socialistparty.org.uk/articles/6395

[70] *Marx is being proved right*, David Cox, The Guardian, 29 January 2007, http://www.guardian.co.uk/commentisfree/2007/jan/29/marxisbeingprovedright

[71] http://news.bbc.co.uk/2/hi/in_depth/8347409.stm

[72] *Communist Party of Nepal'* (http://www.cpnm.org/)

[73] CountryRisk Maintaining Singapore's Miracle (http://www.countryrisk.com/editorials/archives/cat_singapore.html)

[74] Japan's young turn to Communist Party as they decide capitalism has let them down (http://www.telegraph.co.uk/news/worldnews/asia/japan/3218944/Japans-young-turn-to-Communist-Party-as-they-decide-capitalism-has-let-them-down.html) - Daily Telegraph October 18, 2008

[75] "Communism on rise in recession-hit Japan" (http://news.bbc.co.uk/2/hi/asia-pacific/8027397.stm), BBC, May 4, 2009

[76] *Germany's Left Party woos the SPD'* (http://www.wsws.org/articles/2008/feb2008/hess-f15.shtml)

[77] *Germany: Left makes big gains in poll* http://www.greenleft.org.au/2009/813/41841

[78] *Christofias wins Cyprus presidency'* (http://www.elpasotimes.com/nationworld/ci_835244)

[79] http://ekloges.ypes.gr/pages/index.html

[80] *Danish centre-right wins election* http://news.bbc.co.uk/1/hi/world/europe/7091941.stm

[81] *Crow launches NO2EU euro campaign* http://news.bbc.co.uk/1/hi/uk_politics/8059281.stm

[82] *Exclusive: Tommy Sheridan to stand for Euro elections* http://www.dailyrecord.co.uk/news/scottish-news/2009/03/10/exclusive-tommy-sheridan-to-stand-for-euro-elections-86908-21185994/

[83] *RMT Conference: Crisis in Working Class Representation* http://www.rmt.org.uk/Templates/Internal.asp?NodeID=127346&int1stParentNodeID=89731&int2ndParentNodeID=89763

[84] *Has France moved to the right?* http://www.socialismtoday.org/110/france.html

[85] ""Le Nouveau parti anticapitaliste d'Olivier Besancenot est lancé"" (http://www.lepoint.fr/actualites-politique/le-nouveau-parti-anticapitaliste-d-olivier-besancenot-est-lance/917/0/256540). Agence France-Presse. June 29, 2008. .

[86] *Many Venezuelans Uncertain About Chavez' '21st century Socialism'* (http://www.voanews.com/english/2007-07-09-voa37.cfm), Voice of America, Washington 9 July 2007. Accessed 12 July 2007

[87] "Where Are All The Socialists? Here, There and Everywhere" (http://www.commondreams.org/view/2008/12/10-3). *Common Dreams*. December 10, 2008. . Retrieved November 18, 2009.

[88] http://www.rasmussenreports.com/public_content/business/general_business/december_2008/voters_champion_free_market_but_want_more_regulation

[89] Rasmussen Reports http://www.rasmussenreports.com/public_content/politics/general_politics/april_2009/just_53_say_capitalism_better_than_socialism , accessed 23/10/09

[90] *Why Socialism?* (http://www.monthlyreview.org/598einstein.php) by Albert Einstein, *Monthly Review*, May 1949

[91] John Barkley Rosser and Marina V. Rosser, *Comparative Economics in a Transforming World Economy* (Cambridge, MA.: MIT Press, 2004).

[92] Beckett, Francis, *Clem Attlee*, (2007) Politico's.

[93] Socialist Party of Great Britain (1985) (PDF). *The Strike Weapon: Lessons of the Miners' Strike* (http://www.worldsocialism.org/spgb/pdf/ms.pdf). London: Socialist Party of Great Britain. . Retrieved 2007-04-28.

[94] Hardcastle, Edgar (1947). "The Nationalisation of the Railways" (http://www.marxists.org/archive/hardcastle/1947/02/railways.htm). *Socialist Standard* (Socialist Party of Great Britain) **43** (1). . Retrieved 2007-04-28.

[95] http://english.people.com.cn/200507/13/eng20050713_195876.html

[96] http://www.oecd.org/dataoecd/16/3/36174313.pdf

[97] The Role of Planning in China's Market Economy (http://www.adb.org/Documents/Events/2004/PRC_Planning_System_Reform/chow1.pdf)

[98] http://www.forbes.com/2008/07/08/china-enterprises-state-lead-cx_jrw_0708mckinsey.html

[99] http://us.ft.com/ftgateway/superpage.ft?news_id=fto031620081407384075

[100] http://ufirc.ou.edu/publications/Enterprises%20of%20China.pdf

[101] http://news.bbc.co.uk/2/hi/business/8153138.stm

[102] http://www.vietnamembassy-usa.org/news/story.php?d=20031117235404

[103] *Market Economy and Socialist Road* Duan Zhongqiao (http://docs.google.com/gview?a=v&q=cache:Wl8XGM_vQAJ:www.nodo50.org/cubasigloXXI/congreso06/conf3_zhonquiao.pdf+Socialist+planned+commodity+economy&hl=en&gl=us)

[104] Vanek, Jaroslav, *The Participatory Economy* (Ithaca, NY.: Cornell University Press, 1971).

[105] Michael Albert and Robin Hahnel, *The Political Economy of Participatory Economics* (Princeton, NJ.: Princeton University Press, 1991).

[106] Karl Marx, Preface to A Contribution to the Critique of Political Economy, 1859

[107] "At the Afro-Asian Conference in Algeria" (http://www.marxists.org/archive/guevara/1965/02/24.htm) speech by Che Guevara to the Second Economic Seminar of Afro-Asian Solidarity in Algiers, Algeria on February 24, 1965

[108] Marx and Engels, Communist Manifesto

[109] Schaff, Adam, 'Marxist Theory on Revolution and Violence', p. 263. in Journal of the history of ideas, Vol 34, no.2 (Apr-Jun 1973)

[110] *Writings 1932-33, P.96*, Leon Trotsky.

[111] http://catalog.loc.gov/cgi-bin/Pwebrecon.cgi?Search_Arg=HQ504+.E6&Search_Code=CALL_&CNT=5

[112] http://lccn.loc.gov/64011312

[113] http://www.selvesandothers.org/view804.html

[114] http://www.haymarketbooks.org/Merchant2/merchant.mv?Screen=PROD&Store_Code=Haymarket&Product_Code=MSACM

[115] http://lccn.loc.gov/76154260

[116] http://www.jesushuertadesoto.com/pdf_socialismo/indice.pdf

[117] http://www.gavinkitching.com/marx_0.htm

[118] http://lccn.loc.gov/38012882

[119] http://www.monthlyreview.org/builditnow.htm

[120] http://www.monthlyreview.org

[121] http://www.mises.org/books/socialism/contents.aspx

[122] http://www.pbs.org/heavenonearth/resources.html

[123] http://www.polis.cam.ac.uk/contacts/staff/eperreausaussine/what_is_left_of_socialism.pdf

[124] http://www.westviewpress.com/about.html

[125] http://www.newgnosis.co.uk/deep.html

[126] http://lccn.loc.gov/40034338

[127] http://www.marxists.org/archive/marx/works/1880/soc-utop/index.htm

[128] http://www.monthlyreview.org/598einst.htm

[129] http://libcom.org/library/soul-of-man-under-socialism-oscar-wilde

[130] http://www.marxists.org/reference/archive/shaw/works/guide2.htm

[131] http://www.socialism.com/

[132] http://www.socialism.org.uk/

[133] http://www.spartacus.schoolnet.co.uk/socialism.htm

[134] http://www.fordham.edu/halsall/mod/modsbook33.html

[135] http://www.whatnextjournal.co.uk/Pages/History/Articles.html

[136] http://www.anu.edu.au/polsci/marx/contemp/pamsetc/twosouls/twosouls.htm

[137] http://www.monthlyreview.org/0705magdoffs2.htm

[138] http://www.pbs.org/heavenonearth/

[139] http://www.ecn.wfu.edu/~cottrell/socialism_book/new_socialism.pdf

[140] http://21stcenturysocialism.com/

[141] http://www.sussex.ac.uk/Users/ssfa2/newideas.pdf

[142] http://www.wsws.org/about.shtml

[143] http://www.marxists.org

[144] http://www.marxist.net

[145] http://www.marxist.com

[146] http://www.marxist.com/rircontents-5.htm

[147] http://www.marxist.net/sciphil/reasoninrevolt/index.html

[148] http://monthlyreview.org/091109magdoff-yates.php

Anarchist

Anarchism is a political philosophy which considers the state undesirable, unnecessary and harmful, and which promotes instead a stateless society, or anarchy.[1] [2] It seeks, more broadly, to diminish or even abolish the authority principle in the conduct of human relations.[3] Individual anarchists may have additional criteria for what they conceive to be anarchism, over which there can be wide disagreement. *The Oxford Companion to Philosophy* says, "there is no single defining position that all anarchists hold, and those considered anarchists at best share a certain family resemblance."[4]

There are many types and traditions of anarchism, not all of which are mutually exclusive.[5] Strains of anarchism have been divided into the categories of social and individualist anarchism or similar dual classifications.[6] [7] Anarchism is often considered to be a radical left-wing ideology,[8] [9] and much of anarchist economics and anarchist legal philosophy reflect anti-statist interpretations of communism, collectivism, syndicalism or participatory economics; however, anarchism has always included an individualist strain,[10] with that strain supporting a market economy and private property, or unrestrained egoism that bases right on might.[8] [11]

Others, such as panarchists and anarchists without adjectives, neither advocate nor object to any particular form of organization as long as it is not compulsory. Some anarchist schools of thought differ fundamentally, supporting anything from extreme individualism to complete collectivism.[2] The central tendency of anarchism as a social movement have been represented by communist anarchism, with individualist anarchism being primarily a philosophical or literary phenomenon.[12] Some anarchists fundamentally oppose all forms of aggression, supporting self-defense or non-violence, while others have supported the use of some coercive measures, including violent revolution and terrorism, on the path to an anarchist society.[13]

Etymology and terminology

The term *anarchism* derives from the Greek ἄναρχος, *anarchos*, meaning "without rulers",[14] [15] from the prefix ἀν- (*an-*, "without") + ἀρχή (*archê*, "sovereignty, realm, magistracy")[16] + -ισμός (*-ismos*, from the suffix -ιζειν, *-izein* "-izing"). There is some ambiguity with the use of the terms "libertarianism" and "libertarian" in writings about anarchism. Since the 1890s from France,[17] the term "libertarianism" has often been used as a synonym for anarchism and was used almost exclusively in this sense until the 1950s in the United States;[18] its use as a synonym is still common outside the United States.[19] Accordingly, "libertarian socialism" is sometimes used as a synonym for socialist anarchism,[20] [21] to distinguish it from "individualist libertarianism" (individualist anarchism). On the other hand, some use "libertarianism" to refer to individualistic free-market philosophy only, referring to free-market anarchism as "libertarian anarchism."[22] [23]

Origins

Some claim anarchist themes can be found in the works of Taoist sages Laozi[24] and Zhuangzi. The latter has been translated, *"There has been such a thing as letting mankind alone; there has never been such a thing as governing mankind [with success],"* and *"A petty thief is put in jail. A great brigand becomes a ruler of a Nation."*[25] Diogenes of Sinope and the Cynics, and their contemporary Zeno of Citium, the founder of Stoicism, also introduced similar topics.[24] [26]

William Godwin, "the first to formulate the political and economical conceptions of anarchism, even though he did not give that name to the ideas developed in his work",[24]

Modern anarchism, however, sprang from the secular or religious thought of the Enlightenment, particularly Jean-Jacques Rousseau's arguments for the moral centrality of freedom.[27] Although by the turn of the 19th century the term "anarchist" had lost its initial negative connotation,[28] it first entered the English language in 1642 during the English Civil War as a term of abuse used by Royalists to damn those who were fomenting disorder.[28] By the time of the French Revolution some, such as the *Enragés*, began to use the term positively,[29] in opposition to Jacobin centralisation of power, seeing "revolutionary government" as oxymoronic.[28]

From this climate William Godwin developed what many consider the first expression of modern anarchist thought.[30] Godwin was, according to Peter Kropotkin, "the first to formulate the political and economical conceptions of anarchism, even though he did not give that name to the ideas developed in his work",[24] while Godwin attached his anarchist ideas to an early Edmund Burke.[31] Benjamin Tucker instead credits Josiah Warren, an American who promoted stateless and voluntary communities where all goods and services were private, with being "the first man to expound and formulate the doctrine now known as Anarchism."[32] The first to describe himself as an anarchist was Pierre-Joseph Proudhon,[28] a French philosopher and politician, which led some to call him the founder of modern anarchist theory.[33]

Social movement

Anarchism as a social movement has regularly endured fluctuations in popularity. Its classical period, which scholars demarcate as from 1860 to 1939, is associated with the working-class movements of the nineteenth century and the Spanish Civil War-era struggles against fascism.[34] Anarchists were heavily involved in the abolition of slavery, and continue to be active in the labour movement, civil rights, women's liberation, both anti-capitalism and pro-capitalism[11] (with varying definitions of capitalism), the anti-war movement, LGBT rights, both anti-globalization and pro-globalization (with varying definitions of globalization), tax resistance, and other areas.

The First International

In Europe, harsh reaction followed the revolutions of 1848, during which ten countries had experienced brief or long-term social upheaval as groups carried out nationalist uprisings. After most of these attempts at systematic change ended in failure, conservative elements took advantage of the divided groups of socialists, anarchists, liberals, and nationalists, to prevent further revolt.[35] In 1864 the International Workingmen's Association (sometimes called the "First International") united diverse revolutionary currents including French followers of Proudhon,[36] Blanquists, Philadelphes, English trade unionists, socialists and social democrats.

Due to its links to active workers' movements, the International became a significant organization. Karl Marx became a leading figure in the International and a member of its General Council. Proudhon's followers, the mutualists, opposed Marx's state socialism, advocating political abstentionism and small property holdings.[37] [38]

In 1868, following their unsuccessful participation in the League of Peace and Freedom (LPF), Russian revolutionary Mikhail Bakunin and his collectivist anarchist associates and joined the First International (which had decided not to get involved with the LPF).[39] They allied themselves with the federalist socialist sections of the International,[40] who advocated the revolutionary overthrow of the state and the collectivization of property.

Collectivist anarchist Mikhail Bakunin opposed the Marxist aim of dictatorship of the proletariat in favour of universal rebellion, and allied himself with the federalists in the First International before his expulsion by the Marxists.[28]

At first, the collectivists worked with the Marxists to push the First International in a more revolutionary socialist direction. Subsequently, the International became polarised into two camps, with Marx and Bakunin as their respective figureheads.[41] Bakunin characterised Marx's ideas as centralist and predicted that, if a Marxist party came to power, its leaders would simply take the place of the ruling class they had fought against.[42] [43]

In 1872, the conflict climaxed with a final split between the two groups at the Hague Congress, where Bakunin and James Guillaume were expelled from the International and its headquarters were transferred to New York. In response, the federalist sections formed their own International at the St. Imier Congress, adopting a revolutionary anarchist program.[44]

Organised labour

The anti-authoritarian sections of the First International were the precursors of the anarcho-syndicalists, seeking to "replace the privilege and authority of the State" with the "free and spontaneous organization of labor."[45] In 1886, the Federation of Organized Trades and Labor Unions (FOTLU) of the United States and Canada unanimously set 1 May 1886, as the date by which the eight-hour work day would become standard.[46]

In response, unions across America prepared a general strike in support of the event.[46] On 3 May, in Chicago, a fight broke out when strikebreakers attempted to cross the picket line, and two workers died when police opened fire upon the crowd.[47] The next day, 4 May, anarchists staged a rally at Chicago's Haymarket Square.[48] A bomb was thrown by an unknown party near the conclusion of the rally, killing an officer.[49] In the ensuing panic, police opened fire on the crowd and each other.[50] Seven police officers and at least four workers were killed.[51] Eight anarchists directly and indirectly related to the organisers of the rally were arrested and charged with the murder of the deceased officer. The men became international political celebrities among the labour movement. Four of the men were executed and a fifth committed suicide prior to his own execution. The incident became known as the

Haymarket affair, and was a setback for the labour movement and the struggle for the eight hour day. In 1890 a second attempt, this time international in scope, to organise for the eight hour day was made. The event also had the secondary purpose of memorializing workers killed as a result of the Haymarket affair.[52] Although it had initially been conceived as a once-off event, by the following year the celebration of International Workers' Day on May Day had become firmly established as an international worker's holiday.[46]

Propaganda poster by the spanish anarcho-syndicalist trade union Confederación Nacional del Trabajo

In 1907, the International Anarchist Congress of Amsterdam gathered delegates from 14 different countries, among which important figures of the anarchist movement, including Errico Malatesta, Pierre Monatte, Luigi Fabbri, Benoît Broutchoux, Emma Goldman, Rudolf Rocker, and Christiaan Cornelissen. Various themes were treated during the Congress, in particular concerning the organisation of the anarchist movement, popular education issues, the general strike or antimilitarism. A central debate concerned the relation between anarchism and syndicalism (or trade unionism). Malatesta and Monatte were in particular disagreement themselves on this issue, as the latter thought that syndicalism was revolutionary and would create the conditions of a social revolution, while Malatesta did not consider syndicalism by itself sufficient.[53] He thought that the trade-union movement was reformist and even conservative, citing as essentially bourgeois and anti-worker the phenomenon of professional union officials. Malatesta warned that the syndicalists aims were in perpetuating syndicalism itself, whereas anarchists must always have anarchy as their end and consequently refrain from committing to any particular method of achieving it.[54]

The Spanish Workers Federation in 1881 was the first major anarcho-syndicalist movement; anarchist trade union federations were of special importance in Spain. The most successful was the Confederación Nacional del Trabajo (National Confederation of Labour: CNT), founded in 1910. Before the 1940s, the CNT was the major force in Spanish working class politics, attracting 1.58 million members at one point and playing a major role in the Spanish Civil War.[55] The CNT was affiliated with the International Workers Association, a federation of anarcho-syndicalist trade unions founded in 1922, with delegates representing two million workers from 15 countries in Europe and Latin America. The largest organised anarchist movement today is in Spain, in the form of the Confederación General del Trabajo (CGT) and the CNT. CGT membership was estimated to be around 100,000 for the year 2003.[56] Other active syndicalist movements include the US Workers Solidarity Alliance and the UK Solidarity Federation. The revolutionary industrial unionist Industrial Workers of the World, claiming 2,000 paying members, and the International Workers Association, an anarcho-syndicalist successor to the First International, also remain active.

Russian Revolution

Anarchists participated alongside the Bolsheviks in both February and October revolutions, and were initially enthusiastic about the Bolshevik coup.[57] However, the Bolsheviks soon turned against the anarchists and other left-wing opposition, a conflict that culminated in the 1921 Kronstadt rebellion which the new government repressed. Anarchists in central Russia were either imprisoned, driven underground or joined the victorious Bolsheviks; the anarchists from Petrograd and Moscow fled to the Ukraine.[58] There, in the Free Territory, they fought in the civil war against the Whites (a Western-backed grouping of monarchists and other opponents of the October Revolution) and then the Bolsheviks as part of the Revolutionary Insurrectionary Army of Ukraine led by Nestor Makhno, who established an anarchist society in the region for a number of months.

Anarchists Emma Goldman and Alexander Berkman opposed Bolshevik consolidation of power following the Russian Revolution (1917).

Expelled American anarchists Emma Goldman and Alexander Berkman were amongst those agitating in response to Bolshevik policy and the suppression of the Kronstadt uprising, before they left Russia. Both wrote accounts of their experiences in Russia, criticizing the amount of control the Bolsheviks exercised. For them, Bakunin's predictions about the consequences of Marxist rule that the rulers of the new "socialist" Marxist state would become a new elite had proved all too true.[42] [59]

The victory of the Bolsheviks in the October Revolution and the resulting Russian Civil War did serious damage to anarchist movements internationally. Many workers and activists saw Bolshevik success as setting an example; Communist parties grew at the expense of anarchism and other socialist movements. In France and the United States, for example, members of the major syndicalist movements of the CGT and IWW left the organizations and joined the Communist International.[60]

In Paris, the Dielo Truda group of Russian anarchist exiles, which included Nestor Makhno, concluded that anarchists needed to develop new forms of organisation in response to the structures of Bolshevism. Their 1926 manifesto, called the *Organizational Platform of the General Union of Anarchists (Draft)*,[61] was supported. Platformist groups active today include the Workers Solidarity Movement in Ireland and the North Eastern Federation of Anarchist Communists of North America.

Anti-fascist Maquis, who resisted Nazi and Francoist rule in Europe.

Fight against fascism

In the 1920s and 1930s, the rise of fascism in Europe transformed anarchism's conflict with the state. Italy saw the first struggles between anarchists and fascists. Italian anarchists played a key role in the anti-fascist organisation *Arditi del Popolo*, which was strongest in areas with anarchist traditions, and achieved some success in their activism, such as repelling Blackshirts in the anarchist stronghold of Parma in August 1922.[62] In France, where the far right leagues came close to insurrection in the February 1934 riots, anarchists divided over a united front policy.[63]

In Spain, the CNT initially refused to join a popular front electoral alliance, and abstention by CNT supporters led to a right wing election victory. But in 1936, the CNT changed its policy and anarchist votes helped bring the popular front back to power. Months later, the former ruling class responded with an attempted coup causing the Spanish Civil War (1936–1939).[64] In response to the army rebellion, an anarchist-inspired movement of peasants and workers, supported by armed militias, took control of Barcelona and of large areas of rural Spain where they collectivised the land.[65] But even before the fascist victory in 1939, the anarchists were losing ground in a bitter struggle with the Stalinists, who controlled the distribution of military aid to the Republican cause from the Soviet Union. Stalinist-led troops suppressed the collectives and persecuted both dissident Marxists and anarchists.[66]

Contemporary anarchism

A surge of popular interest in anarchism occurred during the 1960s and 1970s.[67] In the United Kingdom this was associated with the punk rock movement, as exemplified by bands such as Crass and the Sex Pistols.[68] The housing and employment crisis in most of Western Europe led to the formation of communes and squatter movements like that of Barcelona, Spain. In Denmark, squatters occupied a disused military base and declared the Freetown Christiania, an autonomous haven in central Copenhagen.

The famous *okupas* squat near Parc Güell, overlooking Barcelona. Squatting was a prominent part of the emergence of renewed anarchist movement from the counterculture of the 1960s and 1970s.

Since the revival of anarchism in the mid 20th century,[69] a number of new movements and schools of thought emerged. Although feminist tendencies have always been a part of the anarchist movement in the form of anarcha-feminism, they returned with vigour during the second wave of feminism in the 1960s. The American Civil Rights Movement and the movement against the war in Vietnam also contributed to the revival of North American anarchism. European anarchism of the late 20th century drew much of its strength from the labour movement, and both have incorporated animal rights activism. Anarchist anthropologist David Graeber has posited a rupture between generations of anarchism, with those "who often still have not shaken the sectarian habits" of the nineteenth century contrasted with the younger activists who are "much more informed, among other elements, by indigenous, feminist, ecological and cultural-critical ideas", and who by the turn of the 21st century formed "by far the majority" of anarchists.[70]

Around the turn of the 21st century, anarchism grew in popularity and influence as part of the anti-war, anti-capitalist, and anti-globalisation movements.[71] Anarchists became known for their involvement in protests against the meetings of the World Trade Organization (WTO), Group of Eight, and the World Economic Forum. Some anarchist factions at these protests engaged in rioting, property destruction, and violent confrontations with police, and the confrontations were selectively portrayed in mainstream media coverage as violent riots. These actions were precipitated by ad hoc, leaderless, anonymous cadres known as *black blocs*; other organisational tactics pioneered in this time include security culture, affinity groups and the use of decentralised technologies such as the internet.[71] A landmark struggle of this period was the confrontations at WTO conference in Seattle in 1999.[71]

Anarchist schools of thought

Anarchist ideas have only occasionally inspired political movements of any size, and "the tradition is mainly one of individual thinkers, but they have produced an important body of theory."[72] Anarchist schools of thought had been generally grouped in two main historical traditions, individualist anarchism and social anarchism, which have some different origins, values and evolution.[2] [6] [73] The individualist wing of anarchism emphasises negative liberty, i.e. opposition to state or social control over the individual, while those in the social wing emphasise positive liberty to achieve one's potential and argue that humans have needs that society ought to fulfill, "recognizing equality of entitlement".[74] In chronological and theoretical sense there are classical — those created throughout the 19th century — and post-classical anarchist schools — those created since the mid-20th century and after.

Portrait of philosopher Pierre-Joseph Proudhon (1809–1865) by Gustave Courbet. Proudhon was the primary proponent of anarchist mutualism, and influenced many later individualist anarchist thinkers.

Beyond the specific factions of anarchist thought is philosophical anarchism, which embodies the theoretical stance that the State lacks moral legitimacy without accepting the imperative of revolution to eliminate it. A component especially of individualist anarchism[75] [76] philosophical anarchism may accept the existence of a minimal state as unfortunate, and usually temporary, "necessary evil" but argue that citizens do not have a moral obligation to obey the state when its laws conflict with individual autonomy.[77] One reaction against sectarianism within the anarchist milieu was "anarchism without adjectives", a call for toleration first adopted by Fernando Tarrida del Mármol in 1889 in response to the "bitter debates" of anarchist theory at the time.[78] In abandoning the hyphenated anarchisms (i.e. collectivist-, communist-, mutualist- and individualist-anarchism), it sought to emphasise the anti-authoritarian beliefs common to all anarchist schools of thought.[79]

Mutualism

Mutualism began in 18th century English and French labour movements before taking an anarchist form associated with Pierre-Joseph Proudhon in France and others in the United States.[80] Proudhon proposed spontaneous order, whereby organization emerges without central authority, a "positive anarchy" where order arises when everybody does "what he wishes and only what he wishes"[81] and where "business transactions alone produce the social order."[82] Mutualist anarchism is concerned with reciprocity, free association, voluntary contract, federation, and credit and currency reform. According to William Batchelder Greene, each worker in the mutualist system would receive "just and exact pay for his work; services equivalent in cost being exchangeable for services equivalent in cost, without profit or discount."[83] Mutualism has been retrospectively characterised as ideologically situated between individualist and collectivist forms of anarchism.[84] Proudhon first characterised his goal as a "third form of society, the synthesis of communism and property."[85]

Individualist anarchism

Individualist anarchism refers to several traditions of thought within the anarchist movement that emphasise the individual and their will over any kinds of external determinants such as groups, society, traditions, and ideological systems.[86] [87] Individualist anarchism is not a single philosophy but refers to a group of individualistic philosophies that sometimes are in conflict.

In 1793, William Godwin, who has often[88] been cited as the first anarchist, wrote *Political Justice*, which some consider to be the first expression of anarchism.[30] [89] Godwin, a philosophical anarchist, from a rationalist and utilitarian basis opposed revolutionary action and saw a minimal state as a present "necessary evil" that would become increasingly irrelevant and powerless by the gradual spread of knowledge.[30] [90] Godwin advocated extreme individualism, proposing that all cooperation in labour be eliminated on the premise that this would be most conducive with the general good.[91] [92] Godwin was a utilitarian who believed that all individuals are not of equal value, with some of us "of more worth and importance" than others depending on our utility in bringing about social good. Therefore he does not believe in equal rights, but the person's life that should be favoured that is most conducive to the general good.[92] Godwin opposed government because he saw it as infringing on the individual's right to "private judgement" to determine which actions most maximise utility, but also makes a critique of all authority over

19th century philosopher Max Stirner, usually considered a prominent early individualist anarchist (sketch by Friedrich Engels).

the individual's judgement. This aspect of Godwin's philosophy, stripped of utilitarian motivations, was developed into a more extreme form later by Stirner.[93]

The most extreme form of individualist anarchism, called "egoism,"[94] or egoist anarchism, was expounded by one of the earliest and best-known proponents of individualist anarchism, Max Stirner.[95] Stirner's *The Ego and Its Own*, published in 1844, is a founding text of the philosophy.[95] According to Stirner, the only limitation on the rights of the individual is their power to obtain what they desire,[96] without regard for God, state, or morality.[97] To Stirner, rights were *spooks* in the mind, and he held that society does not exist but "the individuals are its reality".[98] Stirner advocated self-assertion and foresaw Unions of Egoists, non-systematic associations continually renewed by all parties' support through an act of will[99] , which Stirner proposed as a form of organization in place of the state.[100] Egoist anarchists claim that egoism will foster genuine and spontaneous union between individuals.[101] "Egoism" has inspired many interpretations of Stirner's philosophy. It was re-discovered and promoted by German philosophical anarchist and LGBT activist John Henry Mackay. Individualist anarchism inspired by Stirner attracted a small following of European bohemian artists and intellectuals (see European individualist anarchism). Stirner's philosophy has been seen as a precedent of existentialism with other thinkers like Friedrich Nietzsche and Sören Kierkegaard.

Social anarchism

Russian theorist Peter Kropotkin (1842–1921), who was influential in the development of anarchist communism.

Social anarchism calls for a system with public ownership of means of production and democratic control of all organizations, without any government authority or coercion. It is the largest school of anarchism[102]. Social anarchism rejects private property, seeing it as a source of social inequality, and emphasises cooperation and mutual aid.[103]

Collectivist anarchism, also referred to as "revolutionary socialism" or a form of such,[104] [105] is a revolutionary form of anarchism, commonly associated with Mikhail Bakunin and Johann Most.[106] [107] Collectivist anarchists oppose all private ownership of the means of production, instead advocating that ownership be collectivised. This was to be achieved through violent revolution, first starting with a small cohesive group through acts of violence, or "propaganda by the deed," which would inspire the workers as a whole to revolt and forcibly collectivise the means of production.[106] However, collectivization was not to be extended to the distribution of income, as workers would be paid according to time worked, rather than receiving goods being distributed "according to need" as in anarcho-communism.

This position was criticised by anarchist communists as effectively "uphold[ing] the wages system".[108] Collectivist anarchism arose contemporaneously with Marxism but opposed the Marxist dictatorship of the proletariat, despite the stated Marxist goal of a collectivist stateless society.[109] Anarchist communist and collectivist ideas are not mutually exclusive; although the collectivist anarchists advocated compensation for labour, some held out the possibility of a post-revolutionary transition to a communist system of distribution according to need.[110]

Anarchist communism proposes that the freest form of social organisation would be a society composed of self-managing communes with collective use of the means of production, organised democratically, and related to other communes through federation.[111] While some anarchist communists favour direct democracy, others feel that its majoritarianism can impede individual liberty and favour consensus democracy instead. In anarchist communism, as money would be abolished, individuals would not receive direct compensation for labour (through sharing of profits or payment) but would have free access to the resources and surplus of the commune.[112] [113] Anarchist communism does not always have a communitarian philosophy. Some forms of anarchist communism are egoist and strongly influenced by radical individualism,[114] believing that anarchist communism does not require a communitarian nature at all.

In the early 20th century, anarcho-syndicalism arose as a distinct school of thought within anarchism.[115] With greater focus on the labour movement than previous forms of anarchism, syndicalism posits radical trade unions as a potential force for revolutionary social change, replacing capitalism and the state with a new society, democratically self-managed by the workers. It is often combined with other branches of anarchism, and anarcho-syndicalists often subscribe to anarchist communist or collectivist anarchist economic systems.[116] An early leading anarcho-syndicalist thinker was Rudolf Rocker, whose 1938 pamphlet *Anarchosyndicalism* outlined a view of the movement's origin, aims and importance to the future of labour.[116] [117]

Post-classical currents

Anarchism continues to generate many philosophies and movements, at times eclectic, drawing upon various sources, and syncretic, combining disparate and contrary concepts to create new philosophical approaches. Since the revival of anarchism in the United States in the 1960s,[69] a number of new movements and schools have emerged.[118] Anarcho-capitalism developed from radical anti-state libertarianism and individualist anarchism, drawing from Austrian School economics, study of law and economics and public choice theory,[119] while the burgeoning feminist and environmentalist movements also produced anarchist offshoots. Anarcha-feminism developed as a synthesis of radical feminism and anarchism that views patriarchy (male domination over women) as a fundamental manifestation of compulsory government. It was inspired by the late 19th century writings of early feminist anarchists such as Lucy Parsons, Emma Goldman, Voltairine de Cleyre, and Dora Marsden. Anarcha-feminists, like other radical feminists, criticise and advocate the abolition of traditional conceptions of family, education and gender roles. Green anarchism (or eco-anarchism)[120] is a school of thought within anarchism which puts an emphasis on environmental issues,[121] and

John Zerzan (1943) prominent green anarchist author, he is known for exploring anti-civilization perspectives within anarchism

whose main contemporary currents are anarcho-primitivism and social ecology. Post-left anarchy is a tendency which seeks to distance itself from traditional left-wing politics and to escape the confines of ideology in general. Post-anarchism is a theoretical move towards a synthesis of classical anarchist theory and poststructuralist thought drawing from diverse ideas including post-modernism, autonomist marxism, post-left anarchy, situationism and postcolonialism. Another recent form of anarchism critical of formal anarchist movements is insurrectionary anarchism, which advocates informal organization and active resistance to the state; its proponents include Wolfi Landstreicher and Alfredo M. Bonanno.

Topics of interest in anarchist theory

Intersecting and overlapping between various schools of thought, certain topics of interest and internal disputes have proven perennial within anarchist theory.

Free love

An important current within anarchism is Free love.[122] Free love advocates sometimes traced their roots back to Josiah Warren and to experimental communities, viewed sexual freedom as a clear, direct expression of an individual's self-ownership. Free love particularly stressed women's rights since most sexual laws discriminated against women: for example, marriage laws and anti-birth control measures.[122] The most important American free love journal was *Lucifer the Lightbearer* (1883–1907) edited by Moses Harman and Lois Waisbrooker,[123] but also there existed Ezra Heywood and Angela Heywood's *The Word* (1872–1890, 1892–1893).[122] Also M. E. Lazarus was an important American individualist anarchist who promoted free love.[122]

French individualist Emile Armand (1872–1962), who propounded the virtues of free love in the Parisian anarchist milieu of the early 20th century

In New York's Greenwich Village, bohemian feminists and socialists advocated self-realisation and pleasure for women (and also men) in the here and now. They encouraged playing with sexual roles and sexuality,[124] and the openly bisexual radical Edna St. Vincent Millay and the lesbian anarchist Margaret Anderson were prominent among them. Discussion groups organised by the Villagers were frequented by Emma Goldman, among others. Magnus Hirschfeld noted in 1923 that Goldman "has campaigned boldly and steadfastly for individual rights, and especially for those deprived of their rights. Thus it came about that she was the first and only woman, indeed the first and only American, to take up the defense of homosexual love before the general public."[125] In fact, before Goldman, heterosexual anarchist Robert Reitzel (1849–98) spoke positively of homosexuality from the beginning of the 1890s in his Detroit-based German language journal *Der arme Teufel*.

In Europe the main propagandist of free love within individualist anarchism was Emile Armand.[126] He proposed the concept of *la camaraderie amoureuse* to speak of free love as the possibility of voluntary sexual encounter between consenting adults. He was also a consistent proponent of polyamory.[126] In Germany the stirnerists Adolf Brand and John Henry Mackay were pioneering campaigners for the acceptance of male bisexuality and homosexuality.

More recently, the British anarcho-pacifist Alex Comfort gained notoriety during the sexual revolution for writing the bestseller sex manual *The Joy of Sex*. The issue of free love has a dedicated treatment in the work of french anarcho-hedonist philosopher Michel Onfray in such works as *Théorie du corps amoureux : pour une érotique solaire* (2000) and *L'invention du plaisir : fragments cyréaniques* (2002).

Libertarian education

Francesc Ferrer i Guàrdia, Catalan
anarchist pedagogue

In 1901, Spanish anarchist and free-thinker Francesc Ferrer i Guàrdia established "modern" or progressive schools in Barcelona in defiance of an educational system controlled by the Catholic Church.[127] The schools' stated goal was to "educate the working class in a rational, secular and non-coercive setting". Fiercely anti-clerical, Ferrer believed in "freedom in education", education free from the authority of church and state.[128] Murray Bookchin wrote: "This period [1890s] was the heyday of libertarian schools and pedagogical projects in all areas of the country where Anarchists exercised some degree of influence. Perhaps the best-known effort in this field was Francisco Ferrer's Modern School (Escuela Moderna), a project which exercised a considerable influence on Catalan education and on experimental techniques of teaching generally." [129] La Escuela Moderna, and Ferrer's ideas generally, formed the inspiration for a series of *Modern Schools* in the United States[127], Cuba, South America and London. The first of these was started in New York City in 1911. It also inspired the Italian newspaper *Università popolare*, founded in 1901.

Another libertarian tradition is that of unschooling and the free school in which child-led activity replaces pedagogic approaches. Experiments in Germany led to A. S. Neill founding what became Summerhill School in 1921.[130] Summerhill is often cited as an example of anarchism in practice.[131] However, although Summerhill and other free schools are radically libertarian, they differ in principle from those of Ferrer by not advocating an overtly-political class struggle-approach.[132]

Internal issues and debates

Anarchism is a philosophy which embodies many diverse attitudes, tendencies and schools of thought; as such, disagreement over questions of values, ideology and tactics is common. The compatibility of capitalism,[4] nationalism and religion with anarchism is widely disputed. Similarly, anarchism enjoys complex relationships with ideologies such as Marxism, communism and capitalism. Anarchists may be motivated by humanism, divine authority, enlightened self-interest or any number of alternative ethical doctrines.

The usage of violence is a subject of much
dispute in anarchism.

Phenomena such as civilization, technology (e.g. within anarcho-primitivism and insurrectionary anarchism), and the democratic process may be sharply criticised within some anarchist tendencies and simultaneously lauded in others. Anarchist attitudes towards race, gender and the environment have changed significantly since the modern origin of the philosophy in the 18th century.

On a tactical level, while propaganda of the deed was a tactic used by anarchists in the 19th century (e.g. the Nihilist movement), contemporary anarchists espouse alternative direct action methods such as nonviolence, counter-economics and anti-state cryptography to bring about an anarchist society. About the scope of an anarchist society, some anarchists advocate a global one, while others do so by local ones.[133] The diversity in anarchism has led to widely different use of identical terms among different anarchist traditions, which has led to many definitional concerns in anarchist theory.

Related pages

- Anarchist symbolism
- Lists of anarchism topics
- List of anarchist communities
- List of anarchist movements by region

Further reading

- *Anarchism: A Documentary History of Libertarian Ideas.* Robert Graham, editor.
  - *Volume One: From Anarchy to Anarchism (300CE to 1939)* Black Rose Books, Montréal and London 2005. ISBN 1551642506.
  - *Volume Two: The Anarchist Current (1939–2006)* Black Rose Books, Montréal 2007. ISBN 9781551643113.
- *Anarchism*, George Woodcock (Penguin Books, 1962). OCLC 221147531 [134].
- *Anarchy: A Graphic Guide*, Clifford Harper (Camden Press, 1987): An overview, updating Woodcock's classic, and illustrated throughout by Harper's woodcut-style artwork.
- *The Anarchist Reader*, George Woodcock (ed.) (Fontana/Collins 1977; ISBN 0006340113): An anthology of writings from anarchist thinkers and activists including Proudhon, Kropotkin, Bakunin, Malatesta, Bookchin, Goldman, and many others.
- *Anarchy and the Law: The Political Economy of Choice*, Edward Stringham (Transaction Publishers, 2007; ISBN 1412805791): An overview of the major arguments and historical studies about private property anarchism.
- Schmidt, Michael & van der Walt, Lucien. *Black Flame: The Revolutionary Class Politics of Anarchism and Syndicalism, CounterPower Vol. I.* AK Press. 2009

External links

- "An Anarchist FAQ Webpage" [135] – An Anarchist FAQ
- Anarchist Theory FAQ [136] – by Bryan Caplan
- Infoshop.org [137] – Infoshop.org; anarchist news, information, and online library
- Daily Bleed's Anarchist Encyclopedia [138] – 700+ entries, with short biographies, links and dedicated pages
- Anarchy Archives [139] – information relating to famous anarchists including their writings (see Anarchy Archives).
- KateSharpleyLibrary.net [140] – website of the Kate Sharpley Library, containing many historical documents pertaining to anarchism
- They Lie We Die [141] – anarchist virtual library containing 768 books, booklets and texts
- Anarchy: Libertarian Studies [142] – Mises Institute; online collection of classical books and works about libertarian anarchism.
- About Market Anarchism [143] – Molinari Institute; online booklets and texts about market anarchism.

References

[1] Malatesta, Errico. "Towards Anarchism" (http://www.marxists.org/archive/malatesta/1930s/xx/toanarchy.htm). *MAN!* (Los Angeles: International Group of San Francisco). OCLC 3930443 (http://worldcat.org/oclc/3930443). . Agrell, Siri (2007-05-14). "Working for The Man" (http://www.theglobeandmail.com/servlet/story/RTGAM.20070514.wxlanarchist14/BNStory/lifeWork/home/). *The Globe and Mail.* . Retrieved 2008-04-14. "Anarchism" (http://www.britannica.com/eb/article-9117285). *Encyclopædia Britannica.* Encyclopædia Britannica Premium Service. 2006. . Retrieved 2006-08-29. "Anarchism". *The Shorter Routledge Encyclopedia of Philosophy*: 14. 2005. "Anarchism is the view that a society without the state, or government, is both possible and desirable.". The following sources cite anarchism as a political philosophy: Mclaughlin, Paul (2007). *Anarchism and Authority.* Aldershot: Ashgate. p. 59. ISBN 0754661962. Johnston, R. (2000). *The Dictionary of Human Geography.* Cambridge: Blackwell Publishers. p. 24. ISBN 0631205616.

[2] Slevin, Carl. "Anarchism." *The Concise Oxford Dictionary of Politics.* Ed. Iain McLean and Alistair McMillan. Oxford University Press, 2003.

[3] Ward, Colin (1966). ["Error: no |title= specified when using {{[[Template:Cite web|Cite web (http://www.panarchy.org/ward/
organization.1966.html)]]}}"]. Anarchism as a Theory of Organization. [http://www.panarchy.org/ward/organization.1966.html. Retrieved 1
March 2010.

[4] "Anarchism." *The Oxford Companion to Philosophy*, Oxford University Press, 2007, p. 31.

[5] Sylvan, Richard (1995). "Anarchism". in Goodwin, Robert E. and Pettit. *A Companion to Contemporary Political Philosophy*. Philip.
Blackwell Publishing. p. 231.

[6] Ostergaard, Geoffrey. "Anarchism". *The Blackwell Dictionary of Modern Social Thought*. Blackwell Publishing. p. 14.

[7] Kropotkin, Peter (2002). *Anarchism: A Collection of Revolutionary Writings*. Courier Dover Publications. p. 5.R.B. Fowler (1972). "The
Anarchist Tradition of Political Thought". *Western Political Quarterly* 25 (4): 738–752. doi: 10.2307/446800 (http://dx.doi.org/10.2307/
446800).

[8] Brooks, Frank H. (1994). *The Individualist Anarchists: An Anthology of Liberty (1881–1908)*. Transaction Publishers. p. xi. "Usually
considered to be an extreme left-wing ideology, anarchism has always included a significant strain of radical individualism, from the
hyperrationalism of Godwin, to the egoism of Stirner, to the libertarians and anarcho-capitalists of today"

[9] Joseph Kahn (2000). "Anarchism, the Creed That Won't Stay Dead; The Spread of World Capitalism Resurrects a Long-Dormant
Movement". *The New York Times* (5 August).Colin Moynihan (2007). "Book Fair Unites Anarchists. In Spirit, Anyway". *New York Times* (16
April).

[10] Stringham, Edward (2007). Stringham, Edward. ed. *Anarchy and the Law. The Political Economy of Choice*. (http://www.amazon.com/
dp/1412805791). Transaction Publishers. p. 720.

[11] Tormey, Simon, Anti-Capitalism, A Beginner's Guide, Oneworld Publications, 2004, pp. 118-119.

[12] Skirda, Alexandre. Facing the Enemy: A History of Anarchist Organization from Proudhon to May 1968. AK Press, 2002, p. 191.

[13] Fowler, R.B. "The Anarchist Tradition of Political Thought." *The Western Political Quarterly*, Vol. 25, No. 4. (December, 1972), pp.
743–744.

[14] Anarchy (http://www.merriam-webster.com/dictionary/anarchy). Merriam-Webster online.

[15] Liddell, Henry George, & Scott, Robert, "A Greek-English Lexicon" (http://www.perseus.tufts.edu/cgi-bin/
ptext?doc=Perseus:text:1999.04.0057:entry=#7439).

[16] Liddell, Henry George; Scott, Robert. *A Greek-English Lexicon* (http://www.perseus.tufts.edu/cgi-bin/ptext?doc=Perseus:text:1999.04.
0057:entry=#15894). .

[17] Nettlau, Max (1996). *A Short History of Anarchism*. Freedom Press. p. 162. ISBN 0900384891.

[18] Russell, Dean. *Who is a Libertarian?* (http://www.boogieonline.com/revolution/politics/name.html), Foundation for Economic
Education, "Ideas on Liberty," May, 1955.

• Ward, Colin. Anarchism: A Very Short Introduction. Oxford University Press 2004 p. 62
• Goodway, David. Anarchists Seed Beneath the Snow. Liverpool Press. 2006, p. 4
• MacDonald, Dwight & Wreszin, Michael. Interviews with Dwight Macdonald. University Press of Mississippi, 2003. p. 82
• Bufe, Charles. The Heretic's Handbook of Quotations. See Sharp Press, 1992. p. iv
• Gay, Kathlyn. Encyclopedia of Political Anarchy. ABC-CLIO / University of Michigan, 2006, p. 126
• Woodcock, George. Anarchism: A History of Libertarian Ideas and Movements. Broadview Press, 2004. (Uses the terms interchangeably,
such as on page 10)
• Skirda, Alexandre. Facing the Enemy: A History of Anarchist Organization from Proudhon to May 1968. AK Press 2002. p. 183.
• Fernandez, Frank. Cuban Anarchism. The History of a Movement. See Sharp Press, 2001, page 9.

[20] Perlin, Terry M. (1979). *Contemporary Anarchism*. Transaction Publishers. p. 40.

[21] Noam Chomsky, Carlos Peregrín Otero. Language and Politics. AK Press, 2004, p. 739.

[22] Morris, Christopher. 1992. *An Essay on the Modern State*. Cambridge University Press. p. 61. (Using "libertarian anarchism" synonymously
with "individualist anarchism" when referring to individualist anarchism that supports a market society).

[23] Burton, Daniel C.. *Libertarian anarchism* (http://www.libertarian.co.uk/lapubs/polin/polin168.pdf). Libertarian Alliance.

[24] Peter Kropotkin, "Anarchism" (http://dwardmac.pitzer.edu/Anarchist_Archives/kropotkin/britanniaanarchy.html), *Encyclopædia
Britannica* 1910.

[25] Murray Rothbard. "Concepts of the role of intellectuals in social change toward laissez faire" (http://www.mises.org/journals/jls/9_2/
9_2_3.pdf) (PDF). . Retrieved 2008-12-28.

[26] Cynics (http://www.iep.utm.edu/c/cynics.htm) entry in the *Internet Encyclopedia of Philosophy* by Julie Piering

[27] "Anarchism", *Encarta Online Encyclopedia* 2006 (UK version).

[28] "Anarchism" (http://www.bbc.co.uk/radio4/history/inourtime/inourtime_20061207.shtml), BBC Radio 4 program, In Our Time,
Thursday 7 December 2006. Hosted by Melvyn Bragg of the BBC, with John Keane, Professor of Politics at University of Westminster, Ruth
Kinna, Senior Lecturer in Politics at Loughborough University, and Peter Marshall, philosopher and historian.

[29] Sheehan, Sean. *Anarchism*, London: Reaktion Books Ltd., 2004. p. 85.

[30] " William Godwin (http://plato.stanford.edu/entries/godwin)" article by Mark Philip in the *Stanford Encyclopedia of Philosophy*,
2006-05-20

[31] Godwin himself attributed the first anarchist writing to Edmund Burke's *A Vindication of Natural Society*. "Most of the above arguments
may be found much more at large in Burke's *Vindication of Natural Society*; a treatise in which the evils of the existing political institutions
are displayed with incomparable force of reasoning and lustre of eloquence..." – footnote, Ch. 2 *Political Justice* by William Godwin.

[32] *Liberty* XIV (December, 1900):1).

[33] Daniel Guerin, *Anarchism: From Theory to Practice* (New York: Monthly Review Press, 1970).

[34] Jonathan Purkis and James Bowen, "Introduction: Why Anarchism Still Matters", in Jonathan Purkis and James Bowen (eds), *Changing Anarchist Theory and Practice in a Global Age* (Manchester: Manchester University Press, 2004), p. 3.

[35] Breunig, Charles (1977). *The Age of Revolution and Reaction, 1789–1850*. New York, N.Y: W. W. Norton & Company. ISBN 0-393-09143-0.

[36] Blin, Arnaud (2007). *The History of Terrorism*. Berkeley: University of California Press. p. 116. ISBN 0520247094.

[37] Dodson, Edward (2002). *The Discovery of First Principles: Volume 2*. Authorhouse. p. 312. ISBN 0595249124.

[38] Thomas, Paul (1985). *Karl Marx and the Anarchists*. London: Routledge & Kegan Paul. p. 187. ISBN 0710206852.

[39] Thomas, Paul (1980). *Karl Marx and the Anarchists*. London: Routledge and Kegan Paul. p. 304. ISBN 0710206852.

[40] Bak, Jños (1991). *Liberty and Socialism*. Lanham: Rowman & Littlefield Publishers. p. 236. ISBN 0847676803.

[41] Engel, Barbara (2000). *Mothers and Daughters*. Evanston: Northwestern University Press. p. 140. ISBN 0810117401.

[42] " On the International Workingmen's Association and Karl Marx (http://www.marxists.org/reference/archive/bakunin/works/1872/karl-marx.htm)" in *Bakunin on Anarchy*, translated and edited by Sam Dolgoff, 1971.

[43] Bakunin, Mikhail (1991) [1873]. *Statism and Anarchy*. Cambridge University Press. ISBN 0-521-36973-8.

[44] Graham, Robert ' *Anarchism* (http://www.blackrosebooks.net/anarism1.htm) (Montreal: Black Rose Books 2005) ISBN 1–55164–251–4.

[45] Resolutions from the St. Imier Congress, in *Anarchism: A Documentary History of Libertarian Ideas*, Vol. 1, p. 100 (http://www.blackrosebooks.net/anarism1.htm)

[46] Foner, Philip Sheldon (1986). *May day: a short history of the international workers' holiday, 1886-1986*. New York: International Publishers. p. 56. ISBN 0717806243.

[47] Avrich, Paul (1984). *The Haymarket Tragedy*. Princeton: Princeton University Press. p. 190. ISBN 0691006008.

[48] Avrich. *The Haymarket Tragedy*. p. 193.

[49] "Patrolman Mathias J. Degan" (http://www.odmp.org/officer/3972-patrolman-mathias-j.-degan). The Officer Down Memorial Page, Inc. . Retrieved 2008-01-19.

[50] *Chicago Tribune*, 27 June 1886, quoted in Avrich. *The Haymarket Tragedy*. p. 209.

[51] "Act II: Let Your Tragedy Be Enacted Here" (http://www.chicagohistory.org/dramas/act2/act2.htm). *The Dramas of Haymarket*. Chicago Historical Society. 2000. . Retrieved 2008-01-19.

[52] Foner. *May Day*. p. 42.

[53] Extract of Malatesta's declaration (http://www.fondation-besnard.org/article.php3?id_article=225) (French)

[54] Skirda, Alexandre (2002). *Facing the enemy: a history of anarchist organization from Proudhon to May 1968*. A. K. Press. p. 89. ISBN 1902593197.

[55] Beevor, Antony (2006). *The Battle for Spain: The Spanish Civil War 1936-1939*. London: Weidenfeld & Nicolson. p. 24. ISBN 978-0297-848325.

[56] Carley, Mark "Trade union membership 1993–2003" (International:SPIRE Associates 2004).

[57] Dirlik, Arif (1991). *Anarchism in the Chinese Revolution*. Berkeley: University of California Press. ISBN 0520072979.

[58] Avrich, Paul (2006). *The Russian Anarchists*. Stirling: AK Press. p. 204. ISBN 1904859488.

[59] Goldman, Emma (2003). "Preface". *My Disillusionment in Russia*. New York: Dover Publications. p. xx. ISBN 048643270X. "My critic further charged me with believing that "had the Russians made the Revolution à la Bakunin instead of à la Marx" the result would have been different and more satisfactory. I plead guilty to the charge. In truth, I not only believe so; I am certain of it."

[60] Nomad, Max (1966). "The Anarchist Tradition title = Revolutionary Internationals 1864 1943". in Drachkovitch, Milorad M.. Stanford University Press. p. 88. ISBN 0804702934.

[61] Dielo Trouda (2006) [1926]. *Organizational Platform of the General Union of Anarchists (Draft)* (http://www.anarkismo.net/newswire.php?story_id=1000). Italy: FdCA. . Retrieved 2006-10-24.

[62] Holbrow, Marnie, "Daring but Divided" (http://www.socialistreview.org.uk/article.php?articlenumber=8205) (*Socialist Review* November 2002).

[63] Berry, David. "Fascism or Revolution." *Le Libertaire*. August 1936).

[64] Beevor, Antony (2006). *The Battle for Spain: The Spanish Civil War 1936-1939*. London: Weidenfeld & Nicolson. p. 46. ISBN 978-0297-848325.

[65] Bolloten, Burnett (1984-11-15). *The Spanish Civil War: Revolution and Counterrevolution*. University of North Carolina Press. pp. 1107. ISBN 978-0807819067.

[66] Birchall, Ian (2004). *Sartre Against Stalinism*. Berghahn Books. p. 29. ISBN 1571815422.

[67] Thomas 1985, p. 4

[68] McLaughlin, Paul (2007). *Anarchism and Authority*. Aldershot: Ashgate. ISBN 0754661962.

[69] Williams, Leonard (September 2007). "Anarchism Revived". *New Political Science* 29 (3): 297–312. doi: 10.1080/07393140701510160 (http://dx.doi.org/10.1080/07393140701510160).

[70] David Graeber and Andrej Grubacic, " Anarchism, Or The Revolutionary Movement Of The Twenty-first Century (http://www.zmag.org/content/showarticle.cfm?SectionID=41&ItemID=4796)", ZNet, retrieved 2007-12-13

[71] Rupert, Mark (2006). *Globalization and International Political Economy*. Lanham: Rowman & Littlefield Publishers. p. 66. ISBN 0742529436.

[72] Adams, Ian. Political Ideology Today (http://books.google.com.ec/books?id=apstK1qIvvMC&printsec=frontcover& source=gbs_navlinks_s) p. 115. Manchester University Press, 2001.

[73] Anarchism (http://libertarian-labyrinth.org/archive/Anarchism), The New Encyclopedia of Social Reform (http://www.amazon.co.uk/dp/1855069954) (1908).

[74] Harrison, Kevin and Boyd, Tony. *Understanding Political Ideas and Movements*. Manchester University Press 2003, p. 251.

[75] Outhwaite, William & Tourain, Alain (Eds.). (2003). Anarchism. The Blackwell Dictionary of Modern Social Thought (2nd Edition, p. 12). Blackwell Publishing.

[76] Wayne Gabardi, review (http://links.jstor.org/sici?sici=0003-0554(198603)80:1<300:A>2.0.CO;2-6) of *Anarchism* by David Miller, published in *American Political Science Review* Vol. 80, No. 1. (Mar., 1986), pp. 300-302.

[77] Klosko, George. *Political Obligations*. Oxford University Press 2005. p. 4.

[78] Avrich, Paul. *Anarchist Voices: An Oral History of Anarchism in America*. Princeton University Press, 1996, p. 6.

[79] Esenwein, George Richard "Anarchist Ideology and the Working Class Movement in Spain, 1868–1898" [p. 135].

[80] "A member of a community," *The Mutualist*; this 1826 series criticised Robert Owen's proposals, and has been attributed to a dissident Owenite, possibly from the Friendly Association for Mutual Interests of Valley Forge; Wilbur, Shawn, 2006, "More from the 1826 "Mutualist"?".

[81] Proudhon, *Solution to the Social Problem*, ed. H. Cohen (New York: Vanguard Press, 1927), p. 45.

[82] Proudhon, Pierre-Joseph (1979). *The Principle of Federation*. Toronto: University of Toronto Press. ISBN 0802054587. "The notion of *anarchy* in politics is just as rational and positive as any other. It means that once industrial functions have taken over from political functions, then business transactions alone produce the social order."

[83] "Communism versus Mutualism", *Socialistic, Communistic, Mutualistic and Financial Fragments*. (Boston: Lee & Shepard, 1875) William Batchelder Greene: "Under the mutual system, each individual will receive the just and exact pay for his work; services equivalent in cost being exchangeable for services equivalent in cost, without profit or discount; and so much as the individual laborer will then get over and above what he has earned will come to him as his share in the general prosperity of the community of which he is an individual member."

[84] Avrich, Paul. *Anarchist Voices: An Oral History of Anarchism in America*, Princeton University Press 1996 ISBN 0-69-04494-5, p.6 *Blackwell Encyclopaedia of Political Thought*, Blackwell Publishing 1991 ISBN 0-631-17944-5, p. 11.

[85] Pierre-Joseph Proudhon. *What Is Property?* Princeton, MA: Benjamin R. Tucker, 1876. p. 281.

[86] "What do I mean by individualism? I mean by individualism the moral doctrine which, relying on no dogma, no tradition, no external determination, appeals only to the individual conscience." *Mini-Manual of Individualism* by Han Ryner (http://www.marx.org/archive/ryner/1905/mini-manual.htm)

[87] "I do not admit anything except the existence of the individual, as a condition of his sovereignty. To say that the sovereignty of the individual is conditioned by Liberty is simply another way of saying that it is conditioned by itself.""Anarchism and the State" in *Individual Liberty*

[88] Everhart, Robert B. The Public School Monopoly: A Critical Analysis of Education and the State in American Society. Pacific Institute for Public Policy Research, 1982. p. 115.

[89] Adams, Ian. Political Ideology Today. Manchester University Press, 2001. p. 116.

[90] Godwin, William (1796) [1793]. *Enquiry Concerning Political Justice and its Influence on Modern Morals and Manners*. G.G. and J. Robinson. OCLC 2340417 (http://worldcat.org/oclc/2340417).

[91] *Britannica Concise Encyclopedia*. Retrieved 7 December 2006, from Encyclopædia Britannica Online (http://www.britannica.com/ebc/article-9037183).

[92] Paul McLaughlin. Anarchism and Authority: A Philosophical Introduction to Classical Anarchism. Ashgate Publishing, Ltd., 2007. p. 119.

[93] Paul McLaughlin. Anarchism and Authority: A Philosophical Introduction to Classical Anarchism. Ashgate Publishing, Ltd., 2007. p. 123.

[94] Goodway, David. Anarchist Seeds Beneath the Snow. Liverpool University Press, 2006, p. 99.

[95] " Max Stirner (http://plato.stanford.edu/entries/max-stirner)" article by David Leopold in the *Stanford Encyclopedia of Philosophy*, 2006-08-04

[96] The Encyclopedia Americana: A Library of Universal Knowledge. Encyclopedia Corporation. p. 176.

[97] Miller, David. "Anarchism." 1987. *The Blackwell Encyclopaedia of Political Thought*. Blackwell Publishing. p. 11.

[98] "What my might reaches is my property; and let me claim as property everything I feel myself strong enough to attain, and let me extend my actual property as fas as *I* entitle, that is, empower myself to take…" In Ossar, Michael. 1980. *Anarchism in the Dramas of Ernst Toller*. SUNY Press. p. 27.

[99] Nyberg, Svein Olav. "max stirner" (http://www.nonserviam.com/stirner/philosophy/index.html). *Non Serviam*. . Retrieved 2008-12-04.

[100] Thomas, Paul (1985). *Karl Marx and the Anarchists*. London: Routledge/Kegan Paul. pp. 142. ISBN 0710206852.

[101] Carlson, Andrew (1972). "Philosophical Egoism: German Antecedents" (http://tmh.floonet.net/articles/carlson.html). *Anarchism in Germany*. Metuchen: Scarecrow Press. ISBN 0810804840. . Retrieved 2008-12-04.

[102] "This does not mean that the majority thread within the anarchist movement is uncritical of individualist anarchism. Far from it! Social anarchists have argued that this influence of non-anarchist ideas means that while its "criticism of the State is very searching, and [its] defence of the rights of the individual very powerful," like Spencer it "opens . . . the way for reconstituting under the heading of 'defence' all the functions of the State." Section G - Is individualist anarchism capitalistic? [[An Anarchist FAQ (http://www.infoshop.org/faq/secGint)]]

html)]*]*

[103] Ostergaard, Geoffrey. "Anarchism". A Dictionary of Marxist Thought. Blackwell Publishing, 1991. p. 21.

[104] Morris, Brian. Bakunin: The Philosophy of Freedom. Black Rose Books Ltd., 1993. p. 76.

[105] Rae, John. Contemporary Socialism. C. Scribner's sons, 1901, Original from Harvard University. p. 261.

[106] Patsouras, Louis. 2005. Marx in Context. iUniverse. p. 54.

[107] Avrich, Paul. 2006. Anarchist Voices: An Oral History of Anarchism in America. AK Press. p. 5.

[108] Kropotkin, Peter (2007). "13". The Conquest of Bread. Edinburgh: AK Press. ISBN 9781904859109.

[109] Bakunin, Mikhail (1990). Statism and Anarchy. Cambridge: Cambridge University Press. ISBN 0521361826. "They [the Marxists] maintain that only a dictatorship — their dictatorship, of course — can create the will of the people, while our answer to this is: No dictatorship can have any other aim but that of self-perpetuation, and it can beget only slavery in the people tolerating it; freedom can be created only by freedom, that is, by a universal rebellion on the part of the people and free organization of the toiling masses from the bottom up."

[110] Guillaume, James (1876). "Ideas on Social Organization" (http://www.marxists.org/reference/archive/guillaume/works/ideas.htm). .

[111] Puente, Isaac. "Libertarian Communism" (http://flag.blackened.net/liberty/libcom.html). The Cienfuegos Press Anarchist Review. Issue 6 Orkney 1982.

[112] Miller. Blackwell Encyclopaedia of Political Thought, Blackwell Publishing (1991) ISBN 0-631-17944-5, p. 12.

[113] Graeber, David and Grubacic, Andrej. Anarchism, Or The Revolutionary Movement Of The Twenty-first Century.

[114] Christopher Gray, Leaving the Twentieth Century, p. 88.

[115] Berry, David, A History of the French Anarchist Movement, 1917–1945 p. 134.

[116] Iain Mckay, ed (2008). "Are there different types of social anarchism?" (http://www.infoshop.org/faq/secA3.html#seca32). An Anarchist FAQ. Stirling: AK Press. ISBN 1902593901. OCLC 182529204 (http://worldcat.org/oclc/182529204). .

[117] Anarchosyndicalism (http://www.spunk.org/library/writers/rocker/sp001495/rocker_as1.html) by Rudolf Rocker, retrieved 7 September 2006.

[118] Perlin, Terry M. Contemporary Anarchism (http://books.google.com.ec/books?id=mppLKlwHx7oC&printsec=frontcover& dq=Contemporary+_+Anarchism&ei=vSDBSuXHMo2mM8mu-OsP#v=onepage&q=&f=false). Transaction Books, New Brunswick, NJ 1979

[119] Edward Stringham, Anarchy, State, and Public Choice (http://www.independent.org/publications/tir/article.asp?issueID=53& articleID=686), Cheltenham, UK: Edward Elgar, 2005.

[120] David Pepper (1996). Modern Environmentalism (http://books.google.com.ec/books?id=PQOvkB7UoWgC&pg=PA44&dq=) p. 44. Routledge.

[121] Ian Adams (2001). Political Ideology Today (http://books.google.com.ec/books?id=apstK1qIvvMC&pg=PA130&dq=) p. 130. Manchester University Press.

[122] The Free Love Movement and Radical Individualism By Wendy McElroy (http://www.ncc-1776.org/tle1996/le961210.html)

[123] Joanne E. Passet, "Power through Print: Lois Waisbrooker and Grassroots Feminism," in: Women in Print: Essays on the Print Culture of American Women from the Nineteenth and Twentieth Centuries, James Philip Danky and Wayne A. Wiegand, eds., Madison, WI, University of Wisconsin Press, 2006; pp. 229-50.

[124] Sochen, June. 1972. The New Woman: Feminism in Greenwich Village 1910-1920. New York: Quadrangle.

[125] Katz, Jonathan Ned. Gay American History: Lesbians and Gay Men in the U.S.A. (New York: Thomas Y. Crowell, 1976)

[126] E. Armand and "la camaraderie amoureuse". Revolutionary sexualism and the struggle against jealousy (http://www.iisg.nl/womhist/ manfreuk.pdf)

[127] Geoffrey C. Fidler (Spring/Summer 1985). "The Escuela Moderna Movement of Francisco Ferrer: "Por la Verdad y la Justicia"" (http:// links.jstor.org/sici?sici=0018-2680(198521/22)25:1/2<103:TEMMOF>2.0.CO;2-R&size=LARGE&origin=JSTOR-enlargePage). History of Education Quarterly 25 (1/2): 103–132. doi: 10.2307/368893 (http://dx.doi.org/10.2307/368893). .

[128] Francisco Ferrer's Modern School (http://flag.blackened.net/revolt/spain/ferrer.html)

[129] Chapter 7, Anarchosyndicalism, The New Ferment. In Murray Bookchin, The Spanish anarchists: the heroic years, 1868-1936. AK Press, 1998, p.115. ISBN 187317604X

[130] Purkis, Jon (2004). Changing Anarchism. Manchester: Manchester University Press. ISBN 0719066948.

[131] Andrew Vincent (2010) Modern Political Ideologies, 3rd edition, Oxford, Wiley-Blackwell p.129

[132] Suissa, Judith (September/October 2005). The New Humanist 120 (5). http://newhumanist.org.uk/1288/anarchy-in-the-classroom Anarchy in the classroom.

[133] Ted Honderich, Carmen García Trevijano, Oxford Enciclopedy of Philosophy (http://books.google.es/books?id=s9iwZGv44psC& pg=PA402&dq=Enciclopedia+teorĂ-a+polĂ-tica&lr=&as_brr=3#PPA57,M1).

[134] http://www.worldcat.org/oclc/221147531

[135] http://www.infoshop.org/page/AnAnarchistFAQ

[136] http://www.gmu.edu/departments/economics/bcaplan/anarfaq.htm

[137] http://www.infoshop.org/

[138] http://recollectionbooks.com/bleed/gallery/galleryindex.htm

[139] http://dwardmac.pitzer.edu/Anarchist_Archives/

[140] http://www.katesharpleylibrary.net/

[141] http://www.theyliewedie.org/ressources/biblio/index-en.php

[142] http://mises.org/literature.aspx?action=subject&Id=123
[143] http://praxeology.net/anarcres.htm

Irish people

Irish people

(Éireannaigh)

Bono • Aidan of Lindisfarne • Brian Boru • Daniel O'Connell • Lady Morgan • Catherine Hayes
Augusta, Lady Gregory • George Bernard Shaw • Oscar Wilde • Robert Boyle • Jonathan Swift • James Joyce
Robbie Keane • Bob Geldof • Jonathan Rhys-Meyers • Pierce Brosnan • Enya • Arthur Guinness

Total population
estimated **80,000,000**

Regions with significant populations		

Ireland (Republic of)	3,900,660	
United States	36,495,800	[1]
United Kingdom	14,000,000	[2]
Canada	4,354,155	[3]
Australia	1,900,000	[4]
Argentina	500,000	[5]
Mexico	300,000-600,000	[6]
Other Regions		

Languages
Irish, English, Ulster Scots, Shelta

Religion
Roman Catholicism (majority), Presbyterianism, Anglicanism, Methodism

Related ethnic groups
Bretons, Cornish, Manx, Scottish, Ulster-Scots, English, Welsh

Footnotes
* Around 800,000 Irish born people reside in Britain, with around 14,000,000 people claiming Irish ancestry.[7]

The **Irish people** (Irish: *Muintir na hÉireann, na hÉireannaigh, na Gaedhil*) are a Western European ethnic group who originate in Ireland, in north western Europe. Ireland has been populated for around 9,000 years (according to archaeological studies), with the Irish people's earliest ancestors recorded[8] as the Nemedians, Fomorians, Fir Bolgs, Tuatha Dé Danann and the Milesians (in legend - there is no written historical record before the 6th century)—the last group supposedly representing the "pure" Gaelic ancestry, and still serving as a term for the Irish race today. The main groups that interacted with the Irish in the Middle Ages include the Scottish people and the Vikings, with the Icelanders especially having some Irish descent. The Anglo-Norman invasion of the High Middle Ages, the English plantations and the subsequent English rule of the country introduced the Normans and Flemish into Ireland. Welsh, Picts, Bretons, and small parties of Gauls and even Anglo-Saxons are known in Ireland from much earlier times.

There have been many notable Irish people throughout history. The 6th century Irish monk and missionary Columbanus is regarded as one of the "fathers of Europe",[9] followed by Kilian of Würzburg and Vergilius of Salzburg. The scientist Robert Boyle is considered the "father of chemistry". Famous Irish explorers include Brendan the Navigator, Ernest Shackleton, and Tom Crean. By some accounts, the first European child born in North America had Irish descent on both sides;[10] while an Irishman was also the first to set foot on American soil in Columbus' expedition of 1492.[11]

Until the end of the early modern period, the majority of educated Irish were proficient at both speaking and writing in Latin and Greek.[12] Notable Irish writers in the English language include Bram Stoker, Jonathan Swift, James Joyce, Flann O'Brien, Oscar Wilde, William Butler Yeats, Samuel Beckett, Patrick Kavanagh and Seamus Heaney. Some of the 20th century writers in the Irish language include Brian O'Nolan (aka Flann O'Brien), Máirtín Ó Cadhain, Pádraic Ó Conaire, Tomás Ó Criomhthain, Peig Sayers, Muiris Ó Súilleabháin and Máirtín Ó Direáin.

Large populations of people of Irish ethnicity live in many western countries, particularly in English-speaking countries. Historically, emigration has been caused by politics, famine and economic issues. An estimated 80 million people make up the Irish diaspora today, which includes Great Britain, Australia, Canada, Argentina, Chile, South Africa, New Zealand, Mexico, France, Germany and Brazil. The largest number of people of Irish descent live in the United States—about ten times more than in Ireland itself.

Origins and antecedents

In its summary of their article 'Who were the Celts?' the National Museum Wales note "It is possible that future genetic studies of ancient and modern human DNA may help to inform our understanding of the subject. However, early studies have, so far, tended to produce implausible conclusions from very small numbers of people and using outdated assumptions about linguistics and archaeology."[13]

Prehistoric and legendary ancestors

During the past 8,000 years of inhabitation, Ireland has witnessed many different peoples arrive on its shores. The ancient peoples of Ireland—such as the creators of the Céide Fields and Newgrange—are almost unknown. Neither their languages nor terms they used to describe themselves have survived. As late as the middle centuries of the 1st millennium the inhabitants of Ireland did not appear to have a collective name for themselves. Ireland itself was known by a number of different names, including Banba, Scotia, Fódla, Ériu by the islanders, Hibernia and Scotia to the Romans, and Ierne to the Greeks.

Carrowmore tomb, 6000 BC

Likewise, the terms for people from Ireland—all from Roman sources—in the late Roman era were varied. They included Attacotti, Scoti, and Gael. This last word, derived from the Welsh *gwyddel* (meaning raiders), was eventually adopted by the Irish for themselves. However, as a term it is on a par with Viking, as it describes an activity (raiding, piracy) and its proponents, not their actual ethnic affiliations.

Part of a series on

Irish people

By region or country

Republic of Ireland · Northern Ireland
Irish diaspora

Irish culture

Art · Calendar · Cinema · Clans
Cuisine · Dance · Dress
Education · Flags · Languages
Literature · Mythology · Music · Politics (Republic of Ireland)
Politics (Northern Ireland)
Religion · Sport · Television

Religion

Catholicism · Church of Ireland
Presbyterianism · Methodism
Judaism · Islam · Paganism

Languages and dialects

Irish · Hiberno-English · Ulster English
Ulster Scots · Shelta

History of Ireland

The term *Irish* and *Ireland* is derived from the Érainn, a people who once lived in what is now central and south Munster. Possibly their proximity to overseas trade with western Great Britain, Gaul, and Hispania led to the name of this one people to be applied to the whole island and its inhabitants. A variety of historical ethnic groups have inhabited the island, including the Airgialla, Fir Ol nEchmacht, Delbhna, Fir Bolg, Érainn, Eóganachta, Mairtine, Conmaicne, Soghain, and Ulaid. In the cases of the Conmaicne, Delbhna, and perhaps Érainn, it can be demonstrated that the tribe took their name from their chief deity, or in the case of the Ciannachta, Eóganachta, and possibly the Soghain, a deified ancestor. This practise is parallel by the Anglo-Saxon dynasties claims of descent from Woden, via his sons Wecta, Baeldaeg, Casere and Wihtlaeg.

The Greek mythographer, Euhemerus, originated the concept of Euhemerism, which treats mythological accounts as a reflection of actual historical events shaped by retelling and traditional mores. In the 12th-century, Icelandic bard and historian Snorri Sturluson proposed that the Norse gods were originally historical war leaders and kings, who later became cult figures, eventually set into society as gods. This view is in aggrement with Irish historians such T. F. O'Rahilly and Francis John Byrne; the early chapters of their respective books, *Early Irish history and mythology* (reprinted 2004) and *Irish Kings and High-Kings* (3rd revised edition, 2001), deal in depth with the origins and status of many Irish ancestral deities.

One legend states that the Irish were descended from one "Milesius of Spain", whose sons supposedly conquered Ireland around 1000 BC or later.[14] The character is almost certainly a mere personification of a supposed migration by a group or groups from Hispania to Ireland. It is from this that the Irish were, as late as the 1800s, popularly known as "Milesian".[15] Medieval Irish historians, over the course of several centuries, created the genealogical dogma that all Irish were descendants of Míl, ignoreing the fact that their own works demonstrated inhabitants in Ireland prior to his supposed arrival.

This doctrine was adapted between the 10th and 12th centuries, as demonstrated in the works of Eochaid ua Flainn (936-1004); Flann Mainistrech (died 25 November 1056); Tanaide (died c. 1075; and Gilla Cómáin mac Gilla Samthainde (fl. 1072). Many of their compositions were incorporated into the compendium Lebor Gabála Érenn.

This tradition was enhanced and embedded in the tradition by successive historians such as Dubsúilech Ó Maolconaire (died 1270); Seán Mór Ó Dubhagáin (d.1372); Gilla Íosa MacFhirbhisigh (fl. 1390–1418); Pilip Ballach Ó Duibhgeannáin (fl. 1579–1590) and Flann Mac Aodhagáin (alive 1640).

The first Irish historian who questioned the reliability of such accounts was Dubhaltach Mac Fhirbhisigh (murdered 1671). Nonetheless, it continued to be widely believed as late as the early 20th century.

Genetics

The frequency of Y-DNA haplogroup R1b(the most common Haplogroup in Europe) is highest in the populations of Atlantic Europe and, due to European emigration, in North America, South America, and Australia. In Ireland and the Basque Country its frequency exceeds 90% and approaches 100% in Western Ireland.[16] The incidence of R1b is 70% or more in parts of northern and western England, northern Spain, northern Portugal, western France, Wales and Scotland. R1b's incidence declines gradually with distance from these areas but it is still common across the central areas of Europe. R1b is the most frequent haplogroup in Germany, and is common in southern Scandinavia and in Italy. This has led to some popular writers, such as Stephen Oppenheimer and Brian Sykes, to conclude that the majority of Irish people(and indeed all natives of the British Isles) descend from a pre-Indo-European population living in the Ice Age "Iberian refugium".[17] [18]

However, this haplogroup is now believed to have originated over 12,000 years more recently than previously thought, in Western or Central Asia.[19] It thus follows that Irish and many other European subclades originating several thousand miles to the west of the region of origin will be considerably younger than the maximum age of 18,000 years. The previous estimates, based on improper dating methods, were 30,000+ years, which made it possible to envision R1b as being more indigenous to Western Europe than it actually was. According to recent 2009 studies by Bramanti et al and Malmström et al on mtDNA,[20] [21] related Western European populations appear to be of largely Neolithic and not Paleolithic origins as previously thought.

The association of the Irish with the Basques was in fact challenged as early as 2005,[22] and in 2007 scientists began looking at a Neolithic entrance for R1b into Europe.[23] A new study published in 2010 by Balaresque et al confirms a Neolithic entrance for R1b in Europe.[24]

History

Early expansion and the coming of Christianity

One Roman historian records that the Irish people were divided into "sixteen different nations" or tribes.[25] Traditional histories assert that the Romans never attempted to conquer Ireland, although it may have been considered.[25] The Irish were not, however, cut off from Europe; they frequently raided the Roman territories,[25] and also maintained trade links.[26] Irish regiments, referred to as the *"Primi Scotti"*, are recorded in Roman service along the Rhine front.[25] Carausius, appointed Commander in Gaul by Emperor Diocletian, may also have been an Irishman.[27]

Among the most famous people of ancient Irish history are the High Kings of Ireland, such as Cormac mac Airt and Niall of the Nine Hostages, and the semi-legendary Fianna. The 20th century writer Seamus MacManus wrote that even if the Fianna and the Fenian Cycle were purely fictional, it would still be representative of the character of the Irish people:

> ...such beautiful fictions of such beautiful ideals, by themselves presume and prove beautiful-souled people, capable of appreciating lofty ideals.[28]

Finnian of Clonard imparting his blessing to the "Twelve Apostles of Ireland"

The introduction of Christianity to the Irish people during the 5th century brought a radical change to the Irish people's foreign relations.[29] The only military raid abroad recorded after that century is a presumed invasion of Wales, which according to a Welsh manuscript may have taken place around the 7th century.[29] In the words of Seamus MacManus:

> If we compare the history of Ireland in the 6th century, after Christianity was received, with that of the 4th century, before the coming of Christianity, the wonderful change and contrast is probably more striking than any other such change in any other nation known to history.[29]

However, Christianity in Ireland appears never to have expanded outside the religious sphere of influence, whereas for the English people and the people of continental Europe it became a whole social system. Therefore, the Irish secular laws and social institutions remained in place.[30]

Migration and invasion in the Middle Ages

Around the 5th century, Gaelic language and culture spread from Ireland to what is now the west of Scotland via the Dál Riata. These Gaels soon spread out to most of the rest of the country. "Scoti" is the name given by the Romans earlier in the millennium who encountered the inhabitants of Ireland. The Gaelic cultural and linguistic dominance of northern Britain is the origin of the name "Scotland". The territories of the Gaels and the native Picts merged together to form the Kingdom of Alba. The modern Scottish people have therefore been influenced historically by both the Irish people and the English people to the south. The Isle of Man and the Manx people also came under massive Gaelic influence in their history.

The approximate area of the Dál Riata (shaded)

Irish missionaries such as Saint Columba brought Christianity to Pictish Scotland. The Irishmen of this time were also "aware of the cultural unity of Europe", and it was the 6th century Irish monk Columbanus who is regarded as "one of the fathers of Europe".[9] Another Irish saint, Aidan of Lindisfarne, has been proposed as a possible patron saint of the United Kingdom,[31] while Saints Kilian and Vergilius became the patron saints of Würzburg in Germany and Salzburg in Austria, respectively. Irish missionaries founded monasteries outside Ireland, such as Iona Abbey, the Abbey of St Gall in Switzerland, and Bobbio Abbey in Italy.

Common to both the monastic and the secular bardic schools were Irish and Latin. With Latin, the early Irish scholars "show almost a like familiarity that they do with their own Gaelic".[32] There is evidence also that Hebrew and Greek were studied, the latter probably being taught at Iona.[33]

> "The knowledge of Greek", says Professor Sandys in his History of Classical Scholarship, "which had almost vanished in the west was so widely dispersed in the schools of Ireland that if anyone knew Greek it was assumed he must have come from that country."[34]

Since the time of Charlemagne, Irish scholars had a considerable presence in the Frankish court, where they were renowned for their learning.[35] The most significant Irish intellectual of the early monastic period was the 9th century Johannes Scotus Eriugena, an outstanding philosopher in terms of originality.[35] He was the earliest of the founders of scholasticism, the dominant school of medieval philosophy.[36] He had considerable familiarity with the Greek language, and translated many works into Latin, affording access to the Cappadocian Fathers and the Greek theological tradition, previously almost unknown in the Latin West.[35]

The influx of Viking raiders and traders in the 9th and 10th centuries resulted in the founding of many of Ireland's most important towns, including Cork, Dublin, Limerick, and Waterford (earlier native settlements on these sites did not approach the urban nature of the subsequent Norse trading ports). The Vikings left little impact on Ireland other than towns and certain words added to the Irish language, but many Irish taken as slaves inter-married with the Scandinavians, hence forming a close link with the Icelandic people. In the Icelandic *Laxdæla saga*, for example, "even slaves are highborn, descended from the kings of Ireland."[37] The first name of Njáll Þorgeirsson, the chief protagonist of *Njáls saga*, is a variation of the Irish name Neil. According to *Eirik the Red's Saga*, the first European couple to have a child born in North America was descended from the Viking Queen of Dublin, Aud the Deep-minded, and a Gaelic slave brought to Iceland.[10]

The arrival of the Anglo-Normans brought also the Welsh, Flemish, Anglo-Saxons, and Bretons. Most of these were assimilated into Irish culture and polity by the 15th century, with the exception of some of the walled towns and the Pale areas.[30] The Late Middle Ages also saw the settlement of Scottish gallowglass families of mixed

Gaelic-Norse-Pict descent, mainly in the north; due to similarities of language and culture they too were assimilated.

Surnames

The Irish were among the first people in Europe to use surnames as we know them today.[38] It is very common for people of Gaelic origin to have the English versions of their surnames beginning with "O'" or "Mc" (less frequently "Mac" and occasionally shortened to just "Ma" at the beginning of the name).

"O'" comes from the Gaelic Ó which in turn came from Ua, which means "grandson", or "descendant" of a named person. Names that begin with "O'" include Ó Briain (O'Brien), Ó Ceallaigh (O'Kelly), Ó Conchobhair (O'Connor), Ó Domhnaill (O'Donnell), Ó Cuilinn (Cullen), Ó Máille (O'Malley), Ó Néill (O'Neill), and Ó Tuathail (O'Toole).

"Mac" or "Mc" means "son". Names that begin with Mac include Mac Diarmada (MacDermott), Mac Cárthaigh (MacCarthy), Mac Domhnaill (MacDonnell), and Mac Mathghamhna (MacMahon, MacMahony, etc.). However, "Mac" and "Mc" are not exclusive, so, for example, both "MacCarthy" and "McCarthy" are used.

The Red Hand of the Uí Néill (O'Neill), the dynasty that claimed descent from Niall of the Nine Hostages

While both "Mac" and "O'" prefixes are Gaelic in origin, "Mac" is more common in Scotland and in Ulster than in the rest of Ireland; furthermore, "Ó" is far less common in Scotland than it is in Ireland.

There are a number of Irish surnames derived from Norse personal names, including Mac Suibhne (Sweeney) from Swein and McAuliffe from Olaf. The name Cotter, local to County Cork, derives from the Norse personal name Ottir. The name Reynolds is an Anglicization of the Gaelic Mac Raghnaill, itself originating from the Norse names Randal or Reginald. Though these names were of Viking derivation most of the families who bear them appear to have had native origins.

"Fitz" is an old Norman French variant of the Old French word *fils* (variant spellings filz, fiuz, fiz, etc.), used by the Normans, meaning *son*. The Normans themselves were descendants of Vikings, who had settled in Normandy and thoroughly adopted the French language and culture.[39] Names that begin with Fitz include FitzGerald (Mac Gearailt), Fitzpatrick (Mac Giolla Phádraig), and FitzHenry (Mac Anraf), most of whom descend from the initial Norman settlers. A small number of Irish families of Gaelic origin came to use a Norman form of their original surname—so that Mac Giolla Phádraig became Fitzpatrick — while some assimilated so well that the Gaelic name was dropped in favor of a new, Hiberno-Norman form. Another common Irish surname of Norman Irish origin is the 'de' habitational prefix, meaning 'of' and originally signifying prestige and land ownership. Examples include de Búrca (Burke), de Brún, de Barra (Barry), de Stac (Stack), de Tiúit, de Faoite (White), de Londras (Landers), de Paor (Power). The Irish surname "Walsh")(in Gaelic *Breathnach*) was routinely given to settlers of Welsh origin, who had come during and after the Norman invasion. The Joyce and Griffin/Griffith families are also of Welsh origin.

The Mac Lochlainn, Ó Maol Seachlainn, Ó Maol Seachnaill, Ó Conchobhair Mac Loughlin and Mac Diarmada Mac Loughlin families, all distinct, are now all subsumed together as MacLoughlin. The full surname usually indicated which family was in question, something that has being diminished with the loss of prefixes such as Ó and Mac. Different branches of a family with the same surname sometimes used distinguishing epithets, which sometimes became surnames in their own right. Hence the chief of the clan Ó Cearnaigh (Kearney) was referred to as An Sionnach (Fox), which his descendants use to this day. Similar surnames are often found in Scotland for many reasons, such as the use of a common language and mass Irish migration to Scotland in the late 19th and early to mid-20th centuries.

Late Medieval and Tudor Ireland

The Irish people of the Late Middle Ages were active as traders on the
European continent.[11] They were distinguished from the English
(who only used their own language or French) in that they only used
Latin abroad—a language "spoken by all educated people throughout
Gaeldom".[40] The explorer Christopher Columbus visited Ireland to
gather information about the lands to the west.[11] A number of Irish
names are recorded on Columbus' crew roster, preserved in the
archives of Madrid, and it was an Irishman named Patrick Maguire
who was the first to set foot on American soil in 1492.[11] According to
Morison and Miss Gould, who made a detailed study of the crew list of
1492, no Irish or English sailors were involved in the voyage.[41]

Gaelic Irish soldiers in the Low Countries, from a
drawing of 1521 by Albrecht Dürer

An English report of 1515 states that the Irish people were divided into over sixty Gaelic lordships and thirty
Anglo-Irish lordships.[30] The English term for these lordships was "nation" or "country".[30] The Irish term
"oireacht" referred to both the territory and the people ruled by the lord.[30] Literally, it meant an "assembly", where
the Brehons would hold their courts upon hills to arbitrate the matters of the lordship.[30] Indeed, the Tudor lawyer
Sir John Davies described the Irish people with respect to their laws:

> There is no people under the sun that doth love equal and indifferent (impartial) justice better than the Irish, or
> will rest better satisfied with the execution thereof, although it be against themselves, as they may have the
> protection and benefit of the law upon which just cause they do desire it.[42]

Another English commentator records that the assemblies were attended
by "all the scum of the country"—the labouring population as well as the
landowners.[30] While the distinction between "free" and "unfree"
elements of the Irish people was unreal in legal terms, it was a social and
economic reality.[30] Social mobility was usually downwards, due to
social and economic pressures.[30] The ruling clan's "expansion from the
top downwards" was constantly displacing commoners and forcing them
into the margins of society.[30]

As a clan-based society, genealogy was all important.[30] Ireland 'was
justly styled a "Nation of Annalists"'.[43] The various branches of Irish
learning—including law, poetry, history and genealogy, and
medicine—were associated with hereditary learned families.[44] The
poetic families included the Uí Dhálaigh (Daly) and the MacGrath.[30]

The Gaelic scribes and poets reflected the
broad education of the Irish learned classes.

Irish physicians, such as the O'Briens in Munster or the MacCailim Mor in the Western Isles, were renowned in the
courts of England, Spain, Portugal and the Low Countries.[42] Learning was not exclusive to the hereditary learned
families, however; one such example is Cathal Mac Manus, the 15th century diocesan priest who wrote the *Annals of
Ulster*.[44] Other learned families included the Mic Aodhagáin and Clann Fhir Bhisigh.[44] It was this latter family
which produced Dubhaltach Mac Fhirbhisigh, the 17th century genealogist and compiler of the *Leabhar na
nGenealach*. (see also Irish medical families).

Plantations

After Ireland was subdued by England, the English—under James I of England (reigned 1603–1625), the Lord Protector Oliver Cromwell (1653–1658), William III of England (reigned 1689–1702) and their successors—began the settling of Protestant English and Scottish colonists into Ireland, where they settled most heavily in the northern province of Ulster. The Plantations of Ireland and in particular the Plantation of Ulster in the 17th century introduced great numbers of Scottish, English as well as French Huguenots as colonists.

Many native Irish were displaced during the 17th century plantations. Only in the major part of Ulster did the plantations of mostly Scottish prove long-lived; the other three provinces (Connacht, Leinster, and Munster) remained heavily "Gaelic" or "native" Irish. Eventually, the Anglo-Irish and Protestant populations of those three provinces decreased drastically as a result of the political developments in the early 20th century in Ireland, as well as the Catholic Church's Ne Temere decree for mixed marriages, which obliged the non-Catholic partner to have the children raised as Catholics.

Robert Boyle, Anglo-Irish scientist and father of chemistry, whose family obtained land in the plantations

Enlightenment Ireland

There have been notable Irish scientists. The Anglo-Irish scientist Robert Boyle (1627–1691) is considered the father of chemistry for his book *The Sceptical Chymist*, written in 1661.[45] Boyle was an atomist, and is best known for Boyle's Law. The hydrographer Sir Francis Beaufort (1774–1857), an Irish naval officer of Huguenot descent, was the creator of the Beaufort scale for indicating wind force. George Boole (1815–1864), the mathematician who invented Boolean algebra, spent the latter part of his life in Cork. The 19th century physicist George Stoney introduced the idea and the name of the electron. He was the uncle of another notable physicist, George FitzGerald.

The Irish bardic system, along with the Gaelic culture and learned classes, were upset by the plantations, and went into decline. Among the last of the true bardic poets were Brian Mac Giolla Phádraig (c. 1580-1652) and Dáibhí Ó Bruadair (1625–1698). The Irish poets of the late 17th and 18th centuries moved toward more modern dialects. Among the most prominent of this period were Séamas Dall Mac Cuarta, Peadar Ó Doirnín, Art Mac Cumhaigh Cathal Buí Mac Giolla Ghunna, and Seán Clárach Mac Domhnaill. Irish Catholics continued to receive an education in secret "hedgeschools", in spite of the Penal laws.[46] A knowledge of Latin was common among the poor Irish mountaineers in the 17th century, who spoke it on special occasions, while cattle were bought and sold in Greek in the mountain market-places of Kerry.[47]

Jonathan Swift, one of the foremost prose satirists in the English language

For a comparatively small island, Ireland has made an enormous contribution to literature. Irish literature encompasses the Irish and English languages. Notable Irish writers include Jonathan Swift (1667–1745), Oliver Goldsmith, Bram Stoker, James Joyce. Among the famous Irish poets are William Butler Yeats, Francis Ledwidge, "A.E." Russell and Seamus Heaney. Irish playwrights include Oscar Wilde, Lady Gregory, John Millington Synge, Edward Plunkett, George Bernard Shaw, Samuel Beckett, Sean O'Casey, Brendan Behan and Brian Friel. Some of the 20th century writers in the Irish language include Brian O'Nolan, Peig Sayers, Muiris Ó Súilleabháin, and Máirtín Ó Direáin.

20th century

In 1921, with the formation of the Irish Free State, six counties in the northeast remained in the United Kingdom as Northern Ireland. It is predominately religion, historical, and political differences that divide the two communities of (nationalism and unionism). Four polls taken between 1989 and 1994 revealed that when asked to state their national identity, over 79% of Northern Ireland Protestants replied "British" or "Ulster" with 3% or less replying "Irish", while over 60% of Northern Ireland Catholics replied "Irish" with 13% or less replying "British" or "Ulster".[48] A survey in 1999 showed that 72% of Northern Ireland Protestants considered themselves "British" and 2% "Irish", with 68% of Northern Ireland Catholics considering themselves "Irish" and 9% "British".[49] The survey also revealed that 78% of Protestants and 48% of all respondents felt "Strongly British", while 77% of Catholics and 35% of all respondents felt "Strongly Irish". 51% of Protestants and 33% of all respondents felt "Not at all Irish", while 62% of Catholics and 28% of all respondents felt "Not at all British".[50] [51]

"Ulster-Irish" surnames tend to differ based on which community families originate from. Ulster Protestants tend to have either English or Scottish surnames while Catholics tend to have Irish surnames, although this is not always the case. There are many Catholics in Northern Ireland with surnames such as Emerson, Whitson, Livingstone, Hardy, Tennyson, MacDonald (this surname is also common with Highland Roman Catholics in Scotland), Dunbar, Groves, Legge, Scott, Gray, Page, Stewart, Roberts, Rowntree, Henderson, et al.; almost certainly due to intermarriage.

Recent history

Religions

In the Republic of Ireland, as of 2006, 3,681,446 people or about 86.83% of the population claim to be Roman Catholic.[52] In Northern Ireland about 53.1% of the population are Protestant (21.1% Presbyterian, 15.5% Church of Ireland, 3.6% Methodist, 6.1% Other Christian) whilst a large minority are Catholic at approximately 43.8%, as of 2001.

The 31st International Eucharistic Congress was held in Dublin in 1932, that year being the supposed 1,500th anniversary of Saint Patrick's arrival. Ireland was then home to 3,171,697 Catholics, about a third of whom attended the Congress.[53] [54] It was noted in *Time Magazine* that the Congress' special theme would be "the Faith of the Irish."[53] The massive crowds were repeated at Pope John Paul II's Mass in Phoenix Park in 1979.[55] The idea of faith has affected the question of Irish identity even in relatively recent times, apparently more so for Catholics and Irish-Americans:

> What defines an Irishman? His faith, his place of birth? What of the Irish-Americans? Are they Irish? Who is more Irish, a Catholic Irishman such as James Joyce who is trying to escape from his Catholicism and from his Irishness, or a Protestant Irishman like Oscar Wilde who is eventually becoming Catholic? Who is more Irish... someone like C.S. Lewis, an Ulster Protestant, who is walking towards it, even though he never ultimately crosses the threshold?[56]

This has been a matter of concern over the last century for followers of nationalist ideologists such as DP Moran.

Europe

Ireland joined the European Community in 1973, and Irish citizens became additionally Citizens of the European Union with the Maastricht Treaty signed in 1992. This brought a further question for the future of Irish identity; whether Ireland was "closer to Boston than to Berlin:"

Ireland joined the EU in 1973

> History and geography have placed Ireland in a very special location between America and Europe... As Irish people our relationships with the United States and the European Union are complex. Geographically we are closer to Berlin than Boston. Spiritually we are probably a lot closer to Boston than Berlin. — Mary Harney, Tánaiste, 2000[57]

Celebrities

Famous Irish singers and musicians have included the harpist Turlough O'Carolan (1670–1738), Catherine Hayes; and more recently U2, The Script, The Clancy Brothers, Tommy Makem, The Corrs, Dónal Lunny, Van Morrison, Gilbert O'Sullivan, Rory Gallagher, Phil Lynott, Sinéad O'Connor, Bob Geldof, Shane MacGowan, David King, Enya, The Cranberries, James Galway, Colm Wilkinson, Johnny Logan, Damien Rice, Chris de Burgh, Glen Hansard, Kíla, Boyzone and Westlife.

Famous Irish actors include Maureen O'Hara, Peter O'Toole, Liam Neeson, Richard Harris, Greer Garson, Pierce Brosnan, Spike Milligan, Stephen Boyd, Brendan Gleeson, Cillian Murphy, Colm Meaney, Colin Farrell, Saoirse Ronan, John McNiff and Jonathan Rhys Meyers. One of the most significant national Irish media figures is Gay Byrne, who presented the *Late Late Show* from 1962-1999. There are several other Irish broadcasters of note who developed careers outside of Ireland, such as Terry Wogan and Eamonn Andrews, who are well known internationally.

In sport, modern Irish figures include Colm Cooper, Peter Canavan, Darragh Ó Sé and Pádraic Joyce (Gaelic football), Richard Dunne, Robbie Keane, Roy Keane, Steve Staunton and Martin O'Neill (soccer); Pádraig Harrington,Rory McIlroy, Paul McGinley and Darren Clarke (golf); Steve Collins, Barry McGuigan and Bernard Dunne (boxing); Keith Wood, Brian O'Driscoll, and Paul O'Connell (Rugby Union); Mary Peters, Eamonn Coghlan, John Treacy and Sonia O'Sullivan (athletics); Sean Kelly and Stephen Roche (cycling), Michelle Smith (swimming) Henry Shefflin, Andrew Bree, Joe Canning and Seán Óg Ó hAilpín (hurling), Sheamus O'Shaunessy and Finlay (wrestling).

Ireland has produced many famous comedians, known both nationally and internationally. Many of them draw their humour from being Irish, or from their province, county or locality. Irish comedians who were born or raised in Dublin include Dave Allen, Frank Kelly,Dermot Morgan, Ed Byrne, Andrew Maxwell, Dara Ó Briain, and Jason Byrne. Ulster-born comedians include Colin Murphy, Patrick Kielty, and Ardal O'Hanlon, while Leinster has also produced, Neil Delamere, Tommy Tiernan, Deirdre O'Kane and Dylan Moran. Munster and Connaught have produced comedian Pat Shortt,Graham Norton, and comedienne Pauline McLynn respectively. Comedians of Irish descent, born outside Ireland, include George Carlin, Des Bishop (who performed the first live stand up gig in Irish), Conan O'Brien, and Jimmy Carr.

Irish diaspora

Patrice MacMahon, Marshal of France and first elected President of the French Third Republic

The Irish diaspora consists of Irish emigrants and their descendants in countries such as the United States, Great Britain, Canada, Australia, New Zealand, South Africa, and nations of the Caribbean such as Jamaica and Barbados. These countries, known sometimes as the Anglosphere, all have large minorities of Irish descent, who in addition form the core of the Catholic Church in those countries. People of Irish descent also feature strongly in Latin America, especially in Argentina, Brazil, Chile, and Mexico. In 1995, President Mary Robinson reached out to the "70 million people worldwide who can claim Irish descent."[58] Today the diaspora is believed to contain an estimated 80 million people.[59]

There are also large Irish communities in some mainland European countries, notably in Spain, France and Germany. Between 1585 and 1818, over half a million Irish departed Ireland to serve in the wars on the continent, in a constant emigration romantically styled the "*Flight of the Wild Geese*".[60] In the early years of the English Civil War, a French traveller remarked that the Irish "are better soldiers abroad than at home".[61] Later, Irish brigades in France and Spain fought in the Wars of the Spanish and Austrian Succession and the Napoleonic Wars.[60] In the words of Arthur Wellesley, the Irish born "Iron Duke" of Wellington, a notable representative of the Irish military diaspora, "Ireland was an inexhaustible nursery for the finest soldiers".[62]

The most famous cause of emigration was Irish Potato Famine of the late 1840s. A million are thought to have emigrated to Liverpool as a result of the famine.[63] For both the native Irish and those in the resulting diaspora, the famine entered folk memory[64] and became a rallying point for various nationalist movements.

People of Irish descent are the second largest self-reported ethnic group in the United States, after German Americans. Nine of the signatories of the American Declaration of Independence were of Irish origin.[65] Among them was the sole Catholic signatory, Charles Carroll of Carrollton, whose family were the descendants of Ely O'Carroll, an Irish prince who had suffered under Cromwell.[66] At least twenty-five presidents of the United States have some Irish ancestral origins, including George Washington.[67] [68] [69] [70] Since John F. Kennedy took office in 1961, every American President has had some Irish blood.[71] An Irish-American, James Hoban, was the designer of the White House. Commodore John Barry was the father of the United States Navy.[72]

John F. Kennedy visiting the John Barry Memorial in Wexford, Ireland

In the mid-19th century, large numbers of Irish immigrants were conscripted into Irish regiments of the United States army at the time of the Mexican-American War. The vast majority of the 4,811 Irish-born soldiers served honorably in the American army, but some defected to the Mexican Army, primarily to escape mistreatment by Anglo-Protestant officers and the strong anti-Catholic discrimination in America.[73] These were the *San Patricios*, or Saint Patrick's Battalion—a group of Irish led by Galway-born John O'Riley, with some German, Scottish and American Catholics.[73] They fought until their surrender at the decisive Battle of Churubusco, and were executed outside Mexico City by the American government on 13 September 1847.[73] The battalion is commemorated in Mexico each year on 12 September.[74]

During the 18th and 19th centuries, 300,000 free emigrants and 45,000 convicts left Ireland to settle in Australia.[75] Today, Australians of Irish descent are one of the largest self-reported ethnic groups in Australia, after English and Australian. In the 2006 Census, 1,803,741 residents identified themselves as having Irish ancestry either alone or in combination with another ancestry.[76] However this figure does not include Australians with an Irish background who chose to nominate themselves as 'Australian' or other ancestries. The Australian embassy in Dublin states that up to 30 percent of the population claim some degree of Irish ancestry.[77]

It is believed that as many as 30,000 Irish people emigrated to Argentina between the 1830s and the 1890s, having a "seismic" impact on Argentinian society.[5] Today Irish-Argentines number over 500,000—about 1,2% of the population.[5] Some famous Argentines of Irish descent include Che Guevara, former president Edelmiro Julián Farrell, and admiral William Brown. There are Irish descent people all over South America, such as the Chilean liberator Bernardo O'Higgins and the Peruvian photographer Mario Testino. Although some Irish retained their surnames intact, others were assimilated into the Spanish vernacular. The last name *O'Brien*, for example, became *Obregón*.

People of Irish descent are also one of the largest self-reported ethnic groups in Canada, after English, French and Scottish Canadians. As of 2006, Irish Canadians number around 4,354,155.[3]

See also

- List of expatriate Irish populations
- European ethnic groups
- Genetic history of Europe
- The Ireland Funds
- List of Ireland-related topics
- Lists of Irish Americans

References

Part of a series of articles on

Celts and Modern Celts

Celtic nations · Celtic studies · Celtic Tribes

- Aldous, Richard (2007). *Great Irish Speeches*. London: Quercus Publishing PLC. ISBN 1847241956.
- Davies, Norman (1996). *Europe: A History*. Oxford: Oxford University Press. ISBN 0-19-820171-0.
- Ellis, Steven G. (1985). *Tudor Ireland: Crown, Community, and the Conflict of Cultures, 1470-1603*. Great Britain: Longman. ISBN 0582493412.
- MacManus, Seamus (1921). *The Story of the Irish Race: A Popular History of Ireland*. Ireland: The Irish Publishing Co. ISBN 0-517-06408-1.
- McLaughlin, Mark G. (1980). *The Wild Geese: The Irish Brigades of France and Spain* [78]. Osprey Publishing. ISBN 0850453585.
- Nicholls, Kenneth W. (1972). *Gaelic and Gaelicised Ireland in the Middle Ages*. Gill and Macmillan. ISBN 071710561X.

- Oppenheimer, Stephen (2006). *The Origins of the British: A Genetic Detective Story*. Carroll & Graf. ISBN ISBN 0786718900.
- Sykes, Bryan (2006). *Blood of the Isles: Exploring the Genetic Roots of Our Tribal History*. DNA, Fossil. ISBN 0593056523.
- Toman, Rolf (2007). *The Art of Gothic: Architecture, Sculpture, Painting*. photography by Achim Bednorz. Tandem Verlag GmbH. ISBN 978-3-8331-4676-3.
- Various (2001). *The Sagas of Icelanders* [79]. edited by Smiley, Jane. Penguin. ISBN 9780141000039.

External links

- Irish surname origins [80]
- Irish ancestors [81] on Ireland.com

References

[1] U.S. Census Bureau, 2007 (http://factfinder.census.gov/servlet/ADPTable?_bm=y&-geo_id=01000US&-parsed=true& -ds_name=ACS_2007_1YR_G00_&-_lang=en&-_caller=geoselect&-format=)

[2] One in four Britons claim Irish roots (http://news.bbc.co.uk/2/hi/uk_news/1224611.stm)

[3] "Ethnocultural portrait of Canada" (http://www12.statcan.ca/english/census06/data/highlights/ethnic/pages/Page.cfm?Lang=E& Geo=PR&Code=01&Table=2&Data=Count&StartRec=1&Sort=3&Display=All&CSDFilter=5000). Statistics Canada. 2006. . Retrieved 2008-07-04.

[4] The 2006 Australian Census (http://www.censusdata.abs.gov.au/ABSNavigation/prenav/ViewData?action=404& documentproductno=0&documenttype=Details&order=1&tabname=Details&areacode=0&issue=2006&producttype=Census Tables& javascript=true&textversion=false&navmapdisplayed=true&breadcrumb=TLPD&&collection=Census&period=2006& productlabel=Ancestry (full classification list) by Sex&producttype=Census Tables&method=Place of Usual Residence&topic=Ancestry&) reports 1.9 million people of Irish *ancestry* in the 2001 Census. Up to two ancestries could be chosen. Recent increases in the number who identify as Australian suggest that this number is an underestimate of the true number with Irish ancestry. With that being said, the number claiming Irish ancestry from the previous census actually more than doubled. One reason, an improved image of what it means to be Irish according to the census experts, making Australians more proud to state their Irish ancestry. Also the Australian Embassy in Dublin states that up to 30 percent of Australians have some degree of Irish ancestry. (http://www.ireland.embassy.gov.au/dubl/relations.html).

[5] "Flying the Irish flag in Argentina" (http://www.westernpeople.ie/news/story.asp?j=36054). Western People. 2008-03-14. . Retrieved 2008-07-04.

[6] http://en.wikipedia.org/wiki/Irish_Mexican

[7] "More Britons applying for Irish passports I UK news I guardian.co.uk" (http://www.guardian.co.uk/britain/article/0,,1871753,00.html). Guardian. . Retrieved 2009-12-31.

[8] Boylan, Henry (1998). *A Dictionary of Irish Biography, 3rd Edition*. Dublin: Gill and MacMillan. pp. xvi. ISBN 0-7171-2945-4.

[9] "Pope Calls Irish Monk a Father of Europe" (http://www.zenit.org/rssenglish-22867). Zenit. 2007-07-11. . Retrieved 2007-07-15.

[10] Smiley, p 630

[11] MacManus, p 343-344

[12] MacManus, pp 215; 221-222; 461-462

[13] "Who were the Celts? ... Rhagor" (http://www.museumwales.ac.uk/en/rhagor/article/1939/). *Amgueddfa Cymru – National Museum Wales website*. Amgueddfa Cymru – National Museum Wales. 2007-05-04. . Retrieved 2009-10-14.

[14] Mac Manus, p 1 & 7

[15] MacManus, p 1

[16] "Y-Chromosome Biallelic Haplogroups" (http://www.roperld.com/YBiallelicHaplogroups.htm). Roperld.com. . Retrieved 2009-12-31.

[17] Stephen Oppenheimer, *The Origins of the British - A Genetic Detective Story*, 2006, Constable and Robinson, ISBN 1-84529-158-1

[18] Bryan Sykes, *Blood of the Isles: Exploring the Genetic Roots of Our Tribal History*, 2006, Bantam, ISBN 0593056523

[19] ISOGG 2009 (http://www.isogg.org/tree/ISOGG_HapgrpR09.html)

[20] Bramanti et al 2009 (http://www.sciencemag.org/cgi/content/abstract/1176869)

[21] Malmström et al 2009 (http://www.cell.com/current-biology/abstract/S0960-9822(09)01694-7)

[22] Alonso et al. The Place of the Basques in the European Y-chromosome Diversity Landscape (http://www.nature.com/ejhg/journal/v13/ n12/full/5201482a.html). European Journal of Human Genetics, 13:1293-1302, 2005

[23] B. Arredi, E. S. Poloni and C. Tyler-Smith (2007). "The peopling of Europe". in Crawford, Michael H.. *Anthropological genetics: theory, methods and applications*. Cambridge, UK: Cambridge University Press. p. 394. ISBN 0-521-54697-4.

[24] Balaresque et al. (2010), "A Predominantly Neolithic Origin for European Paternal Lineages" (http://www.ncbi.nlm.nih.gov/pmc/ articles/PMC2799514), *PLoS Biol.* 8 (1), doi: 10.1371/journal.pbio.1000285 (http://dx.doi.org/10.1371/journal.pbio.1000285), PMID PMC2799514 (http://www.ncbi.nlm.nih.gov/pubmed/PMC2799514),

[25] MacManus, p 86

[26] MacManus, p 87

[27] MacManus, pp. 86-87. 'Carausius was native of an Irish city which the Roman historian calls "Menapia in Ireland."'

[28] MacManus, p67

[29] MacManus, p 89

[30] Nicholls

[31] "Home-grown holy man: Cry God for Harry, Britain and... St Aidan" (http://www.independent.co.uk/news/uk/this-britain/
homegrown-holy-man-cry-god-for-harry-britain-and-st-aidan-814057.html). The Independent. 2008-04-23. . Retrieved 2008-07-21.

[32] MacManus, p 221

[33] MacManus, p 221-222

[34] MacManus, p 215

[35] "John Scottus Eriugena" (http://plato.stanford.edu/entries/scottus-eriugena/). Stanford Encyclopedia of Philosophy. Stanford University.
2004-10-17. . Retrieved 2008-07-21.

[36] Toman, p 10: "Abelard himself was... together with John Scotus Erigena (9th century), and Lanfranc and Anselm of Canterbury (both 11th
century), one of the founders of scholasticism."

[37] Smiley, p 274

[38] Woulfe, Patrick (1923) (in English). Sloinnte Gaedheal is Gall: Irish names and surnames (http://books.google.co.uk/
books?id=nWFmAAAAMAAJ&q="ireland+was+the+first+country+after+the+fall"&dq="ireland+was+the+first+country+after+
the+fall"&cd=5). M. H. Gill & son. pp. xx. . Retrieved 20/02/10.

[39] Richard Hooker. "The Normans" (http://www.wsu.edu/~dee/MA/NORMANS.HTM). Washington State University. . Retrieved
2008-07-12.

[40] MacManus, p 340

[41] Paolo Emilio Taviani, Chrstopher Columbus, Page 376, ISBN 085613922X

[42] MacManus, p 348

[43] MacManus, p 352

[44] Jefferies, Dr. Henry A. "Culture and Religion in Tudor Ireland, 1494-1558" (http://multitext.ucc.ie/d/
Culture__Religion_in_Tudor_Ireland_1494-1558). University College Cork. . Retrieved 2008-06-23.

[45] Boyle on Atheism by J.J. MacIntosh (University of Toronto Press ISBN 978-0802090188), page 6

[46] MacManus, p 461

[47] MacManus, p 461-462

[48] in, Social Attitudes in Northern Ireland: The Fifth Report (http://cain.ulst.ac.uk/othelem/research/nisas/rep5c2.htm)

[49] Northern Ireland Life and Times Survey (http://www.ark.ac.uk/nilt/1999/Community_Relations/NINATID.html)

[50] Northern Ireland Life and Times Survey (http://www.ark.ac.uk/nilt/1999/Community_Relations/BRITISH.html)

[51] Northern Ireland Life and Times Survey (http://www.ark.ac.uk/nilt/1999/Community_Relations/IRISH.html)

[52] Population classified by religion for relevant censuses from 1881 to 2006 Summary (http://beyond2020.cso.ie/Census/TableViewer/
tableView.aspx?ReportId=19670), Central Statistics Office

[53] "In Dublin" (http://www.time.com/time/magazine/article/0,9171,753335-1,00.html). Time Magazine. 1932-06-20. . Retrieved
2008-06-23.

[54] John Paul McCarthy. "The 31st International Eucharistic Congress, Dublin, 1932" (http://multitext.ucc.ie/d/
The_31st_International_Eucharistic_Congress_Dublin_1932). University College Cork. . Retrieved 2008-06-23. "Newspapers and
contemporaries estimated that close to a million souls had converged on the Phoenix Park for the climax of the Congress"

[55] The figure 1,250,000 is mentioned on the commemorative stone at the Papal Cross in the Phoenix Park, Dublin; a quarter of the population
of the island of Ireland, or a third of the population of Republic of Ireland

[56] Pearce, Joseph (March/April 2007). "Editorial: The Celtic Enigma". St. Austin Review (Ave Maria University, Naples, Florida: Sapientia
Press) 7 (2): 1.

[57] Aldous, p 185

[58] Ireland's Diaspora (http://www.irelandroots.com/roots4.htm)

[59] The island history (http://www.discoverireland.com/us/about-ireland/history/), discoverireland.com

[60] The Wild Geese (http://www.ospreypublishing.com/text_search.aspx?TextSearch=Wild Geese&Group=1), Men-at-Arms 102, Osprey
Publishing

[61] McLaughlin, p4

[62] Davies, p 832

[63] David Ross, Ireland: History of a Nation, New Lanark: Geddes & Grosset, 2002, p. 226. ISBN 1842051644

[64] The Famine that affected Ireland from 1845 to 1852 has become an integral part of folk legend. Kenealy, This Great Calamity, p. 342.

[65] "Irish-American History Month, 1995" (http://irishamericanheritage.com/ProcWebPages/1995.htm). irishamericanheritage.com. .
Retrieved 2008-06-25.

[66] Maryland Traces Its Irish Roots (http://www.visitmaryland.org/PressRoom/Pages/MarylandTracesitsIrishRootsar.aspx), Maryland
Office of Tourism

[67] "Presidents of the United States with "Irish Roots"" (http://irishamericanheritage.com/Presidents.htm). irishamericanheritage.com. . Retrieved 2008-06-25.

[68] Marck, John T. "William H. Taft" (http://www.aboutfamouspeople.com/article1118.html). aboutfamouspeople.com. . Retrieved 2008-06-25.

[69] "Warren Gamaliel Harding" (http://library.thinkquest.org/TQ0312172/harding.html). thinkquest.com. . Retrieved 2008-06-25.

[70] Marck, John T. "Harry S. Truman" (http://www.aboutfamouspeople.com/article1124.html). aboutfamouspeople.com. . Retrieved 2008-06-25.

[71] "American Presidents with Irish Ancestors" (http://homepage.eircom.net/%7Eseanjmurphy/dir/pres.htm). Directory of Irish Genealogy. . Retrieved 2008-06-25.

[72] John Barry Kelly. "Commodore Barry" (http://www.ushistory.org/people/commodorebarry.htm). . Retrieved 2007-06-25.

[73] Michael G. Connaughton (September 2005). "Beneath an Emerald Green Flag, The Story of Irish Soldiers in Mexico" (http://www.irlandeses.org/sanpatriciosB.htm). The Society for Irish Latin American Studies. . Retrieved 2008-07-12.

[74] Mark R. Day. "The San Patricios: Mexico's Fighting Irish" (http://flag.blackened.net/revolt/mexico/img/more_san_ps.html). . Retrieved 2008-07-12.

[75] Ryan, Sean (2006). "Botany Bay 1791 - 1867" (http://indigo.ie/~wildgees/australia/index.htm). Wild Geese Heritage Museum and Library Portumna, Co. Galway. . Retrieved 2009-05-27.

[76] Australian Bureau of Statistics (25 October 2007). "Australia" (http://www.censusdata.abs.gov.au/ABSNavigation/prenav/LocationSearch?collection=Census&period=2006&areacode=0&producttype=QuickStats&breadcrumb=PL&action=401). *2006 Census QuickStats*. . Retrieved 2007-07-25.

[77] Australia- Ireland relationship - Australian Embassy (http://www.ireland.embassy.gov.au/dubl/relations.html)

[78] http://books.google.com/books?id=fJlzoC_RdhEC&printsec=frontcover

[79] http://us.penguingroup.com/nf/Book/BookDisplay/0,,9780141000039,00.html

[80] http://www.goireland.com/genealogy/html/surname_search.htm

[81] http://www.irishtimes.com/ancestor/

Communism

Communism is a social structure in which classes are abolished and property is commonly controlled, as well as a political philosophy and social movement that advocates and aims to create such a society.[1] Karl Marx, the father of communist thought, posited that communism would be the final stage in society, which would be achieved through a proletarian revolution and only possible after a socialist stage develops the productive forces, leading to a superabundance of goods and services.[2] [3]

"Pure communism" in the Marxian sense refers to a classless, stateless and oppression-free society where decisions on what to produce and what policies to pursue are made democratically, allowing every member of society to participate in the decision-making process in both the political and economic spheres of life. In modern usage, communism is often used to refer to the policies of the various communist states which were authoritarian governments that had ownership of all the means of production and centrally planned economies. Most communist governments based their ideology on Marxism-Leninism.

As a political ideology, communism is usually considered to be a branch of socialism; a broad group of economic and political philosophies that draw on the various political and intellectual movements with origins in the work of theorists of the Industrial Revolution and the French Revolution.[4] Communism attempts to offer an alternative to the problems with the capitalist market economy and the legacy of imperialism and nationalism.

Marx states that the only way to solve these problems is for the working class (proletariat), who according to Marx are the main producers of wealth in society and are exploited by the Capitalist-class (bourgeoisie), to replace the bourgeoisie as the ruling class in order to establish a free society, without class or racial divisions.[1] The dominant forms of communism, such as Leninism, Stalinism, Maoism and Trotskyism are based on Marxism, as well as others forms of communism (such as Luxemburgism and Council communism), but non-Marxist versions of communism (such as Christian communism and Anarchist communism) also exist.

Karl Marx never provided a detailed description as to how communism would function as an economic system, but it is understood that a communist economy would consist of common ownership of the means of production, culminating in the negation of the concept of private ownership of capital, which referred to the means of production in Marxian terminology.

Terminology

In the schema of historical materialism, communism is the idea of a free society with no division or alienation, where mankind is free from oppression and scarcity. A communist society would have no governments, countries, or class divisions. In Marxist theory, the dictatorship of the proletariat is the intermediate system between capitalism and communism, when the government is in the process of changing the means of ownership from privatism, to collective ownership.[5] In political science, the term "communism" is sometimes used to refer to communist states, a form of government in which the state operates under a one-party system and declares allegiance to Marxism-Leninism or a derivative thereof.

Marxist schools of communism

Self-identified communists hold a variety of views, including Marxism-Leninism, Trotskyism, council communism, Luxemburgism, anarchist communism, Christian communism, and various currents of left communism. However, the offshoots of the Marxist-Leninist interpretations of Marxism are the most well-known of these and have been a driving force in international relations during most of the 20th century.[1]

Marxism

The Communist Manifesto.

Like other socialists, Marx and Engels sought an end to capitalism and the systems which they perceived to be responsible for the exploitation of workers. But whereas earlier socialists often favored longer-term social reform, Marx and Engels believed that popular revolution was all but inevitable, and the only path to the socialist state.

According to the Marxist argument for communism, the main characteristic of human life in class society is alienation; and communism is desirable because it entails the full realization of human freedom.[6] Marx here follows Georg Wilhelm Friedrich Hegel in conceiving freedom not merely as an absence of restraints but as action with content.[7] According to Marx, Communism's outlook on freedom was based on an agent, obstacle, and goal. The agent is the common/working people; the obstacles are class divisions, economic inequalities, unequal life-chances, and false consciousness; and the goal is the fulfillment of human needs including satisfying work, and fair share of the product.[8] [9] They believed that communism allowed people to do what they want, but also put humans in such conditions and such relations with one another that they would not wish to exploit, or have any need to. Whereas for Hegel the unfolding of this ethical life in history is mainly driven by the realm of ideas, for Marx, communism emerged from material forces, particularly the development of the means of production.[7]

Marxism holds that a process of class conflict and revolutionary struggle will result in victory for the proletariat and the establishment of a communist society in which private ownership is abolished over time and the means of production and subsistence belong to the community. Marx himself wrote little about life under communism, giving only the most general indication as to what constituted a communist society. It is clear that it entails abundance in which there is little limit to the projects that humans may undertake. In the popular slogan that was adopted by the communist movement, communism was a world in which each gave according to their abilities, and received according to their needs. *The German Ideology* (1845) was one of Marx's few writings to elaborate on the communist future:

> "In communist society, where nobody has one exclusive sphere of activity but each can become accomplished in any branch he wishes, society regulates the general production and thus makes it possible for me to do one thing today and another tomorrow, to hunt in the morning, fish in the afternoon, rear cattle in the evening, criticise after dinner, just as I have a mind, without ever becoming hunter, fisherman, herdsman or critic."[10]

Marx's lasting vision was to add this vision to a theory of how society was moving in a law-governed way toward communism, and, with some tension, a political theory that explained why revolutionary activity was required to bring it about.[7]

In the late 19th century, the terms "socialism" and "communism" were often used interchangeably. However, Marx and Engels argued that communism would not emerge from capitalism in a fully developed state, but would pass through a "first phase" in which most productive property was owned in common, but with some class differences remaining. The "first phase" would eventually evolve into a "higher phase" in which class differences were eliminated, and a state was no longer needed. Lenin frequently used the term "socialism" to refer to Marx and Engels' supposed "first phase" of communism and used the term "communism" interchangeably with Marx and Engels' "higher phase" of communism.

These later aspects, particularly as developed by Vladimir Ilyich Lenin, provided the underpinning for the mobilizing features of 20th century Communist parties.

Marxism-Leninism

Marxism-Leninism is a version of socialism adopted by the Soviet Union and most Communist Parties across the world today. It shaped the Soviet Union and influenced Communist Parties worldwide. It was heralded as a possibility of building communism via a massive program of industrialization and collectivization. Historically, under the ideology of Marxism-Leninism the rapid development of industry, and above all the victory of the Soviet Union in the Second World War occurred alongside a third of the world being lead by Marxist-Leninist inspired parties. Despite the fall of the Soviet Union and Eastern Bloc countries, many communist Parties of the world today still lay claim to uphold the Marxist-Leninist banner. Marxism-Leninism expands on Marxists thoughts by bringing the theories to what Lenin and other Communists considered, the age of capitalist imperialism, and a renewed focus on party building, the development of a socialist state, and democratic centralism as an organizational principle.

Lenin adapted Marx's urban revolution to Russia's agricultural conditions, sparking the "revolutionary nationalism of the poor".[11] The pamphlet *What is to be Done?* (1902), proposed that the (urban) proletariat can successfully achieve revolutionary consciousness only under the leadership of a vanguard party of professional revolutionaries — who can achieve aims only with internal democratic centralism in the party; tactical and ideological policy decisions are agreed via democracy, and every member must support and promote the agreed party policy.

To wit, capitalism can be overthrown only with revolution — because attempts to *reform* capitalism from within (Fabianism) and from without (democratic socialism) will fail because of its inherent contradictions. The purpose of a Leninist revolutionary vanguard party is the forceful deposition of the incumbent government; assume power (as agent of the proletariat) and establish a dictatorship of the proletariat government. Moreover, as the government, the vanguard party must educate the proletariat — to dispel the societal false consciousness of religion and nationalism that are culturally instilled by the bourgeoisie in facilitating exploitation. The dictatorship of the proletariat is governed with a de-centralized direct democracy practised via soviets (councils) where the workers exercise political power (cf. soviet democracy); the fifth chapter of *State & Revolution*, describes it:

> ". . . the dictatorship of the proletariat — i.e. the organisation of the vanguard of the oppressed as the ruling class for the purpose of crushing the oppressors. . . . An immense expansion of democracy, which

for the first time becomes democracy for the poor, democracy for the people, and not democracy for the rich: . . . and suppression by force, i.e. exclusion from democracy, for the exploiters and oppressors of the people — this is the change which democracy undergoes during the *transition* from capitalism to communism."[12]

The Bolshevik government was hostile to nationalism, especially to Russian nationalism, the "Great Russian chauvinism", as an obstacle to establishing the proletarian dictatorship.[13] The revolutionary elements of Leninism — the disciplined vanguard party, a dictatorship of the proletariat, and class war.

Stalinism

"Stalinism" refers to the political system of the Soviet Union, and the countries within the Soviet sphere of influence, during the leadership of Joseph Stalin. The term usually defines the style of a government rather than an ideology. The ideology was "Marxism-Leninism theory", reflecting that Stalin himself was not a theoretician, in contrast to Marx and Lenin, and prided himself on maintaining the legacy of Lenin as a founding father for the Soviet Union and the future Socialist world. Stalinism is an interpretation of their ideas, and a certain political regime claiming to apply those ideas in ways fitting the changing needs of society, as with the transition from "socialism at a snail's pace" in the mid-twenties to the rapid industrialization of the Five-Year Plans.

The main contributions of Stalin to communist theory were:

*   The groundwork for the Soviet policy concerning nationalities, laid in Stalin's 1913 work *Marxism and the National Question*,[14] praised by Lenin.
*   Socialism in One Country,
*   The theory of aggravation of the class struggle along with the development of socialism, a theoretical base supporting the repression of political opponents as necessary.

Trotskyism

Trotsky and his supporters organized into the *Left Opposition* and their platform became known as *Trotskyism*. Stalin eventually succeeded in gaining control of the Soviet regime and Trotskyist attempts to remove Stalin from power resulted in Trotsky's exile from the Soviet Union in 1929. During Trotsky's exile, world communism fractured into two distinct branches: Marxism-Leninism and Trotskyism.[1] Trotsky later founded the Fourth International, a Trotskyist rival to the Comintern, in 1938.

Leon Trotsky reading *The Militant*.

Trotskyist ideas have continually found a modest echo among political movements in some countries in Latin America and Asia, especially in Argentina, Brazil, Bolivia and Sri Lanka. Many Trotskyist organizations are also active in more stable, developed countries in North America and Western Europe. Trotsky's politics differed sharply from those of Stalin and Mao, most importantly in declaring the need for an international proletarian revolution (rather than socialism in one country) and unwavering support for a true dictatorship of the proletariat based on democratic principles.

However, as a whole, Trotsky's theories and attitudes were never accepted in worldwide mainstream Communist circles after Trotsky's expulsion, either within or outside of the Soviet bloc. This remained the case even after the Secret Speech and subsequent events critics claim exposed the fallibility of Stalin.

Some criticize Trotskyism as incapable of using concrete analysis on its theories, rather resorting to phrases and abstract notions.[15] [16] [17]

Maoism

Maoism is the Marxist-Leninist trend of Communism associated with Mao Zedong and was mostly practiced within the People's Republic of China. Khrushchev's reforms heightened ideological differences between the People's Republic of China and the Soviet Union, which became increasingly apparent in the 1960s. As the Sino-Soviet Split in the international Communist movement turned toward open hostility, China portrayed itself as a leader of the underdeveloped world against the two superpowers, the United States and the Soviet Union.

This poster shows Mao Zedong as continuing the legacy set by former Communist leaders.[18]

Parties and groups that supported the Communist Party of China (CPC) in their criticism against the new Soviet leadership proclaimed themselves as 'anti-revisionist' and denounced the CPSU and the parties aligned with it as revisionist "capitalist-roaders." The Sino-Soviet Split resulted in divisions amongst communist parties around the world. Notably, the Party of Labour of Albania sided with the People's Republic of China. Effectively, the CPC under Mao's leadership became the rallying forces of a parallel international Communist tendency. The ideology of CPC, Marxism-Leninism-Mao Zedong Thought (generally referred to as 'Maoism'), was adopted by many of these groups.

After Mao's death and his replacement by Deng Xiaoping, the international Maoist movement diverged. One sector accepted the new leadership in China; a second renounced the new leadership and reaffirmed their commitment to Mao's legacy; and a third renounced Maoism altogether and aligned with Albania.

Hoxhaism

Another variant of anti-revisionist Marxism-Leninism appeared after the ideological row between the Communist Party of China and the Party of Labour of Albania in 1978. The Albanians rallied a new separate international tendency. This tendency would demarcate itself by a strict defense of the legacy of Joseph Stalin and fierce criticism of virtually all other Communist groupings as revisionism. Critical of the United States, Soviet Union, and China, Enver Hoxha declared the latter two to be social-imperialist and condemned the Soviet invasion of Czechoslovakia by withdrawing from the Warsaw Pact in response. Hoxha declared Albania to be the world's only Marxist-Leninist state after 1978. The Albanians were able to win over a large share of the Maoists, mainly in Latin America such as the Popular Liberation Army, but also had a significant international following in general. This tendency has occasionally been labeled as 'Hoxhaism' after him.

After the fall of the Communist government in Albania, the pro-Albanian parties are grouped around an international conference and the publication 'Unity and Struggle'.

Titoism

Elements of Titoism are characterized by policies and practices based on the principle that in each country, the means of attaining ultimate communist goals must be dictated by the conditions of that particular country, rather than by a pattern set in another country. During Tito's era, this specifically meant that the communist goal should be pursued independently of (and often in opposition to) the policies of the Soviet Union.

The term was originally meant as a pejorative, and was labeled by Moscow as a heresy during the period of tensions between the Soviet Union and Yugoslavia known as the *Informbiro* period from 1948 to 1955.

Unlike the rest of East Europe, which fell under Stalin's influence post-World War II, Yugoslavia, due to the strong leadership of Marshal Tito and the fact that the Yugoslav Partisans liberated Yugoslavia with only limited help from the Red Army, remained independent from Moscow. It became the only country in the Balkans to resist pressure from Moscow to join the Warsaw Pact and remained "socialist, but independent" right up until the collapse of Soviet socialism in the late 1980s and early 1990s. Throughout his time in office, Tito prided himself on Yugoslavia's independence from Russia, with Yugoslavia never accepting full membership of the Comecon and Tito's open rejection of many aspects of Stalinism as the most obvious manifestations of this.

Eurocommunism

Since the early 1970s, the term Eurocommunism was used to refer to moderate, reformist Communist parties in western Europe. These parties did not support the Soviet Union and denounced its policies. Such parties were politically active and electorally significant in Italy (PCI), France (PCF), and Spain (PCE).

Council communism

Council communism is a far-left movement originating in Germany and the Netherlands in the 1920s. Its primary organization was the Communist Workers Party of Germany (KAPD). Council communism continues today as a theoretical and activist position within both left-wing Marxism and libertarian socialism.

The central argument of council communism, in contrast to those of social democracy and Leninist Communism, is that democratic workers' councils arising in the factories and municipalities are the natural form of working class organisation and governmental power. This view is opposed to both the reformist and the Leninist ideologies, with their stress on, respectively, parliaments and institutional government (i.e., by applying social reforms), on the one hand, and vanguard parties and participative democratic centralism on the other).

The core principle of council communism is that the government and the economy should be managed by workers' councils composed of delegates elected at workplaces and recallable at any moment. As such, council communists oppose state-run authoritarian "State socialism"/"State capitalism". They also oppose the idea of a "revolutionary party", since council communists believe that a revolution led by a party will necessarily produce a party dictatorship. Council communists support a worker's democracy, which they want to produce through a federation of workers' councils. Council communism (and other types of "anti-authoritarian and Anti-leninist Marxism" such as Autonomism) are often viewed as being similar to Anarchism because they criticize Leninist ideologies for being authoritarian and reject the idea of a vanguard party.

Luxemburgism

Luxemburgism, based on the writing of Rosa Luxemburg, is an interpretation of Marxism which, while supporting the Russian Revolution, as Luxemburg did, agrees with her criticisms of the politics of Lenin and Trotsky; she did not see their concept of "democratic centralism" as democracy.

The chief tenets of Luxemburgism are commitment to democracy and the necessity of the revolution taking place as soon as possible. In this regard, it is similar to Council Communism, but differs in that, for example, Luxemburgists don't reject elections by principle. It resembles anarchism in its insistence that only relying on the people themselves as opposed to their leaders can avoid an authoritarian society, but differs in that it sees the importance of a revolutionary party, and mainly the centrality of the working class in the revolutionary struggle. It resembles Trotskyism in its opposition to the totalitarianism of Stalinist government while simultaneously avoiding the reformist politics of modern Social Democracy, but differs from Trotskyism in arguing that Lenin and Trotsky also made undemocratic errors.

Luxemburg's idea of democracy, which Stanley Aronowitz calls "*generalized* democracy in an unarticulated form", represents Luxemburgism's greatest break with "mainstream communism", since it effectively diminishes the role of the Communist Party, but is in fact very similar to the views of Karl Marx ("*The emancipation of the working classes must be conquered by the working classes themselves*"). According to Aronowitz, the vagueness of Luxembourgian democracy is one reason for its initial difficulty in gaining widespread support. However, since the fall of the Soviet Union, Luxemburgism has been seen by some socialist thinkers as a way to avoid the totalitarianism of Stalinism. Early on, Luxemburg attacked undemocratic tendencies present in the Russian Revolution.

Juche

In 1992, Juche replaced Marxism-Leninism in the revised North Korean constitution as the official state ideology, this being a response to the Sino-Soviet split. Juche was originally defined as a creative application of Marxism-Leninism, but after the 1991 collapse of the Soviet Union (North Korea's greatest economic benefactor), all reference to Marxism-Leninism was dropped in the revised 1998 constitution. The establishment of the Songun doctrine in the mid-1990s has formally designated the military, not the proletariat or working class, as the main revolutionary force in North Korea. All reference to communism had been dropped in the 2009 revised constitution.[19]

According to Kim Jong-il's *On the Juche Idea*, the application of Juche in state policy entails the following:

1. The people must have independence (*chajusong*) in thought and politics, economic self-sufficiency, and self-reliance in defense.
2. Policy must reflect the will and aspirations of the masses and employ them fully in revolution and construction.
3. Methods of revolution and construction must be suitable to the situation of the country.
4. The most important work of revolution and construction is molding people ideologically as communists and mobilizing them to constructive action.

Prachandapath

Prachanda, giving a speech at the Nepalese city of Pokhara.

Prachanda Path refers to the ideological line of the Communist Party of Nepal (Maoist). This thought doesn't make an ideological break with Marxism, Leninism and Maoism but it is an extension of these ideologies totally based on home-ground politics of Nepal. The doctrine came into existence after it was realized that the ideology of Marxism, Leninism and Maoism couldn't be practiced completely as it was done in the past. And an ideology suitable, based on the ground reality of Nepalese politics was adopted by the party.

After five years of armed struggle, the party realized that none of the proletarian revolutions of the past could be carried out on Nepal's context. So moving further ahead than Marxism, Leninism and Maoism, the party determined its own ideology, Prachanda Path.

Having analyzed the serious challenges and growing changes in the global arena, the party started moving on its own doctrine. Prachanda Path in essence is a different kind of uprising, which can be described as the fusion of a protracted people's war strategy which was adopted by Mao in China and the Russian model of armed revolution. Most of the Maoist leaders think that the adoption of Prachanda Path after the second national conference is what nudged the party into moving ahead with a clear vision ahead after five years of 'people's war'.

Senior Maoist leader Mohan Vaidya alias Kiran says, 'Just as Marxism was born in Germany, Leninism in Russia and Maoism in China and Prachanda Path is Nepal's identity of revolution. Just as Marxism has three facets-philosophy, political economy and scientific socialism, Prachanda Path is a combination of all three totally in Nepal's political context.' Talking about the party's philosophy, Maoist chairman Prachanda says, 'The party considers Prachanda path as an enrichment of Marxism, Leninism and Maoism.' After the party brought forward its new doctrine, the government was trying to comprehend the new ideology, Prachanda Path.

see also: 'People's Revolution' In Nepal

Non-Marxist schools

The dominant forms of communism, such as Leninism, Trotskyism and Maoism, are based on Marxism, but non-Marxist versions of communism (such as Christian communism and anarchist communism) also exist and are growing in importance since the fall of the Soviet Union.

Anarcho-communism

Some of Marx's contemporaries espoused similar ideas, but differed in their views of how to reach to a classless society. Following the split between those associated with Marx and Mikhail Bakunin at the First International, the anarchists formed the International Workers Association.[20] Anarchists argued that capitalism and the state were inseparable and that one could not be abolished without the other. Anarchist-communists such as Peter Kropotkin theorized an immediate transition to one society with no classes. Anarcho-syndicalism became one of the dominant forms of anarchist organization, arguing that labor unions, as opposed to Communist parties, are the organizations that can change society. Consequently, many anarchists have been in opposition to Marxist communism to this day.

Anarchist communists propose that the freest form of social organisation would be a society composed of self-governing communes with collective use of the means of production, organized by direct democracy, and related to other communes through federation.[21] However, some anarchist communists oppose the majoritarian nature of direct democracy, feeling that it can impede individual liberty and favor consensus democracy.[22]

Christian communism

Christian communism is a form of religious communism centered on Christianity. It is a theological and political theory based upon the view that the teachings of Jesus Christ urge Christians to support communism as the ideal social system. Christian communists trace the origins of their practice to teachings in the New Testament, such as this one from Acts of the Apostles at chapter 2 and verses 42, 44, and 45:

> **42** *And they continued steadfastly in the apostles' doctrine and in fellowship [...]* **44** *And all that believed were together, and had all things in common;* **45** *And sold their possessions and goods, and parted them to all men, as every man had need.* (King James Version)

Christian communism can be seen as a radical form of Christian socialism. Also, due to the fact that many Christian communists have formed independent stateless communes in the past, there is also a link between Christian communism and Christian anarchism. Christian communists may or may not agree with various parts of Marxism.

Christian communists also share some of the political goals of Marxists, for example replacing capitalism with socialism, which should in turn be followed by communism at a later point in the future. However, Christian communists sometimes disagree with Marxists (and particularly with Leninists) on the way a socialist or communist society should be organized.

History

Early communism

Karl Heinrich Marx saw primitive communism as the original, hunter-gatherer state of humankind from which it arose. For Marx, only after humanity was capable of producing surplus, did private property develop.

In the history of Western thought, certain elements of the idea of a society based on common ownership of property can be traced back to ancient times . Examples include the Spartacus slave revolt in Rome.[23] The fifth century Mazdak movement in what is now Iran has been described as "communistic" for challenging the enormous privileges of the noble classes and the clergy, criticizing the institution of private property and for striving for an egalitarian society.[24]

At one time or another, various small communist communities existed, generally under the inspiration of Scripture.[25] In the medieval Christian church, for example, some monastic communities and religious orders shared their land and other property (see religious communism and Christian communism). These groups often believed that concern with private property was a distraction from religious service to God and neighbor.

Communist thought has also been traced back to the work of 16th century English writer Thomas More. In his treatise *Utopia* (1516), More portrayed a society based on common ownership of property, whose rulers administered it through the application of reason. In the 17th century, communist thought arguably surfaced again in England. In 17th century England, a Puritan religious group known as the Diggers advocated the abolition of private ownership of land. Eduard Bernstein, in his 1895 *Cromwell and Communism*[26] argued that several groupings in the English Civil War, especially the Diggers espoused clear communistic, agrarian ideals, and that Oliver Cromwell's attitude to these groups was at best ambivalent and often hostile.[27]

Criticism of the idea of private property continued into the Age of Enlightenment of the 18th century, through such thinkers as Jean Jacques Rousseau in France. Later, following the upheaval of the French Revolution, communism emerged as a political doctrine.[28] François Noël Babeuf, in particular, espoused the goals of common ownership of land and total economic and political equality among citizens.

Various social reformers in the early 19th century founded communities based on common ownership. But unlike many previous communist communities, they replaced the religious emphasis with a rational and philanthropic basis.[25] Notable among them were Robert Owen, who founded New Harmony in Indiana (1825), and Charles Fourier, whose followers organized other settlements in the United States such as Brook Farm (1841–47).[25] Later in the 19th century, Karl Marx described these social reformers as "utopian socialists" to contrast them with his program of "scientific socialism" (a term coined by Friedrich Engels). Other writers described by Marx as "utopian socialists" included Saint-Simon.

In its modern form, communism grew out of the socialist movement of 19th century Europe. As the Industrial Revolution advanced, socialist critics blamed capitalism for the misery of the proletariat — a new class of urban factory workers who labored under often-hazardous conditions. Foremost among these critics were the German philosopher Karl Marx and his associate Friedrich Engels. In 1848, Marx and Engels offered a new definition of communism and popularized the term in their famous pamphlet *The Communist Manifesto.*[25] Engels, who lived in Manchester, observed the organization of the Chartist movement (*see History of British socialism*), while Marx departed from his university comrades to meet the proletariat in France and Germany.

Growth of modern communism

Vladimir Lenin, following his return to Petrograd.

In the late 19th century, Russian Marxism developed a distinct character. The first major figure of Russian Marxism was Georgi Plekhanov. Underlying the work of Plekhanov was the assumption that Russia, less urbanized and industrialized than Western Europe, had many years to go before society would be ready for proletarian revolution to occur, and a transitional period of a bourgeois democratic regime would be required to replace Tsarism with a socialist and later communist society. (EB)

In Russia, the 1917 October Revolution was the first time any party with an avowedly Marxist orientation, in this case the Bolshevik Party, seized state power. The assumption of state power by the Bolsheviks generated a great deal of practical and theoretical debate within the Marxist movement. Marx predicted that socialism and communism would be built upon foundations laid by the most advanced capitalist development. Russia, however, was one of the poorest countries in Europe with an enormous, largely illiterate peasantry and a minority of industrial workers. Marx had explicitly stated that Russia might be able to skip the stage of bourgeoisie capitalism.[29] Other socialists also believed that a Russian revolution could be the precursor of workers' revolutions in the West.

The moderate Mensheviks opposed Lenin's Bolshevik plan for socialist revolution before capitalism was more fully developed. The Bolsheviks' successful rise to power was based upon the slogans "peace, bread, and land" and "All power to the Soviets", slogans which tapped the massive public desire for an end to Russian involvement in the First World War, the peasants' demand for land reform, and popular support for the Soviets.

The usage of the terms "communism" and "socialism" shifted after 1917, when the Bolsheviks changed their name to the Communist Party and installed a single party regime devoted to the implementation of socialist policies under Leninism. The Second International had dissolved in 1916 over national divisions, as the separate national parties that composed it did not maintain a unified front against the war, instead generally supporting their respective nation's role. Lenin thus created the Third International (Comintern) in 1919 and sent the Twenty-one Conditions, which included democratic centralism, to all European socialist parties willing to adhere. In France, for example, the majority of the French Section of the Workers' International (SFIO) party split in 1921 to form the French Section of the Communist International (SFIC). Henceforth, the term "Communism" was applied to the objective of the parties founded under the umbrella of the Comintern. Their program called for the uniting of workers of the world for revolution, which would be followed by the establishment of a dictatorship of the proletariat as well as the development of a socialist economy. Ultimately, if their program held, there would develop a harmonious classless society, with the withering away of the state.

During the Russian Civil War (1918–1922), the Bolsheviks nationalized all productive property and imposed a policy of *war communism*, which put factories and railroads under strict government control, collected and rationed food, and introduced some bourgeois management of industry. After three years of war and the 1921 Kronstadt rebellion, Lenin declared the New Economic Policy (NEP) in 1921, which was to give a "limited place for a limited time to capitalism." The NEP lasted until 1928, when Joseph Stalin achieved party leadership, and the introduction of the first

A map of countries who declared themselves to be socialist states under the Marxist-Leninist or Maoist definition (in other words, "communist states") in 1980. The map also includes Communist alignment: either to the Soviet Union, China or independent

Five Year Plan spelled the end of it. Following the Russian Civil War, the Bolsheviks formed in 1922 the Union of Soviet Socialist Republics (USSR), or Soviet Union, from the former Russian Empire.

Following Lenin's democratic centralism, the Communist parties were organized on a hierarchical basis, with active cells of members as the broad base; they were made up only of elite cadres approved by higher members of the party as being reliable and completely subject to party discipline.[30]

After World War II, Communists consolidated power in Eastern Europe, and in 1949, the Communist Party of China (CPC) led by Mao Zedong established the People's Republic of China, which would later follow its own ideological path of Communist development. Cuba, North Korea, Vietnam, Laos, Cambodia, Angola, and Mozambique were among the other countries in the Third World that adopted or imposed a pro-Communist government at some point. Although never formally unified as a single political entity, by the early 1980s almost one-third of the world's population lived in Communist states, including the former Soviet Union and People's Republic of China. By comparison, the British Empire had ruled up to one-quarter of the world's population at its greatest extent.[31]

Communist states such as the Soviet Union and China succeeded in becoming industrial and technological powers, challenging the capitalists' powers in the arms race and space race and military conflicts.

Cold War years

By virtue of the Soviet Union's victory in the Second World War in 1945, the Soviet Army had occupied nations in both Eastern Europe and East Asia; as a result, communism as a movement spread to many new countries. This expansion of communism both in Europe and Asia gave rise to a few different branches of its own, such as Maoism.

USSR postage stamp depicting the communist state launching the first artificial satellite Sputnik 1.

Communism had been vastly strengthened by the winning of many new nations into the sphere of Soviet influence and strength in Eastern Europe. Governments modeled on Soviet Communism took power with Soviet assistance in Bulgaria, Czechoslovakia, East Germany, Poland, Hungary and Romania. A Communist government was also created under Marshal Tito in Yugoslavia, but Tito's independent policies led to the expulsion of Yugoslavia from the Cominform, which had replaced the Comintern. Titoism, a new branch in the world communist movement, was labeled *deviationist*. Albania also became an independent Communist nation after World War II.

By 1950, the Chinese Communists held all of Mainland China, thus controlling the most populous nation in the world. Other areas where rising Communist strength provoked dissension and in some cases led to actual fighting through conventional and guerrilla warfare include the Korean War, Laos, many nations of the Middle East and Africa, and notably succeeded in the case of the Vietnam War against the military power of the United States and its allies. With varying degrees of success, Communists attempted to unite with nationalist and socialist forces against what they saw as Western imperialism in these poor countries.

Fear of communism

A 1947 propaganda book published by the Catechetical Guild Educational Society "warning of the dangers" of a Communist takeover.

With the exception of the Soviet Union's, China's and the Italian resistance movement's great contribution in World War II, communism was seen as a rival, and a threat to western democracies and capitalism for most of the twentieth century. This rivalry peaked during the Cold War, as the world's two remaining superpowers, the United States and the Soviet Union, polarized most of the world into two camps of nations (characterized in the West as "The Free World" vs. "Behind the Iron Curtain"); supported the spread of their economic and political systems (capitalism and democracy vs. communism); strengthened their military power, developed new weapon systems and stockpiled nuclear weapons; competed with each other in space exploration; and even fought each other through proxy client nations.

Near the beginning of the Cold War, on February 9, 1950, Senator Joseph McCarthy from Wisconsin accused 205 Americans working in the State Department of being "card-carrying Communists".[32] The fear of communism in the U.S. spurred aggressive investigations and the red-baiting, blacklisting, jailing and deportation of people suspected of following Communist or other left-wing ideology. Many famous actors and writers were put on a "blacklist" from 1950 to 1954, which meant they would not be hired and would be subject to public disdain.[33]

After the collapse of the Soviet Union

In 1985, Mikhail Gorbachev became leader of the Soviet Union and relaxed central control, in accordance with reform policies of glasnost (openness) and perestroika (restructuring). The Soviet Union did not intervene as Poland, East Germany, Czechoslovakia, Bulgaria, Romania, and Hungary all abandoned Communist rule by 1990. In 1991, the Soviet Union itself dissolved.

A map of countries who declare themselves to be socialist states under the Marxist-Leninist or Maoist definition (in other words, "communist states") today. The map also includes Communist alignment: either to China or independent

By the beginning of the 21st century, states controlled by Communist parties under a single-party system include the People's Republic of China, Cuba, Laos, Vietnam, and informally North Korea. Communist parties, or their descendant parties, remain politically important in many countries. President Dimitris Christofias of Cyprus is a member of the Progressive Party of Working People, but the country is not run under single-party rule. In South Africa, the Communist Party is a partner in the ANC-led government. In India, communists lead the governments of three states, with a combined population of more than 115 million. In Nepal, communists hold a majority in the parliament.[34]

The People's Republic of China has reassessed many aspects of the Maoist legacy; and the People's Republic of China, Laos, Vietnam, and, to a far lesser degree, Cuba have reduced state control of the economy in order to stimulate growth. The People's Republic of China runs Special Economic Zones dedicated to market-oriented enterprise, free from central government control. Several other communist states have also attempted to implement market-based reforms, including Vietnam.

A tableau in a communist rally in Kerala, India, of a young farmer and worker.

Theories within Marxism as to why communism in Eastern Europe was not achieved after socialist revolutions pointed to such elements as the pressure of external capitalist states, the relative backwardness of the societies in which the revolutions occurred, and the emergence of a bureaucratic stratum or class that arrested or diverted the transition press in its own interests. (Scott and Marshall, 2005) Marxist critics of the Soviet Union, most notably Trotsky, referred to the Soviet system, along with other Communist states, as "degenerated" or "deformed workers' states", arguing that the Soviet system fell far short of Marx's communist ideal and he claimed the working class was politically dispossessed. The ruling stratum of the Soviet Union was held to be a bureaucratic caste, but not a new ruling class, despite their political control. Anarchists who adhere to Participatory economics claim that the Soviet Union became dominated by powerful intellectual elites who in a capitalist system crown the proletariat's labor on behalf of the bourgeoisie.

Non-Marxists, in contrast, have often applied the term to any society ruled by a Communist Party and to any party aspiring to create a society similar to such existing nation-states. In the social sciences, societies ruled by Communist Parties are distinct for their single party control and their socialist economic bases. While some social and political scientists applied the concept of "totalitarianism" to these societies, others identified possibilities for independent political activity within them,[35] [36] and stressed their continued evolution up to the point of the dissolution of the Soviet Union and its allies in

Eastern Europe during the late 1980s and early 1990s.

Today, Marxist revolutionaries are conducting armed insurgencies in India, Philippines, Peru, Bangladesh, Iran, Turkey, and Colombia.

Criticism

A diverse array of writers and political activists have published criticism of communism, such as:

- Soviet bloc dissidents Lech Wałęsa, Aleksandr Solzhenitsyn and Václav Havel;
- Social theorists Hannah Arendt, Raymond Aron, Ralf Dahrendorf, Seymour Martin Lipset, and Karl Wittfogel;
- Economists Ludwig von Mises, Friedrich Hayek, and Milton Friedman;
- Historians and social scientists Robert Conquest, Stéphane Courtois, Richard Pipes, and R. J. Rummel;
- Anti-Stalinist leftists Ignazio Silone, George Orwell, Saul Alinsky, Richard Wright, Arthur Koestler, and Bernard-Henri Levy;
- Russian-born novelist and philosopher Ayn Rand
- Philosophers Leszek Kołakowski and Karl Popper.

Part of this criticism is on the policies adopted by one-party states ruled by Communist parties (known as "Communist states"). Critics are specially focused on their economic performance compared to market based economies. Their human rights records are thought to be responsible for the flight of refugees from communist states, and are alleged by some scholars to be responsible for famines, purges and warfare resulting in deaths far in excess of previous empires, capitalist or Axis regimes.[37] [38] [39]

Some writers, such as Courtois, argue that the actions of Communist states were the inevitable (though sometimes unintentional) result of Marxist principles;[40] thus, these authors present the events occurring in those countries, particularly under Stalin and Mao, as an argument against Marxism itself. Some critics were former Marxists, such as Wittfogel, who applied Marx's concept of "Oriental despotism" to Communist states such as the Soviet Union,[41] Silone, Wright and Koestler (among other writers) who contributed essays to the book *The God that Failed* (the title refers not to the Christian God but to Marxism).[42] Czesław Miłosz, author of the influential essay *The Captive Mind*, was an example of a sceptic holding a party post, that of cultural attaché.[43]

There have also been more direct criticisms of Marxism, such as criticisms of the labor theory of value or Marx's predictions. Nevertheless, Communist parties outside of the Warsaw Pact, such as the Communist parties in Western Europe, Asia, Latin America, and Africa, differed greatly.

Economic criticisms of communal and/or government property are described under criticisms of socialism.

References

Notes

[1] " Communism (http://www.encyclopedia.com/topic/communism.aspx)". *Columbia Encyclopedia*. 2008.

[2] Schaff, Kory (2001). *Philosophy and the problems of work: a reader*. Lanham, Md: Rowman & Littlefield. pp. 224 (http://books.google.com/books?id=mdLh5EMehwgC&pg=PA224&dq=isbn=0742507955&source=gbs_search_r&cad=0_1& sig=ACfU3U2S6uiRNCig9mq_bY4yKB7877tY4A). ISBN 0-7425-0795-5.

[3] Walicki, Andrzej (1995). *Marxism and the leap to the kingdom of freedom: the rise and fall of the Communist utopia*. Stanford, Calif: Stanford University Press. p. 95. ISBN 0-8047-2384-2.

[4] "Socialism." Columbia Electronic Encyclopedia. Columbia University Press. 03 Feb. 2008.<reference.com http://www.reference.com/browse/columbia/socialis>.

[5] "Critique of the Gotha Programme--IV" (http://www.marxists.org/archive/marx/works/1875/gotha/ch04.htm). *Critique of the Gotha Programme*. . Retrieved 2009-10-18.

[6] Stephen Whitefield. "Communism." *The Concise Oxford Dictionary of Politics*. Ed. Iain McLean and Alistair McMillan. Oxford University Press, 2003.

[7] McLean and McMillan, 2003.

[8] Ball and Dagger 118

[9] Terence Ball and Richard Dagger. "Political Ideologies and the Democratic Ideal." Pearson Education, Inc.:2006.

[10] Karl Marx, (1845). *The German Ideology*, Marx-Engels Institute, Moscow. ISBN 978-1-57392-258-6. Sources available at The German Ideology (http://www.marxists.org/archive/marx/works/1845/german-ideology/ch01a.htm) at www.marxists.org.

[11] *Faces of Janus* p. 133.

[12] Hill, Christopher *Lenin and the Russian Revolution* (1971) Penguin Books:Londonp. 86.

[13] Harding, Neil (ed.) *The State in Socialist Society*, second edition (1984) St. Antony's College: Oxford, p. 189.

[14] "Marxism and the National Question" (http://www.marxists.org/reference/archive/stalin/works/1913/03.htm)

[15] "On Trotskyism" (http://www.marx2mao.com/Other/OT73NB.html). Marx2mao.com. . Retrieved 2009-10-18.

[16] "Swedish FRP on anti-Marxist-Leninist dogmas of Trotskyism" (http://home.flash.net/~comvoice/32cTrotskyism.html). Home.flash.net. . Retrieved 2009-10-18.

[17] "What's Your Line?" (http://web.archive.org/web/20080201115440/http://www.etext.org/Politics/MIM/wim/wyl/). Web.archive.org. . Retrieved 2009-10-18.

[18] This poster has been jokingly referred to as "The History of Shaving" Stefan Landsberger's Chinese Propaganda Poster Pages-Ideological Foundations (http://www.iisg.nl/~landsberger/if.html)

[19] http://www.reuters.com/article/latestCrisis/idUSSEO253213

[20] Marshall, Peter. "Demanding the Impossible — A History of Anarchism" p. 9. Fontana Press, London, 1993 ISBN 978-0-00-686245-1

[21] Puente, Isaac. "Libertarian Communism" (http://flag.blackened.net/liberty/libcom.html). *The Cienfuegos Press Anarchist Review*. Issue 6 Orkney 1982.

[22] Graeber, David and Grubacic, Andrej. *Anarchism, Or The Revolutionary Movement Of The Twenty-first Century*.

[23] "Historical Background for Spartacus" (http://www.vroma.org/~bmcmanus/spartacus.html). Vroma.org. . Retrieved 2009-10-18.

[24] *The Cambridge History of Iran* Volume 3, The Seleucid, Parthian and Sasanian Period (http://web.archive.org/web/20080611075040/http://www.derafsh-kaviyani.com/english/mazdak.html), edited by Ehsan Yarshater, Parts 1 and 2, p1019, Cambridge University Press (1983)

[25] "Communism." *Encyclopædia Britannica*. 2006. Encyclopædia Britannica Online.

[26] Eduard Bernstein: Cromwell and Communism (1895) (http://www.marxists.org/reference/archive/bernstein/works/1895/cromwell/)

[27] Eduard Bernstein, (1895). *Kommunistische und demokratisch-sozialistische Strömungen während der englischen Revolution*, J.H.W. Dietz, Stuttgart. OCLC 36367345 (http://www.worldcat.org/oclc/36367345) Sources available at Eduard Bernstein: Cromwell and Communism (1895) (http://www.marxists.org/reference/archive/bernstein/works/1895/cromwell/) at www.marxists.org.

[28] "Communism" *A Dictionary of Sociology*. John Scott and Gordon Marshall. Oxford University Press 2005. Oxford Reference Online. Oxford University Press.

[29] Marc Edelman, "Late Marx and the Russian road: Marx and the 'Peripheries of Capitalism'" - book reviews. *Monthly Review*, Dec., 1984. Late Marx and the Russian road: Marx and the "Peripheries of Capitalism." - book reviews Monthly Review Find Articles at BNET (http://findarticles.com/p/articles/mi_m1132/is_v36/ai_3537723) at www.findarticles.com.

[30] Norman Davies. "Communism" *The Oxford Companion to World War II*. Ed. I. C. B. Dear and M. R. D. Foot. Oxford University Press, 2001.

[31] Hildreth, Jeremy (2005-06-14). "The British Empire's Lessons for Our own" (http://online.wsj.com/article/SB111870387824258558.html). *The Wall Street Journal*. . Retrieved 2009-10-18.

[32] Adams, John G. (1983). *Without Precedent*. New York, N.Y.: W. W. Norton & Company. p. 285. ISBN 0-393-01616-1.

[33] Georgakas, Dan (1992). "The Hollywood Blacklist". *Encyclopedia of the American Left*. University of Illinois Press.

[34] "Nepal's election The Maoists triumph Economist.com" (http://www.economist.com/displaystory.cfm?story_id=11057207&src=nwl). Economist.com. 2008-04-17. . Retrieved 2009-10-18.

[35] H. Gordon Skilling (April 1966). "Interest Groups and Communist Politics". *World Politics* **18** (3): 435–451. doi: 10.2307/2009764 (http://dx.doi.org/10.2307/2009764).?UNIQ3ab34e171166e61b-HTMLCommentStrip7c7dfbc41ccbeb7000000002

[36] J. Arch Getty (1985). *Origins of the Great Purges: The Soviet Communist Party Reconsidered: 1933–1938*. Cambridge University Press. ISBN 978-0-521-33570-6.

[37] Rosefielde, Steven (2009). *Red Holocaust*. Routledge. ISBN 978-0-415-77757-5.

[38] Daniel Jonah Goldhagen. *Worse Than War: Genocide, Eliminationism, and the Ongoing Assault on Humanity*. PublicAffairs, 2009. ISBN 1586487698 p. 54: "...in the past century communist regimes, led and inspired by the Soviet Union and China, have killed more people than any other regime type."

[39] Benjamin A. Valentino. *Final Solutions: Mass Killing and Genocide in the Twentieth Century*. Cornell University Press, 2004. p.91 (http://books.google.com.au/books?id=LQfeXVU_EvgC&pg=PA91#v=onepage&q=&f=false) ISBN 0801439655

[40] Nicolas Werth, Karel Bartošek, Jean-Louis Panne, Jean-Louis Margolin, Andrzej Paczkowski, Stéphane Courtois, *The Black Book of Communism: Crimes, Terror, Repression*, Harvard University Press, 1999, hardcover, 858 pages, ISBN 978-0-674-07608-2

[41] Wittfogel, Karl *Oriental Despotism*, Vintage, 1981

[42] Crossman, Richard, ed., *The God That Failed*. Harper & Bros, 1949

[43] Czeslaw Milosz, Poet and Nobelist Who Wrote of Modern Cruelties, Dies at 93 (http://www.nytimes.com/2004/08/15/obituaries/15milosz.html?pagewanted=all), *The New York Times*, accessed 3 January 2010.

Further reading

- Reason in Revolt: Marxism and Modern Science By Alan Woods and Ted Grant (http://www.marxist.com/rircontents-5.htm)
- Forman, James D., "Communism from Marx's Manifesto to 20th century Reality", New York, Watts. 1972. ISBN 978-0-531-02571-0
- Books on Communism, Socialism and Trotskyism (http://www.marxist.com/marxist-books.htm)
- Furet, Francois, Furet, Deborah Kan (Translator), "The Passing of an Illusion: The Idea of Communism in the Twentieth Century", University of Chicago Press, 2000, ISBN 978-0-226-27341-9
- Daniels, Robert Vincent, "A Documentary History of Communism and the World: From Revolution to Collapse", University Press of New England, 1994, ISBN 978-0-87451-678-4
- Marx, Karl and Friedrich Engels, "Communist Manifesto", (Mass Market Paperback - REPRINT), Signet Classics, 1998, ISBN 978-0-451-52710-3
- Dirlik, Arif, "Origins of Chinese Communism", Oxford University Press, 1989, ISBN 978-0-19-505454-5
- Beer, Max, "The General History of Socialism and Social Struggles Volumes 1 & 2", New York, Russel and Russel, Inc. 1957
- Adami, Stefano, 'Communism', in Encyclopedia of Italian Literary Studies, ed. Gaetana Marrone - P.Puppa, Routledge, New York- London, 2006

External links

- European Parliament resolution on European conscience and totalitarianism (http://www.europarl.europa.eu/news/expert/infopress_page/019-53246-091-04-14-902-20090401IPR53245-01-04-2009-2009-false/default_en.htm)
- In Defense of Marxism (http://www.marxist.com/)
- Anarchy Archives (http://dwardmac.pitzer.edu/anarchist_archives/index.html) Includes the works of anarchist communists.
- Libertarian Communist Library (http://www.libcom.org/library)
- Marxists Internet Archive (http://www.marxists.org/)
- Marxist.net (http://www.marxist.net/)
- The Mu Particle in "Communism" (http://www.wumingfoundation.com/english/outtakes/communism.htm), a short etymological essay by Wu Ming.
- Open Society Archives (http://www.osaarchivum.org/guide/fonds/communismandcoldwar.shtml), one of the biggest history of communism and cold war archives in the world.
- Islam and Communism (http://www.quran-miracle.info/Quran-Communism.htm)

Blackshirts

Part of the Politics series on

Fascism

Fascism portal
Politics portal

For other uses and meanings see Blackshirts (disambiguation).

The **Blackshirts** (Italian: *camicie nere*, *CCNN*, or *squadristi*) were Fascist paramilitary groups in Italy during the period immediately following World War I and until the end of World War II. Blackshirts were also known as the National Security Volunteer Militia (*Milizia Volontaria per la Sicurezza Nazionale*, or *MVSN*).

The term was later applied to a similar group serving the British Union of Fascists before World War II and to members of a quasi-political organization in India.

Inspired by Giuseppe Garibaldi's Redshirts, the Fascist Blackshirts were organized by Benito Mussolini as the military tool of his political movement. The founders of the paramilitary groups were nationalist intellectuals, former army officers or members of the special corp *Arditi*, young landowners opposing peasants' and country labourers' unions. Their methods became harsher as Mussolini's power grew, and they used violence and intimidation against Mussolini's opponents.

The ethos and sometimes the uniform were later copied by others who shared Mussolini's political ideas, including Adolf Hitler in Nazi Germany, who issued brown shirts to the "Storm Troops" (*Sturmabteilung*) and black uniforms to the "Shield Squadron" (*Schutzstaffel*, also colloquially known as "Brownshirts", because they wore black suit-like tunics with brown shirts), Sir Oswald Mosley in the United Kingdom (whose British Union of Fascists were also known as the "Blackshirts"), William Dudley Pelley in the United States (Silver Legion of America or "Silver Shirts"), in Mexico the Camisas Doradas or "Golden Shirts", Plínio Salgado in Brazil (whose followers wore green shirts), and Eoin O'Duffy in the Irish Free State (Army Comrades Association or "Blueshirts"). "Blueshirts" can also refer to Canadian fascists belonging to the Canadian National Socialist Unity Party; And blue were, also, the shirts of the members of Falange Española, the party which ruled Spain during Franco's dictatorship. The paramilitary fascist Iron Guard members in Romania also wore green shirt.

History

The Blackshirts were established as the *squadristi* in 1919 and consisted of many disgruntled former soldiers which may have numbered 200,000 by the time of Mussolini's March on Rome from October 27 to October 29, 1922. In 1922 the *squadristi* were reorganized into the *milizia* and formed numerous *bandiere*, and on 1 February 1923 the Blackshirts became the Volunteer Militia for National Security (*Milizia Volontaria per la Sicurezza Nazionale*, or MVSN), which lasted until the Italian Armistice in 1943. The Italian Social Republic, located in the areas of northern Italy occupied by Germany, reformed the MVSN into the Republican National Guard (*Guardia Nazionale Repubblicana*, or GNR).

Organization

Benito Mussolini was the leader, or Commandant-General, of the blackshirts, but executive functions were carried out by the Chief of Staff, equivalent to an army general. The MVSN was formed in imitation of the ancient Roman army, as follows:

Basic Organization

The terms after the first are not words common to European armies (e.g., the Italian *battaglione* has cognates in many languages). Instead, they derive from the structure of the armies of ancient Rome.

- Zona (Zone) = division
- Legione (Legion) = regiment, each legion was a militia unit consisting of a small active cadre and a large reserve of civilian volunteers.
- Coorte (Cohort) = battalion
- Centuria (Centuria) = company
- Manipolo (Maniple)= platoon
- Squadra (Squad) = squad

These units were also organized on the triangular principle as follows:

- 3 squadre = 1 manipolo (maniple)
- 3 manipoli = 1 centuria (centurie)
- 3 centurie = 1 coorte (cohort)
- 3 coorti − 1 legione (legion)
- 3 legioni = 1 divisioni (field division)
- 3 or more legioni = 1 zona (zone - an administrative division)

Territorial Organization

The MVSN original organization consisted of 15 zones controlling 133 legions (one per province) of three cohorts each and one Independent Group controlling 10 legions. In 1929 it was reorganized into four *raggruppamenti*, but later in October 1936 it was reorganized into 14 zones controlling only 133 legions with two cohorts each, one of men 21 to 36 years old and the other of men up to 55 years old, plus special units in Rome, on Ponza Island and the black uniformed *Moschettieri del Duce* ("The Leader's Musketeers", Mussolini's Guard) and the Albanian Militia (four legions) and Colonial Militia in Africa (seven legions). Special militias were also organized to provide security police functions, these included:

Security Militia

- Anti-aircraft and Coastal Artillery Militia, a combined command which controlled two militias:
  - Anti-Aircraft Militia
  - Coastal Artillery Militia
- Forestry Militia
- Frontier Militia
- Highway Militia
- Port Militia
- Posts and Telegraph Militia
- Railway Militia
- University Militia

Ethiopian Campaign

During the 1935-36 Abyssinian Campaign seven CCNN Divisions were organized:

- 1st (23rd of March) CCNN Division
- 2nd (28th of October) CCNN Division
- 3rd (21 April) CCNN Division
- 4th (3rd of January) CCNN Division
- 5th (1st of February) CCNN Division
- 6th (Tevere) CCNN Division

The first six Divisions were sent to Ethiopia and participated in the war.

- 7th (Cirene) CCNN Division - The 7th CCNN Division "Cirene" was never deployed overseas or even fully equipped before it was disbanded.[1]

Organization of 1935 Blackshirts Divisions:

- Divisional HQ
- 3 x Legions each with:
  - 1 Legionary Machine Gun Company with 16 Machine Guns
  - 2 Legionary Infantry Battalions, each with 1 Machine Gun Company (8x8mm Breda Machine Guns) and 3 Infantry Companies (9 Light Machine Guns and 3 45mm Mortars)
  - 1 pack-artillery battery with 4x65mm L17 each.[2]
- 1 x Artillery Battalion (Army) with 3 batteries (65L17)
- 1 x Engineers company (mixed Army and Blackshirts)
- 2 x Replacements Battalions (1 Infantry, 1 Mixed)
- 1 x Medical Section
- 1 x Logistics Section (food)
- 1 x Pack-Mules unit (1600 mules)
- 1 x Mixed Trucks unit (80 light trucks)

The Blackshirts Rifle Battalions had three rifle companies but no MMG company. The rifle companies had three platoons (three squads with one LMG each). Each Legion had a MMG company with four platoons of three weapons each (plus two spare ones). The Blackshirts replacements battalions were organized as the Blackshirts Rifle Battalions, but its platoon were overstrength (60 men each) and with only 1 x LMG in each platoon.[3]

Blackshirts Division Organization - 10 June 1940

- Division Command
- 2 Black Shirt Legions - each

- 3 Battalions
- 1 81mm Mortar Company
- 1 Accompanying Battery 65mm/17 Mtn guns
- 1 Machine Gun Battalion
- 1 Artillery Regiment:
  - 2 Artillery Groups (75mm/27)
  - 1 Artillery Group (100mm/17)
  - 2 AA Batteries 20mm
- 1 Mixed Engineering Battalion
  - 1 Ambulance Section Sanita
  - 3 Field Hospitals (Planned when available)
  - 1 Supply Section
- 1 Section Mixed Transport[4]

Spanish Civil War

Three CCNN Divisions were sent to Spain to participate in the Civil War there as part of the Corpo Truppe Volontarie. The Blackshirt (Camicie Nere, or CCNN) Divisions contained regular soldiers and volunteer militia from the Fascist Party. The CCNN divisions were semi-motorised.

- 1st CCNN Division "Dio lo Vuole" (*"God wants it"*)
- 2nd CCNN Division "Fiamme Nere" (*"Black Flames"*)
- 3rd CCNN Division "Penne Nere" (*"Black Feathers"*)

The 3rd CCNN Division was disbanded and consolidated with the 2nd CCNN Division in April 1937 after the Battle of Guadalajara. After the northern campaigns in October 1937, the 2nd CCNN Division was consolidated with the 1st CCNN and renamed the XXIII de Marzo Division "Llamas Negras".

World War II

In 1940 the MVSN was able to muster 340,000 first-line combat troops, providing three divisions (1st, 2nd and 4th - all three of which were lost in the North African Campaign) and, later in 1942, a fourth division ("M") and fifth division *Africa* were forming.

Mussolini also pushed through plans to raise 142 MVSN combat battalions of 650 men each to provide a *Gruppo di Assalto* to each army division. These Gruppi consisted of two cohorts (each of three *centurie* of 3 *manipoli* of 2 *squadre* each) plus Gruppo Supporto company of two heavy machine gun *manipoli* (with three HMG each) and two 81 mm mortar *manipoli* (with 3 Mortars each).

Later 41 Mobile groups were raised to become the third regiment in Italian Army divisions as it was determined through operational experience that the Italian arm's binary divisions were too small in both manpower and heavy equipment. These mobile groups suffered heavy casualties due to being undermanned, under equipped and under trained. The three divisions were destroyed in combat in North Africa. The MVSN fought in every theater where Italy did.

Ranks

Mussolini as *Comandante Generale* was made *Primo Caporale Onorario* (First Honorary Corporal) in 1935 and Adolf Hitler was made *Caporale Onorario* (Honorary Corporal) in 1937. All other ranks closely approximated those of the old Roman army as follows:

Generals:

- Comandante Generale = General (Commander-in-chief)
- Luogotenente Generale Capo di S.M. = First Lieutenant General of the S.M. (Chief of Staff)
- Luogotenente Generale = Lieutenant General
- Console Generale = Brigadier General

Commissoned Officers:

- Console Comandante = Colonel (Commander of a Legion)
- Primo Seniore = Lieutenant Colonel
- Seniore = Major (Commander of a Cohort)
- Centurione = Captain (Commander of a Centuria)
- Capomanipolo = First Lieutenant
- Sottocapomanipolo = Second Lieutenant
- Aspirante Sottocapomanipolo = Officer Cadet

Other Ranks:

- Primo Aiutante = Master Warrant Officer
- Aiutante Capo = Chief Warrant Officer

Benito Mussolini as First Honorary Corporal of the MVSN.

- Aiutante = Warrant Officer
- Primo Capo Squadra = First Sergeant
- Capo Squadra = Sergeant (Squad/Section Leader)
- Vicecapo Squadra = Corporal (Vice Squad Leader)
- Camicia Nera Scelta = Black Shirt Private First Class
- Camicia Nera = Black Shirt Private

See also

- Blackshirts - Albania
- Blueshirts - Canada
- Brownshirts - Germany
- Blackshirts - India
- Blueshirts - Ireland
- Greenshirts - Ireland
- Gestapo - Nazi Germany
- Redshirts - Italy
- Goldshirts - Mexico
- Greyshirts - ethnically Dutch South Africans
- Greenshirts - Romania
- Blackshirts - United Kingdom
- Silvershirts - United States

- Purpleshirts-SEIU-United States
- Black Brigades
- Blue Shirts Society - Taiwan (Kuomintang)
- Italian Social Republic
- Militia
- Paramilitary
- Political color
- Political uniform
- Squadrismo
- Integralismo
- Black Shorts – parody of the blackshirts in the writings of P.G. Wodehouse

External links

- Axis History Factbook/Italy/Militia [5]
- Comando Supremo [6]

References

[1] The Blackshirt Division Order of Battle comes from "Storia delle Unità Combattenti della MVSN 1923-1943" by Ettore Lucas and Giorgio de Vecchi, Giovanni Volpe Editore 1976 pages 63 to 116 plus errata.

[2] Italian Army Infantry Regulation of 1939 (Page 472/473)I

[3] The Blackshirts Division TO&E comes from an original document (order sheet "Ministero della Guerra, Comando del Corpo di Stato Maggiore - Ufficio Ordinamento e Mobilitazione . Prot.2076 del 18-06-1935").

[4] The Blackshirts Division TO&E comes from an original document (order sheet "Ministero della Guerra, Comando del Corpo di Stato Maggiore - Ufficio Ordinamento e Mobilitazione. dated 1939").

[5] http://www.axishistory.com/index.php?id=4311

[6] http://www.comandosupremo.com/Blackshirts.html

National Socialist Party of America v. Village of Skokie

National Socialist Party v. Skokie	
Supreme Court of the United States	
Decided June 14, 1977	
Full case name	*National Socialist Party of America et al. v. Village of Skokie*
Docket nos.	76-1786 [1]
Citations	432 U.S. 43 (*more*) 97 S. Ct. 2205; 53 L. Ed. 2d 96; 1977 U.S. LEXIS 113; 2 Media L. Rep. 1993
Holding	
If a state seeks to impose an injunction in violation of First Amendment rights, it must provide strict procedural safeguards, including immediate appellate review. Absent such review, a stay must be granted.	
Court membership	
Case opinions	
Per curiam.	
Concur/dissent	White
Dissent	Rehnquist, joined by Burger, Stewart
Laws applied	
First Amendment of the United States Constitution	

National Socialist Party of America v. Village of Skokie, 432 U.S. 43 (1977) (sometimes referred to as the **Skokie Affair**), was a United States Supreme Court case dealing with freedom of assembly.

Facts of the case

The National Socialist Party of America (a Neo-Nazi group) planned a march in the town of Skokie, Illinois, a largely Jewish community. Some Skokie residents were Holocaust survivors. The neo-Nazi leader, Frank Collin, originally had proposed a march in Marquette Park on Chicago's Southwest side where their headquarters was located. The Park District asked for a huge insurance bond to indemnify them against any damage caused by the anticipated violence hoping that this requirement would dissuade them from marching. The neo-Nazis then threatened to march in Skokie.

Prior history

On behalf of the NSPA, the ACLU sued for the right of the National Socialists to march. The case was ultimately brought to the Illinois Supreme Court where they overturned the ruling of the District court. Afterwards, it was brought to the U.S. Supreme Court. On June 14, 1977, the Supreme Court ordered Illinois to hold a hearing on their ruling against the Nazis. Illinois decided that the county court decision violated the First Amendment. Since other people were allowed to march without paying insurance, the neo-Nazis should be allowed to march too. A major side question, however, was whether the swastika should be allowed. One concentration camp survivor angrily declared, "I do not know if I could control myself if I saw the swastika in a parade." Skokie attorneys argued that for Jews, seeing the swastika was just like being physically attacked.

The United States Supreme Court sympathized with the Skokie residents, but allowed the National Socialist Party to march anyway. The Court ruled that the use of the swastika is a symbolic form of free speech entitled to First Amendment protections and determined that the swastika itself did not constitute "fighting words."

Effect of the decision

In the summer of 1978, the Nazis finally held three rallies, but not in Skokie. All were in the Chicago area: Lincolnwood (near Skokie), the downtown Chicago Federal Center, and Marquette Park on the city's Southwest side. Attendance at the three rallies was very low, but the national attention brought on by the Supreme Court case gave them enough press coverage as to make a Skokie rally redundant.

Also as a response to the court's decision, Holocaust survivors set up a museum on Main Street to commemorate the people who died in the genocide.

Significance

The Skokie case shows that the First Amendment not only protects the views that most citizens support, but also unpopular beliefs. The First Amendment makes possible what Justice Oliver Wendell Holmes called "a marketplace of ideas" where all views can be expressed whether they were popular or not.

See also

- Skokie (Movie)
- Neo-Nazi groups of the United States
- List of United States Supreme Court cases, volume 432
- Battle of Cable Street

Sources

- National Socialist Party v. Skokie, 432 U.S. 43 (1977) - findlaw.com [2]
- Chronology of Events [3]
- Attempted Nazi March 1977 and 1978 in Skokie digitized document and recordings archive [4]

References

[1] http://www.supremecourtus.gov/docket/76-1786.htm
[2] http://caselaw.lp.findlaw.com/scripts/getcase.pl?court=US&vol=432&invol=43
[3] http://www.skokiehistory.info/chrono/nazis.html
[4] http://skokiepubliclibrary.info/s_info/in_biography/attempted_march/index.asp

Article Sources and Contributors

Battle of Cable Street *Source*: http://en.wikipedia.org/w/index.php?oldid=345641495 *Contributors*: 80.255, A3RO, Adam Bishop, AlistairMcMillan, Big bunny, Bowbrick, Brianiii, Cgingold, Cheeky Films, Chzz, Colin S, D6, DJ Silverfish, Dahn, Date delinker, Del Trotter, Doniago, E0N, Ed Poor, Emoscopes, Fonzy, G-Man, Gil Gamesh, Gramscis cousin, Horses In The Sky, Hugo999, Hux, JK the unwise, Kbthompson, Keresaspa, Kierant, Kuralyov, Lapsed Pacifist, MRSC, Manticore126, Mattstan, Modest Genius, Murray McDonald, Nev1, Newprogressive, Nuttyskin, Onevalefan, Raymond1922, Rayray, Redzen, Remuel, Richard Allen, Richje, Ronnie Biggs, Ryan4314, Serein (renamed because of SUL), Smerus, Squiddy, Steinsky, Stevejackswan, The Anome, The Four Deuces, ThievingGypsy, Tim!, Triquetra, Trugster, Ua747sp, Wasteofspace, Wobble, 64 anonymous edits

Cable Street *Source*: http://en.wikipedia.org/w/index.php?oldid=314723907 *Contributors*: *isa*, Acmthompson, B3virq3b, Businessman332211, Cactus.man, Carcharoth, DuncanHill, Dweller, Gwernol, Ian Pitchford, James Frankcom, Kbthompson, Kritikos99, Kwamikagami, MRSC, Mahlum, Mikecupcake, Ogg, P Ingerson, Paulbrock, Pearle, Plastikspork, RJFJR, Regan123, Richard Allen, Rje, Road Wizard, Ross Burgess, Rpyle731, Ruziklan, Saga City, Sparkit, Thomas Blomberg, Wereon, Yohan euan o4, 18 anonymous edits

East End of London *Source*: http://en.wikipedia.org/w/index.php?oldid=344616026 *Contributors*: 1924, 21655, Altzinn, Andy Marchbanks, Andycjp, Ani td, Antonio Lopez, AuburnPilot, Badudoy, Barticus88, Bbbco, Bcorr, Beetstra, Bellhalla, Biruitorul, Bluebird999, Borgx, BrainyBabe, Brilliantine, CalJW, CanisRufus, Carl.bunderson, Carlwev, CarolGray, Casliber, Cave laborem, Cavie78, Cedders, Chesdovi, Chocolatechipcookie91, Chuck Marean, Colin4C, CommonsDelinker, Coralmizu, Cyfal, David Straub, David Underdown, Dawn Bard, Dbarnes99, Derek.cashman, Digdogyo, Digest, Dumelow, EamonnPKeane, Edward, Ekamaloff, Eliz81, EmersonLowry, Epbr123, Error, Esthameian, F-402, Fieldday-sunday, Formeruser-81, Francs2000, Fratrep, Fys, G F Williams, Gareth Wyn, Gil Gamesh, GoScoutUK, GossamerBliss, Grafen, Graham87, Grahamec, GreatWhiteNortherner, Ground Zero, Hadžija, Halaf, Heron, Hitman012, Icemuon, Imnotminkus, Instinct, Iridescent, JDG, JPD, Jamorama, Jj137, Jmabel, Joel7687, Johnmarkh, Jooler, JusticeGuy, Justinc, Jza84, Kaare, Karada, Kbthompson, Ken Gallager, Kirk Hilliard, Knapspank, Kozuch, Ksenon, Kukini, LAX, Lacrimosus, Lightmouse, LittleOldMe, Luk, Lynntoniolondon, MJCdetroit, MRSC, Mahlum, Mas 18 dl, Mezzanine, Michael Devore, Middayexpress, Mikkeyg, MisfitToys, Morwen, MykReeve, Natl1, NawlinWiki, Neelix, Neropolis, Nevilley, Nihiltres, Nomadologist, Nono64, Old Moonraker, Ondewelle, One Night In Hackney, Papppfaffe, Paul W, Paularblaster, Pcpcpc, Peter Shearan, Peter cohen, Philopedia, Piledhigheranddeeper, Pinkpunks, PoisonedPigeon, Primitivojumento, Pterre, R. fiend, Radon210, Rhillman, Richard D. LeCour, Rigadoun, Rjwilmsi, Robertgreer, Ross Diamond, SandyGeorgia, Sannse, SimonD, SimonP, SimonTrew, Sjc, Skomorokh, Slawojarek, Smerus, Sony9, Squiddy, Ssilvers, Sswonk, Starrycupz, Steeev, Stephenb, Sue Wallace, Suruena, Swanny18, TN55, Tagishsimon, Tarquin, Tarquin Binary, Tawniz, Tedder, The Anome, Thebeginning, ThievingGypsy, Tim riley, Tintagle, Tmangray, Todd661, Tony1, Tpbradbury, Trieste, Ttotto, Tusitala, Uk-art-online, Val11214, Vanished user, Ventolin, Websitedesigners, Wereon, WhisperToMe, Wimstead, WolfmanSF, Wwoods, XLerate, YUL89YYZ, ZimZalaBim, Zscout370, 147 anonymous edits

Metropolitan Police Service *Source*: http://en.wikipedia.org/w/index.php?oldid=345201754 *Contributors*: A More Perfect Onion, AMPERIO, ASJ94, Aaron7chicago, Aatox, Adambro, Ado, Ahoerstemeier, Ajpralston1, Allstarecho, An Siarach, An13sa, Andrea105, Andrew Yong, Andy Marchbanks, Another Believer, ArmadilloProcess, Arpingstone, Ashtonstreet01, Asim18, Astonwiki, Aude, Aumnamahashiva, B1link82, Barek, Bayerischermann, Beeblebrox, Bibliomaniac15, Birdhurst, BlaiseFEgan, Bobanny, Bobblewik, Brianlucas, BritishWatcher, CPBOOTH, Cahk, CalJW, Callumfh, CanadianLinuxUser, Canley, Canterbury Tail, Carabinieri, CarolGray, Carschten, Cenarium, Centrx, ChickenFalls, Chris j wood, ChrisTheDude, Clarky1991, Closeapple, Cnbrb, Colin4C, Craigy144, DabMachine, DanDud88, Dancingwombatsrule, Dark wingstalker, Date delinker, DeadEyeArrow, DeadlyAssassin, Delpino, DeluxNate, Dep. Garcia, Dibble999, Discospinster, Displaced Brit, DoubleBlue, Dpaajones, Duffman, Duroy, Dynamup, Eastmain, Ed g2s, EdC, Edward Breslin, Emmanuel Chanel, EoGuy, Epbr123, EpicDream86, Eric-Wester, Ericamick, Escaper2007, Escaper27, Escaper7, Esrever, Eva Destruction, Everyking, Extols, Favonian, Fences and windows, Fifth Fish Finger, Foodman, G-Man, Gaius Cornelius, Garryq, Gerald Farinas, GiollaUidir, Giraffedata, GomiTaroGeorge42, Grim23, Grstain, HTUK, HaeB, Hammersfan, HappyCamper, Happynoodleboycey, Hardouin, Hexatonic, Hightower25, Hmains, Hotspur23, Hydraton31, Icurok, Ikescs, Imc, Indon, Iorek85, Iridescent, Iridescent 2, Ixfd64, J.delanoy, Jackus2008, Jacob.l345, Jamacfarlane, Jamesblythe, Jangli, Jaraalbe, Jaranda, Jcmo, Jcmurphy, Jeltz, Jemthepen, JimVC3, Jlamos, Jocasta shadow, JoeSmack, John, Jooler, Joseph Solis in Australia, Josh477, Jumaha, Jvhertum, Jwrosenzweig, JzG, Kaisershatner, Katherine Shaw, Kbthompson, Keilana, Keith Edkins, Keithjbailey, Klemen Kocjancic, Klenod, Kungfuadam, LilHelpa, Linehanfamily, Lost tourist, MBRZ48, MJCdetroit, MRSC, Macphisto12, Maedin, Mais oui!, Majyr, Malepheasant, Marc osborne, Matt520269, Mauls, Mb1000, McGeddon, Michael Hardy, Midx1004, Mintguy, Mirv, Mnbf9rca, Molui, Moondog88, Morwen, Mowthegrass, Mr Larrington, Mr. Brownstone, Nasnema, Nathanfrank, Ncik, Necrothesp, Neilbeach, Neutrality, Nick Cooper, Ninetyone, Ninja Scaley, Niteowlneils, Nono64, NorthenMonkey, Nv8200p, Ohconfucius, Ohnoitsjamie, Ojcookies, Olborne, Olegwiki, OlgaOnal, Olliebzt, Oneeye, Orangepippen, Paki.tv, Phantomsteve, Piledhigheranddeeper, Police,Mad,Jack, PoliceChief, Possum, Preada, ProfPhys, Proteus, Quadell, RFBailey, RadioFan, Razorflame, Rebelduder69, Red Thunder, Rich Farmbrough, Richard Weil, Rif Winfield, Rjwilmsi, Rm uk, Robbskey, Rollgypsyroll, Ronaldccwong, Rooboy715, Sandstein, Sango123, Sapient, Sardanaphalus, SasiSasi, SchuminWeb, Shploom, Signalhead, Simesa, SimonP, Sjorford, Skapur, Skcpublic, Sketchmoose, Smartse, Smomo, Snigbrook, Soulresin, Ssilvers, SteinbDJ, SunDragon34, Swan41, Tabletop, Tagishsimon, TakuyaMurata, Tanthalas39, Tellyaddict, The Anome, The Giant Puffin, Tide rolls, Timothy Titus, Timrollpickering, Tokufan, Tonebarry, TonyDodson, Travelbird, Trevyn, Trodaikid1983, Tt 225, Ukexpat, Undzeichnete, Vegaswikian, WLU, Warrington123, Wavelength, Wik, Willy on WheeLs, Wnjr, Xevious, Xienyao, Xsharksx, Yhinz17, Ynhockey, You're Having A Giraffe, Zir, 212, 334 anonymous edits

British Union of Fascists *Source*: http://en.wikipedia.org/w/index.php?oldid=346493995 *Contributors*: 4u1e, 80.255, Adam Carr, Adam Keller, Alansohn, Altenmann, Amcalabrese, AndreasPraefcke, Ant, Antodav2007, Aranel, Arwel Parry, Asav, AuntFlo, Balsa10, Benson93, Big bunny, Bigturtle, Bonadea, BritishKnight, BrownHairedGirl, Chmod007, Chris Roy, Chris the speller, Colin4C, Coyets, Crablogger, DNewhall, Dahn, DanKeshet, Del Trotter, Dexterj, Deyyaz, Dthomsen8, Edward Wakelin, FictionalEmu, Flarkins, G-Man, Garik, Geoff97, GeorgeFormby1, Gogo Dodo, Gr8opinionater, Ground Zero, Hadal, Hajor, HenrYrneHenry, Herostratus, HighKing, Honeycake, Hotlorp, Ianhowlett, JAF1970, JK the unwise, Jackytar, James500, JennaPseudonym, Jmorrison230582, Joehaer, Jza84, Karada, Kbthompson, Keresaspa, Killing Vector, Kpjas, Kuralyov, Kxh, Les woodland, Lususromulus, Lynch derance, MeltBanana, MeteorMaker, Mintguy, Monkey Tennis, Morwen, MrHill, Neutrality, Nickieee, Nikodemos, Nopira, Norvo, Pandora, PatGallacher, Patrickcm, PaulVIF, Pgk, Phil pf, Philip Trueman, Pigsonthewing, Plastikspork, Rancebesnuffed, Ranceinnoose2, Rayray, RobMBrown, Rosalbissima, S ellinson, SE7, Saforrest, Saluton, Sam Korn, Secretlondon, Sir Cueball, Skier Dude, Slimerance, Spidey oh man, Sugarbat, Superiority, Susanmcpherson, SwiftlyTilt, TUF-KAT, Tallicfan20, Tdgtdg, TharkunColl, The Anome, The Crying Orc, The Four Deuces, TheoloJ, Toiletfacerance, UNSC Trooper, Uncle Dick, Unfree, Vanished User 03, Vsion, Warofdreams, Wehwalt, White Guard, Wik, Woohookitty, Writtenonsand, Zzuuzz, °, 206 anonymous edits

Oswald Mosley *Source*: http://en.wikipedia.org/w/index.php?oldid=346961307 *Contributors*: (, 2fort5r, 6afraidof7, 80.255, Activevocabulary, Adam Holland, Alansohn, Albertvanbiljon, AndreasPraefcke, Apterygial, Arbeit Sockenpuppe, Avalon, BTLizard, Bee Coz, Best name, Bhadani, Binary TSO, Biruitorul, Bjones, Blue520, Bluewind, Bobfrombrockley, Bobsbobbins, Bookbayou, Bornintheguz, Brenont, Britannicus, Bronks, BrownHairedGirl, Brutaldeluxe, CBM, Can't sleep, clown will eat me, Capricorn42, Cardzplaya32, Carmeld1, Ceedjee, Chase me ladies, I'm the Cavalry, Cheesemite, Choess, Chris Roy, Cjrother, Commonlaw504, Counter-revolutionary, Craigy144, D6, DH85868993, DJ Clayworth, Damifb, Darrelljon, David Gerard, David Straub, Deiz, Del Trotter, Demiurge, Demophon, DerHexer, Dfrg.msc, Djrobgordon, Ed g2s, Edward J. Picardy, Elmarko5, Enchanter, EncyclopediaUpdaticus, ErinKM, Foofbun, Formeruser-81, Formeruser-82, Fys, Fyyer, G.-M. Cupertino, GABaker, GANDALF1992, GCarty, Glampers, Goldenlane, Gonçalo-Manuel, GregorB, Grepnork, Ground Zero, Grytviken, GusF, Gwernol, H2g2bob, Hajor, Haldraper, Hashomer, Henning M, Heron, Hobartimus, Hooperbloob, Hydraton31, Ian Dalziel, IceDragon64, Ineuw, Intelligent Mr Toad, Intolerrance, InvisibleK, Irishaodhan, Irunongames, Jac16888, JackofOz, Janinho, Jay-W, Jed keenan, Jellyman, Jevansen, Jheald, John Kenney, John Lunney, Johnbibby, Johnhousefriday, Jontomkittredge, Jpbowen, Jph, KatherineK, Kauffner, Keegan, Kel-nage, Kelisi, Keresaspa, Kernel Saunters, Kingstowngalway, Kittybrewster, Kuralyov, LaurenManchester, Lightmouse, Lipothymia, Lord Cornwallis, Lord Emsworth, Luk, M Johnson, MER-C, Mackensen, Manticore126, Marcosw, Marcus334, MarkGallagher, Martinscholes, Mathsci, Matt.T, Mauls, Mhenneberry, Mild Bill Hiccup, Montrealais, Morwen, Moyabrit, Mtiedemann, Muppeteer, Mxcatania, Mynamespatrick, NatC, Nedrutland, Newprogressive, Nicke L, Nickhk, Nickieee, Nickirk84, Old Nol, PatGallacher, Patrick lovell, Peter cohen, Peterlewis, Phl3djo, Pirmasis, Proteus, Pterodactyler, Puark, Puragus, QueenCake, Qwm, RFBailey, Ranceinnoose2, Randy2063, Regan123, Relata refero, Rich Farmbrough, Richard David Ramsey, Rje, Rklisowski, Rlevse, Rms125a@hotmail.com, RobinCarmody, RodC, Rodolph, SE7, SGBailey, Sam Korn, Shoemaker's Holiday, Sirmylesnagopaleentheda, Sjc, Skier Dude, Skysmith, Slatersteven, Spidey oh man, SteveSims, Sus scrofa, Susanmcpherson, Ta bu shi da yu, Tai kit, Teatreez, Tedickey, The Crying Orc, The Four Deuces, Thelibrarian, ThievingGypsy, Thingg, Thomasolson, Timrollpickering, Todowd, Toph99, Trekphiler, Tripod86, True as Blue, Tryde, Uncia, VKokielov, Valenciano, Vanished User 03, Wavehunter, Wes Pacek, Writtenonsand, Xxanthippe, Yeanold Viskersenn, YeshuaDavid, Zazpot, Zzuuzz, °, 245 anonymous edits

Anti-fascist *Source*: http://en.wikipedia.org/w/index.php?oldid=16468968 *Contributors*: 12345e, 97036, Admiral Norton, Adreamsoul, AidenWolf, Aksi great, AlexiusHoratius, Amire80, Andreas1968, Article19, Barticus88, Ben-Al-Harr, Black Cat, Bloomfield, Bobfrombrockley, BritishNationalist, Bronks, C mon, Canadian-Bacon, Cground, Cjs56, Coentor, Cs32en, Dh2k, Dopex, DukePatton, Ed4444, Emmisa, Enders on, Fawkes1, Formeruser-81, Fourdee, Freako, GCarty, Gaius Cornelius, Giancarlo Rossi, Hanshans23, Isolani, Joy, K. Lastochka, Ka34, Kaibabsquirrel, Kbthompson, Kenyon, Koavf, La goutte de pluie, Lapaz, Lapsed Pacifist, Legionas, Liftarn, Little Mountain 5, Lord Eru, Lucio Di Madaura, MSJapan, Magnus Colossus, Mamalujo, Marcos G. Tusar, Martpol, MegX, Miacek, Mister X, Moeron, Mrahman1917, Ne0Freedom, Nikodemos, Orgullomoore, Outercell, Owen, Picus viridis, Piotrus, Poke-Dude1995, Primalchaos, Revolución, Rje, Rskellner, Sadistik, Sebasbronzini, Shermozle, Smg 777, Snigbrook, SpeedyGonsales, Spylab, Stor stark7, SummerWithMorons, Superiority, TYRXrus, Tawker, Tazmaniacs, TexasDex, The Ungovernable Force, Thingg, Thorburn, Türa, Vanished User 03, VengeancePrime, Viator slovenicus, Walton One, West Brom 4ever, Wmahan, Xdiabolicalx, Yahel Guhan, Yanksox, Zenohockey, Zoe, Zzuuzz, £, Шизомби, 164 anonymous edits

Jew *Source*: http://en.wikipedia.org/w/index.php?oldid=340235600 *Contributors*: -the-muffin-man-, 1297, 169-254-13-37, 16@r, 172, 200.255.83.xxx, 2007apm, 209.240.222.xxx, 25, 7pac, 8888845375T, A Sniper, A Toyota's A Toyota, A suyash, A-kshay, A8UDI, ABCD, AGGoH, AGM2513, ALE!, Aaron Brenneman, Aaron Mendelson, AaronMicael, Abc45678, Abc45678910, Abductive, Abhishekbh, Acbarkhan, Ace101, Aceofspades4, Achaemenes, Acidburn24m, Adam Bishop, Adam1213, Adam7davies, Adambro, Adarsharon, Adashiel, Adawar, Adinas, Administer, Adolf hitler, Adolf23141234343454535243, Adolph Hitler, Adrian, AdultSwim, Aeonimitz, After Midnight, Ahines7777, Ahmadandyoung, Ahoerstemeier, Aieff, Ak47225, Akamad, Akseli, Al Ameer son, Al-Andalus, Alberuni, Albion13, Alejandroak, Alex S, Alex groos, AlexH, Alexander Domanda, Alice Mudgarden, Alison, All Hallow's Wraith, All portals, AllyUnion, Alphabetagamnma, Alphachimp, Altenmann, Amberrock, Amoruso, AnOddName, Andre Engels, Andres, Andrevan, Andrew Levine, Andrewa, Andrewpmk, Android79, Andrwsc, Andy Marchbanks, Andy5, Anetode, Angela, Angelo De La Paz, Angelofevil13, Angr, Ani td, Anilocra, Anonymous Dissident, Anonymus1, Ant101123, Antandrus, Anthb06, Anthony

Appleyard, AntiJew, Antifa, Antonio Di Dio, AntonioMartin, Anyac, Anárion, Aperakh, Aquintero82, Arcturus, Ares06, Ari777il, Arjun01, Arker, Arminius, ArnoLagrange, Art LaPella, Artaxiad, Artura56, Arvindn, Arwel Parry, AryanPower, Asbestos, Asbl, Asidemes, Attackoftheclones, Audiosmurf, Avi (usurped), Avraham, AxelBoldt, Axis101, Aytakin, AzaToth, B. Peppers, B3verything, BD2412, BL, Bachrach44, Badanedwa, Bampro, Banes, Barbara Shack, Barista, Baristarim, Baronnet, Barrettman2000, Baylink, Bbatsell, Bcorr, Bdavid, Beaverbroc, Beit Or, Ben D., Ben0385, Benami, Benjil, Benmoshe, Bensaccount, Benson85, Benstown, Berrowj03, Betacommand, Bezalela, Bfinn, Bh3u4m, Bhadani, Bibi Saint-Pol, Big balls ben 28, BigHairRef, Billybud989, Biruitorul, Bjbarker1988, Bjelleklang, Blackangel25, Blaineeee, BlankVerse, Blankfaze, Blarg2.0, Blightsoot, Bludevil260 yah, Blue520, Bluemask, Blurkom, Blurp, Bmicomp, Bnwwf91, Bnynms, Bobblehead, Bobblewik, Bobby the Milligan, Bodnotbod, Bogdangiusca, Boodlesthecat, Boothy443, Boutboul, BoxingWear, BozMo, Brad theory, Bradeos Graphon, Brandmeister, Bratsche, Brian0918, Brianski, Brim, BrokenSegue, BrokenSphere, BrownBean, Brsomogyi, Buckyboy314, Buickid, Bumcheekcity, Bumstuffersgonewild, Burgundavia, Burningblood11, Bus stop, Bush Sucks, Bw213, CJCurrie, CONFIQ, CZmarlin, Cactus.man, Calidore Chase, Camoboy1290, Can't sleep, clown will eat me, Canderson7, Carbonbase, Carolmooredc, CasualObserver'48, Cathwon, Causa sui, Cbmccarthy, Cdc, Cecropia, Celestra, Cellsy, Celtise, Centrx, Cfsenel, Cgl712, Chabad, ChanochGruenman, Chanting Fox, Chcoc, Chedorlaomer, Cheesygordito, Chemical harmony, Chesdovi, Chillum, Chimrae, Chinese3126, Chocoforfriends, Chowbok, Chris Bulgin, Chris Roy, Chrishills91, Christopher Parham, Chuq, Claudio90, Clavecin, Clay70, ClemMcGann, Cliche-29, Closedmouth, Clubjuggle, Cmdrjameson, Cncs wikipedia, Cometstyles, CommonGround, Comperr, Comradebrightsmile, ConstAchilles, Consumed Crustacean, Contributor777, Conversion script, Cookie1456, Cool157, Coolcat68976897, Cooldud7, Cooper Cronk, Copperboom, Coragma, Correogsk, Cprompt, Craftypants, Crippsicle of tha nation, Crusadeonilliteracy, Cserlajos, Csl77, Cuks 22, Curps, Cutler, Cyan, Cyberevil, Cyde, D Monack, D6, DGtal, DMacks, DO'Neil, DVD R W, DaGizza, Dabomb691, Dagestan, Damiyiddish, Dan100, DanKeshet, DanPMK, Danc, Danfeder, Danntm, Danny, Danski14, Darimore, Dark Shikari, Darkildor, Darkohead, Darkyoshi, Darth Anne Jaclyn Sincoff, Darth Vortex, Daverocks, David Gerard, David Kernow, David Shankbone, David.Monniaux, Davidrose24, Dawn Bard, Db3737, Dbachmann, Dbratton, Dchall1, DeMingtang, DeSales, DeadEyeArrow, Deadmanwalking2006, Deb, December21st2012Freak, Deejay114, Deepred6502, DeirYassin, Delirium, Delldot, Delos, Deltabeignet, Dem466, Dementedd, Demiurge, Demomoke, Den fjättrade ankan, Denisutku, Dennv, DerHexer, Derek Ross, Dezidor, Dfranks77, Dharmabum420, Dianelos, Dickius, Dina, Dinopup, Diremarc, Dittaeva, Dj iET, Dkostic, Dmackey2, Dmerrill, Doc Tropics, Doc glasgow, Docu, Donny11, DoomsDay349, Dori, Dota Gosu, DouglasGreen, Dr. Fujita, Drago-skott, DragonflySixtyseven, DreamOfMirrors, Drewz2, Drini, Dsmets88, Dstnwltn, Ducker, Duhon, Dukedevil91390, Duncharris, Dureo, Dwaipayanc, Dzoxar, EBruchmann, EDGE, EJRaven, ESkog, Ealbert, Earl Turner, Ebizur, Ed g2s, EdH, EdIrving, Edcolins, Eddie Voco-Turner, Edirving, Edo 555, Eequor, Efghij, EhavEliyahu, Ekotekk, El C, Elan26, Eleassar777, Eleland, Elias Enoc, EliasAlucard, Elipongo, Eliyak, Eliyyahu, EllG73, Ellzyboy, Elnuevomercurio, Eloquence, Eltrentoro, Elven warlord, Emadyeah, Emma1001, Emmawoolf, Emojones, Enkiduk, EnragedAlbinoYak, Enwright09, Epbr123, Epeefleche, Epson291, Ericbbbbb, Eridani, Ertz, Etymologian, Eugene van der Pijll, Evercat, Evertype, Everyking, Evil Monkey, Evil saltine, EvilZak, Ewawer, ExRat, Ezra Wax, FEastman, Faddyk, Falafelboy, Falvo 8, Fantastic4boy, FateClub, Fayenatic london, Fcpremix23, Fdssdf, Fedor, Feedmecereal, Feer, Feitclub, Fennec, Fennessy, Ferkelparade, Fidsah, FinsternisKatzchen, Fipplet, Firthy2002, Fivetrees, Fjbfour, FlavrSavr, Flockmeal, Flowerparty, FlushinQwnzNyc, Flymeoutofhere, Fnorp, FocalPoint, FolkenFanel, Font, Foobar, Fourtildas, Francs2000, Freakofnurture, Freddieandthedreamers, Fredrik, Freedom skies, FreplySpang, Friedchikinz, Friedo, Fru1tbat, FrummerThanThou, Fs, Fsdhfhkssij, Fugimugim, Fugocci7211, FunkMonk, Futhark, Fuzheado, Fvw, Fys, Gabr-el, Gadfium, Gahunt, Gaius Cornelius, Galizia, Galoubet, Gamaliel, GangstaNate91, Gareth E Kegg, Gargantuan Cat, Gatemansgc, Gazpacho, Geagea, Geni, Germzmonster, GhostBoy66, GhostPirate, Gidonb, Gilgamesh, Gilisa, Gilliam, Ginga123, Gnarlodious, Goalie1998, Gogo Dodo, Goodoldpolonius, Goodoldpolonius2, Goosehumper, Goudzovski, GraemeL, Graham87, Granpuff, Grant65, Grantsky, Grantyboy14, Gravitan, Green Giant, Greg Grahame, GregAsche, Grenavitar, Grendelkhan, Grika, Grm wnr, Grunt, Grutter, Gscshoyru, Guanaco, Gugilymugily, Guy Montag, Gwernol, Gzuckier, H, H7asan, HDCase, HGB, Hadal, Haham hanuka, Haiduc, Hairymon, Hajhouse, Halaqah, HalfMoonFan, HalfShadow, Hall Monitor, Hanastop, Hanchen, Hanchi, Haplogroup2010, Happy08, HaravM, Hardytlc, HarisM, Harro5, HarvardOxon, Hasdrubal, Haukurth, Haveronjones, Hayden5650, Haytxa 911, Heel033, HeikoEvermann, Heine, Hellcat fighter, HelloDollars!, Hells Terrror, Hemanshu, Henburylaughs, HereToHelp, Hernandez5874, Heron, Hertz1888, Herut, Heymanawesome, Hiflyer9453, Hisbonenus, Historian932, Hkelkar, Hmains, Hmclithium, Hoboklown, Holling, Hollowed Ground, HomerJay603, Honesttoyou, HooperBandP, Humus sapiens, Hungaria777, Husond, HussainAbbas, Hut 8.5, Hveziris, I'mDown, IAMTHEPEOPLESCHAMP, IZAK, Ian Pitchford, Ian13, IceKarma, Iceager, Iceaxejuggler, Idontknow610, Igiffin, Iijjccoo, Ikhveysnit, Ilbisaac, IlyaHaykinson, Imalegend, Imediting4noreason, ImmortalYawn, ImperatorExercitus, Impfac, InShaneee, Infrogmation, Inigmatus, Instinct42, Intelligentsium, Inter, Ipathshoes1981, Iridescent, IrishJew, IsaacAA, Isomorphic, Istvan, Italianskoddy, Itsabouttime, Itzse, Ixfd64, Izehar, J intela, J.delanoy, J04n, JDC Marcom, JHMM13, JLogan, JRM, JRWalko, JYOuyang, Jack, Jack O'Lantern, Jackgats, Jackk, Jacobolus, Jacquerie27, Jag123, Jagged 85, Jaksmith, Jamiecole, Jaranda, JarlaxleArtemis, Jawg, Jaxl, Jay, JayHenry, Jayflex, Jayjg, Jaymarcos, Jbabrams2, Jbamb, Jc37, Jd2718, Jdavidb, Jdc1266, Jdhunt, Jdsteakley, JeMa, Jecar, Jenexica, Jengod, JeremyA, Jeremyrishe, Jerome Charles Potts, Jerryseinfeld, Jets1632, Jets1832, Jets1862, Jew, JewBoy, Jewboy6039, Jewish spain, Jez, Jfdwolff, Jgold03, Jgritz, Jguk, Jguk 2, Jheald, Jiddisch, JimCollaborator, Jimbo33, Jimderkaisser, Jimmybob12, Jj137, Jkuciiii, Jm083b, Jmabel, Jmlk17, Jndrline, Jni, JoanneB, Jobe6, Joeanderson85, Joel7687, Joerg25, JoergenG, Joergg, Johann Wolfgang, John Carter, John Hyams, John T. Henry, John T. Vogerson, John254, JohnAFlynn, JohnClarknew, Johnleemk, Johnny1988, JohnnyTwain, Joly roger, Jon513, Jonesjim5, Jonnabuz, Jordanrozum, Jordz, Josepages web, Joshbainbridge, Joshman62, JoshuaZ, Jossi, Jpeob, Jpgordon, Jprg1966, Jptdrake, Jredmond, Jtdirl, Jtkiefer, Jtucker007, Judaism123, Juliancolton, Just Another Dan, Justin Eiler, Justincarpenter, Jwinters, Jwissick, Jwrosenzweig, Jza84, K wedge, KBrown143, KF, Kaaveh Ahangar, Kafziel, Kaihsu, Kaisershatner, KaliqX, Karada, Karaites-USA, Karatenerd, Karimarie, Karl-Henner, Kat73, Katefan0, Kayeth1, Kbdank71, Kbh3rd, Kbolino, Keith H., Keith from Calgary, Keithd, Kelisi, Kelly Martin, Kemet, Kesla, Kevdev59, Kewp, Kf4bdy, Khoikhoi, Kidkash102, Kidpoker15, KillerChihuahua, Kimon, King kong922, Kingpin13, Kingturtle, Kingvinvin, Kinslayer3210, Kirill Lokshin, Knowledge Seeker, KnowledgeOfSelf, Koavf, Kosebamse, Kotzker, Koyaanis Qatsi, Kpalion, KpopSe7en, Krazy boi nat, Krazykane, Kross, Krukouski, Kshep64, Kubigula, Kungfuadam, Kuratowski's Ghost, Kuru, Kuzaar, Kwamikagami, Kyorosuke, Lalalanothing69, Lam3l, LamaXX, Lanolin, Lapsed Pacifist, LarryGilbert, Laubz83, LeaW, Leandrod, LeeMulod333, Leflyman, Leifern, LeighvsOptimvsMaximvs, Lemmey, LeoNomis, LepVektor, Lepenseur09, Leroy odoosh, Lev, Lewisxxxusa, Lexi Marie, Lexicon, Lightdarkness, Lightmouse, Liist, Liist5, Lilashy11238, Lily15, Ling.Nut, Linuxbeak, LittleDan, LittleOldMe, Loadmaster, Lockesdonkey, Lollerpop, Lord Anubis, LordAmeth, Lorrane, Louisblackwell1000, Lucas606, Lukobe, Lunz2121, Lupo, Luprecal, Lvivske, M5891, MC MasterChef, MCLE0012, MK8, ML-Est, MPerel, MZMcBride, Mac Davis, Mackers2006, Madbiggie00, Magicianxox, Magnus Manske, Maijinsan, Mailer diablo, Malik Shabazz, Mallaccaos, Mallerd, Malo, Mamndassan, Man vyi, Maphisto86, Marcadams99, Marcika, Marcus2, Mareino, MarkSutton, Markalex, Maroux, Martin S Taylor, Masterbeefy, Masterhomer, MathKnight, Mathew5000, Matiasab87, Matt Heard, Matt Yeager, Matthew Woodcraft, Mattnicho, Matttaplin, Mattwu, Maurice45, Mav, Mavromatis, Maxell2k1, Maximus Rex, Maxsendziak, Maxshanly, Mbassan, Mbecker, Mbeki, Mbn85, Mboverload, Mbz1, McFizzle, McKorn, Mcdonald23, Mcgeester, Mcorazao, Meetwursti, MehrdadNY, Mel Etitis, Mellum, Merzul, Metadon, Metb82, MeteorMaker, Meursault2004, Micahmn, Michael Devore, Michael Hardy, Michael Snow, Mikalchaos7, Mike 7, Mike Rosoft, Mikeage, Mild Bill Hiccup, Militant-54, Millerboyz999@aol.com, Mindmatrix, Mindspillage, Minesweeper, Mintguy, Mirv, Miskin, Misza13, Mitchumch, Miteymite27, Mjchonoles, Mkmcconn, Mloclam901, Mmsarfraz, Mo-Al, Modest Genius, Moe Epsilon, Moeron, Mogly, Mohdh, Moltrasi, Momojeng, Moncrief, Monedula, Monkeys can fly, Monosig, Moochie9000, Moplord359, Moreh Qanaa, Morgan Wright, Moroboshi, MosheA, Mpolo, Mporch, Mprudhom, Mr Adequate, Mr. Lefty, Mr. Sombrero, MrSomeone, Msheflin, Mttll, Muchosucko, Mukadderat, Musical Linguist, Musicloverisrael, Mustaafaa, Mustafaa, MyPulseReverberates, MylesRudin, Mynameisstanley, Mynameisstlawson, Myok, Mysidia, Mythatom, Mythras, NJ, NSLE, NSM88, Nakon, Natalie Erin, Nato187, Naus, Navijation, NawlinWiki, Nbafreakman, Neddyseagoon, Nehrams2020, NeilN, Neilc, Neilfein, Netizen, Neutrality, NewEnglandYankee, Newman Luke, Newrob20, Newtman, Nhoj123, Nice Santa, Nicetomeetyou, Nicholasngkm, NickBush24, Nicoholowko, Nicool333, Nimnar, Nishidani, Nishkid64, Njaard, No-Chance-ThreeSixteen, Nomadicface, Nomist, NordicThunder88, Normankev, Nothos, Notjustanumber, Nufy8, Nunh-huh, Nuttycoconut, Oballin619, Oberiko, Oemb1905, Oggmaster, Ogress, Ohnoitsjamie, Ohwell32, Okedem, Olaffpomona, Old Moonraker, Oldknowall, Olivier, Olve Utne, Omgomgdylan, Omicronpersei8, Omnie, OneVoice, Oneworld25, Oo64eva, Oodus, Opticon, Oren.tal, Oreo Priest, Orlanu Brecker, Orrin Hatch, Ortonmc, OvenFreshJew, OwenX, P4k, PDH, PMLF, Pabix, Pablo Alcayaga, Pak21, Paleo dragon, Pan Dan, Pangmeister, Pangmiester, Papageorgio, Pasd, Pathoschild, Patrickm1990, Patton123, Patxi lurra, Paukrus, Paul August, Pauljoffe, Paysonsrt, Pcpcpc, PenguinJockey, Persian Poet Gal, Peruvianllama, PeteVine, Pgk, Pharos, Phenz, Phil Sandifer, Phil326, PhilHibbs, Philfus, Philgp, PhilipBrower, PhilipO, Philwelch, Pigglywiggly30945, Pilotguy, PinchasC, Pintele Yid, Plasticup, Plutochaun, Poetaris, Politician, Pollinator, Polyhister, Pooooooooooooooooop, Pop up pirate, Popcontest, Popenfresh123, PorkHole, Possum, Postdlf, Praze Allah, Prezbo, Prime Entelechy, Prise fightr, Prodego, Prosfilaes, Proteus, Protocolz, Psy guy, Psychless, Psychomelodic, Ptcamn, Pwd1990, Pwntabi, Pylambert, Pyrospirit, Quade999, Quadell, Quebec99, Quinsareth, Qxz, R'n'B, RBSIS24, RG2, RJN, RK, RM, Rabin, Rachaellloyd, Rackbar, Raffyfan93, Raguks, Rajanr imposter, Randy Johnston, Rapfan67, Raphael26, Raul654, Raven4x4x, RaviC, Rayc59, RdFlcnz, Rdskns4eva, Rdsmith4, Realywierd, RebCoh, Rebecca, RebekahThorn, Recato, Red Thunder, RedWolf, Redvers, Redwingchamp98, Reenem, Reid A., Reinis, Remiel, Remort, Renji22, Rentaferret, Retired username, Retune, RexNL, Rexwarrior, ReyBrujo, Rgbutler, Rhbeatz, Rhobite, Rich Farmbrough, Rich Janis, Richard David Ramsey, RickK, Rickterp, Rickyrab, Rightfully in First Place, Rimsrus, Ripman, Rishartha555, RisingSun96815, Rje, Rjm656s, Rjwilmsi, Rmhermen, Roadrunner, Rob Hooft, Robchurch, Robinbirk, RobtheGate, Rockfang, RolandH, Roleplayer, Roman Zacharij, Romanm, Rorypunkrock, RoseParks, Rosedora, Rosencomet, Rosencrantz1, Rosnum, Ross Burgess, Rovibroni, RoyBoy, Rpetit, Rrjanbiah, RucasHost, Rudjek, RxS, Ryan4, Rydel, Ryecatcher773, Ryulong, Rémih, SEOXpert, SEWilco, SKEAM, Sam Hocevar, Sam Spade, Sam Vimes, Sammermpc, Sammich, Sandahl, Sangil, Sango123, Sannse, Sanoysalvo, Sardanaphalus, Sbluen, Scarface02, Scavanger, Scepia, Sceptre, Schaefer, Scheinermann, Scherfk, Schissel, Schmloof, Schneelocke, Scifiintel, Scohoust, Scoopsos, Scurra, Scythian1, Scythian99, Sean.hoyland, Seantrac, Search4Lancer, Seba, Sebastiankessel, Secretlondon, Seicer, Seong0980, Seth Ilys, Shaitan Al Mahdi, ShameOnTerrorists, Shamir1, Shanel, Shanes, Shaul, Shaul avrom, Shilonite, Shinmawa, Shirik, Shirulashem, Shlomke, Shoaler, ShortBus, Shortstopmmc, Shpakovich, Shqiptar nga Kosova, Shykee, Sietse Snel, SilentKoala, Silentkillr, Silly rabbit, Silsor, Simon J Kissane, SimonArlott, SimonP, Sinabtin, Singhalawap, Sirmylesnagopaleentheda, Siroxo, Sirre, Sj, Sjaim, Sjakkalle, Sktrc9, Slakr, SlavPoland, SlimVirgin, Slkjord, Slowking Man, Slrubenstein, Smokizzy, Smyth, Snoyes, Somepostman, Sonic1218, Sopranosmob781, Soumyasch, Spartaz, Speekmonkey, Spencer195, Spicy marmalade, Splash, Spliffy, Sportguy91, Spread your legs, SpuriousQ, Sputnikcccp, SqueakBox, Squiddy, Squizzislame, Sroulik, Ssmith619, Stabilityx, Star-of-David92, Startaq, Steel, Steerpike, Stephen Bain, Stephen C. Carlson, Stephenb, Steve Bauer, Steven J. Anderson, Steven2000, Stevenj, Stevenplunkett, Stevertigo, Stewartadcock, Stud896, StuffOfInterest, Stusutcliffe, Stwalkersock, Stylishman, Sucene, Superman1408, Supersexyspacemonkey, Supreme Bananas, Suptaiy, Svan1188, Swatjester, Syvanen, Syynapse, Szyslak, THEONe, THF, TOO, TPK, TShilo12, TUF-KAT, Ta bu shi da yu, Taamu, Tactik, Tad Lincoln, Tallicfan20, Tamafrmtaupo, Tangotango, Tannin, Targeman, Tariqabjotu, Tartutic17, Tatarian, Taxman, Teamferby, Tequendamia, Teryx, TexasAndroid, TexasDex, Texture, The Anome, The Behnam, The Hybrid, The Judaic Jedi, The Mad Bomber, The Ogre, The Prince Manifest, The number c, The way, the truth, and the light, The wub, TheBrandon, TheCuriousGnome, TheDarkArchon, TheDoctor10, TheEmoEater, TheKMan, TheObtuseAngleOfDoom, TheYmode, Theadolescent, Thedraz, Thegame06, Thelovebugy, Themindsurgeon, Theresa knott, Thetruthbelow, Thewall544, Thewebthsp, Threeafterthree, ThuranX, Thursiya, Tibbsy, Tide rolls, TigerShark, Tillasly, Tim Starling, Timwi, Tintinlover123, Titoxd, Tkynerd, Tlogmer, Tobby72, Toejam117, Tofubar, Tom harrison, TomPhil, Tomfreelance, Tomlillis, Tony Sidaway, Tony1, TonySt, Tonylemesmer, Torontobwoi, Trashanaut, Trevor MacInnis, Trojan51, Trotsky05, TsiyonNassi, Ttwaring, Tuhoy, Tukes, Tullie, Turbinator, Turm, Tvaughn05, Twoheel, Tyciol, Tyomitch, Ubervinny, Ucanlookitup, Uconnhoopz123, Ucucha, Udoq, Udzu, Ugen64, Ukraina, Uncle J, Undead Herle King, Upsetparent, Uremum234, Uriel8, Uriyan, Used2BAnonymous, Usedbook, User2004, Usergreatpower, UtherSRG, Uunl, Vague Rant, Valleyofdawn, Valyer, Vaniba12, Varan619, Varangian, Vasile, Vaubin, Vdegroot, Vedek Dukat, Veinor, Ventur, Vikodan31, Vilerage, Vince251, Viriditas, Vizcarra, Vmrgrsergr, VonBluvens, Vonones, Voyevoda, Vuvar1, WBardwin, WWGB, WX 0, WanderSage, Ward3001, Wassamatta, Wassermann, Wattsv03, Wavelength, Wayiran, Wayward, Waz187, Wb678, Wclark, Wellminesthesun, Welsh, Wetman, Weyes, White Cat, Whitlockj1, Wicksie86, Wiki alf, Wiki1609, WikiCats, Wikieditor06, Wikimike, Wikinger, Wikix, Wikizach, Wildnox, William Howard Hart, Wilson frederick, Wimt, Winhunter, Wissam24, Wiwaxia, Wjec, Wknight94, Wmahan, Wmgamd, Wolfman, Woohookitty, Working for Him, Wormbird1, WpZurp, XParadigm777x, XSG, Xaosflux, Xeverett, Xsuperlative, Xxchrisukxx, Xxxxxxxxx, Xy7, YUL89YYZ, Yahel Guhan, Yamamoto Ichiro, Yancyfry jr, Ybbor, YellowMonkey, Yelyos, YeshuaDavid, Yisraelee, Ynhockey, Yoninah, Yosefgun9, Yoshiah ap, Yoyochris924, Ysangkok, Yukirat, Yuval a, Yuvn86, Zachwoo, Zain engineer, Zandweb, Zantolak, Zaorish, Zapvet, Zargulon, Zeiden, Zenohockey, Zero0000, Zestauferov, Zhiwa odzer, Zigger, ZimZalaBim, Zinck, Zoe, Zondor, Ztrawhcs, Zzuuzz, Zzyzx11, , Александър, Саша Стефановић, 1835 anonymous edits

Socialist *Source*: http://en.wikipedia.org/w/index.php?oldid=247160690 *Contributors*: $yD!, 172, 213.67.126.xxx, 2D, 3.1415, 3fo3, 52 Pickup, 62.253.64.xxx, A Man In Black, A-rock, A3RO, A8UDI, ABF, AED, ATGUHBT, Aaron McDaid, Abrech, Academic Challenger, Acroterion, Acs4b, Adam Carr, Adambro, Adamburton, Adashiel, Addihockey10, Addshore, AdjustShift, Adrachd, Aeonite, Aetheling, Afitillidie13, Agüeybaná, Ahoerstemeier, Airplaneman, Aitias, Akanemoto, Alansohn, Aldaron, Alemily, Alex Bakharev, Alex S, Alex Shih, Alex4827, AlexWaelde, Alexander the Lame, Alexb102072, AlexiusHoratius, Alkiede, All Is One, Allixpeeke, Alpheus, Altenmann, Alun Ephraim, Am088, Ameliorate!, Amnonc, Amphytrite, Amplitude101, Anarcho-capitalism, Anarchopedia, Andre Engels, Andrea105, Andreave1977, Andrevan, Andy Marchbanks, Andysoh, Angela, Angr, Animum, Antandrus, Anthon.Eff, Anthony.bradbury, Antonio Lopez, Anurag devilz, Apjohns54, Apollonius 1236, Appleboy, Arakunem, Aram33, ArcticYoshi, ArielGold, Aristophanes68, Arjun01, Aron1, Arrest traitor rance, Arrest traitor rance12, Aryder779, Ashenai, Ashriner, Astanhope, Asterion, Astral, Atacm middle east, Atif.t2, Atlant, Austiiinnnn, Auswiger, Avsn, AxelBoldt, BL, Baa, Bacchiad, Backburner001, Badlermd, Bahahs, Bang it hard8, Barek, Baristarim, Barnaby banger, Basawala, Bash rrance, Battlecry, Bballballer, Beantwo, Bedwetting rrance, Behead rrance2, Behead rrance3, Behead rrance6, Behead rrance9, Bella Swan, Belovedfreak, Benjaburns, Betterusername, Bhadani, BibleThumper4 3rdHeaven&Earth, Big Brother 1984, BigCow, Bigred1973, Biker Biker, Bill j, Billare, Billy Ego, Binary TSO, Bingbingbung, Bingomzan, Bitch696969, Bitemerance45, Bitemerance51, Bitemerance67, Bjr35, BlaBlaDK, Black Khaos, Blackdraq, Blockader, Blue Tie, Blue520, BlueResistance, Bluerain, Bluerasberry, Bobblehead, Bobfrombrockley, Bobisbob2, Bobo192, Bogey97, Bolivian Unicyclist, Bonadea, Bongwarrior, Boothy443, BorgHunter, BorgQueen, Born2cycle, BrentJ277, Brianlucas, Briannine, Brighterorange, Brokenchairs, Brothejr, Brozen, Bryan Derksen, Bryan024, Bsskchaitanya, Bubsadaddy, Burntsauce, Buzoo, Bwahlsbo, Bwumster, C mon, C'est moi, CALR, CJ, CJCurrie, CJK, CPMcE, Cactus.man, Cadillac, Cadr, Cafeirlandais, Cafzal, Calibas, Calmer Waters, Calvin5557, CambridgeBayWeather, Camilo Rubinos, Camw, Can't sleep, clown will eat me, Can'tStandYa, Canadian-Bacon, CanadianLinuxUser, Canderson7, Canthusus, Capricorn42, Captain Disdain, Captainblack1199, CardinalDan, Carlosguitar, Carroteater117, Cast, Cat13cvd, Catgut, Causa sui, Cause of death, Cavscorvette32, Cberlet, Cbohus, Cdc, Cerebrith, Cfailde, Chamal N, Chanting Fox, Charles Matthews, Che y Marijuana, Chegwozdziowski, ChessPlayer, Chewdiss, Chewshyt rrance, Chimeric Glider, Chowbok, Chris G, ChrisG, Chrisch, Christian List, Christofurio, Chriswiki, Chuckiesdad, Chzz, CiTrusD, Cielomobile, Cilstr, Citizen Premier, Civilized Man, Cjberryman, ClockworkSoul, Closedmouth, Clutch, Cmart, Cncs wikipedia, Cobra2cobra, Cobracool, Cochise the Restorer, Coffee, Cohesion, Colchicum, Cometstyles, Commander Keane, Commodevoncommode, CommonsDelinker, Comraderedoctober, Conversion script, Cool 2002, Cool bortherqw, Cool3, Coopkev2, Cordell, Corvus cornix, Cosmic Latte, Cosmosmariner, Couki, Counterheg, Cpuwhiz11, Craitman17, Crashmcbean, CrazyChemGuy, Cretog8, Cureden, Curps, Curufinwe, Cwolfsheep, D, DA3N, DMcM, DNS246, DROOPz, DRSANGLE, DVD R W, Da monster under your bed, Dabeastintheeast888999, DanKeshet, Dancter, Daniel Olsen, Daniel Quinlan, DanielCD, Dannycas, Danski14, Dark Charles, Darrelljon, Darth Panda, Dasha14, Datheisen, David Igra, David.Monniaux, Davidlawrence, Dawn Bard, Dbader000, Dbader50, Dbfirs, Dc2005silk, Ddoner, De-Chomskidize, DeadEyeArrow, Debresser, Dee's Nuts, Defenestrating Monday, Dekisugi, Delaybased, Delirium, Delita Hyral, Demigod Ron, Demolish RRance, Demolish rolie, DennisDaniels, DerHexer, DerekDD, Detox runcie, Deviledknight, DickClarkMises, Diderot, Dieselfuel6, Dinga Bell, Dire straits, Discospinster, Djinn112, Djr xi, Dlohcierekim, Dogtownclown, Don't dream it's over, Doniago, Donkeyluva, Donmccullen, Donnachadelong, Doonhamer, DoubleBlue, DouglasGreen, Dougofborg, Downtown deadbeat, Doyley, Dozer0987, Dp462090, Dpu, Dr. Berg, Dr3w505, Dreadstar, Dream of Goats, Drewbyh, Drini, Drmies, Dthomsen8, Dullfig, Dylan Lake, Dylan anglada, Dysepsion, EBY3221, ERcheck, ESkog, Earth, Eastlaw, Eatmydyk rancie, Economizer, Ed Poor, Edgarie, EgbertMcDunk, Egon Bauwelinck, EhJJ, Eiffelle, Eirik (usurped), El C, ElKevbo, Elaqero, Eldooshbag, Electrified mocha chinchilla, Elfie67, Elian, EliasAlucard, Elliskev, Eloquence, Elsacs, Emmisa, Emre D., EnglishEfternamn, Enviroboy, Epbr123, Erendwyn, Error fixer7, Escobar600ie, Esperant, Eubulides, Eulen, Evan Robidoux, Evercat, Everyking, Excirial, Explodicle, Ezgeez, FCSundae, FISHERAD, Fang 23, Fantastic4boy, Fartface12345, Fatla00, Faustus Tacitus, FayssalF, Fbd, Fcueto, Ferkelparade, Ferocious osmosis, Fetchmaster, Ffolldd, Fieldday-sunday, Fightindaman, FighttheleftSD, Figureskatingfan, Finlay McWalter, Fipplethitsback, Fipps revenge4, Fire 55, Fireman sam, Firing squad34, Fixer40, Fizban, Floquenbeam, Flushawayrance, FlyingToaster, Foegle, Folome, Fooling noone, Foolinthewind, Fooltocry, ForgetfulDoryFish, Formeruser-81, FrancisTyers, FrancoGG, Francomemoria, Francs2000, Frankenpuppy, Franz.87, Franzose, Fred Bauder, Fredrik, Freeway, FreplySpang, Friendlyjack67, Frosted14, FrozenUmbrella, Frykommies, Full Shunyata, Funkymuskrat, Funnykid777, Funnymonkey91210, Fusionmix, Fvw, Fygde, Fys, G-Man, GSMR, GTBacchus, Gadfium, Gaelen S., Gail, Gaius Cornelius, Gallowaysbooger, Gangsterls, Garycompugeek, Garzo, Gasull, Gatoclass, Gatoclass is a homo, Gatoclass is a loser, Gatoclass stinks, Gatoclass sucks, Gcom, Gene93k, George dubya Bush, Ghmyrtle, Ghostbear616, Giant guppy, Gilliam, Giovanni33, Gitmo 4jaz, Gitmo 4rancie, Globalization, Gnowor, Gobonobo, Gogo Dodo, Gorrilla radio, Gr8N8, Gr8opinionater, GraemeL, Graham87, Grant65, Grcaphistory, Green01, Greensteintony, GregAsche, GregMaughan, Gregbard, GreggW, Grick, Grika, Grrrlriot, Gtyron, Gudeldar, Guitarist1897, Gunderiffic, Gurch, Guy Peters, Guðsþegn, HJMG, Haham hanuka, Haipa Doragon, HamburgerRadio, Handle 2001, Hang traitors2, Hang traitors4, Hang traitors6, Hang traitors8, Hangdatbastard, Hardys, Harryboyles, Hawkwild, Hdt83, Hectorthebat, Helpful Dave, Helvetius, Herostratus, HexaChord, Heyche, Hmains, Hobartimus, HobbesPDX, Hockeyman384925, Hogeye, Hopiakuta, Hordaland, Howcheng, Hqb, Hu, Humbabba, Husond, Hut 8.5, Hydrargyrum, Hydrogen Iodide, Hydrostatic, I am cool123456, I am the novagenerata, I'mDown, IanManka, Icseaturtles, Ig0774, Igoldste, Ihateyou12, Ilovesnow2012, Ilyanep, Ilyushka88, Im a real wild one, Im soooooooooo coool, Imarealwildone, Imprison RRance, Improper Bostonian, Inbloom2, Indiawilliams, Infinity0, InfinityO, Inomyabcs, Inspectasobies, Intangible, Intangible2.0, Intelligentsium, Inter, Introman, Iridescent, Irishguy, IronChris, Isis07, Itanesco, Ivy Shoots, Ixfd64, J Milburn, J.R. Hercules, J.delanoy, JCapone, JDPhD, JFG, JForget, JFreeman, JHunterJ, JK., JKWithers, JONJONAUG, JTravisRolko, Jacek Kendysz, Jackbirdsong, Jackfork, Jackie chan11, Jacob Haller, Jahiegel, Jake Wartenberg, James uk, James086, JamesAM, Jared Preston, Jayjg, Jcchat66, Jdaniel456, Jdeugwillo, Je suis desole, JeanColumbia, Jecar, Jeendan, Jeff G., Jeremy221, Jessemonroy650, JesusGuest, Jetman3, Jiang, Jimbo46, Jimmi Hugh, Jimmiey, Jimmyjohn222, Jimphilos, Jjoseph8907, Jkeene, Jlannon11, Jmabel, Jman1984, Jmccabe871, Jmundo, Jni, Jnothman, JoanneB, JodyB, JoeBlogsDord, Joel50, Joel55, Joel8, Joey blackwell94, John, John Kenney, John.john.1234567, John254, JohnDoe0007, JohnFitzpatrick, JohnGalt1812, Johnleemk, Joklolk, Jorvik, Joselondono, Joseph Solis in Australia, Journalist, Jouvenel, Joy, Joyous!, Jsan, Jt white93, Jtnelson, Julia.dullien, Juliancolton, Junes, Jusdafax, Jwrosenzweig, Jxsmith, JzG, KBaileyMN, KC109, KJS77, Kaboom911, Kaihsu, Kaisershatner, Kano156, Kappa, Kara123, Karada, Karl Naylor, Katalaveno, Kbdank71, Keberic, Keegan, Keelm, KeepItClean, Keilana, Kelaos, Kelly Martin, Kevin Neel, Kevin wong, Kevinsneel, Keycard, Khoikhoi, Khukri, Kim Bruning, Kingpin13, Kinston eagle, Kiss the razor's edge, KoRnholio8, Konulu, Koool, Korin, Kostisl, Kowey, Kp7, Krich, Kronecker, Kronos1996, Kubigula, Kukini, Kulak revenge, Kungfuadam, Kuru, Kurykh, Kvan1st, KyraVixen, LKodaL, LLcopp, Lacrimosus, Lala939, Lambiam, Lancemurdoch, Landon1980, Lapsed Pacifist, Lar, Larklight, Latka, Laurinavicius, Laurusnobilis, Lawrence Cohen, Le vin blanc, LeaveSleaves, Lee Daniel Crocker, Leebo, Leejasonc, Legoktm, Lemmey, LeoO3, Lesouris, Lev lafayette, Levineps, Lexor, Liberal Freemason, LiberalFascist, Lickprik rrance, Liftarn, Liftarn is a homo, Lightmouse, Lights, Lightyear69, LilHelpa, Linkspamremover, Lir, LittleDan, Livajo, Lloyd rm, Localist, Lord Emsworth, Loremaster, Loren.wilton, Lorenzarius, Lradrama, Luffmodular, Luis rib, Luk, Luke4545, LukeTheSpook, Lumidek, Luna Santin, Lupin, Lvken7, Lycurgus, Lynch derance2, Lynxmb, M.V.E.i., M1ss1ontomars2k4, M4rk, MBisanz, MER-C, MWOAP, MacRusgail, Macai, Macy, Madhava 1947, Madhero88, Magioladitis, Malcolm, Malinaccier, Manchester Liberal, Mandarax, Mani1, Manway, Marcel63, March3yahoo, Marek69, Marj Tiefert, Markaci, Martg76, Martin Wisse, Martin451, Martintg, MarxistJiggers, Mas 18 dl, Massacretraitors, Master Jay, Master Wikiman, Masterpiece2000, Matt Lewis, Mattfox82, MattieTK, Mattisse, Mattum, Matty, Maurreen, Mav, Max rspct, MaxSem, Maxis ftw, Mc6809e, Meck islander, Meekywiki, Meelar, Megamix, Mentifisto, Merc owner, Merope, Mhazard9, Michael Devore, Michael Hardy, Michael Snow, Michael40, Michaelm, Michaelwuzthere, Middle east man, Middle man from the east plus conflict, Midnightblueowl, Mike Rosoft, Mike5904, Millerc, Minesweeper, Miquonranger03, Mirror Vax, MisterActually, Mjk2357, Mnemeson, Modulatum, Molindo, MondoWanda, Monedula, Moosehead46, MorganaFiolett, Mprudhom, Mpty0624, Mr.TotallyAwesome, MrBosnia, MrTrev, Mrdthree, Mtaylor848, Mtndewwatkins, MutantPlatypus, Mysdaao, N-k, N5iln, NSH001, NWOG, NaBUru38, Nach0king, Nakon, Nanite1018, Nanousis, Natalie Erin, NathanV, Naturenet, NatusRoma, Naufana, Naveen Sankar, NawlinWiki, Ndenison, Necromantic666, NeilTarrant, Neko-chan, Nema Fakei, Nerdyned22, NewEnglandYankee, Nhart, NickelShoe, NietzscheFan, Nikodemos, Nimbusania, Nirvana2013, Nishkid64, Nivix, Nlu, Nmpenguin, Noisy, Nonamer98, Noonesaboobwiththepeoplescube, NorVegan, Nosedung, Nrcprm2026, Nsaa, Ntennis, Nubiatech, Obamah8r, Obamahater, ObeliskBJM, Octane, Ohnoitsjamie, Olivier, Omicronpersei8, One, Ong saluri, Operation Spooner, Ophy4, Other, OverlordQ, Owen, Oxymoron83, PAK Man, PCHS-NJROTC, Passdarifle, Passportguy, PasswordUsername, PatPeter, Paul Markel, Paul Spicker, Pde, Pedro Paulo Vasconcellos, Perry anderson, Persian Poet Gal, Peter G Werner, Peter Stalin, Peterwats, Pexise, Pezntboy, Pgk, PhJ, Pharos, Phil Sandifer, Philip Trueman, Phinicky, Phookqu rance, Phort99, Piano non troppo, Picapica, Pigman, Pillow talk6, Pilotguy, Pingveno, Pinkadelica, Pinklitigation, Piotrus, Pir, Pisson trots, Plain regular ham, Plasticup, PlatonicIdeas, PoccilScript, Pokharasam, Political Guru, Polonium, Polpotsguppy, Pompy, Ponce de Leon 2nd, Pontificalibus, Poorsod, Portalian, Possum, Pparader, Prashanthns, Pratyeka, PrestonH, Princeofexcess, PrincessofLlyr, Ps3queen, Psicorps, Psychonaut, Puchiko, PyroGamer, Quadpus, Quetzaquotal, Qwerty21, Qwertyuiop23, Qwertyus, Qxz, R Lowry, R-41, RED DAVE, RG2, RJASE1, RJHall, RJII, RJaguar3, Rabin, RadiantRay, Raider lovin jew, RainbowOfLight, Rance intrance, Ranceindumpster, Ranceinnoose, Ranceon endofrope, Rancie shthead, Rancie sooks, RandomCritic, Rangerdude, Rankiri, Rantsie raus, Rantsie raus2, Rantsongallows, RaseaC, Rawling, RayAYang, Rd232, Rdsmith4, Rebecca, Rebroad, Red, Red Bastard, Red Deathy, Red Wing, Red square 44, Redneckpaul, Redsoxfan08, Redstar1987, Redthoreau, Redvers, Regicollis, Res2216firestar, RetiredWikipedian789, Rettetast, RexNL, Rhodog, RichardF, Rigosantana3, Rjd0060, Rjm656s, Rjwilmsi, Rkeys, Rlevse, Rmartin16, Roadrunner, Roastytoast, Rob1n, Robert I, Robert K S, Robert plant fan, RobertG, Robinrobin, Robomaeyhem, Robyn6913, Rocket Socket, Rodentrance, Rogerjung, Rokbas, Roland dykhead, Roland rancidity, RolandR, Rolandrance shythead, Rolands foreskin, Rolandsukks, Roleplayer, Roliecoaster, Roliejurkingoff, Roliesukks, Ronhjones, Roninbk, Ronithkasukar, RookZERO, Rosattin, Rrance buggerizer, Rror, Rtdrury, Ruhrjung, Rward71, RxS, Ryoutou, Ryulong, SJP, SWAdair, Sagaciousuk, SaltyBoatr, Sam Korn, Sam Spade, Sam akba, SamB135, Samadam, Sampi, Samuel Blanning, Sango123, Sanmartin, Sarcastic Avenger, Sardanaphalus, Sausagehiders, Savidan, Sbowers3, Scam-Wow, Scartol, Sceptre, SchfiftyThree, Schzmo, Scott Burley, Secretlondon, Seidenstud, Seijihyouronka, Selimtheslim, Serlin, Serpent-A, Sesel, Sfmammamia, Shane Kenyon, Shanel, Shanes, Sharkface217, Sharpieyellow, Shell Kinney, Shii, Shirazz, Shoeofdeath, Shopping freak, Shreeniwasiyer, Shytbrain rrance, Silverback, SimonArlott, Simonm223, Singhalawap, Sjakkalle, Sky hook hanger, Slakr, Slimerance, Slipoutside, Slowking Man, Sluzzelin, Smackrance, Smilingsami, Smite rrants, Snigbrook, Snowded, Snoyes, Snuffrants, SoCalJustice, SoWhy, Solid Rancher, Soliloquial, Solo1234, Someone who isn't MECM, Songbordie, SpLoT, SpaceFlight89, Spellcast, Spike2321, Spot2112, Spylab, Squiddy, Stalins douche, Stalynsboy, Stalynutsy, Startstop123, Stealth031, Stemonitis, Stephenb, Steven Zhang, Stevertigo, Sting au, Storm Rider, Stormie, Strangerer, Strongsauce, Stwalkerster, Subpar, Subversive, Sukdyk rrance, Sumatrik, Sundar1, Sundiii, Sunray, SuperByelich, SuperHamster, Superiority, Swarm, SwitChar, Sycthos, Synchronism, TDC, TDS, TINAxTURNER, TJive, Ta bu shi da yu, Tainted Conformity, TakuyaMurata, Tannin, Tarc, Tarshish, Taw, Tawker, Tcncv, Telex, Tgv8925, The Anome, The Four Deuces, The Hokkaido Crow, The Land, The Middle East Conflict Dude, The Middle East Conflict Man, The Negotiator (usurped), The Peacemaker, The Person Who Is Strange, The Thing That Should Not Be, The Ungovernable Force, The middle man, The middle west conflict man, The8thbit, TheCatalyst31, TheKMan, TheMadBaron, TheOtherJesse, ThePedro, TheTrueSora, TheWeakWilled, Theman84, Thepeoplescube, Thewolf37, Thewolfstar, Thingg, Thomas.macmillan, Threefourninesixnineeight, Tiddly Tom, Tide rolls, TigerShark, Tillwe, Tim Ivorson, Tim010987, TimothyPilgrim, Tipmra, Titansolaris, Tito-, Titoxd, Tmh, Tocino, Tohd8BohaithuGh1, Tom Radulovich, Tom harrison, Tomb24, Tompagenet, Tony1, Tonysgirlfriend, Toomanysmilies, Topbanana, Tothebarricades.tk, Tova Hella, Tpbradbury, Train guard, Traitorsinjail, Trash stalinazis, TravisTX, Trevor MacInnis, Trey Stone, Treyjp, TriniSocialist, Trnj2000, Trothunter, Trotskys tooches, Trust Is All You Need, Truthnamerica, Tsunaminoai, TutterMouse, TwelveStones,

TwinsFan48, Twthmoses, Tyler, Tylerh33, Tymun, Tzartzam, UNSC Trooper, Ugen64, Ugur Basak, Uhdcj98, Ukexpat, Ultimus, Ultramarine, Uncle Dick, Universe=atom, Upex, Uruiamme, Utcursch, Utility Monster, Utinomen, Valip, Valley2city, Valois bourbon, Vegaswikian, Venceremos, Versus22, Viajero, Victoriaedwards, Violent Proletarian, Vision Thing, Viskonsas, Vivalareaganrevolution, Vivisect rance, VladimirVUL, Voltairine, Votemoose, Vvibbert, WAS 4.250, WGee, Waggers, Washburnmav, Wassermann, Waterboard Rance12, Waterboard Rance17, Waterboarder2, Wayward, Wcp07, Wetman, Whichmore, Whiskey Rebellion, Who, Whpq, Whywhenwhohow, Wigren, Wik, Wiki alf, Wikidea, Wikidemon, Wikifan3543, Wikifanatic28, Wikiscient, Wilfried Derksen, Will Beback, Willdw79, WilliamThweatt, Williambeaufoy, Wimt, Windchaser, Winxrockswitchsux, Wisamhamoui, Wisco, Wmahan, Wolbo, Woohookitty, Wordmonkey, Working Poor, Woverbie, Writtenonsand, Wtmitchell, Wuhwuzdat, Xcentaur, Xe Cahzytr Ryz, Xenophrenic, Xero-7, Xiner, Xnux, Xornok, Xram lrak, Xrchz, Xy7, Yamamoto Ichiro, Yanivg, Yankee stadium, Yazman, YellowMonkey, Yespm, Yidisheryid, Yonghokim, Yoooooooooooooo, Yossarian, Youradhere, Yourafool, Youzwan, ZX81, Zachalope, Zaharous, Zazaban, Zd12, Zenohockey, Zenwhat, ZeropwnzOr, Zhang He, Zimbardo Cookie Experiment, Zizzybaluba, Zleitzen, Zorkmid, Zsinj, Zzuuzz, Τις, Саша Стефановић, 2907 anonymous edits

Anarchist *Source*: http://en.wikipedia.org/w/index.php?oldid=235939043 *Contributors*: ...---...SOS, 0, 100110100, 11thedition, 15.22, 1984, 216.39.146.xxx, 4twenty42o, 895cxi, A Clown in the Dark, A-giau, A8UDI, ABCD, AFA, ARxDelp, Aardvark3, AaronS, AaronSw, Aaronhill, Aaronwinborn, Abductive, Abudhurr, Abyy, Academician, Acanon, Accurizer, Achilles, Acroterion, Adam Conover, AdamRaizen, AdamRetchless, Adamantios, Adambiswanger1, Addshore, Aelffin, Aenar, Aeusoes1, Afitillidie13, Aggelophoros, Ahoerstemeier, Akanemoto, Alai, Alan Liefting, Alansohn, Albamuth, AlexiusHoratius, Allixpeeke, AllyUnion, Alonlaudon, Alpheus, Altenmann, Alxndr, Amcbride, Amcfreely, AnarChrist, Anaraug, Anarchist92, Anarcho Egoism, Anarcho hipster, Anarcho-capitalism, Anarchocelt, Anarkisto, AndonicO, Andre Engels, Andrea Parton, Andres, Andres rojas22, Andrew c, AndrewFleming72, Andrewlp1991, Andy Marchbanks, Anna Quist, AnnaAniston, AnnaFrance, Anonymous editor, Antaeus Feldspar, Antandrus, Anthony, Aqwis, Arinaya, Ark30inf, Army1987, Armyaware, Art LaPella, Arturus, Arvindn, Asa Winstanley, AstroHurricane001, AstroNomer, Asultanpur, Atomela, Atreyu42, Aunt Cudjoe, Aurush kazemini, Axon, BD2412, Babedacus, Bacchiad, Bachrach44, Barbara Shack, Barking Mad, Barkingdoc, Bart133, Bastin, Battlecry, Beeboe, Behemote, Beland, Belovedfreak, Ben Kidwell, Benc, Bengalski, Benny Boros, Beno1000, Beta m, Betacommand, Bhadani, Bigjake, Bikepunk2, Bill j. Billinghurst, Binary TSO, Birmdogs, Bjorn Martiz, Bk0, Black Butterfly, BlackFlag, Blah99, Blahblahblahblahblahblah, Blockader, Blocknew, Bloomfield, Blueboar, Bmicomp, Bobblewik, Bobdobbs1723, Bobfrombrockley, Bobo192, Bodnotbod, Bomac, Bookandcoffee, Booyabazooka, Borchamps, Born2cycle, Boss Big, Bpt, BradBeattie, Brandonbb13, Brennen, Brianfedirko, Brillig20, Brinkost, Brion VIBBER, Brisvegas, BryanG, Btljs, Buchanan-Hermit, Bucktoothie, Bugmenot42, Bumm13, Butros, C9cflute2wall, CB319, CJWilly, CJames745, CWii, Cactus.man, Caesaraix, CalebNoble, CambridgeBayWeather, Camembert, Cameron Nedland, Can't sleep, clown will eat me, Canaen, Cander0000, Canderson7, CanisRufus, CapitalR, CapitalistAnarchist, Capnquackenbush, Captainj, Carabinieri, Carnildo, Carolmooredc, Carterab, Cast, Catch, Cedders, Cenarium, Centrx, CesarB, Cews, Chaikney, Chairboy, Chameleon, Chaos, Che y Marijuana, Chelman, Chendy, ChihuahuaAssassin, Childhoodsend, ChildofMidnight, Chris Acheson, Chris Capoccia, Chris Roy, Chrisbang, Christiaan, Christofurio, Christopher Connor, Christopher Parham, Chromaticity, Chuck Smith, Chuck0, Churchofmau, Cielomobile, Cj, Clockwork, Clore, Closedmouth, Cmdrjameson, Cobaltbluetony, Coconut sprinkles, Cocytus, Colak, Collabi, Colonel panic, Colonies Chris, CommonsDelinker, Contributor777, Conversion script, Coredesat, Correogsk, Corvun, Corvus cornix, Costho, Cowdog, Crashola, Crashtip, CrazyLucifer, Creagh, Crimzonsol, Crudo, Crvst, Ctmkevlee, Ctmt, Cwolfsheep, Cybercobra, CyclopsX, D-Rock, DTC, DabMachine, Dachshund, Dale R. Gowin, Dalta, Dan Gardner, Dan100, DanKeshet, Daniel, Daniel Wootton, Danneskjold, Dannyno, DarkBlackGod, Darklilac, Darrennn, Darth Panda, Dasha14, David depaoli, Davidw, Dawn Bard, Dayv, Dbachmann, Dcoetzee, Dcooper, Deb, Debresser, Decepty, Deicidus, Dekimasu, Deleting Unnecessary Words, Deli nk, Delirium, Delldot, Denelson83, Der Eberswalder, Derek Ross, Descendall, Deus Ex, Dglynch, Dietary Fiber, Disquietude, Dmanning, Doctors without suspenders, Dogstar11, Dominio, Donnachadelong, Donnial, Doonhamer, Doright, DoubleBlue, DougsTech, Dpknauss, Dragon Master 666, Drake Dun, Dralwik, Dreadstar, Drowner, DryGrain, Dsp13, Dtobias, Dunkstr, Dwaipayanc, Dylan Lake, E235, EDGE, ES Sage, ESkog, Earth, EbonyTotem, Eclecticology, Economist198, Ed Poor, EdGl, Edivorce, Eduen, Edward, Edwinstearns, Efe, Ejosse1, Ekserevnitis, El C, Electionworld, ElectricRay, Elehack, Eleland, Elementart123, Elodoth, Emmisa, Emuzesto, Encephalon, Epbr123, Erebus Morgaine, Eric-Wester, Ericamick, Erik9, Escobar600ie, Etcetc, Evercat, Everyking, Evil Monkey, Ewlyahoocom, Exander, Excirial, Exir Kamalabadi, Extra Rock, Fang 23, Faré, Fatal, Father Inire, Fatmouse, Fbd, Ffirehorse, Fieldday-sunday, Fifelfoo, Fightindaman, Finlandssvensk, Finlay McWalter, Firebug, Fjulle, Flauto Dolce, Flexxx, FluteyFlakes88, FlyingToaster, Foant, Fplay, Fram, Francis Tyers, FrancisTyers, Frank Shearar, FrankGrigg, FrankoBoy, Freakofnurture, Fredrik, Free Bear, FreeJohnG, Freedomeagle, Frymaster, Full Shunyata, Funkybeat, Furrykef, Fuzheado, Fvw, G00df311a, GD, Gabr, Gadfium, Gaius Cornelius, Galanskov, Generica, Geni, Geoffg, Getcrunk, Ghimboueils, Ghostbear616, Giantcalledgrawp, Giantgrawp, Ginsengbomb, Givegains, Glenn, Glevern, GlobeGores, Goalyoman, Gohiking, Gomm, Good Intentions, Grace Note, GraemeL, Graft, Graham87, Grandgrawper, Granpuff, Grapenuts90, Grawp, Grawp the Giant, Green Giant, Gregbard, GregorB, Grenavitar, Griot, Gronky, Grumpyyoungman01, Guaka, Guanaco, Gurch, Guy M, Guðsþegn, Gwernol, Gzornenplatz, Hackwrench, Hadal, Haeleth, Haemo123, Hajor, Hans castorp81, Happy-melon, Harburg, Hard Sin, Hardys, Harmil, Harris88, Harry Potter, Harry491, Harrypotter, Haseo9999, Hayduke2000, Hdante, Headbomb, Heah, HeikoEvermann, Heliogabalus1, Hellogoodbye96, Helpful Dave, Hephaestus@freeq.com, Hetar, HiEverybodyHiDoctorNick, Hiddenfromview, Hiding, Hixx, Hogeye, Hongkyongnae, Ht1848, Hu, Hughdbrown, Huku-chan, Humanitarian, I already forgot, I ate jelly, IRP, Ian Pitchford, Iflylow, Imagination débridée, Imroy, IndividualistAnarchist, Indon, Infinity0, Inkani, Inky, Intangible, Intangible2.0, Introman, Iridescent, Iris lorain, Irish South African, Iroll, Iseedeadfood, J.delanoy, JLMadrigal, JaGa, Jackl, Jackriter, Jacob Haller, JacobCurtis, Jadabocho, JaffeBoyet, Jamesburrow, JamieJones, Jaranda, Jaredwf, Jason Ford, JayJasper, Jeeny, JeffWaxman, Jeffq, Jelly FTW, Jemmy Button, JeremyA, JeremySavage, Jersey Devil, Jhfrontz, Jiddisch, Jim Yar, Jizzbug, Jketola, Jklin, Jkschroeder27, Jni, JoanneB, Joel.a.davis, John Broughton, John Stevenson, JohnOwens, Johnleemk, JonasRH, Jonathunder, Joseph Solis in Australia, Josh Grosse, Josh Parris, JoshHeitzman, Joyous!, Jpers36, Jpgordon, Jrtayloriv, Jtkiefer, JulesCollins, Jwulsin, Kaihsu, Kaldari, Kaliz, Kalogeropoulos, Karenjc, Karl, KathrynLybarger, Kazvorpal, Kbthompson, Kelly Martin, Ken Gallager, KesheR, Kevehs, Khamm, Khin2718, Khoikhoi, KingTT, KingWen, Kingpin13, Kipala, Kiteinthewind, Knight of BAAWA, Koavf, Komap, Korey Kaczynski, Korg, Koroesu, Kosebamse, Kotjze, KrakatoaKatie, Krator, Kristaga, Kross, Krukouski, Kubra, Kukini, Kumioko, Kurykh, Kyle Barbour, L1ttleTr33, LGagnon, LM1973, LOL, Lamahater, Lancemurdoch, Landon1980, Lapsed Pacifist, Latics, Laurusnobilis, Lee Daniel Crocker, Lee J Haywood, Lemmey, Lentower, Li-sung, Libertatia, LibertyFirst, Liftarn, Lightmouse, Ligulem, Lingeron, Linkspamremover, Lir, Lisasmall, Little guru, Livajo, Llamadog903, Llosoc, Localist, Lockeownzj00, Loof Lirpa, Lowellian, Lquilter, Lranatunga, Lucidish, Luis rib, Lulu of the Lotus-Eaters, Lussmu, Luxdormiens, Lygophile, Lynch1989, M A V Delacey, MANiAC, MECU, MER-C, MONGO, Macai, Macho, Madhava 1947, Magicker71, MakeRocketGoNow, Malcolm Farmer, Malik Shabazz, Mani1, MapsMan, MarcMyWords, Marcika, Mardavich, Marketorama, Martin451, MartinHarper, Martpol, Marudubshinki, Marumari, Marxist leon, MastCell, Master of Puppets, Mathx314, Mattergy, Matthew Stannard, Mav, Max rspct, MaxSem, Maximus Rex, Mayooranathan, Mayumashu, Maziotis, Mboverload, McNick, Mcelroy, Meatloafx, Meelar, Memotype, Mennonot, Mentifisto, MeteorMaker, Mgarriss, Michael Hardy, Michaelm, Midnightblueowl, Miguel, Mike Dillon, Mike R, Mike Serfas, Millerc, Millosh, Mindgrime, Mini-Geek, Mirv, Mister X, Mnemisis, Modern inferno, Modernist, MojoTas, Mooseofshadows, Moreschi, Moriori, Mortimerghadibalo, Moshe Constantine Hassan Al-Silverburg, Motorizer, Mousy, Mr.Z-man, MrRadioGuy, MrVoluntarist, Msrasnw, Mumia-w-18, Munci, Murderbike, Mushroom, Mwanner, Mykenism, Mysid, Mzajac, N-k, N1h1l, NWOG, NYCJosh, Naddy, Nagy, Nakon, Nakore, Nappyrash, Naraht, Nat Krause, Naval Scene, NawlinWiki, Necromancing, Neelix, NeilHynes, Neilbeach, Nema Fakei, NeuronExMachina, NeutralAndObjective, Neutrality, Nick, Nihila, Nihilo 01, Nikodemos, Ninja Fred, Nirvana2013, Niteowlneils, Nixdorf, Nlu, Nmpenguin, No Guru, Nom de guerre, Noone, NotACow, NuclearWarfare, Nunh-huh, Nurg, Nwe, O-Boy, Oatmeal batman, Oberst, OceanDepths, Ohnoitsjamie, OlEnglish, Olathe, OleMaster, Oleg326756, Oliver Crow, Olivier, Olorin28, Omnipaedista, Operation Spooner, Optim, Organ123, Otolemur crassicaudatus, Ottershrew, Ottre, Owen, OwenX, Owl, Oxymoron83, PJM, Pak21, Pariah, ParkerHiggins, Parkwells, Part Time Security, Pascal666, Patstuart, Paul Martin, Paxsimius, Pbadams, Pearle, Peemil, Pekinensis, Per Hedetun, Peruvianllama, Peter Winnberg, Peter cohen, Petri Krohn, Pgagge, Pgan002, Pgk, Pharos, Phil Sandifer, PhilLiberty, Philippe, Philwelch, Phttttt, Physicistjedi, Piano non troppo, PierreAbbat, Pigman, Pir, Piyushrajput, Pizza Puzzle, Plasticup, PlayersPlace, Plrk, Pokrajac, Political Guru, Polotet, PoptartKing, Postdlf, Praxeo, Prebendclarion, Pro66, Professor rat, Prometheus7Unbound, Pseudomonas, Psi36, Psychomelodic, Ptans, Puckish boy, Pwd, Qst, Quebec99, Quercusrobur, Quintote, R'n'B, R. fiend, RJII, Radical Mallard, Raditzman, RainbowOfLight, RandomP, Randy6767, Rangek, Rankiri, Ratesspace, Raul654, Ravichandar84, Rdsmith4, RealGrouchy, Recall, Red&black revolt, RedCoat10, Rehpotsirhc, RememberingLife, Renamed user 832, RepublicanJacobite, Rettetast, Revkat, Revolution Guy, RexNL, Rhodog, Rich Farmbrough, Richard Blatant, Richard a b, RichiH, Ricky81682, Riki, Risker (Anne Criske) is old & has gray hair & wears glasses. 16, Ristonet, Rjwilmsi, Rkr1991, Rlove, Rmrfstar, Roadcollective, RobertMillan, Robertgreer, Robgraham, Rodentrance, Rogerz, RolandR, Rollo44, Rory096, Rossami, Rotem Dan, RoyBoy, RubyQ, Rustanddust, Ruy Lopez, Ryulong, SARAHFANDRICKSDONGBAG, SJP, ST47, Sabbut, Saebjorn, Sageo, Saii, Salsb, Sam Blacketer, Sam Clark, Sam Francis, Sam Hocevar, Sam Spade, Sam gheiace, Samar, Sannse, Sardanaphalus, Sasquatch, Saswann, Savidan, SchfiftyThree, SchuminWeb, Scientizzle, Scimitar, Sciurinæ, Scm83x, Sdornan, SeanLegassick, Seanmwalsh10, Sebaxxxtian, Secretlondon, Selket, Senator Palpatine, Sether, Sethmahoney, SgtSchumann, Shahab, ShaneKing, Shanes, Shino Baku, Shrume72, Si, Sietse Snel, Signatory, Silverback, SimonP, Singwaste, Sir Paul, Sir Richardson, Sjakkalle, Sjjb, Skateraw, Skittleys, Skomorokh, Sloth monkey, Sluzzelin, SmileToday, Smooth O, Snoyes, Softparadigm, Soja, Soman, Someoneinmyheadbutit'snotme, Soxwon, SparrowsWing, Speakhandsforme, Spidern, Splash, Spleeman, Spyfan, Spylab, Stan Still, Steambadger, Steel, SteinbDJ, Stephen B Streater, Steppley, Steve802, Steven Walling, Steven X, Stevenmitchell, Stevertigo, Stewartadcock, Stifle, Stirling Newberry, Storkk, Strait, Suckitman, Sudasana, SummerWithMorons, Sundar, Sundiiiiii, Sunray, Super propane, Superbeecat, Supersheep, Susan Mason, Susurrus, SwitChar, Synergy, T-rex, THINMAN, TKD, TZOTZIOY, Ta bu shi da yu, Tabletop, Tachyon01, Taco325i, Tallus, Tamfang, Tannin, Tasc, Tastemyhouse, Tawker, Tazmaniacs, TeamZissou, TedE, TelemachusSneezed, TenOfAllTrades, TexasDawg, Th1rt3en, That'sHot, Thatsrightthatsright, The Cunctator, The JPS, The Nameless, The Rambling Man, The Thin Man Who Never Leaves, The Transhumanist, The Ungovernable Force, The Writer, The truth, TheEternalMan, TheIndividualist, TheKMan, TheSlash, TheSolomon, TheTrueSora, Thedjatclubrock, Theelf29, Theoldanarchist, Theslash, Thingg, Thomas H. Larsen, Thomas.giovanni, ThompsonFest, Thorne, Thumperward, Thunderhead, Tide rolls, Tim Ivorson, TimMony, Timir2, Timwi, Tins128, Tito-, Titoxd, Tlim7882, Tobi Obito Kakashi, Toby Bartels, Tom, Tomorrowsashes, Tompsci, Tony Sidaway, Tony1, TonyClarke, TonySt, Tonyfaull, Topbanana, Tothebarricades.tk, Trachys, Trackstand, Travelbird, Treisijs, Trevor W. McKeown, Triskaideka, Trusilver, Tumblingsky, Turkeyplucker, Twas Now, Twobitsprite, Tzartzam, Ultramarine, Unbreakable MJ, Uncle G, Unforgiven666, Unschool, Urthogie, User2004, Userafw, Vampyrecat, Van helsing, Vanguard4life, Vanished User 03, Vargklo, VegKilla, Venu62, Veritas Noctis, Versus22, Vert et Noir, VertetNoir, VeryVerily, Viajero, Victorgrigas, Vikingstad, Vision Thing, Viskonsas, Voice of All, Voiceinsideyou, VolatileChemical, VoluntarySlave, Voyagerfan5761, WGee, WHEELER, WODUP, WakeUpAndLive, Warhorus, Wassermann, Wayland, Wayward, Wellingwebsite, Weregerbil, WhatamIdoing, Whiskey Rebellion, White Cat, WickedWanda, Wiki alf, Wikiklrsc, Wildsoda, Wilfried Derksen, Williamroy3, Wimt, Winder side, Wingspeed, WinterSpw, Witchkraut, Wmahan, Wnt, Wobean, WolfgangMoeselecker, Woohookitty, Writtenright, Wutschwlllm, XaViER, Xaosflux, Xcentaur, Xdenizen, Xeresblue, Xhaoz, Xiahou, Xiaopo, Xosé, Xy7, YellowMonkey, Yill577, Yingdan, Yono, Yossarian, Yuckfoo, Yummifruitbat, Zachorious, Zazaban, Zenohockey, Zoe, Zoicon5, Zundark, Zweidinge, ^demon, Αναρχία, Александър, 2596 anonymous edits

Irish people *Source*: http://en.wikipedia.org/w/index.php?oldid=346917141 *Contributors*: 2006already, ABF, Aaker, Acesmitty121, Adam mumaniac 8, Adam7davies, Agadant, Agape25, Agathoclea, AgentZZZ, Al-Andalus, Alai, Alainejosey, Alansohn, Alensha, Alex.muller, Alison, Altenmann, Amcbride, Amcguinn, Andes Man, Andrewsthistle, Angr, Angular, Angusmclellan, Annalise, AnonGuy, Antandrus, Anthon.Eff, Anthony.bradbury, Antidote, Aquintero82, Ardfern, Arnie587, Arniep, Aruton, Avenue, BRUTE, Backslash Forwardslash, Barneyboyd, Barticus88, Bastique, Bdegfcunbbfv, Beach drifter, Bedford, Beginning, Beland, Belligero, Ben Ben, BernardBernard, Beta, Betacommand, BigDunc, Biker Biker, Bill Tegner, Billfoolsgold, Biruitorul, Black Kite, Blacksands, Blind Man Walking, Bluemoose, Bluflores, Bobblehead, Bobo192, Bogger, Bohemianroots, Bonadea, Bongwarrior, Boothy443, Bostonsux122, Brian Boru is awesome, Brianlacey, BritishWatcher, BrittonLaRoche, BrokenSegue, BrownHairedGirl, Brylcreem2, Bucketsofg, Buenos-Aires City, Bukalemun3, Bunnydance08, Burntsauce, C777, CALR,

CactusWriter, CambridgeBayWeather, Camshron, Can't sleep, clown will eat me, CanisRufus, Capricorn42, CaptainVindaloo, CardinalDan, Catchpole, Catgut, Celtus, Ceoil, Ceyockey, Cfslattery1, Chaldean, Charles Matthews, Chibbleshotofnot, ChicXulub, Chuunen Baka, Citizen keane, ClemMcGann, Cloigeann, Coccyx Bloccyx, Cocytus, Coldphinger, Colin "All Your Base" Heaney, Colonies Chris, Commander Keane, CommonsDelinker, Comrade42, Concaff, Constantlysmiling, Cooku Caca, Cool Blue, Cormacross, Corregere, Cowbud2004, Cpl Syx, Cracker llama, Crazyinsaneman, Crimson Observer, Culnacreann, D.de.loinsigh, D6, DO'Neil, Dabbler, Daftestpunk, Daicaregos, Danno uk, Darcy16, Darranc, Darthgriz98, David Fuchs, David Kernow, Dawn Bard, Dbachmann, Deacon of Pndapetzim, Declan77, Decomcgrath, Delirium, Demiurge, Denzillacey, DerHexer, Dermo69, Derry Boi, Deville, Diddims, Dimadick, Dimitrii, DinDraithou, Djcam, Djegan, Dmitri Lytov, Domer48, Domsparrow, Dougweller, Downunda, Dppowell, Dpv, Drmies, Dspradau, Dubhdara, Dubhthach, Dueyfinster, Dundean19, Durrus, EANationalist, EamonnPKeane, Earl Andrew, Eastpaw, Ecuadorian Stalker, Edgar181, Editor32, Edzedd, Eireland09, Either way, El Gringo, Elipongo, Emperor Mudd, Enzedbrit, Eoj nhoj, Epbr123, Epf, Epson291, EronMain, Esanchez7587, Everyking, Ewalshe, Ezeu, FLORIDA101, Fabhcún, FaerieInGrey, Faolan101126, Farmsex11, Fasach Nua, Felixboy, Fercho85, Fergananim, Fergus mac Róich, Feydey, Ff22, Fieldday-sunday, Filastin, Finnrind, Fionnuala.Leclerc, FisherQueen, Fleming60, Flowerpotman, Fox, Fratrep, Freakofnurture, FreplySpang, Friesland NL, FruitMonkey, Fuhghettaboutit, GRBerry, Gail, Gaillimh, Gaius Cornelius, Gardar Rurak, Gareth E Kegg, Garret Beaumain, Garymcg, Gav108, Gazh, Genius4usa, GeoffGeorge, George Burgess, Gerard Doyle, Gerry Lynch, Ghmyrtle, Gil Gamesh, Gilliam, Gimmetrow, GiollaUidir, Globe01, Gnevin, Gocanada, Gold heart, Goldstar68, Gr8opinionater, Graham87, GreyPoint, Griffinofwales, Grim23, Grimhelm, Gtstricky, Guanaco, Guat6, Guliolopez, Gurch, GusF, Gustav von Humpelschmumpel, HMIPG, HalfShadow, Hamza883, HappyInGeneral, Hashmi, Usman, Henrymark, HeteroZellous, Hibernian, HighKing, Hintgergedanı, Historian19, Hmains, Hohenloh, Homework diary.v2, Honkytonkangel, Hoovernj, Hottentot, Hu, IJA, Iamlondon, Ian Cheese, Iridescent, Irish Lad, Irish Pearl, Irish.avenger, Irish4life91, IrishGirl25, IrishHermit, IrishPete, Irishguy, Irishredsox, Ironcorona, IslandShader, Ixfd64, J-stan, J.delanoy, J.smith, J04n, JForget, JHMM13, JMHamo, Jack Bhan, Jackets 3, James086, James57, Jamesbx, Java7837, Jcaragonv, Jdorney, Jeff3000, Jeroen, Jerry, Jkelly, Jll, Johann Wolfgang, John, John254, Johnny 0, Johnny45irish, JohnnyRush10, Johnwcowan, Jon Holly, Jon Kay, Jonesy1289, Joseph Solis in Australia, Jossi, Jusdafax, Jvlm.123, K1Bond007, KFP, Kaeso Dio, Kanags, Karenjc, Kartano, Kashk, Kathryn NicDhàna, Kbdank71, KeineLust90, Keithgreer, Kell0911, Kelly Martin, Kesac, Kevin McE, Kevlar67, Kevyn, Kgaughan, Khashkilla, Khoikhoi, Kidbrother, Kingpin13, Kipoc, Kman543210, KnowledgeOfSelf, Korovioff, Kozuch, Kristod, KudukGirl, Kuifjeenbobbie, Kukini, Kungfuadam, Kuyabribri, LSLM, La Fuente, Lacrimosus, Lapsed Pacifist, Le Anh-Huy, Leuko, LevenBoy, LevoTyro, LibLord, Lightmouse, Likemike23, Ling.Nut, Llort, Lofty, Londium, Lord Melvin, Lorn10, Lradrama, Lucky Mitch, Luckyion15, Luna Santin, M.V.E.i., M5891, MONGO, MacedonianLights, Madunne, Mais oui!, Man vyi, Mandarax, ManfromDelmonte, Manticore126, Martin451, MartinRobinson, Matticus78, Mattis, MaxPride, Mboverload, Mczack26, Mdebets, Meegs, MegX, MelForbes, MellBourne, Menlivetogether, Michael Hardy, Michaelsanders, Mike Rosoft, Millars, Milligan2, Million Little Gods, Mira, Missvain, Mmounties, Monre, Moon822, Mooretwin, Moydow, Mr Stephen, Mrdoylehasfunkyjumpers, Mttll, Mufanatic2, Murphys Law, MusicInTheHouse, Muuuuuur, Mwanner, MyMindSpoken, Mysticshade, NawlinWiki, Nehrams2020, Neilc, Neutrality, Neverquick, NewEnglandYankee, Nhoulihan, NickMartin, NickW557, Nikzbitz, Nilbud14, Nlu, NotMuchToSay, Notuncurious, Nposs, Nua eire, Nuclare, O Fenian, OBO7, Oda Mari, Odie5533, Odonan06, OekelWm, Ohainbhthin, Onorem, Opie, Opinoso, Optakeover, Osioni, Osm agha, OwenX, Oxymoron83, Oz MH, PMK1, Paddy More, PaddyBriggs, Palmiro, Pan-ethnic, Pat Mustard, Pathoschild, Patrick Denny, PatrickStar LaserPants, PaulGarner, Pentasyllabic, Perkeleperkele, Peruvianllama, Peter Clarke, Pharaoh of the Wizards, Pharillon, Phgao, Philip Baird Shearer, Philip Trueman, Picaroon, Pingu, Plrk, Polluxian, Polyhymnia, Pondle, PookeyMaster, Poolservice, Porto Madera, Possum, Prashanthns, PrestonH, Pro66, Proofreader77, Provocateur, Pwqn, Queezbo, Quintote, R9tgokunks, RPIRED, Radon210, Raid85, Random cupcake thief, RandomP, Rannpháirtí anaithnid, Rannpháirtí anaithnid (old), RashersTierney, Raven4x4x, Rbpolsen, Rdngchris, Realm of Shadows, RebekahThorn, Red Director, Red blaze, Red dwarf, Revolución, RexNL, Riana, Ric78, Richardcavell, Rickyrab, RingtailedFox, Risker, Rjwilmsi, Rmhermen, Rnt20, Ro2000, Roaeannexo, Roidhrigh, Romanm, Ropers, Ryano, Rye1967, Ryulong, S Hunter Haggard, SFC9394, SM, Saforrest, Saint-Paddy, Saintpatricksday, Salmon hunter, Samtheboy, Sandahl, Sarah, Sasha l, Saskia89, Sblj44, Scienceman123, Seabhcan, Search4Lancer, Secrowl, Selket, SeoR, Setanta747, Setanta747 (locked), Shawn M. O'Hare, Shoreranger, Sigma 7, Sigurd Dragon Slayer, Simhedges, SiobhanHansa, Skomorokh, Skunkboy74, Smcmod, SmilesALot, Smobri, Snappy, Snowded, Soliloquial, Sorcha niri, Soumyasch, Specter01010, Spenster, Splash, Springeragh, SpuriousQ, St Petersburgh, Steffenwood, Stephenchou0722, Stevebritgimp, Steven J. Anderson, Stevenb123, Stevenmitchell, Stpaul, Sttf01, Sugaar, Sunburntface, Superdan3000, Superdude99, Superfopp, Supermanpig, Swirlface, Taamu, Tabletop, TacoMan, Taketa, Tameamseo, Tankred, Teacherjjlee, Ted Bettler, Tempodivalse, Terrifictriffid, Tesscass, Tewapack, Tfz, Thch33, The Thing That Should Not Be, The undertow, TheIntersect, TheSun, TheTypoPatrol, Thecat21, Theniallmcgrane, Thunderboltz, Tiddly Tom, Tim1357, Timo, Tingiwingi, TintoDeSerrano, Tiocfaidh Ár Lá, Tiptoety, Tofts, Tohd8BohaithuGh1, Tom harrison, Tomassoroberto, Tombseye, Tone, TornVictor, Totemruby, Tpbradbury, Trasman, True as Blue, Twas Now, Ukabia, Ultraexactzz, Ulysses54, Upthera23, Urselius, Vald, Valfarly, Vanished188, Vary, Vegagb, Vekoler, Veledan, Vintagekits, Vizcarra, Vono, Waggers, Waker913, Wayland, Wayward, Weenieman13, Weevilo, Weird Whodi, WhoopeeDoo, Whytecypress, Wiggywalsh, Wiki01916, Wikipediaman44, WikipedianProlific, Willie Stark, Winchelsea, Windyjarhead, Wisdom89, Wj32, Wobble, Woohookitty, Ww2censor, Wysprgr2005, Xaosflux, Xavierized, Xezbeth, Xiahou, Xy7, Yellowneck, Yman88, Yolgnu, Yorkshirian, Zeno Izen, Zerophyte, ZhaoHong, Zocky, Zscout370, Zvn, Zymurgy, Zzuuzz, Александљр, 石, 1849 anonymous edits

Communism *Source*: http://en.wikipedia.org/w/index.php?oldid=346196202 *Contributors*: 05theben, 08toi, 0o64eva, 10qwerty, 172, 200.255.83.xxx, 213.67.126.xxx, 24.93.53.xxx, 4u1e, 5M4R7Y, 6birc, 98smithg2, A bit iffy, A-giau, A.Beaz, A.K.A.47, A.M., ALL YOUR STUPID IDEAS ARE BELONG TO US, ANTI COMMUNIST 16, AaronF2, Aaronw, Abu-Fool Danyal ibn Amir al-Makhiri, Accurizer, Acetic Acid, Ackoz, Acros037, Adam Carr, Adhib, Adis44, Adrian, Aeusoes1, Afitillidie13, Afterword, Aggie Jedi, Ahoerstemeier, Ahs gurl2012, Ahuitzotl, Ainlina, Aitias, Aiwendil42, Aksi great, Al3xil, Alakhriveion, Alansohn, Alex Peppe, Alex S, Alexper, Alhutch, Allenc28, Allstarecho, AlphaEta, Alphachimp, Alrasheedan, Altenmann, Amberrock, Anarchist-communist, Anarchopedia, AndonicO, Andre Engels, Andres, Andrewlp1991, Andrewpmk, Android79, Andy Marchbanks, Andypandy.UK, Andysoh, Angela, Anger22, Anime Editor, Anna969, Anonymous editor, Anonymous from the 21th century, Anoopkn, Another disinterested reader, Antandrus, Anthony Appleyard, Apeloverage, Aphaia, Apollonius 1236, Aprogressivist, Aqualung, Arctic-Editor, Arhiv, Aris Katsaris, Arjun01, Arkhiver, Arrest pol pot stoogerance, Arrest traitor rance12, Arronax50, Arwel Parry, Asams10, AsgdafdgadgasfdfQ!!!!!!!!!, Ashlux, Ashockey77, Ask123, Asn, Assbackward, Astroceltica, Athaenara, Atlant, AtrusTheGuildmaster, Attilios, Auno3, Auswiger, Average Earthman, Avernet, Avia, Awesomo Jefray, Az1568, AzaToth, AzureFury, B. Fairbairn, BAR1543, BD2412, BTraven, Babajobu, Babij, Bachcell, Badgerpatrol, Badinfinity, Balu.muthu, Bamboodragon, BananaFiend, Banes, Banjotime, Bantosh, Barnaby dawson, Bash rrance, Basidd1, Battlecry, Bawolff, Bbatsell, Bdevoe, Beanluc, Bearcat, Beeblebrox, Beland, Belligero, Benipinga, Beno1000, Berek, Bhadani, Big Bird, Bigeholt990, Bigjimr, Bigtop, BillCosby, Billysucksyay, Biruitorul, Biscuit and crunch, Bjorn Martiz, Bkwillwm, Bl0wme, Blake-, Blockader, Blog Mav Rick, Bluemoose, Bluenwhite341, Bmicomp, BobFromBrockley, Bobblewik, Bobbybrown, Bobet, Bobfrombrockley, Bobianite, Bobisbob, Bobisbob2, Bobo192, Bodnotbod, Bomac, Bombastus, Bonadea, Bongwarrior, Boothman, Boothy443, Boraczek, Boris 1991, Bornhj, BostonMA, Branislavk, BrendelSignature, Bristow1, Broken Segue, BrokenSegue, Bronks, Buchanan-Hermit, Bucketsofg, Bulltastrophy, BurritoLuca, Burschik, C mon, C.J. Griffin, CART fan, CHS BULLDOGS 75, CJCurrie, CJK, CJLL Wright, CJWilly, Cactus.man, CambridgeBayWeather, Can't sleep, clown will eat me, Canderson7, Capone, Captain panda, CardinalDan, Causa sui, Cdc, Celebration1981, Centrx, Cesar Tort, Cflm001, Chairman S., Chancemill, Changing of the guard, Chanting Fox, Charles Matthews, CharlotteWebb, Chato, Che y Marijuana, Chenzw, ChildofMidnight, Chinaleftcom, Chinesearabs, Chino, Chitrapa, Chowbok, Chowells, Chris Roy, Chris the speller, ChrisMorgan, Chrislk02, Chrisrmason, Christian List, Christofurio, Christopher Kraus, Christopherjamesgraham, Chunkofwhores, Claire andrade, Clamwave, Clanposse, Clarencedarrow, Clilly, Clockwork Soul, ClockworkSoul, Cloggedone, CloudNine, Cloudcoverboy, Clq, CmrdMariategui, Codij51, Colchicum, Comandante, Cometstyles, Commander Keane, Commiessuck, Commodore Kevles, CommonsDelinker, Communist Monkey, CommunistLeague, Complex (de), Computerjoe, Concon26, Conscious, Constanz, Conversion script, Cool3, Coolcaesar, Corporal Tunnel, Cosmic Latte, Cowie1337, Cranium225, Crazycomputers, Crazytales, Crc32, Cremepuff222, Critik, Crito2161, Crocodealer, CryptoDerk, Csmcsm, Curps, Curufinwe, Cybercobra, CyrilB, Cyrius, DHN, DJ Clayworth, DNewhall, DVD R W, Dak, Damicatz, Daniel Case, Daniel Olsen, Daniel Quinlan, DanielCD, Danis1911, Danny, Darcrist, Darsh13, Dash Hause, Dasha14, Dave6, Davenbelle, David.Mestel, David.Monniaux, Davidstrauss, Dawn Bard, Dazcue, Dbtfz, DeadEyeArrow, Decora, Deedubzed, Deeptrivia, Delldot, Delphii, Deltabeignet, Den fjättrade ankan, DennyColt, Der Ausländer, Derek Ross, Derfuehrer, Descendall, Destroy101, Dfrg.msc, Diagonalfish, Dickiedudeles, Diligens, DirkvdM, Discospinster, Dissident, Diza, Dizzytheegg, Dlohcierekim's sock, Dmerrill, DocWatson42, Doctors without suspenders, Dolda2000, Dominic, Domthedude001, Donnachadelong, Donthaveacowman, DoomsDay349, Dormantfascist, Downpayment, Dp462090, Dr. Yingst, DragonflySixtyseven, Dragracer89, DreamGuy, Drini, Drlcartman, Droll, DrowningInRoyalty, Dskluz, Dudtz, Dullfig, DuncanBCS, Duncharris, Dycedarg, Dylansmrjones, Dynesclan, Dysepsion, Dysprosia, Dzhugashvili, E-Carl, ESkog, Earle Martin, Easygardener, EatAlbertaBeef, Eberswim49, Ecadre, Eclecticology, Ed Fitzgerald, Ed Poor, Eddyrule3, Edidi, Edivorce, Edwy, Egern, Eirik (usurped), Ejercito Rojo 1967, El C, El presidente, Electionworld, Elembis, Elliskev, Elostirion, Elustran, Elvenscout742, Emishi, Emperorbma, Emuzesto, Enrico Pallazzo, Enviroboy, EoGuy, Equa olien, Eremin, Esanchez7587, Escobar600ie, Estel, Estumadre, EugeneZelenko, Evannator, Evercat, Everyking, Evil Monkey, Evilphoenix, Exir Kamalabadi, Exploding Boy, Eyeflash, FCYTravis, Fact check, Fang 23, Fangfyre, Fanofranz, Fargonite, Fearisstrong, Fennessy, Ferkelparade, FieryPhoenix, Fifelfoo, Fishal, FisherQueen, Flcelloguy, Flesh, Flowerpotman, Formeruser-81, Fpahl, FrancisTyers, FrancoGG, Francomemoria, Francs2000, Frank, Frankman, Franz.87, Fratrep, Freakofnurture, Fred Bauder, Fredbauder, Frederick, Fredrik, Freedomtroll, Freerick, FreplySpang, Freyr, Frigo, Frosty0814snowman, FrozenUmbrella, Frymaster, Fsotrain09, Func, FunkyRatDemon, Furrykef, Future usaf, Fuzbaby, Fuzheado, Fvw, G-Man, GHe, GMB, GRACCHVS, GTBacchus, GTubio, Gabbe, Gadfium, Galactor213, Galaxy413, Galoubet, Gannondork, GaryJolt, Garzo, Gaytan, Gdo01, Geoffj981, Georgecostanza, Georgiaisastate, Gerrish, Gerrit, Getoar, Gewehr, GhostPirate, Ghostbear616, Giovanni33, Glen, Globalization, Gmanunoman, Gmax0505, Goaredstar, Goatasaur, Gogo Dodo, GoldenTorc, Goochelaar, Good Olfactory, Goodboy8, Goplat, GraemeL, Graham87, Grandpafootsoldier, Granpuff, Grant65, Great Demon Lord, Green caterpillar, GregAsche, Gregbard, Grenavitar, Grey Shadow, Griffjam, Grlrocker777, Ground Zero, Grunt, Guanaco, Gugilymugily, Gundersen53, Gunmetal, Gurch, Gurubrahma, Gutza, Guy M, Guðsþegn, Gwernol, Gzornenplatz, H, HAPPYBIRTHDAY1010, Hacker6798, Hacktivist, Hadal, Hagedis, Haipa Doragon, Hairy Dude, Hajor, Haloman1013, Hammer Raccoon, Hardyplants, Hardys, Haroldpennywink, Hawaiian717, HeikoEvermann, Heimstern, Hellblazer112, Hellboy2hell, Hephaestos, Heqwm, Hetar, Hgrenbor, Hierophantasmagoria, HiramvdG, History Genius, Historymasterdotcom, Historypre, Hmrox, Hoerth, Hojimachong, Holocron, Hu, Hu!tz!l0p0chtl!, HubertCumberdale, Humbabba, Husond, Hvn0413, Hydrostatic, Hysteria2424, I Am Not Willy On Wheels, I'mDown, IJA, IZAK, Ian Evil, Ian Pitchford, Icarus3, Icewedge, IgorekSF, Iliev, Ilyanep, Imaginationac, InSaNe 48163264, InShaneee, Inbloom2, Infinity0, Infrogmation, Instinct, Intangible, Inter, Intheshade, Intimidated, Intrigue, Ioannes Pragensis, Ion-weapon, Irendraca, Iridescence, Irishguy, Irk, IronGargoyle, Isndez, Isolani, Isomorphic, Itsmejudith, Itsmine, Ittan, Ixfd64, Izehar, J Crow, J Di, J.J., J.delanoy, J.reed, J4V4, JAGEagent, JBKramer, JForget, JHMM13, JIMBO WALES, JImbo Wales, JMaxwell, JMeijer, JRI, JTBX, Jack Cox, Jack Holbrook, Jackalope darko, Jackbirdsong, Jackk, Jadam12345678910, Jag123, Jagged 85, James A. Donald, Jamsterlavery, JasonAQuest, Jauerback, Jaxl, Jaysiii, Jazzeur, Jcr2, Jecar, Jedravent, Jeeves, Jeff Silvers, Jemmy Button, Jensbn, JeremyA, Jersey Devil, JesseHogan, Jesusfive, Jiang, Jigesh, Jigsaw Jimmy, Jim Douglas, Jim62sch, Jimbo D. Wales, Jimmy D Wales, Jimmy da tuna, Jimothytrotter, Jiravo, Jittat, Jj137, Jklin, Jmabel, Jmlk17, JoanneB, Job L, Jobe6, JoeCarson, Joebear29, Johanneswilm, John, John Fader, John Vandenberg, John254, JohnGalt1812, JohnOwens, Johncmullen1960, Jorge1000xl, Jose77, Joseph Solis in Australia, Joshbuddy, Joshklipp, JoshuaD1991, JoshuaZ, Jossi, Journalist, Jouvenel, Joyous!, João Neves, Jpgordon, Jrash, Jredmond, Js.rad-dawg-man, Jtkiefer, Jumbo Wales, Jungykanglolipop, Jusjih, Jvgama, Jxg, KAOSv.s.CONTROL, KDRGibby, KI, Kablammo, Kajasudhakarababu, Kaliz, Kane69, Karl, Karmafist, Katalaveno, Katana314, Kaylor17351, Kaze no Kae, KeepItClean, Kelly Martin, Kennyisinvisible, Kewp, Kharoon, Khoikhoi, Khukri, Kikodawgzz, Kilimac, Killedbymanbearpig, Kindling5, Kinema, Kingfisherswift, Kinst, Kiske, Kman543210, Knightofni79, Knowledge Seeker, KnowledgeOfSelf, Knucmo2, Kokiri, Korg, Kpjas, KrakatoaKatie, Kukini, Kungfuadam, Kuntz12, Kuru, Kurykh, Kveerlarka, Kwekubo, Kwekwc, KyraVixen, Kzzl, La goutte de pluie, Lachelt, Lachlan12, Lacrimosus, LaggedOnUser, LahDeeDah7, Lancemurdoch, Landroo, Lapinmies, Lapsed

Pacifist, Laurenalyssa, Laurusnobilis, Lcarscad, Lebanese blond, LenBudney, Leo50, LeobenConoy, Leoboudv, Leolaursen, Leon7, Letter 7, Lewis.denholm, Liang9993, Libertas, Lick Spittle RRance, Lightdarkness, Lightmouse, Ligulem, Lijealso, Lingeron, Linuxlad, Lir, LittleOldMe, Livajo, Lkesteloot, Llort, Llywelyn, Llywrch, Localzuk, Looper5920, Lord Voldemort, LordRattor, LordZarglif555, Loremaster, LotSolarin, Lowe4091, Lowellian, Lradrama, Luckyherb, Luis rib, Lumidek, Luna Santin, Lupin, Lupo, Luthinya, Lycurgus, M a s, MC MasterChef, MER-C, MITB, MONGO, MZMcBride, MacGyverMagic, Macai, Machu505, Mackensen, Madcat87, Madhava 1947, Magioladitis, Mahal11, Mailer diablo, Mailliw115, Maire, Majin Takeru, Majorly, Malaysian Nazi Party representative, Malcolm Farmer, Malo, Mamalujo, Man vyi, Mangwanani, Mani1, Manic19, Manjithkaini, Manscher, ManuelGR, MarXidad, Marc Mongenet, Marek69, Marj Tiefert, MarkS, MarnetteD, Martin Wisse, MartinHarper, Marxist Revolutionary, MarxistNapoleon, Marysunshine, Master Jay, Master adam, Master of Puppets, Mastercomputerpro9999, Matijap, Matt Crypto, Matthew Fennell, Matticus78, Mattley, MauroVan, Mav, Mavaddat, Max rspct, Maxmc, Mayis, McCorrection, Mcarling, Mdwh, Measure, Meisterkoch, Mekong Bluesman, Melaen, MeltBanana, Mentifisto, Metageek, Mgw, Michael B. Trausch, MichaelBillington, Michaelas10, MichaelsProgramming, Midnightblueowl, Midnite Critic, Mihai Capotă, Mike Rosoft, MikeGogulski, Mikeandtom, Mikegrant, Mikker, Millerc, Miltonkeynes, Mindspillage, MindstormsKid, Minimin, Mirv, Miss Madeline, Mista-X, Mjk2357, Mjollnir111, Mjpieters, Mkwiatko, Mo0, MoOnY, Mocu, Mohonu, Momo117, Monalisa2, Mond, MonicaTTmed, Moohasha, Morwen, Motorizer, Mount Paektu, Mpstanco, Mr Adequate, Mr R Lopez, Mr.Rocks, MrBosnia, MrFish, MrWotUp, Mrdarklight, Mrdie, Mrdthree, Mrobby93, Mrs God, Mschel, Msikma, Msinummoc, Mtndewwatkins, Muchness, Mugarmugar, Musamo, Muscovite99, Musicianman11, Muéro, Mwanner, Mário, NGerda, NPPyzixBlan, NWOG, Naddy, Nakon, Nat, NatC, Natalina smpf, Natty4bumpo, NawlinWiki, Nazism isn't cool, Neenish, Nefariouski, Neil9999, Nemu, Neo Communist, Neo-Jay, Nerd101010, Netsumdisc, Neutrality, Newone, Nexxen, Nhandler, Niallharkin, Nibuod, NicAgent, Niccos, Nicholas Tan, Nick, Nick125, Nicolaibrown, Nigholith, NightOnEarth, Nikodemos, Nirvana2013, Njk, Nlu, Nmnmnm, No Guru, Nodnarbl.lad, Noik, Nono64, Normski3000, Nospamme2000, Notinasnaid, NubKnacker, Nut1917, Nuttycoconut, Nvek, Nyenyec, O918273645, ONEder Boy, ObiterDicta, Oblivious, Ocatecir, Oceanhahn, Octeron, Oda Mari, Ohmylord, Ohnoitsjamie, OleMaster, Olivier, Olly150, Omegatron, Onionpersei8, Ondrejk, Ong saluri, Optichan, Orange Flowerpot, Orbis Tertius, OrbitOne, Orderinchaos, Orionsky1, Ossmann, Otolemur crassicaudatus, Owen, Oxyman803, PRODUCER, Paine Ellsworth, Paki.tv, Paleocon, Palmiro, Palthrow, Paranoid, ParticleMan, Passargea, PasswordUsername, Pat Payne, Pathoschild, Patricius Augustus, Patrick, Patrick0Moran, Paul August, Paul-L, Paulink, Paxfeline, Pbannister, Pearle, Pedro, Pelicans Eating Fish, Penubag, Penwhale, Peptuck, Perníček, Persian Poet Gal, Peruvianllama, Peterwats, Petorian, Petri Krohn, Pevarnj, Pgan002, Pgk, PhJ, PhilKnight, Philfaebuckie, Philip Baird Shearer, Philip Cross, Philip Trueman, Philipb, Philthecow, Philwelch, PhotoBox, Phyzome, Piali, Pigenator, Pikiwedia, Pill, Pilotguy, Piotrus, Pir, Pjoef, Pleasantville, Pmanderson, PoccilScript, Podoksik, Pol pot stoogerance, Politepunk, Political Analysis, Political Guru, Polluxian, Polylerus, Pomte, Poor Yorick, Pranjalghimire, Prattmic, Pravda1987, PrestonH, Private Butcher, Proofreader, Proteus, Protos99, Psy guy, Psycho Kirby, Psychotic Panda, Puchiko, Purple people eater, Quadell, Que-Can, Queen bee1, Questioning81, Qwerty1234, Qxz, QzDaddy, R-41, RJASE1, RJII, RYNORT, RacerboyGTR, Rachlin92, Racjsingamac53, Radeksz, Radgeek, RadioKirk, Radoneme, Rafter Man, Railer 353, Railer 731, Rallye, Ran, Randalllin, RandomP, Randomlychaotic, Randroide, Randy Johnston, Raul654, Rayoflight278, Rdsmith4, Rebroad, Red Deathy, Redrocketboy, Redshoe2, Redthoreau, Reedy, Reeveorama, Regaler, RenegadeSniper7, Reverted edits by Regaler (talk) to last version by Pgk, RexNL, Riana, Richboy45, RickK, Rizdaddy, Rizzierizz, Rjbonacolta, Rjd0060, Rje, Rjwilmsi, Rklawton, Roadrunner, Rob99324, Robchurch, Robert I, Robert K S, RobertG, RobertHuaXia, Robth, RockerAndRoller, RockerAndRollerRevived, Rogpyvbc, Roland2, Rolandsukks, Roleplayer, Romanm, Ron Burgundy, Ronburgundy67, Ronnyberry28645, Roorootru96, Ropez, RossenV, Rotem Dan, Rrburke, Rsm99833, Runoble, Rursus, Ruy Lopez, Ryanaxp, Ryanbomber, Ryane26, Ryulong, SIEG HEIL!, SJP, ST47, SU Linguist, SV Resolution, Sade, Sagaciousuk, Sam Spade, Samer791, Sammyjay23, Samuel Blanning, Samy Merchi, Sanbeg, Sancak, Sandahl, Sango123, Sanmartin, Sannse, Sapdutta, Sardanaphalus, SauliH, Savant1984, Scallawaged, Sceptre, Schatzman, SchfiftyThree, Schzmo, Scohoust, Scott Ritchie, ScottishPinko, Scoutersig, Sdaconsulting, Sdorman, Sdr, Secretlondon, Seeleschneider, Seifip, Semila58, Semperf, Seqsea, Seraphimbelial616, Seraphimblade, Serpent-A, Sesel, Shadoom1, Shadow1, Shadowblade, Shanel, Shanes, Sharonlees, Shellwood, Shimgray, Shizhao, Shmooshkums, Shoeofdeath, Shoessss, Shorne, Shoshonna, Shruti14, Shwoo5, Sibemaster, Sietse Snel, Signalhead, Silly rabbit, Silsor, Silverback, SimonP, Singhalawap, Sir Lewk, Sir Nicholas de Mimsy-Porpington, Sir chris 2, Sjakkalle, Skdeewan, Skew-t, Skins88, Skomorokh, Slakr, Slof, Slrubenstein, Slythfox, Smalljim, Smallman12q, Smellyfishfart, Smilingman, Smoove Z, Smurfoid, Snatchaquarious Hunter, Snow Shoes, So Hungry, Sodarn Insane, Solipsist, Solitude, Soman, SonofRage, Sorpigal, Sottolacqua, Soulpatch, SparqMan, Spellcast, Spinach Monster, Splash, Spliffy, Spookfish, SpudHawg948, Spylab, Spywriter, Squirepants101, Srijon, Srikeit, Sshap36, Stanley Accrington, Stanley011, Star Wars117, Stars4change, Stdout, Steamrunner, Steel, Steelhammer, Stemonitis, Stephenb, Stephenchou0722, Stepupthefun, Steven Zhang, Stevobowdo, Stevoman69, Stlcards, Stomp rance, Stormie, Student7, Stumpyraccoon, Stwalkerster, Subcommandante, Supergeo, Superm401, Suwa, Sunholm, SwitChar, Sydney2006, Synergy, SyntaxError55, Syvanen, TBadger, TDC, TJDay, Tacoman359, Takenrocks, Talamor, Talkie tim, Tangotango, Tannin, Tapir Terrific, Taroaldo, Tarret, Tarshish, Tasc, Tasudrty, Tatarian, Taw, Tawker, Tazmaniacs, Tbasherizer, TedE, Teeninvestor, Tekmatic38, Tentu, Terence, Termer, Tero, Tfl, Thane Eichenauer, That Guy, From That Show!, That-Vela-Fella, The Anome, The Halo, The High Commander, The Rambling Man, The Transhumanist, The Trolls of Navarone, The Ungovernable Force, The dark lord trombonator, The monkeyhate, The sunder king, The wub, The8thbit, TheBilly, TheCatalyst31, TheDJ, TheFix63, TheGrza, TheInquisitor, TheKMan, TheLamprey, TheOngmanALT12, TheOtherJesse, TheSeer, TheTick, TheTrueSora, Thea Corona's party, Thedoorhinge, TheeT29, Thekckid79, Thompson3217, Thunk00, Timir2, Timothy Usher, Titoxd, Tkmasta, Tocoageorgia, Tocino, Toddgarsden, Tom harrison, Tom mayfair, Tomandlu, Tommybtennis, Tommybtennis2, Tonster, Tonym88, Tothebarricades.tk, Toya, Travelbird, Travellingstone, Travйrsa, Trblsldr, Tree Biting Conspiracy, Triacylglyceride, Triona, Tristanb, Trogdawr, Trotskys tooches, Troyboy69, Trunk68, Trust Is All You Need, Tulninfarv, Tuncrypt, Twosocks, Typelighter, Tzartzam, UNSC Trooper, US Patriot 1776, UberScienceNerd, Ulric1313, Ultramarine, Umkhontto, Union6, Unixer, Upsidedownalways, Urocyon, UserGoogol, Uusitunnus, V10, Vacuum, Vadac, Vald, Valentinian, Valois bourbon, VampWillow, Vand.account, Vanderdecken, Vargon, Vary, VegaDark, Veinor, Verdadero, VeryVerily, Viajero, Victor, Vildricianus, Viridae, Vision Thing, Vivio Testarossa, Vmenkov, VolatileChemical, VoluntarySlave, Von Fiszman, VonWoland, VoodooSteve, Vslashg, Vsmith, WCar1930, WGee, WJBscribe, WODUP, Walaby211, Walkiped, Warhorus, Warofdreams, Wassamatta, Wassermann, Waterboarder17, Wayland, Wayward, Wcp07, Welsh, Wenteng, Weyes, Whassuo, Where, White Cat, White Guard, Whiteheadj, Who, Wi-king, WiiGamer, Wiki alf, Wiki-vr, Wikiklrsc, Wikipedia Admin, Wikipedia Administration, Wikipedia is Communism, Wikipedia is Marxism, Wildhartlivie, Wilfried Derksen, WillQuan, Willdw79, Wilson44691, Wilt, Wimt, Wingman1331, Wink wank, WinterSpw, Wisc06, Wknight94, Wolfkeeper, X Tron 13, X201, XXXVANDELXXX, Xaosflux, Xasthuresque, Xciiio, Xdcdx, Xed, Xevi, Xiahou, Xiner, Xixve, Xnuala, Xvandelx, Xx236, Xy7, Yacht, Yahel Guhan, Yamaguchi先生, Yamamoto Ichiro, Yaml, Natalie Erin, Necrothesp, Neutrality, Ninetyone, Numerousfalx, Orzetto, PFHLai, Panairjdde, Pat Payne, Paul August, Pen of bushido, Phydend, Piececrowd, Pramzan, Prittglue, Ricebowl09, Rjwilmsi, Rmhermen, Saint-Paddy, Sam Hocevar, Sardanaphalus, SchnappM, Shoeofdeath, Skysmith, Slambo, Slarre, Sm8900, Smalljim, Smgold92, Sobolewski, Stewartadcock, Tazmaniacs, The Crying Orc, Tidaress, Tomtom, Treybien, Vanished User 03, Will2k, Woohookitty, Yerpo, Ángel Luis Alfaro, 210 anonymous edits

Blackshirts *Source:* http://en.wikipedia.org/w/index.php?oldid=343419872 *Contributors:* Akrusemark, Amcalabrese, Antixt, Aranel, Asiaticus, Attilios, Babajobu, Biruitorul, Bloodofox, Bobo192, Bpselvam, Brian Sayrs, Cacycle, CambridgeBayWeather, Caramesc, Cloj, Coentor, CommonsDelinker, Coyr, DNewhall, DO'Neil, Dahn, Daufer, Detruncate, Dudeman5685, Eequor, Everyking, Femmina, FlagSteward, Flankk, Frecklefoot, GCarty, Gennarous, Golbez, Greenshed, Grendelkhan, Hajor, Hmains, Ian Spackman, Infrogmation, Irt78, Jackliddle, Jason M, Jiang, Josh Parris, Jpbrenna, Jpgordon, Jvano, Kaliz, Karada, Kazubon, Kmaster, Koshki, KrakatoaKatie, Kuralyov, Llywrch, Lvcipriani, Mangrove22, Marco polo, MauroVan, Michael Hardy, Mitsukai, Mixcoatl, Mkpumphrey, Mole, Moncrief, NEMT, Nadiral, Natalie Erin, Necrothesp, Neutrality, Ninetyone, Numerousfalx, Orzetto, PFHLai, Panairjdde, Pat Payne, Paul August, Pen of bushido, Phydend, Piececrowd, Pramzan, Prittglue, Ricebowl09, Rjwilmsi, Rmhermen, Saint-Paddy, Sam Hocevar, Sardanaphalus, SchnappM, Shoeofdeath, Skysmith, Slambo, Slarre, Sm8900, Smalljim, Smgold92, Sobolewski, Stewartadcock, Tazmaniacs, The Crying Orc, Tidaress, Tomtom, Treybien, Vanished User 03, Will2k, Woohookitty, Yerpo, Ángel Luis Alfaro, 210 anonymous edits

National Socialist Party of America v. Village of Skokie *Source:* http://en.wikipedia.org/w/index.php?oldid=344183576 *Contributors:* Albrozdude, Alksub, Amalas, BD2412, Cberlet, Cdogsimmons, Cgingold, Chaser, Ckatz, Cubman4444, Cyrillic, Delldot, Eliyak, Eric-Wester, Erik the Red 2, Fashnable1, Fnorth, Gilliam, Jbapowell, Jsgoodman, MZMcBride, MosheA, Nutiketaiel, Petdance, Qmwne235, RayvnEQ, RevelationDirect, Richardshusr, Rjwilmsi, RussNelson, Shell Kinney, Tad Lincoln, The Thing That Should Not Be, Thecomputermedic, ThreeOneFive, Tim!, USN1977, WRK, Xeno, Zorro CX, 55 anonymous edits

Image Sources, Licenses and Contributors

Image:CableStreet.jpg *Source*: http://en.wikipedia.org/w/index.php?title=File:CableStreet.jpg *License*: unknown *Contributors*: Hux, Murray McDonald

Image:Battle-of-Cable-Street-red-plaque.png *Source*: http://en.wikipedia.org/w/index.php?title=File:Battle-of-Cable-Street-red-plaque.png *License*: unknown *Contributors*: GeorgHH, Liftarn, Man vyi, Mu, Nard the Bard, Oosoom, Roomba, Wst

Image:WilliamPerkinBluePlaque.png *Source*: http://en.wikipedia.org/w/index.php?title=File:WilliamPerkinBluePlaque.png *License*: GNU Free Documentation License *Contributors*: Burn, Captmondo, GeorgHH, Man vyi, Oosoom, Roomba

Image:Jack-Berg-blue-plaque.png *Source*: http://en.wikipedia.org/w/index.php?title=File:Jack-Berg-blue-plaque.png *License*: Public Domain *Contributors*: Richard Allen

Image:Ch ch spitalfields.400px.jpg *Source*: http://en.wikipedia.org/w/index.php?title=File:Ch_ch_spitalfields.400px.jpg *License*: GNU Free Documentation License *Contributors*: Original uploader was MykReeve at en.wikipedia

Image:1745 Roque Map.jpg *Source*: http://en.wikipedia.org/w/index.php?title=File:1745_Roque_Map.jpg *License*: unknown *Contributors*: Original uploader was Kbthompson at en.wikipedia

Image:1882 Reynolds Map.jpg *Source*: http://en.wikipedia.org/w/index.php?title=File:1882_Reynolds_Map.jpg *License*: unknown *Contributors*: Original uploader was Kbthompson at en.wikipedia

Image:Williambooth.jpg *Source*: http://en.wikipedia.org/w/index.php?title=File:Williambooth.jpg *License*: unknown *Contributors*: Mgallege, Polarlys, Wst, 3 anonymous edits

Image:Angela Georgina Burdett-Coutts.jpg *Source*: http://en.wikipedia.org/w/index.php?title=File:Angela_Georgina_Burdett-Coutts.jpg *License*: Public Domain *Contributors*: User:Magnus Manske

Image:Sylvia Pankhurst 1909.jpeg *Source*: http://en.wikipedia.org/w/index.php?title=File:Sylvia_Pankhurst_1909.jpeg *License*: Public Domain *Contributors*: ElRaki, Ferengi, Kaldari, Svencb

Image:IKBrunelChains.jpg *Source*: http://en.wikipedia.org/w/index.php?title=File:IKBrunelChains.jpg *License*: Public Domain *Contributors*: Robert Howlett

Image:West India Docks Microcosm edited.jpg *Source*: http://en.wikipedia.org/w/index.php?title=File:West_India_Docks_Microcosm_edited.jpg *License*: Public Domain *Contributors*: Oneblackline, Wimstead

Image:Minories stationLBR.jpg *Source*: http://en.wikipedia.org/w/index.php?title=File:Minories_stationl.BR.jpg *License*: unknown *Contributors*: User:Oxyman

Image:Captainjamescookportrait.jpg *Source*: http://en.wikipedia.org/w/index.php?title=File:Captainjamescookportrait.jpg *License*: unknown *Contributors*: Nathaniel Dance

Image:Boundary est Bandstand.JPG *Source*: http://en.wikipedia.org/w/index.php?title=File:Boundary_est_Bandstand.JPG *License*: Creative Commons Attribution 2.5 *Contributors*: Original uploader was Kbthompson at en.wikipedia

Image:Dornier Do17Z over West Ham.jpg *Source*: http://en.wikipedia.org/w/index.php?title=File:Dornier_Do17Z_over_West_Ham.jpg *License*: unknown *Contributors*: Kbthompson

Image:WWII London Blitz East London.jpg *Source*: http://en.wikipedia.org/w/index.php?title=File:WWII_London_Blitz_East_London.jpg *License*: Creative Commons Attribution 3.0 *Contributors*: Sue Wallace

Image:Prefabfront.jpg *Source*: http://en.wikipedia.org/w/index.php?title=File:Prefabfront.jpg *License*: Creative Commons Attribution-Sharealike 2.5 *Contributors*: Sfan00 IMG, Wyrdlight

Image:Brick Lane 2005.jpg *Source*: http://en.wikipedia.org/w/index.php?title=File:Brick_Lane_2005.jpg *License*: Creative Commons Attribution-Sharealike 2.0 *Contributors*: User:Justinc

Image:BritishBrothersLeaguePoster(1902).jpg *Source*: http://en.wikipedia.org/w/index.php?title=File:BritishBrothersLeaguePoster(1902).jpg *License*: Public Domain *Contributors*: Unknown

Image:police.boat.london.arp.jpg *Source*: http://en.wikipedia.org/w/index.php?title=File:Police.boat.london.arp.jpg *License*: Public Domain *Contributors*: User:Arpingstone

Image:William Hogarth - Gin Lane.jpg *Source*: http://en.wikipedia.org/w/index.php?title=File:William_Hogarth_-_Gin_Lane.jpg *License*: Public Domain *Contributors*: William Hogarth/Samuel Davenport

Image:Princess alice collision in thames.jpg *Source*: http://en.wikipedia.org/w/index.php?title=File:Princess_alice_collision_in_thames.jpg *License*: Public Domain *Contributors*: Original uploader was Ydorb at en.wikipedia

Image:Curtain Theatre.jpg *Source*: http://en.wikipedia.org/w/index.php?title=File:Curtain_Theatre.jpg *License*: Public Domain *Contributors*: Cirt, Galileo01, Jennavecia

Image:1867 NationalStandardTheatre.jpg *Source*: http://en.wikipedia.org/w/index.php?title=File:1867_NationalStandardTheatre.jpg *License*: Public Domain *Contributors*: Original uploader was Kbthompson at en.wikipedia

Image:Hoxton Hall.JPG *Source*: http://en.wikipedia.org/w/index.php?title=File:Hoxton_Hall.JPG *License*: Creative Commons Attribution 2.5 *Contributors*: User:BotMultichill

Image:Canary Wharf complex.jpg *Source*: http://en.wikipedia.org/w/index.php?title=File:Canary_Wharf_complex.jpg *License*: GNU Free Documentation License *Contributors*: Original uploader was Henrygb at en.wikipedia

Image:London Olympic Stadium (Nov 2007).jpg *Source*: http://en.wikipedia.org/w/index.php?title=File:London_Olympic_Stadium_(Nov_2007).jpg *License*: unknown *Contributors*: Kbthompson, Paralympic, SGBailey, 1 anonymous edits

Image:1899 Gus Ellen.jpg *Source*: http://en.wikipedia.org/w/index.php?title=File:1899_Gus_Ellen.jpg *License*: Public Domain *Contributors*: Kbthompson, Peachey88, Relen

Image:Met-police-logo.svg *Source*: http://en.wikipedia.org/w/index.php?title=File:Met-police-logo.svg *License*: unknown *Contributors*: User:Smomo

Image:Metropolitan Police Flag.gif *Source*: http://en.wikipedia.org/w/index.php?title=File:Metropolitan_Police_Flag.gif *License*: GNU Free Documentation License *Contributors*: http://hu.wikipedia.org/wiki/User:Sancho (on Hungarian Wiki)

Image:Image-EnglandPoliceMetropolitan.png *Source*: http://en.wikipedia.org/w/index.php?title=File:Image-EnglandPoliceMetropolitan.png *License*: GNU Free Documentation License *Contributors*: User Morwen on en.wikipedia

Image:UK-police-01.PNG *Source*: http://en.wikipedia.org/w/index.php?title=File:UK-police-01.PNG *License*: Creative Commons Attribution-Sharealike 3.0 *Contributors*: User:Timothy Titus

Image:UK-police-02.PNG *Source*: http://en.wikipedia.org/w/index.php?title=File:UK-police-02.PNG *License*: Creative Commons Attribution-Sharealike 3.0 *Contributors*: User:Timothy Titus

Image:UK-police-03.PNG *Source*: http://en.wikipedia.org/w/index.php?title=File:UK-police-03.PNG *License*: Creative Commons Attribution-Sharealike 3.0 *Contributors*: User:Timothy Titus

Image:UK-police-04.PNG *Source*: http://en.wikipedia.org/w/index.php?title=File:UK-police-04.PNG *License*: Creative Commons Attribution-Sharealike 3.0 *Contributors*: User:Timothy Titus

Image:UK-police-05.PNG *Source*: http://en.wikipedia.org/w/index.php?title=File:UK-police-05.PNG *License*: Creative Commons Attribution-Sharealike 3.0 *Contributors*: User:Timothy Titus

Image:UK-police-06.PNG *Source*: http://en.wikipedia.org/w/index.php?title=File:UK-police-06.PNG *License*: Creative Commons Attribution-Sharealike 3.0 *Contributors*: User:Timothy Titus

Image:UK-police-07.PNG *Source*: http://en.wikipedia.org/w/index.php?title=File:UK-police-07.PNG *License*: Creative Commons Attribution-Sharealike 3.0 *Contributors*: User:Timothy Titus

Image:UK-police-08.PNG *Source*: http://en.wikipedia.org/w/index.php?title=File:UK-police-08.PNG *License*: Creative Commons Attribution-Sharealike 3.0 *Contributors*: User:Timothy Titus

Image:UK-police-09.PNG *Source*: http://en.wikipedia.org/w/index.php?title=File:UK-police-09.PNG *License*: Creative Commons Attribution-Sharealike 3.0 *Contributors*: User:Timothy Titus

Image:UK-police-10.PNG *Source*: http://en.wikipedia.org/w/index.php?title=File:UK-police-10.PNG *License*: Creative Commons Attribution-Sharealike 3.0 *Contributors*: User:Timothy Titus

Image:UK-police-11.PNG *Source*: http://en.wikipedia.org/w/index.php?title=File:UK-police-11.PNG *License*: Creative Commons Attribution-Sharealike 3.0 *Contributors*: User:Timothy Titus

Image:Metofficer.JPG *Source*: http://en.wikipedia.org/w/index.php?title=File:Metofficer.JPG *License*: Public Domain *Contributors*: User:Ronaldccwong

Image:DSC05638.JPG *Source*: http://en.wikipedia.org/w/index.php?title=File:DSC05638.JPG *License*: Creative Commons Attribution-Sharealike 2.5 *Contributors*: Rebelduder69, 2 anonymous edits

Image:Met Police Blue Lamp.jpg *Source*: http://en.wikipedia.org/w/index.php?title=File:Met_Police_Blue_Lamp.jpg *License*: Public Domain *Contributors*: Avron, Canley, Mattes

Image:British Union of Fascists flag.ant.svg *Source*: http://en.wikipedia.org/w/index.php?title=File:British_Union_of_Fascists_flag.ant.svg *License*: Public Domain *Contributors*: user:masturbius

Image:Blackshorts.svg *Source*: http://en.wikipedia.org/w/index.php?title=File:Blackshorts.svg *License*: Public Domain *Contributors*: User:Kxh, User:Masturbius

file:OMosley.jpg *Source*: http://en.wikipedia.org/w/index.php?title=File:OMosley.jpg *License*: unknown *Contributors*: Counter-revolutionary

Image:101st with members of dutch resistance.jpg *Source*: http://en.wikipedia.org/w/index.php?title=File:101st_with_members_of_dutch_resistance.jpg *License*: Public Domain *Contributors*: User:W.wolny

Image:Antifa !!.jpg *Source*: http://en.wikipedia.org/w/index.php?title=File:Antifa_!!.jpg *License*: Creative Commons Attribution-Sharealike 2.5 *Contributors*: Original uploader was Jcarax68 at en.wikipedia

License

GNU Free Documentation License Version 1.2, November 2002 Copyright (C) 2000,2001,2002 Free Software Foundation, Inc. 59 Temple Place, Suite 330, Boston, MA 02111-1307 USA Everyone is permitted to copy and distribute verbatim copies of this license document, but changing it is not allowed.

0. PREAMBLE

The purpose of this License is to make a manual, textbook, or other functional and useful document "free" in the sense of freedom: to assure everyone the effective freedom to copy and redistribute it, with or without modifying it, either commercially or noncommercially. Secondarily, this License preserves for the author and publisher a way to get credit for their work, while not being considered responsible for modifications made by others. This License is a kind of "copyleft", which means that derivative works of the document must themselves be free in the same sense. It complements the GNU General Public License, which is a copyleft license designed for free software. We have designed this License in order to use it for manuals for free software, because free software needs free documentation: a free program should come with manuals providing the same freedoms that the software does. But this License is not limited to software manuals; it can be used for any textual work, regardless of subject matter or whether it is published as a printed book. We recommend this License principally for works whose purpose is instruction or reference.

1. APPLICABILITY AND DEFINITIONS

This License applies to any manual or other work, in any medium, that contains a notice placed by the copyright holder saying it can be distributed under the terms of this License. Such a notice grants a world-wide, royalty-free license, unlimited in duration, to use that work under the conditions stated herein. The "Document", below, refers to any such manual or work. Any member of the public is a licensee, and is addressed as "you". You accept the license if you copy, modify or distribute the work in a way requiring permission under copyright law. A "Modified Version" of the Document means any work containing the Document or a portion of it, either copied verbatim, or with modifications and/or translated into another language. A "Secondary Section" is a named appendix or a front-matter section of the Document that deals exclusively with the relationship of the publishers or authors of the Document to the Document's overall subject (or to related matters) and contains nothing that could fall directly within that overall subject. (Thus, if the Document is in part a textbook of mathematics, a Secondary Section may not explain any mathematics.) The relationship could be a matter of historical connection with the subject or with related matters, or of legal, commercial, philosophical, ethical or political position regarding them. The "Invariant Sections" are certain Secondary Sections whose titles are designated, as being those of Invariant Sections, in the notice that says that the Document is released under this License. If a section does not fit the above definition of Secondary then it is not allowed to be designated as Invariant. The Document may contain zero Invariant Sections. If the Document does not identify any Invariant Sections then there are none. The "Cover Texts" are certain short passages of text that are listed, as Front-Cover Texts or Back-Cover Texts, in the notice that says that the Document is released under this License. A Front-Cover Text may be at most 5 words, and a Back-Cover Text may be at most 25 words. A "Transparent" copy of the Document means a machine-readable copy, represented in a format whose specification is available to the general public, that is suitable for revising the document straightforwardly with generic text editors or (for images composed of pixels) generic paint programs or (for drawings) some widely available drawing editor, and that is suitable for input to text formatters or for automatic translation to a variety of formats suitable for input to text formatters. A copy made in an otherwise Transparent file format whose markup, or absence of markup, has been arranged to thwart or discourage subsequent modification by readers is not Transparent. An image format is not Transparent if used for any substantial amount of text. A copy that is not "Transparent" is called "Opaque". Examples of suitable formats for Transparent copies include plain ASCII without markup, Texinfo input format, LaTeX input format, SGML or XML using a publicly available DTD, and standard-conforming simple HTML, PostScript or PDF designed for human modification. Examples of transparent image formats include PNG, XCF and JPG. Opaque formats include proprietary formats that can be read and edited only by proprietary word processors, SGML or XML for which the DTD and/or processing tools are not generally available, and the machine-generated HTML, PostScript or PDF produced by some word processors for output purposes only. The "Title Page" means, for a printed book, the title page itself, plus such following pages as are needed to hold, legibly, the material this License requires to appear in the title page. For works in formats which do not have any title page as such, "Title Page" means the text near the most prominent appearance of the work's title, preceding the beginning of the body of the text. A section "Entitled XYZ" means a named subunit of the Document whose title either is precisely XYZ or contains XYZ in parentheses following text that translates XYZ in another language. (Here XYZ stands for a specific section name mentioned below, such as "Acknowledgements", "Dedications", "Endorsements", or "History".) To "Preserve the Title" of such a section when you modify the Document means that it remains a section "Entitled XYZ" according to this definition. The Document may include Warranty Disclaimers next to the notice which states that this License applies to the Document. These Warranty Disclaimers are considered to be included by reference in this License, but only as regards disclaiming warranties: any other implication that these Warranty Disclaimers may have is void and has no effect on the meaning of this License.

2. VERBATIM COPYING

You may copy and distribute the Document in any medium, either commercially or noncommercially, provided that this License, the copyright notices, and the license notice saying this License applies to the Document are reproduced in all copies, and that you add no other conditions whatsoever to those of this License. You may not use technical measures to obstruct or control the reading or further copying of the copies you make or distribute. However, you may accept compensation in exchange for copies. If you distribute a large enough number of copies you must also follow the conditions in section 3. You may also lend copies, under the same conditions stated above, and you may publicly display copies.

3. COPYING IN QUANTITY

If you publish printed copies (or copies in media that commonly have printed covers) of the Document, numbering more than 100, and the Document's license notice requires Cover Texts, you must enclose the copies in covers that carry, clearly and legibly, all these Cover Texts: Front-Cover Texts on the front cover, and Back-Cover Texts on the back cover. Both covers must also clearly and legibly identify you as the publisher of these copies. The front cover must present the full title with all words of the title equally prominent and visible. You may add other material on the covers in addition. Copying with changes limited to the covers, as long as they preserve the title of the Document and satisfy these conditions, can be treated as verbatim copying in other respects. If the required texts for either cover are too voluminous to fit legibly, you should put the first ones listed (as many as fit reasonably) on the actual cover, and continue the rest onto adjacent pages. If you publish or distribute Opaque copies of the Document numbering more than 100, you must either include a machine-readable Transparent copy along with each Opaque copy, or state in or with each Opaque copy a computer-network location from which the general network-using public has access to download using public-standard network protocols a complete Transparent copy of the Document, free of added material. If you use the latter option, you must take reasonably prudent steps, when you begin distribution of Opaque copies in quantity, to ensure that this Transparent copy will remain thus accessible at the stated location until at least one year after the last time you distribute an Opaque copy (directly or through your agents or retailers) of that edition to the public. It is requested, but not required, that you contact the authors of the Document well before redistributing any large number of copies, to give them a chance to provide you with an updated version of the Document.

4. MODIFICATIONS

You may copy and distribute a Modified Version of the Document under the conditions of sections 2 and 3 above, provided that you release the Modified Version under precisely this License, with the Modified Version filling the role of the Document, thus licensing distribution and modification of the Modified Version to whoever possesses a copy of it. In addition, you must do these things in the Modified Version: A. Use in the Title Page (and on the covers, if any) a title distinct from that of the Document, and from those of previous versions (which should, if there were any, be listed in the History section of the Document). You may use the same title as a previous version if the original publisher of that version gives permission. B. List on the Title Page, as authors, one or more persons or entities responsible for authorship of the modifications in the Modified Version, together with at least five of the principal authors of the Document (all of its principal authors, if it has fewer than five), unless they release you from this requirement. C. State on the Title page the name of the publisher of the Modified Version, as the publisher. D. Preserve all the copyright notices of the Document. E. Add an appropriate copyright notice for your modifications adjacent to the other copyright notices. F. Include, immediately after the copyright notices, a license notice giving the public permission to use the Modified Version under the terms of this License, in the form shown in the Addendum below. G. Preserve in that license notice the full lists of Invariant Sections and required Cover Texts given in the Document's license notice. H. Include an unaltered copy of this License. I. Preserve the section Entitled "History", Preserve its Title, and add to it an item stating at least the title, year, new authors, and publisher of the Modified Version as given on the Title Page. If there is no section Entitled "History" in the Document, create one stating the title, year, authors, and publisher of the Document as given on its Title Page, then add an item describing the Modified Version as stated in the previous sentence. J. Preserve the network location, if any, given in the Document for public access to a Transparent copy of the Document, and likewise the network locations given in the Document for previous versions it was based on. These may be placed in the "History" section. You may omit a network location for a work that was published at least four years before the Document itself, or if the original publisher of the version it refers to gives permission. K. For any section Entitled "Acknowledgements" or "Dedications", Preserve the Title of the section, and preserve in the section all the substance and tone of each of the contributor acknowledgements and/or dedications given therein. L. Preserve all the Invariant Sections of the Document, unaltered in their text and in their titles. Section numbers or the equivalent are not considered part of the section titles. M. Delete any section Entitled "Endorsements". Such a section may not be included in the Modified Version. N. Do not retitle any existing section to be Entitled "Endorsements" or to conflict in title with any Invariant Section. O. Preserve any Warranty Disclaimers. If the Modified Version includes new front-matter sections or appendices that qualify as Secondary Sections and contain no material copied from the Document, you may at your option designate some or all of these sections as invariant. To do this, add their titles to the list of Invariant Sections in the Modified Version's license notice. These titles must be distinct from any other section titles. You may add a section Entitled "Endorsements", provided it contains nothing but endorsements of your Modified Version by various parties--for example, statements of peer review or that the text has been approved by an organization as the authoritative definition of a standard. You may add a passage of up to five words as a Front-Cover Text, and a passage of up to 25 words as a Back-Cover Text, to the end of the list of Cover Texts in the Modified Version. Only one passage of Front-Cover Text and one of Back-Cover Text may be added by (or through arrangements made by) any one entity. If the Document already includes a cover text for the same cover, previously added by you or by arrangement made by the same entity you are acting on behalf of, you may not add another; but you may replace the old one, on explicit permission from the previous publisher that added the old one. The author(s) and publisher(s) of the Document do not by this License give permission to use their names for publicity for or to assert or imply endorsement of any Modified Version.

5. COMBINING DOCUMENTS

You may combine the Document with other documents released under this License, under the terms defined in section 4 above for modified versions, provided that you include in the combination all of the Invariant Sections of all of the original documents, unmodified, and list them all as Invariant Sections of your combined work in its license notice, and that you preserve all their Warranty Disclaimers. The combined work need only contain one copy of this License, and multiple identical Invariant Sections may be replaced with a single copy. If there are multiple Invariant Sections with the same name but different contents, make the title of each such section unique by adding at the end of it, in parentheses, the name of the original author or publisher of that section if known, or else a unique number. Make the same adjustment to the section titles in the list of Invariant Sections in the license notice of the combined work. In the combination, you must combine any sections Entitled "History" in the various original documents, forming one section Entitled "History"; likewise combine any sections Entitled "Acknowledgements", and any sections Entitled "Dedications". You must delete all sections Entitled "Endorsements".

6. COLLECTIONS OF DOCUMENTS

You may make a collection consisting of the Document and other documents released under this License, and replace the individual copies of this License in the various documents with a single copy that is included in the collection, provided that you follow the rules of this License for verbatim copying of each of the documents in all other respects. You may extract a single document from such a collection, and distribute it individually under this License, provided you insert a copy of this License into the extracted document, and follow this License in all other respects regarding verbatim copying of that document.

7. AGGREGATION WITH INDEPENDENT WORKS

A compilation of the Document or its derivatives with other separate and independent documents or works, in or on a volume of a storage or distribution medium, is called an "aggregate" if the copyright resulting from the compilation is not used to limit the legal rights of the compilation's users beyond what the individual works permit. When the Document is included in an aggregate, this License does not apply to the other works in the aggregate which are not themselves derivative works of the Document. If the Cover Text requirement of section 3 is applicable to these copies of the Document, then if the Document is less than one half of the entire aggregate, the Document's Cover Texts may be placed on covers that bracket the Document within the aggregate, or the electronic equivalent of covers if the Document is in electronic form. Otherwise they must appear on printed covers that bracket the whole aggregate.

8. TRANSLATION

Translation is considered a kind of modification, so you may distribute translations of the Document under the terms of section 4. Replacing Invariant Sections with translations requires special permission from their copyright holders, but you may include translations of some or all Invariant Sections in addition to the original versions of these Invariant Sections. You may include a translation of this License, and all the license notices in the Document, and any Warranty Disclaimers, provided that you also include the original English version of this License and the original versions of those notices and disclaimers. In case of a disagreement between the translation and the original version of this License or a notice or disclaimer, the original version will prevail. If a section in the Document is Entitled "Acknowledgements", "Dedications", or "History", the requirement (section 4) to Preserve its Title (section 1) will typically require changing the actual title.

9. TERMINATION

You may not copy, modify, sublicense, or distribute the Document except as expressly provided for under this License. Any other attempt to copy, modify, sublicense or distribute the Document is void, and will automatically terminate your rights under this License. However, parties who have received copies, or rights, from you under this License will not have their licenses terminated so long as such parties remain in full compliance.

10. FUTURE REVISIONS OF THIS LICENSE

The Free Software Foundation may publish new, revised versions of the GNU Free Documentation License from time to time. Such new versions will be similar in spirit to the present version, but may differ in detail to address new problems or concerns. See http://www.gnu.org/copyleft/. Each version of the License is given a distinguishing version number. If the Document specifies that a particular numbered version of this License "or any later version" applies to it, you have the option of following the terms and conditions either of that specified version or of any later version that has been published (not as a draft) by the Free Software Foundation. If the Document does not specify a version number of this License, you may choose any version ever published (not as a draft) by the Free Software Foundation. ADDENDUM: How to use this License for your documents To use this License in a document you have written, include a copy of the License in the document and put the following copyright and license notices just after the title page: Copyright (c) YEAR YOUR NAME. Permission is granted to copy, distribute and/or modify this document under the terms of the GNU Free Documentation License, Version 1.2 or any later version published by the Free Software Foundation; with no Invariant Sections, no Front-Cover Texts, and no Back-Cover Texts. A copy of the license is included in the section entitled "GNU Free Documentation License". If you have Invariant Sections, Front-Cover Texts and Back-Cover Texts, replace the "with...Texts." line with this: with the Invariant Sections being LIST THEIR TITLES, with the Front-Cover Texts being LIST, and with the Back-Cover Texts being LIST. If you have Invariant Sections without Cover Texts, or some other combination of the three, merge those two alternatives to suit the situation. If your document contains nontrivial examples of program code, we recommend releasing these examples in parallel under your choice of free software license, such as the GNU General Public License, to permit their use in free software.

Lightning Source UK Ltd.
Milton Keynes UK

178280UK00001B/39/P